The War in Ukraine and International Law

Masahiko Asada • Dai Tamada
Editors

The War in Ukraine and International Law

Springer

Editors
Masahiko Asada
Faculty of Law
Doshisha University
Kyoto, Japan

Dai Tamada
Graduate School of Law
Kyoto University
Kyoto, Japan

ISBN 978-981-97-2503-8   ISBN 978-981-97-2504-5   (eBook)
https://doi.org/10.1007/978-981-97-2504-5

© The Editor(s) (if applicable) and The Author(s), under exclusive license to Springer Nature Singapore Pte Ltd. 2024
This work is subject to copyright. All rights are solely and exclusively licensed by the Publisher, whether the whole or part of the material is concerned, specifically the rights of translation, reprinting, reuse of illustrations, recitation, broadcasting, reproduction on microfilms or in any other physical way, and transmission or information storage and retrieval, electronic adaptation, computer software, or by similar or dissimilar methodology now known or hereafter developed.
The use of general descriptive names, registered names, trademarks, service marks, etc. in this publication does not imply, even in the absence of a specific statement, that such names are exempt from the relevant protective laws and regulations and therefore free for general use.
The publisher, the authors and the editors are safe to assume that the advice and information in this book are believed to be true and accurate at the date of publication. Neither the publisher nor the authors or the editors give a warranty, expressed or implied, with respect to the material contained herein or for any errors or omissions that may have been made. The publisher remains neutral with regard to jurisdictional claims in published maps and institutional affiliations.

This Springer imprint is published by the registered company Springer Nature Singapore Pte Ltd.
The registered company address is: 152 Beach Road, #21-01/04 Gateway East, Singapore 189721, Singapore

If disposing of this product, please recycle the paper.

Introduction

Masahiko Asada and Dai Tamada

At the time of writing, the war in Ukraine was fast approaching its second anniversary since its commencement on 24 February 2022. As we discuss in detail in this book, there are multiple international legal issues that arise and require addressing. What is more, the very international legal order is under threat, insofar as international law obligations are not being complied with and international rules are ignored in the face of such blatant aggression as is the war in Ukraine.

As an introductory remark to this book, we would like to sketch out the outline that frames the ensuing discussion on the war in Ukraine from an international law perspective.

Importance of the Legal Evaluation of the War in Ukraine

Scholarly debate—particularly, international legal evaluations of the war in Ukraine—is expected to bring a variety of impacts. First, scholarly evaluations could be directed to Russia's civil society, which may not necessarily be familiar or open to objective evaluations of Russia's role in the war from an international legal perspective. Russians reportedly believe that the threat of NATO encroachment to Russia is considerable, and that the population of Donbas has experienced genocide at the hands of Ukraine. An objective, legal evaluation of the facts may help make Russians critical towards their government's war propaganda. Second, scholarly evaluations could also be directed to ordinary citizens in the West who may now be sceptical about their States continuing to both militarily and economically support Ukraine and to impose economic sanctions against Russia. To maintain their motivation in thwarting Russia's efforts, it may be necessary to emphasise issues of legitimacy. Third, scholarly evaluations may also be directed to the 'Global South' which does not currently participate in global economic sanction efforts against Russia. For the moment, economic sanctions against Russia are one of the most realistic means of weakening Russia's war capacity and, eventually, of ending the war. To make sanctions effective, persuading abstaining States, mainly from the Global South, to join the sanctions is the key. For this, international legal discussions may foster perceptions of legitimacy when it comes to sanctions and those who take such action against Russia.

On the other hand, international legal evaluations must be based on impartiality and conducted consistently, in the sense that international law must be applied equally to all similar sets of circumstances. At the time of writing, another conflict was under way in the Gaza Strip since 7 October 2023. Against a gruesome attack carried out by Hamas, Israel commenced full-scale military action, resulting in considerable loss of civilian life among the population of Gaza. These hostilities have given rise to calls as to why the chorus of, for the most part, Western States seems not to have attempted to prevent Israel from committing international crimes, including war crimes, crimes against humanity and genocide, in the way that it has when it comes to Russia. Many States, from the Global South, may regard such disparity as Western double standards that disincentivises them from joining efforts to sanction Russia. Being law, international law must be uniformly and consistently cited and applied to various situations, even when the realities surrounding the reach (or even possibility) of judicial scope mean that some situations are unlikely to ever come before some adjudicative competent body. Otherwise, criticisms of Russia risk being perceived as matters of political expediency and thus becoming devoid of legal substance.

Overview of the Book

This book attempts to showcase and analyse various aspects of international law engaged by the war in Ukraine. While some of the articles herein are openly critical of Russian aggression, they nonetheless adhere to scholarly standards of objectivity, following the positivist approach to international law.

Chapter 'The War in Ukraine Under International Law: Its Use of Force and Armed Conflict Aspects' (Masahiko Asada) deals with the main issues of *jus ad bellum*, United Nations law, and the law of neutrality and belligerency, as the basis for discussion. Chapter 'Use of Force by Russia and *jus ad bellum*' (Tatsuya Abe) analyses the use of force by the USSR and Russia and their legal justifications, to conclude that they have breached international law. Chapter 'Russia's War of Aggression Against Ukraine and the Crime of Aggression' (Claus Kreß) focuses on the crime of aggression in the context of the war in Ukraine, in light of the possibility to punish it before the ICC and a Special Tribunal for the Crime of Aggression against Ukraine. Chapter 'War in Ukraine and the International Court of Justice: Provisional Measures and the Third-Party Right to Intervene in Proceedings' (Dai Tamada) analyses the current two International Court of Justice Orders in the

Allegations of Genocide case, to clarify the dilemma that the ICJ has faced. Chapter 'Economic Sanctions Against Russia: Questions of Legality and Legitimacy' (Mika Hayashi and Akihiro Yamaguchi) examines questions of legality of the autonomous economic sanctions against Russia unsettled despite the apparent legitimacy of these sanctions. Chapter 'Freezing, Confiscation and Management of the Assets of the Russian Central Bank and the Oligarchs: Legality and Possibility Under International Law' (Kazuhiro Nakatani) explains and analyses the financial aspects of sanctions against Russia, with a particular focus on the freezing of Russian assets. Chapter 'Trade Sanctions Against Russia and Their WTO Consistency: Focusing on Justification Under National Security Exceptions' (Fujio Kawashima) analyses the question as to whether trade sanctions against Russia satisfy the requirements of the security exception under Article XXI of the GATT. Chapter 'WTO Dispute Settlement and Trade Sanctions as Permissible Third-Party Countermeasures Under Customary International Law' (Satoru Taira) focuses on the permissibility of sanctions against Russia within the context of WTO dispute settlement under customary international law on third-party countermeasures. Chapter 'War in Ukraine and Implications for International Investment Law' (Dai Tamada) analyses the investment arbitration cases that have arisen and are likely to arise from the war in Ukraine, including the annexation of Crimea. Concluding section (Martin Paparinskis) makes comments on each chapter for situating it in a broader context of international law in relation to the war in Ukraine.

In total, this book grapples with and sheds light on key issues of international law arising from the war in Ukraine, covering not only the use of force by Russia but in particular the legal evaluation of economic sanctions against Russia. We hope this book will contribute meaningfully to the legal discussion on the war in Ukraine, as well as bear some practical impact, however minute, to the ending of the ongoing war.

Acknowledgment

This book is an achievement of the joint research supported by the JSPS KAKENHI Grant-in-Aid for Scientific Research (A), Number 21H04384. The group held an online seminar twice, one in September 2022 and the other in February 2024.

Contents

Part I   Military and Criminal Aspects

The War in Ukraine Under International Law: Its Use of Force and Armed Conflict Aspects   3
Masahiko Asada

Use of Force by Russia and *jus ad bellum*   33
Tatsuya Abe

Russia's War of Aggression Against Ukraine and the Crime of Aggression   55
Claus Kreß

War in Ukraine and the International Court of Justice: Provisional Measures and the Third-Party Right to Intervene in Proceedings   79
Dai Tamada

Part II   Economic Aspects

Economic Sanctions Against Russia: Questions of Legality and Legitimacy   109
Mika Hayashi and Akihiro Yamaguchi

Freezing, Confiscation and Management of the Assets of the Russian Central Bank and the Oligarchs: Legality and Possibility Under International Law   137
Kazuhiro Nakatani

Trade Sanctions Against Russia and Their WTO Consistency: Focusing on Justification Under National Security Exceptions   157
Fujio Kawashima

WTO Dispute Settlement and Trade Sanctions as Permissible Third-Party Countermeasures Under Customary International Law . . . 185

Satoru Taira

War in Ukraine and Implications for International Investment Law . . . 217

Dai Tamada

Part III Conclusion

Reflections on War in Ukraine and International Law 239

Martins Paparinskis

Editors and Contributors

About the Editors

Masahiko Asada (LL.M. and LL.D., Kyoto University) is Professor of International Law at the Faculty of Law, Doshisha University, and Professor Emeritus at Kyoto University. He served as President of the Japanese Society of International Law from 2018 to 2020, and President of the Japan Association of Disarmament Studies from 2013 to 2015. He was a member of the UN Panel of Government Experts on Verification from 2005 to 2007 and of the Panel of Experts for DPRK Sanctions from 2009 to 2010. Professor Asada has also served as a member (and occasionally Vice Chairperson or Chairperson) of the Confidentiality Commission of the Organisation for the Prohibition of Chemical Weapons (OPCW) since 1997. He was elected as an associate member of the Institut de Droit International (IDI) and as a member of the UN International Law Commission (ILC) both in 2021. In his country, he has been a member (and occasionally Chairperson) of various Advisory Councils and Committees of the government, including the Ministry of Foreign Affairs, Ministry of International Trade and Industry, Ministry of Economy, Trade and Industry, Ministry of Defense and the Science and Technology Agency as well as the Prime Miniter's Office and the Cabinet Office. His areas of research cover the use of force, United Nations law, arms control and disarmament, international humanitarian law, law of treaties, law of the sea, law of State responsibility, law of State succession, law of international organisations, and the settlement of disputes. His publications include *Post-War Reparations between Japan and China under International Law* (Toshindo, 2015, in Japanese), *Economic Sanctions in International Law and Practice* (Routledge, 2020, editor), and 'International Law of Nuclear Non-Proliferation and Disarmament', *Recueil des cours*, Vol. 424 (2022).

Dai Tamada is Professor of International Law at Graduate School of Law, Kyoto University. He holds LL.M. (Kyoto University 2000) and Ph.D. (Kyoto University 2014). His research areas cover international dispute settlement, international investment law, the law of treaties, and the law of the sea. He has been committee member in Ministry of Foreign Affairs (MOFA), Ministry of Economy, Trade and Industry (METI), and Ministry of Justice (MOJ) of Japan. His recent publications include Malgosia Fitzmaurice and Dai Tamada (eds.), *Whaling in the Antarctic: Significance and Implications of the ICJ Judgment* (Brill/Nijhoff, 2016), Dai Tamada and Philippe Achilleas (eds.), *Theory and Practice of Export Control: Balancing International Security and International Economic Relations* (Springer, 2017), and Piotr Szwedo, Richard Peltz-Steele and Dai Tamada (eds.), *Law and Development: Balancing Principles and Values* (Springer, 2019), and Dai Tamada and Keyuan Zou (eds.), *Implementation of the United Nations Convention on the Law of the Sea: State Practice of China and Japan* (Springer, 2021).

Contributors

Tatsuya Abe School of International Politics, Economics, and Communication, Aoyama Gakuin University, Tokyo, Japan

Masahiko Asada Faculty of Law, Doshisha University, Kyoto, Japan

Mika Hayashi Graduate School of International Cooperation Studies, Kobe University, Kobe, Japan

Fujio Kawashima Graduate School of Law, Kobe University, Kobe, Japan

Claus Kreß Faculty of Law, University of Cologne, Cologne, Germany

Kazuhiro Nakatani Faculty of Law, Tokai University, Hiratsuka, Japan

Martins Paparinskis UCL, London, UK
International Law Commission, Geneva, Switzerland

Satoru Taira Osaka City University, Osaka, Japan

Dai Tamada Graduate School of Law, Kyoto University, Kyoto, Japan

Akihiro Yamaguchi Graduate School of International Cooperation Studies, Kobe University, Kobe, Japan

Part I
Military and Criminal Aspects

The War in Ukraine Under International Law: Its Use of Force and Armed Conflict Aspects

Masahiko Asada

Abstract More than two years have passed since the Russian aggression against Ukraine started in February 2022. However, there appears to be no prospect for a ceasefire. The long duration of this situation, which fundamentally undermines the prohibition of the use of force and flatly disregards rules on armed conflict, was unexpected. The international order thus faces a critical situation, but a calm and objective analysis is still necessary. Such a perspective is significant as it helps to maintain the rule of law in the international community over the long run, while simultaneously shedding light on possible constraints that other States have in relation to the aggressor State. This article analyzes the legal aspects of the war in Ukraine, focusing on rules concerning the prohibition of the use of force and the law of neutrality.

1 Introduction

More than two years have elapsed since the Russian armed forces started to invade Ukraine on 24 February 2022. While the conflict on the ground is constantly evolving, there appears to be no prospect for a ceasefire, at least at the time of this writing. The long duration of this situation, which fundamentally undermines the prohibition of the use of force and flatly disregards rules on armed conflict, was rather unexpected. The international order thus faces a critical situation, but a calm and objective analysis, including with regard to the claims of justification by Russia, is still necessary. Such a perspective is valuable as it helps to maintain the rule of law in the international community over the long run while simultaneously shedding light on possible constraints that other States have in relation to the aggressor State. This article, therefore, analyzes the legal aspects of the war in Ukraine, focusing on rules concerning the prohibition of the use of force and the law of neutrality.

M. Asada (✉)
Faculty of Law, Doshisha University, Kyoto, Japan

© The Author(s), under exclusive license to Springer Nature Singapore Pte Ltd. 2024
M. Asada, D. Tamada (eds.), *The War in Ukraine and International Law*,
https://doi.org/10.1007/978-981-97-2504-5_1

2 Prohibition of the Use of Force

2.1 Justification by Russia

2.1.1 Individual and Collective Self-Defense

Russia called its invasion a "special military operation", but it was nothing other than a use of force under international law. This characterization can be confirmed by Russia's own letter to the UN Secretary-General sent on the day of the invasion.[1] It referred to the "measures taken in accordance with Article 51 of the Charter of the United Nations in exercise of the right of self-defence".[2] The letter took the unusual form of simply attaching the text of President Putin's speech to the Russian people on the same day (the "Putin speech"). The Putin speech was also later attached to the Russian document[3] sent to the International Court of Justice (ICJ) in an effort to deny the Court's jurisdiction over the case brought by Ukraine on 26 February 2022 (*Allegations of Genocide* case). Thus, the speech can be seen as a central argument for legal justification by Russia.

Despite the lack of legal clarity given its context as a public address, the Putin speech primarily based the Russian use of force on the right of individual and collective self-defense. By referring to the expansion of the North Atlantic Treaty Organization (NATO) to the east,[4] the speech argued that there was a "real threat" to

---

[1] UN Doc. S/2022/154, 24 February 2022.

[2] Ibid., p. 1. For a detailed analysis of the Soviet and Russian history of invasion, see Chapter 'Use of Force by Russia and *jus ad bellum*' (Tatsuya Abe) of this volume. For the question on the crime of aggression, see Chapter 'Russia's War of Aggression Against Ukraine and the Crime of Aggression' (Claus Kress).

[3] ICJ, "Document (with annexes) from the Russian Federation Setting Out Its Position regarding the Alleged 'Lack of Jurisdiction' of the Court in the Case" (7 March 2022), at https://icj-cij.org/case/1 82/other-documents. The body of the document points out, *inter alia*, that Article IX of the Genocide Convention does not provide the basis for jurisdiction over the present dispute as the Convention does not regulate either the use of force between States or the recognition of States, that the "special military operation" is based on the right of self-defense under the UN Charter and customary international law, and that the recognition of the Donetsk and Luhansk Peoples' Republics is related to the right to self-determination. Ibid., paras. 10, 12, 13, 15, 17, 19.

[4] In December 2021, Russia even proposed a treaty between Russia and NATO countries, in which all NATO member States would "commit themselves to refrain from any further enlargement of NATO, including the accession of Ukraine as well as other States". "Agreement on Measures to Ensure the Security of the Russian Federation and Member States of the North Atlantic Treaty Organization", 17 December 2021, Art. 6, at https://augengeradeaus.net/wp-content/uploads/2021/12/20211217_Draft_Russia_NATO_security_guarantees.pdf. It is ironic that Finland and Sweden applied for NATO membership both on 18 May 2022, after Russia's invasion of Ukraine. Finland was admitted on 4 April 2023 and Sweden on 7 March 2024. NATO Parliamentary Assembly, "Finland and Sweden Accession", (date not given), at https://www.nato-pa.int/content/finland-sweden-accession; NATO, "Finland Joins NATO as 31st Ally", 4 April 2023, at https://www.nato.int/cps/en/natohq/news_213448.htm. And now even Ukraine seems poised to gain membership in the future. NATO, "Vilnius Summit Communiqué", 11 July 2023, para. 11, at https://www.nato.int/cps/en/natolive/official_texts_217320.htm.

Russia's interests and to its "very existence". It was followed by a statement that there was "no other way to defend Russia", suggesting that it was an exercise of the right of individual self-defense.

At the same time, the speech referred to a "genocide" that was allegedly taking place in the Donbas region of eastern Ukraine, to appeals for help from the two "People's Republics of Donbass", and to the Treaties of Friendship, Cooperation and Mutual Assistance Russia had concluded with both "Republics".[5] These explanations allegedly justified the Russian decision to conduct a special military operation "in accordance with Article 51 ... of the Charter of the United Nations", clearly relying on the right of collective self-defense.[6]

However, it is not possible for Russia to resort to the right of individual self-defense in the absence of an armed attack *against Russia*. Even if one recognizes the doctrine of anticipatory self-defense against an imminent armed attack,[7] it cannot be said that such a threat *against Russia* existed at that time.

Regarding the right of collective self-defense, the Russian justification for its use of force against Ukraine referred to the requests by the two "Republics" in Donbas. This appears to have followed the ICJ's *Nicaragua* judgment of 1986, which stated that "in customary international law, ... there is no rule permitting the exercise of collective self-defence in the absence of a *request* by the State which regards itself as the victim of an armed attack"[8] (emphasis added). However, such a request must come from a sovereign State. In the same judgment, the ICJ also stated that "[the principle of non-intervention] would certainly lose its effectiveness as a principle of law if intervention were to be justified by a mere request for assistance made by an *opposition group* in another State"[9] (emphasis added). This statement was made in the context of the principle of non-intervention, but it seems to apply equally or *a fortiori* to the case of collective self-defense.

This statehood prerequisite is also important in relation to the requirement of an armed attack in self-defense. In its advisory opinion in the *Israeli Wall* case of 2004 (though it was an individual self-defense case), the ICJ stated that "Article 51 of the [UN] Charter thus recognizes the existence of an inherent right of self-defence in the

---

[5] The treaties were signed on 21 February 2022, the day Russia recognized both Republics as States, and on the following day, the parliaments of all the "States" concerned approved them. For their texts, see UN Doc. A/76/740-S/2022/179, 7 March 2022.

[6] In fact, the two treaties contain a provision agreeing to afford each other the necessary assistance in the exercise of the right of collective self-defense (Art. 4). Ibid., pp. 3, 9.

[7] The Russian Defense Ministry suggested early in March 2022, after the invasion commenced, that the special military operation was a pre-emptive response to Ukraine's alleged plans to launch a major offensive in the Donbas region. James A. Green, Christian Henderson and Tom Ruys, "Russia's Attack on Ukraine and the *Jus ad Bellum*", *Journal on the Use of Force and International Law*, Vol. 9, No. 1 (2022), p. 20.

[8] *Military and Paramilitary Activities in and against Nicaragua (Nicaragua v. United States of America)*, Merits, Judgment, *ICJ Reports 1986*, p. 105, para. 199.

[9] Ibid., p. 126, para. 246.

case of armed attack by *one State against another State*"[10] (emphasis added). Therefore, the initially attacked entity must be a "State".

However, the statehood of the two "Republics" in Donbas is questionable. The two "Republics", as puppet States of Russia, have not satisfied all the requirements for an entity to be a State under international law as contained in Article 1 of the 1933 Montevideo Convention on the Rights and Duties of States.[11] The fact that Russia is virtually the only country that has recognized the two "Republics" as independent States additionally provides strong evidence that they have not achieved statehood.[12] Indeed, Resolution ES-11/1 of the UN General Assembly's emergency special session of 2 March 2022 "[d]eplore[d]" Russia's recognition of the two "Republics" as a "violation of the territorial integrity and sovereignty of Ukraine", and "[d]emand[ed]" Russia "immediately and unconditionally reverse the decision related to the status of . . . the Donetsk and Luhansk regions of Ukraine".[13] Although both "Republics" declared independence in May 2014, the Minsk Agreement II of 12 February 2015 (signed by representatives of the OSCE, Ukraine, Russia, Donetsk and Luhansk and aimed at an immediate and comprehensive ceasefire in Donbas) specifically envisaged no more than a "special status" for the two regions, not independent statehood.[14]

Russia recognized both "Republics" as sovereign States only on 21 February 2022, three days before the invasion of Ukraine, and the Putin speech referred to the "genocide" in Donbas as the main reason for the recognition. This claim, along with the subsequent reference to the right to self-determination in the speech, suggests that President Putin may have had in mind so-called "remedial secession", the right to external self-determination when a people is blocked from the meaningful exercise of its right to self-determination internally.[15]

For an entity within an existing State to become an independent State under international law, it is required to be in circumstances where it could lawfully

---

[10] *Legal Consequences of the Construction of a Wall in the Occupied Palestinian Territory*, Advisory Opinion, *ICJ Reports 2004*, p. 194, para. 139.

[11] Article 1 of the Montevideo Convention enumerates as qualifications for a State as a person of international law: (a) a permanent population, (b) a defined territory, (c) government and (d) capacity to enter into relations with the other States. It seems that the two "Republics" do not satisfy qualification (d).

[12] In addition to mutual recognition by the two "Republics", they have been recognized as sovereign States by South Ossetia and Abkhazia. See "South Ossetia Recognizes 'Luhansk People's Republic", *Radio Free Europe/Radio Liberty*, 19 June 2014, at https://www.rferl.org/a/south-ossetia-recognizes-luhansk-peoples-republic/25427651.html; "Abkhazia Recognises Ukraine's Donetsk and Luhansk", *OC Media*, 26 February 2022, at https://oc-media.org/abkhazia-recognises-ukraines-donetsk-and-luhansk/.

[13] UN Doc. A/RES/ES-11/1 (2 March 2022), 18 March 2022, paras. 5, 6.

[14] "Minsk Agreement: Full Text in English", 12 February 2015, para. 11, at https://www.unian.info/politics/1043394-minsk-agreement-full-text-in-english.html.

[15] For an argument supporting remedial secession as positive law, see Christian Tomuschat, "Secession and Self-Determination", in Marcelo G. Kohen (ed.), *Secession: International Law Perspectives* (Cambridge U.P., 2006), pp. 38–42.

exercise the right to external self-determination. However, it is unclear whether remedial secession has been established as such a right under international law, as pronounced by the Supreme Court of Canada in the 1998 "Secession of Quebec" case. According to the Court, while the right to exercise external self-determination for colonial peoples as well as peoples subject to alien subjugation, domination or exploitation is undisputed, "it remains unclear" whether remedial secession actually reflects an established international law standard.[16]

Russia itself, in its written statement in the 2010 *Kosovo* case of the ICJ, in which remedial secession was discussed, stated that remedial secession is only permitted in "truly extreme circumstances, such as an outright armed attack by the parent State, threatening the very existence of the people in question", and argued that there were no such extreme circumstances in Kosovo[17] (the Court, however, did not rule on this point because it thought the issue was beyond the scope of the question posed[18]).

Concerning the situation in Donbas, neither the Organization for Security and Co-operation in Europe (OSCE) nor the UN High Commissioner for Human Rights (UNHCHR) reported that the Donbas region faced circumstances that blocked its peoples from meaningfully exercising self-determination internally.[19] The ICJ, in its order on provisional measures in the case of *Allegation of Genocide (Ukraine v. Russian Federation)* in March 2022, also stated that "the Court is not in possession of evidence substantiating the allegation of the Russian Federation that genocide has been committed on Ukrainian territory".[20]

While it is true that there have been repeated armed clashes between the Ukrainian forces and pro-Russian armed groups in the Donbas region, this is not sufficient to satisfy the requirements for secession (even if one recognizes the

---

[16]"Supreme Court of Canada: Reference re Secession of Quebec [August 20, 1998]", *International Legal Materials*, Vol. 37, No. 6 (November 1998), pp. 1372–1373, paras. 131–138, esp. para. 135.

[17]ICJ, "Accordance with International Law of the Unilateral Declaration of Independence by the Provisional Institutions of the Self-Government of Kosovo: Written Statement by the Russian Federation", 16 April 2009, paras. 88, 98, 99.

[18]*Accordance with International Law of the Unilateral Declaration of Independence in respect of Kosovo*, Advisory Opinion, *ICJ Reports 2010*, p. 438, paras. 82–83.

[19]The OSCE monitoring mission reported that there were some 1500 civilian casualties in the Donbas region in 2016–2021, but with a sharp decrease since 2018, with just 91 total cases (16 killed and 75 injured) in 2021. Organization for Security and Co-operation in Europe, "2021 Trends and Observations from the Special Monitoring Mission to Ukraine", at https://www.osce.org/files/f/documents/2/a/511327.pdf. Also, the Office of the UN High Commissioner for Human Rights reported 3100 civilian deaths (excluding some 300 deaths on board Malaysian Airlines flight MH17 on 17 July 2014) in Ukraine in 2014–2021, with the overwhelming majority occurring in 2014 and 2015. Office of the High Commissioner for Human Rights, United Nations Human Rights Monitoring Mission in Ukraine, "Conflict-related Civilian Casualties in Ukraine", 27 January 2022, at https://ukraine.un.org/sites/default/files/2022-02/Conflict-related%20civilian%20casualties%20 as%20of%2031%20December%202021%20%28rev%2027%20January%202022%29%20corr%20EN_0.pdf.

[20]*Allegations of Genocide under the Convention on the Prevention and Punishment of the Crime of Genocide (Ukraine v. Russian Federation)*, Provisional Measures, Order, 16 March 2022 [hereinafter cited as "*Allegations of Genocide*, Provisional Measures"], para. 59.

doctrine of remedial secession). If one were to assume that this alone satisfies the requirements for secession, then it would permit rebel groups an almost unrestricted right to secession as long as they could stage an armed uprising.

It is true, as the Canadian Court stated, that "an illegal act may eventually acquire legal status if . . . it is recognized on the international plane".[21] However, as noted above, the number of recognitions of the two "Republics" as independent States is not such that their secession can be legalized. Thus, their recognition by Russia, which was legally dubious, should be viewed primarily as a steppingstone taken by Russia to justify its military intervention in response to the requests for assistance by the "Republics". This seems particularly plausible when one recalls the date of recognition (three days before the invasion). Thus, the Russian justification of its use of force in collective self-defense, relying on the *request* by two "Republics" against which an *armed attack* allegedly occurred, cannot be sustained.

On a related note, a "request" for assistance from another State may be (i) one of the requirements for the lawful exercise of the right of collective self-defense, or (ii) used as an independent justification for the use of force on its own.[22] While the two can be distinguished conceptually, it can be harder in practice to draw the distinction, particularly when the use of force is limited exclusively to the territory of the requesting State.

In the present case, however, both cases are difficult to sustain, even setting aside the statehood issue of the requesting entity. In relation to (i) above, the "Republics" failed to satisfy the requirement of a preceding armed attack. With regard to (ii), such a request would not justify the use of force against a State (the other regions of Ukraine which Russia invaded) other than the requesting "States" (the "Republics").

2.1.2 Protection of Nationals Abroad and Humanitarian Intervention

The Putin speech may potentially offer other justifications beyond the right of self-defense, including the use of force to protect nationals abroad. After stating that he had decided to conduct a "special military operation" in accordance with Article 51 of the UN Charter, President Putin stated that the purpose of the operation was to "protect people who have been subjected to abuse and genocide by the Kiev regime". To this end, he would seek the "demilitarization and de-Nazification of Ukraine" as well as the "prosecution of those who have committed numerous bloody crimes against the civilians", "including citizens of the Russian Federation".[23]

In the last quoted part above, he was highlighting the protection of Russian nationals living in Donbas, to whom Russia granted nationality by providing Russian passports. This policy of "passportization", which previously had been

---

[21] "Supreme Court of Canada", supra note 16, paras. 141, 146.

[22] See ILA, "Use of Force: Military Assistance on Request, Proposal for an ILA Committee", pp. 2–4, at https://www.ila-hq.org/en_GB/documents/background-information.

[23] UN Doc. S/2022/154, supra note 1, p. 6.

The War in Ukraine Under International Law: Its Use of Force and...

implemented in South Ossetia and Crimea, is a popular practice of Russia. In the Donbas region, approximately 720,000 passports were reportedly fast-tracked between April 2019 and February 2022.[24]

It still appears overly simplistic to consider that such actions could justify the use of force on the ground of protection of nationals abroad. The scope of a State to extend its nationality to whomsoever it wishes is unlimited in principle, but this is true only insofar as it is not inconsistent with international law.[25] Additionally, while the Russian Constitution contains a provision that has been interpreted as supporting the legality of the use of force to protect nationals abroad,[26] this principle has notably been the subject of a long-running debate in international law. A plea by a State justifying its use of force as necessary to protect its nationals does not receive broad support in scholarship nor among States.[27]

---

[24] See Green, Henderson and Ruys, "Russia's Attack on Ukraine and the *Jus ad Bellum*", supra note 7, p. 15. See also James A. Green, "Passportisation, Peacekeepers and Proportionality: The Russian Claim of the Protection of Nationals Abroad in Self-Defence", in James A. Green and Christopher P.M. Waters (eds.), *Conflict in the Caucasus: Implications for International Legal Order* (Palgrave Macmillan, 2010), pp. 66–68. It is reported that the Russian government issued some 2.82 million Russian passports in the four annexed "Republics" and oblasts in Donbas by September 2023. *Yomiuri Shimbun*, 1 October 2023.

[25] James Crawford, *Brownlie's Principles of Public International Law*, 9th ed. (Oxford U.P., 2019), pp. 495–511. The practice of passportization may not in itself be completely without question from the viewpoint of the principle of "effective nationality" or the "genuine link" doctrine in relation to the provision of diplomatic protection. *Nottebohm (Liechtenstein v. Guatemala)*, Second Phase, Judgment, *ICJ Reports 1955*, pp. 20–24. However, the Articles on Diplomatic Protection adopted by the International Law Commission (ILC) in 2006 provides for that principle only in cases of the exercise of diplomatic protection by one State against the other where an individual possesses dual nationality (Art. 7). *Yearbook of the International Law Commission, 2006*, Vol. II, Pt. 2, pp. 34–35.

[26] Article 61 (2) of the Russian Constitution provides that "[t]he Russian Federation shall guarantee to its citizens protection and patronage abroad", which Russia has interpreted to provide for a right of armed intervention when it is necessary to protect Russian citizens. Tamás Hoffmann, "War or Peace? - International Legal Issues concerning the Use of Force in the Russia-Ukraine Conflict", *Hungarian Journal of Legal Studies*, Vol. 63, No. 3 (September 2022), p. 215.

[27] See, generally, Tom Ruys, "The 'Protection of Nationals' Doctrine Revisited", *Journal of Conflict and Security Law*, Vol. 13, No. 2 (2008), pp. 233–272. During the drafting of the Articles on Diplomatic Protection in the ILC, draft Article 2 ("The threat or use of force is prohibited as a means of diplomatic protection, except in the case of rescue of nationals where . . .") proposed by the Special Rapporteur, John R. Dugard, was deleted due to overwhelming opposition in the ILC as well as in the UN General Assembly's Sixth Committee. The Commentary on Article 1 ("diplomatic protection consists of the invocation by a State, through diplomatic action or other means of peaceful settlement, of the responsibility of another State . . .") of the adopted Articles on Diplomatic Protection clearly states that "[t]he use of force, prohibited by Article 2, paragraph 4, of the Charter of the United Nations, is not a permissible method for the enforcement of the right of diplomatic protection". *Yearbook of the International Law Commission, 2000*, Vol. II, Pt. 1, p. 218; *Yearbook of the International Law Commission, 2006*, Vol. II, Pt. 2, pp. 27–28, Article 1, Commentary, para. 8. It is said that only one member of the ILC did not challenge draft Article 2, and Italy was the only country which supported it in the Sixth Committee. Olivier Corten, *The Law against War: The Prohibition on the Use of Force in Contemporary International Law,* 2nd ed. (Hart, 2021), pp. 515–516. For arguments against or doubtful of the "protection of nationals"

As quoted above, President Putin in his speech stated that the operation was warranted to "protect people who have been subjected to abuse and genocide by the Kiev regime for eight years". This can be viewed as a justification relying on the doctrine of "humanitarian intervention". However, not only is the fact of genocide highly questionable, as pointed out earlier in relation to "remedial secession", but also whether humanitarian intervention can be recognized as an exception to the prohibition of the use of force is a matter of debate under international law; negative voices seem dominant.[28] Indeed, the ICJ, in its order on provisional measures in the *Allegations of Genocide* case, seems to have denied the legality of the unilateral use of force even in the case of genocide.[29]

Moreover, such a justification would be inconsistent with what Russia has done in Donbas, particularly its practice of granting Russian nationality to people in the region by providing passports. If "humanitarian intervention" was one of the justifications for Russia to use force against Ukraine, the alleged massive human rights violations must have been committed by Ukraine against the Ukrainian population

---

doctrine, see, e.g., Josef Mrazek, "Prohibition of the Use and Threat of Force: Self-Defence and Self-Help in International Law", *Canadian Yearbook of International Law*, Vol. 27 (1989), p. 97; Albrecht Randelzhofer, "Article 51", in Bruno Simma et al. (eds.), *The Charter of the United Nations: A Commentary*, 2nd ed. Vol. 1 (Oxford U.P., 2002), pp. 798–799; Crawford, *Brownlie's Principles of Public International Law*, 9th ed., supra note 25, p. 729. On the other hand, some commentators argue or suggest that the use of force to protect nationals abroad is not prohibited under Article 2 (4) of the UN Charter, and is permissible on the basis of the right of self-defense or as an independent exception to the prohibition of the use of force, subject to certain conditions. See, e.g., Louis Henkin, *How Nations Behave: Law and Foreign Policy,* 2nd ed. (Columbia U.P., 1979), p. 145; Oscar Schachter, "The Right of States to Use Armed Force", *Michigan Law Review*, Vol. 82, Nos. 5–6 (April/May 1984), pp. 1629–1633; Natalino Ronzitti, "Rescuing Nationals Abroad Revisited," *Journal of Conflict and Security Law*, Vol. 24, No. 3 (Winter 2019), pp. 431–448.

[28] In its judgment in the *Nicaragua* case, the ICJ stated that the use of force "could not be the appropriate method to monitor or ensure . . . respect [for human rights]" (*Military and Paramilitary Activities in and against Nicaragua (Nicaragua v. United States of America)*, supra note 8, p. 134, para. 268). In addition, the 2005 UN World Summit Outcome document took a negative position on humanitarian intervention as a unilateral measure taken by individual States. It stated that, while each individual State has the responsibility to protect its populations from genocide, war crimes, ethnic cleansing and crimes against humanity, the international community, through the United Nations, also has the responsibility to use peaceful means to help to protect populations and that the international community is prepared to "take collective action, in a timely and decisive manner, *through the Security Council, in accordance with the [UN] Charter, including Chapter VII,* on a case-by-case basis . . ., should peaceful means be inadequate and national authorities are manifestly failing to protect their populations . . ." (emphasis added). UN Doc. A/RES/60/1, 24 October 2005, paras. 138–139. Moreover, while a handful of States, such as the UK, recognize the legality of humanitarian intervention under very limited conditions, member States of the Non-Aligned Movement have repeated their "rejection of the 'right' of humanitarian intervention, which has no basis either in the UN Charter or in international law". Malcolm N. Shaw, *International Law*, 9th ed. (Cambridge U.P., 2021), pp. 1017–1019; Corten, *The Law against War,* supra note 27, p. 512.

[29] The Court states that "it is doubtful that the Convention . . . authorizes a Contracting Party's unilateral use of force in the territory of another State for the purpose of preventing or punishing an alleged genocide". *Allegations of Genocide*, Provisional Measures, supra note 20, para. 59.

on the Ukrainian territory, by definition.[30] However, from the Russian point of view, that was not the case as most victims are the "Russian" population and the location is in the newly established "Republics". Therefore, assuming President Putin's thinking was coherent, one should question whether he really had humanitarian intervention in mind as a justification for the use of force in Ukraine.

In any event, this section clearly concludes that none of the claims made by Russia, including self-defense as its primary justification, could justify its use of force against Ukraine.[31]

2.2 Act of Aggression and the UN Response

The Security Council is the principal UN organ that should respond to situations involving the use of force. However, the current situation involves force used by Russia, a permanent member of the Security Council with veto power. On 25 February 2022, the Security Council failed to adopt a resolution condemning Russia[32] (co-sponsored by 82 States) due to a veto cast by Russia (11 in favor, 1 against [Russia], and 3 abstentions [China, India, UAE]).[33] The Security Council then adopted Resolution 2623 (2022) (co-sponsored by Albania and the United

---

[30] For the discussions based on the concept of humanitarian intervention being for the protection of the population of the target State, not the nationals of the intervening State, see, e.g., Anthony Clark Arend and Robert J. Beck, *International Law and the Use of Force* (Routledge, 1993), pp. 113–114; Sean D. Murphy, *Humanitarian Intervention: The United Nations in an Evolving World Order* (University of Pennsylvania Press, 1996), pp. 15–16; Stanimir A. Alexandrov, *Self-Defense against the Use of Force in International Law* (Kluwer, 1996), p. 204; Tarcisio Gazzini, *The Changing Rules on the Use of Force in International Law* (Manchester U.P., 2005), p. 173; Yoram Dinstein, *War, Aggression and Self-Defence*, 6th ed. (Cambridge U.P., 2017), p. 279; Christine Gray, *International Law and the Use of Force*, 4th ed. (Oxford U.P., 2018), pp. 40–44; Christian Henderson, *The Use of Force and International Law* (Cambridge U.P., 2018), p. 379; Shaw, *International Law*, 9th ed., supra note 28, p. 1016. The use of force to protect nationals abroad is sometimes discussed within the framework of humanitarian intervention. See, e.g., Schachter, "The Right of States to Use Armed Forces", supra note 27, p. 1629; Corten, *The Law against War*, supra note 27, p. 491.

[31] There are, however, a handful of States which argue that Russia has a right to invade or otherwise express support for the Russian invasion, such as Cuba, DPRK, Syria and Venezuela. "State Responses to Russian Invasion of Ukraine", (date not given), at http://opiniojuris.org/wp-content/uploads/State-Reactions-to-Russian-Invasion-of-Ukraine.pdf.

[32] UN Doc. S/2022/155, 25 February 2022. The draft resolution, like the UN General Assembly's emergency special session resolution (to be discussed below), used the phrase "[d]eplores in the strongest terms the Russian Federation's aggression against Ukraine in violation of Article 2, paragraph 4 of the United Nations Charter" (para. 2). It would have further "[d]ecide[d]" that Russia "shall immediately cease its use of force against Ukraine" and "shall immediately, completely, and unconditionally withdraw all of its military forces from the territory of Ukraine" (paras. 3 and 4). But an earlier draft reportedly contained harsher language under Chapter VII of the UN Charter. See below.

[33] UN Doc. S/PV. 8979, 25 February 2022, p. 6.

States) on 27 February based on the 1950 "Uniting for Peace" resolution, with the same voting result but without the blocking power in the Russian negative vote,[34] and it decided to hold an emergency special session of the UN General Assembly. Despite the procedure expressly stipulated in the 1950 resolution,[35] the eleventh emergency special session was convened while the General Assembly was apparently "in session".[36] The Security Council may have intended this procedural abnormality to signal that this was an "emergency" situation.

With regard to the veto, Russia perhaps should have abstained from voting entirely as it was a party to the dispute. This calls into question the validity of the veto itself. Article 27 (3) of the UN Charter provides that "in decisions under Chapter VI, and paragraph 3 of Article 52, a party to a dispute shall abstain from voting". This mandatory abstention only applies to a decision for the peaceful settlement of disputes, not for an enforcement action under Chapter VII.

Looking to the drafting history of the abortive Council resolution against Russia, there is additional support for the argument that Russia should have abstained. The original draft resolution, proposed by Albania and the United States, which condemned Russia's aggression against Ukraine and its decision to recognize the Donetsk and Luhansk "People's Republics", reportedly contained explicit reference to a breach of international peace and security as well as Chapter VII of the UN Charter. However, in response to China's preference for a Chapter VI resolution, all references to Chapter VII were removed.[37] Assuming this history is accurate, the draft resolution vetoed by Russia should have been considered as falling within the purview of Chapter VI rather than Chapter VII, and Article 27 (3) should have applied. In fact, Norway raised this point at the very Council meeting when the draft was vetoed.[38]

In 2014, there would have been a stronger argument for demanding Russia's abstention from voting because the vetoed draft resolution (concerning the referendum on the status of Crimea) urged all parties to pursue the "peaceful resolution of this dispute through direct political dialogue".[39] But the Article 27 (3) issue was not

---

[34] UN Docs. S/2022/160, 27 February 2022; S/RES/2623(2022), 27 February 2022; S/PV.8980, 27 February 2022, p. 2.

[35] The "Uniting for Peace" resolution stipulates that if the General Assembly is "not in session", an emergency special session may be convened.

[36] The 76th regular session opened on 14 September 2021 and closed on 13 September 2022. See https://www.un.org/en/ga/76/. In the case of Crimea, the General Assembly *in regular session* adopted a resolution concerning its status after a draft resolution was vetoed in the Security Council. UN Doc. A/RES/68/262 (27 March 2014), 1 April 2014. See also UN Docs. S/2014/189, 15 March 2014; S/PV.7138, 15 March 2014, p. 3.

[37] "In Hindsight: Ukraine and the Tools of the UN", *Security Council Report*, March 2022 Monthly Forecast.

[38] Norway stated that "in the spirit of the Charter, as a party to a dispute Russia should have abstained from voting on the draft resolution". UN Doc. S/PV. 8979, supra note 33, pp. 7–8.

[39] UN Doc. S/2014/189, supra note 36, para. 2.

raised at that time,[40] and scholars have pointed out that this mandatory abstention requirement has been ignored for more than 60 years in practice.[41]

In any event, on 2 March 2022, Resolution ES-11/1 (co-sponsored by 96 countries), almost identical in content to the one rejected by the Security Council, was adopted by the General Assembly with 141 votes in favor (including UAE this time) and 5 against (Russia, Belarus, North Korea, Eritrea and Syria) with 35 abstentions (including China and India). In the Resolution, the General Assembly:

(i) "[d]eplore[d] in the strongest terms the aggression by the Russian Federation against Ukraine in violation of Article 2 (4) of the [UN] Charter" (para. 2);

(ii) "[d]emand[ed] that the Russian Federation immediately cease its use of force against Ukraine ..." (para. 3); and

(iii) "demand[ed] that the Russian Federation immediately, completely and unconditionally withdraw all of its military forces from the territory of Ukraine within its internationally recognized borders" (para. 4).[42]

Subsequently, between 23–27 September 2022, Russia held so-called "referenda" in the Donetsk and Luhansk "People's Republics" as well as in the oblasts of Zaporizhzhya and Kherson (the latter two neither declaring independence nor receiving State recognition), and signed "treaties" annexing the four "Republics" and oblasts on 30 September. All procedures for annexation were completed on 5 October, but the date of annexation was set for 30 September.[43]

In response to this development as well as the rejection by a Russian veto[44] of a draft Security Council resolution seeking to invalidate the "referenda",[45] the emergency special session of the General Assembly on 12 October 2022 adopted Resolution ES-11/4 (co-sponsored by 44 States) with a vote of 143 in favor (including UAE again) and 5 against (Russia, Belarus, North Korea, Nicaragua and Syria) with 35 abstentions (including China, Eritrea and India). The Resolution, after referring to Russia's "unlawful actions" with regard to the "illegal so-called referenda" taken in parts of Ukraine's regions of Luhansk, Donetsk, Kherson and

---

[40] Enrico Milano, "Russia's Veto in the Security Council: Whither the Duty to Abstain under Art. 27(3) of the UN Charter?", *Zeitschrift für ausländisches öffentliches Recht und Völkerrecht*, Vol. 75 (2015), p. 230. At a subsequently held General Assembly meeting, however, Liechtenstein raised this point. UN Doc. A/68/PV.80, 27 March 2014, p. 8.

[41] It is said that the last few occasions on which the obligatory abstention from voting was arguably applied include that of the determination concerning the dispute between Argentina and Israel over the kidnapping of Eichmann in 1960. Milano, "Russia's Veto in the Security Council", supra note 40, pp. 222–224; "In Hindsight", supra note 37. See also Benedetto Conforti and Carlo Focarelli, *The Law and Practice of the United Nations*, 5th ed. (Brill, 2016), pp. 94–101.

[42] UN Docs. A/RES/ES-11/1, supra note 13, paras. 2–4; A/ES-11/PV.5, 2 March 2022, pp. 14–15.

[43] "Putin Signs Annexation of Ukrainian Regions as Losses Mount", *Japan News*, 6 October 2022, at https://japannews.yomiuri.co.jp/news-services/ap/20221006-62664/; *Yomiuri Shimbun*, 6 October 2022.

[44] UN Doc. S/PV.9143, 30 September 2022, p. 4. The vote result was 10 in favor, 1 against (Russia) and 4 abstentions (Brazil, China, Gabon and India).

[45] UN Doc. S/2022/720, 30 September 2022, para. 3.

Zaporizhzhya, declared that they "can have no validity and cannot form the basis for any alteration of the status of these regions of Ukraine, including any purported annexation".[46]

These developments within the UN are substantively similar to what occurred in 2014 following Russia's annexation of Crimea. Nevertheless, the voting results in the current context demonstrate that the international community has united in stronger opposition to, and condemnation of, Russia's actions. General Assembly Resolution 68/262, invalidating the referendum held in Crimea and Sevastopol in 2014, was adopted with just 100 votes in favor, 11 against and 58 abstentions.[47]

Resolution ES-11/1 is particularly noteworthy in its description of Russia's actions as "aggression". While it is difficult to deny that aggression occurred in light of Article 3 of the 1974 "Definition of Aggression" resolution of the General Assembly,[48] such a declaration by the UN General Assembly arguably represents the "public opinion" of the international community.

Under the UN Charter, the Security Council has the authority to determine the existence of an act of aggression (Art. 39). However, it seems that under Article 10 of the Charter, on which the "Uniting for Peace" resolution is also based, the General Assembly could equally determine the existence of an act of aggression. In accordance with the "Uniting for Peace" resolution, the General Assembly is entitled to make recommendations for "collective measures" (i.e., enforcement measures), and thus it follows that, as a precondition for such recommendations, the General Assembly is entitled to make determinations on the existence of an act of aggression just like the Security Council. This point is also important in relation to the obligation of neutrality and its qualifications, which will be discussed in Sect. 3.1 below.

2.3 Possible Limit on the Ukrainian Use of Force in Self-Defense

2.3.1 Recovery of Crimea

One additional question to be addressed in connection with the Russian aggression against Ukraine is to what extent Ukraine is allowed to use force in self-defense. More specifically, the question is whether Ukraine's right of self-defense may cover

---

[46] UN Docs. A/RES/ES-11/4 (12 October 2022), 13 October 2022, para. 3; A/ES-11/PV.14, 12 October 2022, pp. 11–12.

[47] UN Docs. A/RES/68/262, supra note 36, para. 5; A/68/PV.80, supra note 40, p. 17. Those voted against were Russia, Armenia, Belarus, Bolivia, Cuba, North Korea, Nicaragua, Sudan, Syria, Venezuela and Zimbabwe.

[48] UN Doc. A/RES/3314(XXIX), 14 December 1974, Annex, Article 3 refers to: (a) the invasion or attack by the armed forces of a State of the territory of another State and (b) bombardment by the armed forces of a State against the territory of another State, etc.

The War in Ukraine Under International Law: Its Use of Force and. . .

the forceful recovery of its Crimean territory having been occupied by Russia since 2014. This is not a hypothetical question as it has been reported that Ukraine has carried out attacks on Russian-occupied Crimea several times, and Ukraine acknowledged its involvement in some of the cases.[49]

The exercise of the right of self-defense is subject to several conditions and requirements, including not only the occurrence of an armed attack as provided for in Article 51 of the UN Charter, but also necessity, proportionality and immediacy under customary international law.[50] The requirement of immediacy means that there must not be undue time-lag between the initial armed attack and the use of force in self-defense.[51] Although the ICJ has not expressly recognized this requirement, it seems to have included this element within the requirement of "necessity", as it found in the *Nicaragua* case that the condition of necessity was not fulfilled because the United States action against Nicaragua commenced several months after the major offensive had been completely repulsed.[52]

In the Ukraine case, no problem in this regard would arise in relation to the Russian invasion commenced on 24 February 2022. However, Crimea may be different as it was invaded by Russia in March 2014 without much resistance on the Ukrainian side,[53] and it has been occupied for some eight years before the subsequent Russian invasion started in February 2022. Since then, the Ukrainian government has repeatedly been calling for the "restoration of Ukraine's territorial integrity", as exemplified by President Volodymyr Zelenskyy's 10-point peace plan announced on the occasion of the summit of the Group of Twenty (G20) in November 2022[54]—a statement implying his determination to recover Crimea.[55]

---

[49] *Asahi Shimbun*, 22 July 2023. On 22 September 2023, Ukraine attacked the headquarters of Russia's Black Sea fleet in Crimea, reportedly killing 34 officers including the fleet's commander. "Russian Black Sea Fleet Commander Killed in Crimea Strike, Ukraine Claims", *VOA News*, 25 September 2023.

[50] See, e.g., Dinstein, *War, Aggression and Self-Defence*, 6th ed., supra note 30, pp. 249–252.

[51] Ibid., p. 252.

[52] *Military and Paramilitary Activities in and against Nicaragua (Nicaragua v. United States of America)*, supra note 8, p. 122, para. 237.

[53] Michael Kofman, Katya Migacheva, Brian Nichiporuk, Andrew Radin, Olesya Tkacheva, and Jenny Oberholtzer, *Lessons from Russia's Operations in Crimea and Eastern Ukraine* (RAND Corporation, 2017), pp. xii, 9, 10, 11, 16, 31.

[54] President of Ukraine (Official Website), "Ukraine Has Always Been a Leader in Peacemaking Efforts; If Russia Wants to End This War, Let it Prove it with Actions - Speech by the President of Ukraine at the G20 Summit", 15 November 2022, at https://www.president.gov.ua/en/news/ukrayina-zavzhdi-bula-liderom-mirotvorchih-zusil-yaksho-rosi-79141.

[55] President Zelenskyy has also specifically referred to Crimea. President of Ukraine (Official Website), "The World Should Know: Respect and Order Will Return to International Relations Only When the Ukrainian Flag Returns to Crimea – Address of President Volodymyr Zelenskyy", 7 April 2023, at https://www.president.gov.ua/en/news/svit-maye-znati-lishe-todi-povernutsya-v-mizhnarodni-vidnosi-82153. See also Veronika Melkozerova, "Ukraine Gives Russia Two Options: Leave Crimea Peacefully or Be Ready for Battle", *Politico*, 6 April 2023, at https://www.politico.eu/article/ukraine-russia-crimea-war-peace-volodymyr-zelenskyy/.

2.3.2 Use of Force to Recover Illegally Occupied Territories

The question is whether it is permissible under international law for a State to use force to recover its territory that has been unlawfully occupied for some or many years by another State as a result of an invasion or armed attack. It may be argued that if it is not permissible, then the occupied territory would be, in a sense, assimilated to the occupying State's own territory. At the same time, the rules on the use of force may operate independently from the question of who has the valid title to the territory; and the status quo on the ground may assume importance, particularly where the legitimate title holder is unclear.

A somewhat telling case in this respect may be found in an arbitral award of 2005 in the dispute between Eritrea and Ethiopia over Badme.[56] Badme was controlled by Ethiopia but was also claimed by Eritrea. In May 1998, fighting broke out between the two around Badme. There was a fundamental disagreement between the two States as to the origin of the conflict: while Ethiopia claimed that Eritrea had carried out an unprovoked violation of Ethiopian sovereignty in May 1998, Eritrea argued that Ethiopian troops had used force to occupy the area in July 1997 and installed an Ethiopian administration there, thus continuing aggression against Eritrea.[57]

The Eritrea-Ethiopia Claims Commission found that Eritrea violated Article 2 (4) of the UN Charter by resorting to armed force on 12 May 1998. While Eritrea contended that Ethiopia was unlawfully occupying Eritrean territory in the area around Badme, citing the decision of the Eritrea-Ethiopia *Boundary Commission* of 2002 attributing the territory to Eritrea, the *Claims Commission* in its 2005 award stated that "self-defense cannot be invoked to settle territorial disputes", and noted that "border disputes between States are so frequent that any exception to the prohibition of the threat or use of force for territory that is allegedly occupied unlawfully would create a large and dangerous hole in a fundamental rule of international law".[58] Thus, it hinted that even if Eritrea held a valid title of sovereignty over the disputed territory, this could not condone the illegality of its resort to force against Ethiopia.

When the Eritrean armed forces attacked Badme in 1998, the attribution of the area was unsettled as it was yet to be determined by the Boundary Commission. Therefore, this case arguably has less bearing in a case justifying the use of force to reclaim territory that is "illegally occupied". The strict and precise implication of the

---

[56]This Partial Award is heavily criticized by Christine Gray. See Christine Gray, "The Eritrea/Ethiopia Claims Commission Oversteps Its Boundaries: A Partial Award?", *European Journal of International Law*, Vol. 17, No. 4 (2006), pp. 699–721.

[57]Ibid., pp. 700, 701, 718.

[58]"Eritrea-Ethiopia Claims Commission, Partial Award, Jus ad Bellum, Ethiopia's Claims 1–8, 19 December 2005" [hereinafter cited as "Eritrea-Ethiopia Claims Commission, Partial Award, Jus ad Bellum"], *International Legal Materials*, Vol. 45 (2006), pp. 430–435, esp. p. 433, para. 10. See also Constantinos Yiallourides, Markus Gehring and Jean-Pierre Gauci, *The Use of Force in relation to Sovereignty Disputes over Land Territory* (British Institute of International and Comparative Law, 2018), p. 66, para. 127. For other relevant cases, see ibid., pp. 66–70, paras. 128–136.

The War in Ukraine Under International Law: Its Use of Force and... 17

Commission's award seems that where the legitimate title holder of the territory is unclear or at least unsettled, resorting to force to materialize a State's claim to the territory is illegal.[59]

The Ukrainian situation is somewhat different. Although it may be said that there currently exists a territorial "dispute" in a judicial sense,[60] there seems little doubt about the Ukrainian sovereignty over Crimea. This was not only agreed between Russia and Ukraine in the 1997 Treaty on Friendship, Cooperation and Partnership,[61] but also recognized by UN General Assembly Resolution 68/262 of 27 March 2014, declaring that the referendum held in Crimea earlier in March had no validity and underscoring that it cannot form the basis for any alteration of the status of Crimea.[62] This fact still may not necessarily legitimize Ukraine's recovery of its territorial control over Crimea by force. Whether it is permissible to use force in self-defense to recover the territory *unlawfully* occupied for some or many years by another State has been subject to keen and inconclusive debate.[63]

Dapo Akande argues that "[w]here occupation follows from an unlawful armed attack, the occupation is a continuing armed attack, and the attacked state does not lose its right of self-defence simply because of passage of time".[64] On the other hand, Tom Ruys states that the combined effect of the immediacy requirement (as part of necessity requirement in self-defense) and the principle of the non-use of force to settle territorial disputes[65] is that "a state cannot invoke the right of self-defence to

---

[59] In fact, the Award stated that all the places Eritrean forces initially invaded were either undisputed Ethiopian territory or within territory that was "peacefully administered" by Ethiopia. Eritrea-Ethiopia Claims Commission, Partial Award, Jus ad Bellum, supra note 58, para. 15. As a side note, the Group of Seven (G7) Foreign Ministers' Communiqué adopted in April 2023 includes a similar but slightly different formulation. In the Communiqué, they "strongly oppose any unilateral attempts to change the *peacefully established* status of territories by force or coercion anywhere in the world" (emphasis added). "G7 Japan 2023: Foreign Ministers' Communiqué, 18 April, 2023, Karuizawa, Nagano", pp. 10–11, at https://www.mofa.go.jp/files/100492731.pdf. The same formula was adopted in the G7 Summit declaration of the same year. "G7 Hiroshima Leaders' Communiqué, 20 May 2023", p. 2, at https://www.mofa.go.jp/mofaj/files/100506875.pdf. These seem to have had the Ukraine situation (particularly Crimea) in mind.

[60] UNCLOS Annex VII Arbitral Tribunal, *Dispute Concerning Coastal State Rights in the Black Sea, Sea of Azov, and Kerch Strait*, Preliminary Objections, Award, 21 February 2020, paras. 188–189.

[61] Article 2 of the Treaty provides that the two States "shall respect each other's territorial integrity and confirm the *inviolability of their common borders*" (emphasis added). UN Doc. A/52/174, 9 June 1997, Annex I, p. 3.

[62] UN Doc. A/RES/68/262, supra note 36, para. 5.

[63] Eliav Lieblich, "Wars of Recovery", *European Journal of International Law*, Vol. 34, No. 2 (2023), pp. 349–381.

[64] Dapo Akande and Antonios Tzanakopoulos, "Legal: Use of Force in Self-Defence to Recover Occupied Territory", *European Journal of International Law*, Vol. 32, No. 4 (2021), p. 1299.

[65] This latter principle refers to a provision in the Friendly Relations Declaration, which states that every State has the duty to refrain from the use of force as a means of solving territorial disputes. UN Doc. A/RES/2625 (XXV), 24 October 1970, Annex. See also UN Doc. S/RES/1177 (1998), 26 June 1998 (on the situation between Eritrea and Ethiopia), pre. para. 3.

recover occupied land when the territory has been peacefully administered by another state for a prolonged period of time".[66]

The fundamental difference between the two lies in their approach to the notion of a "continuing armed attack", particularly after the lapse of considerable time since the initial attack. Contrary to its appearance, Akande's above contention does not ignore the necessity requirement in self-defense; he argues that if an armed attack leads to occupation of territory, then it is continuing, and that the lapse of time "may actually mean that the use of force in self-defence is necessary".[67]

However, a counter-argument that "[w]ithout [temporal] limitation, self-defense would sanction armed attacks for countless prior acts of aggression and conquest"[68] seems to carry weight. At the same time, Ruys does not completely rule out the possibility of using force in self-defense after the lapse of time between an armed attack and an attempt to respond: his argument is that a victim State ultimately forfeits its right of self-defense "if it fails to act within a *reasonable* time and after a new status quo has materialized"[69] (emphasis added). What is "reasonable" would depend on each particular situation.

Ukraine, it seems, may be able to argue that it has resisted Russia's invasion in its exercise of the right of self-defense ever since 2014. In fact, the armed conflict in the Donbas region of Ukraine began well before the February 2022 invasion by Russia. In spite of continuing denial by the Russian government, direct Russian military intervention in Donbas likely began as early as August 2014.[70] If so, it can be said that Ukraine's exercise of its right of self-defense against Russia started in the year of Russian annexation of Crimea.

Moreover, the delay of Ukraine's full response to the Crimean situation may be attributed to the transition of the Ukraine government at the time, following the ouster of former President Yanukovych, as well as the inexperience of Ukraine's provisional government and its unwillingness to take action for fear of escalation.[71] Furthermore, Ukraine was attempting to resolve the dispute by conducting truly

---

[66] Tom Ruys and Felipe Rodriguez Silvestre, "Illegal: The Recourse to Force to Recover Occupied Territory and the Second Nagorno-Karabakh War", *European Journal of International Law*, Vol. 32, No. 4 (2021), p. 1294.

[67] Akande and Tzanakopoulos, "Legal", supra note 64, pp. 1305–1306. This statement may be challenging to understand, but it appears to suggest that the use of force is necessary because the State resorting to force has *no other means* of bringing the armed attack and occupation to an end, which is shown by the passage of time. However, then, it might follow that a State using force after a significant lapse of time could always justify itself by claiming it became "necessary" as a last resort, as far as the necessity requirement is concerned. This situation might effectively eliminate that requirement.

[68] Oscar Schachter, "The Lawful Resort to Unilateral Use of Force", *Yale Journal of International Law*, Vol. 10, No. 2 (Spring 1985), p. 292.

[69] Ruys and Rodriguez Silvestre, "Illegal", supra note 66, p. 1296.

[70] Ivan Katchanovski, "The Separatist War in Donbas: A Violent Break-up of Ukraine?", *European Politics and Society*, Vol. 17, No. 4 (2016), pp. 481, 482.

[71] Kofman, Migacheva, Nichiporuk, Radin, Tkacheva, and Oberholtzer, *Lessons from Russia's Operations in Crimea and Eastern Ukraine*, supra note 53, p. 19.

The War in Ukraine Under International Law: Its Use of Force and... 19

intensive consultations (something to be exhausted before responding by force in self-defense[72]). According to Ukraine's Foreign Minister Dmytro Kuleba, the State engaged in more than 100 rounds of consultation and attempts at a ceasefire since Russia's annexation of Crimea in 2014, but these only led to the full-scale invasion of Ukraine in February 2022.[73]

Thus, Ukraine's possible recovery of Crimea by force as an extension of the ongoing military operations could be justified as a lawful exercise of the right of self-defense.[74] What is more, since there exists an armed conflict between Ukraine and Russia, the law of international armed conflict applies in the whole territory of both States,[75] which may mean that Ukraine's military operations against Russian-occupied Crimea or even Russia proper would not legally be ruled out, if they are otherwise consistent with international law.[76]

---

[72] The necessity requirement implies that the defending State can only resort to force when peaceful means have reasonably been exhausted and no practical alternative means of redress are available. See, e.g., Henderson, *The Use of Force and International Law*, supra note 30, p. 230; Dinstein, *War, Aggression and Self-Defence*, 6th ed., supra note 30, p. 251; Tom Ruys, *'Armed Attack' and Article 51 of the UN Charter: Evolutions in Customary Law and Practice* (Cambridge U.P., 2010), p. 95; Judith Gardam, *Necessity, Proportionality and the Use of Force by States* (Cambridge U.P., 2004), pp. 148–155; Oscar Schachter, *International Law in Theory and Practice* (Nijhoff, 1991), p. 152; Chris O'Meara, *Necessity and Proportionality and the Right of Self-Defence in International Law* (Oxford U.P., 2021), pp. 38–42, 95–96; Roberto Ago, "Addendum to the Eighth Report on State Responsibility", *Yearbook of the International Law Commission, 1980*, Vol. II, Pt. 1, p. 69, para. 120.

[73] Carien du Plessis, "Ukraine Rejects Calls to 'Freeze' Conflict, Foreign Minister Says", *Reuters*, 7 June 2023, at https://www.reuters.com/world/europe/ukraine-rejects-calls-freeze-conflict-for eign-minister-says-2023-06-07/.

[74] The following facts may lend further support to the perception that Russia's aggression against Ukraine has continued from 2014 through 2022. In response to the Russian invasion of Ukraine in 2022, the Security Council continues to use the same agenda item as the one used in 2014 for the situation in Crimea. "In Hindsight", supra note 37. In his statement on the issuance of arrest warrants against President Putin and Ms. Lvova-Belova, Prosecutor Karim A.A. Khan of the ICC said that "most acts in this pattern of deportations were carried out in the context of the *acts of aggression* committed by Russian military forces against the sovereignty and territorial integrity of Ukraine *which began in 2014*" (emphasis added). ICC, "Statement by Prosecutor Karim A. A. Khan KC on the Issuance of Arrest Warrants against President Vladimir Putin and Ms Maria Lvova-Belova", 17 March 2023, at https://www.icc-cpi.int/news/statement-prosecutor-karim-khan-kc-issuance-arrest-warrants-against-president-vladimir-putin.

[75] ICTY, Case No. IT-94-1-AR72 (*The Prosecutor v. Tadic*), Decision on the Defence Motion for Interlocutory Appeal on Jurisdiction, Appeals Chamber, 2 October 1995, *International Legal Materials*, Vol. 35, No. 1 (January 1996), p. 54, para. 70.

[76] This would mainly concern *jus in bello* aspects of international law. For discussions that it may also concern *jus ad bellum*, see Christopher Greenwood, "The Relationship between *ius ad bellum* and *ius in bello*", *Review of International Studies*, Vol. 9, No. 4 (October 1983), pp. 223–225; UK Ministry of Defence, *The Manual of the Law of Armed Conflict* (Oxford U.P., 2004), pp. 348–349, para. 13.3; Keiichiro Okimoto, *The Distinction and Relationship between Jus ad Bellum and Jus in Bello* (Hart, 2011), pp. 31–35.

3 Military Assistance from NATO Members

3.1 Military Assistance and Neutrality Obligations

3.1.1 Current State of Law of Neutrality

Given the significant gap in military power between Russia and Ukraine, it was envisaged at the initial stage that Russia would win in the short term. The Russian side, at least, believed this would occur, but the reality has been quite different. One main reason for Ukraine's unexpectedly successful resistance was military assistance rendered by Western countries, particularly the United States and other NATO member States. In total, at least 30 States have provided lethal weapons to Ukraine and other countries have provided non-lethal materials.[77] The question is whether such assistance violates the law of neutrality[78] and whether it thus renders those States parties to the conflict, specifically as co-belligerents of Ukraine.[79]

According to traditional international law, in the event of war, States other than the belligerents/parties to the war stand in the position of a neutral State and are subject to the obligations of neutrality,[80] including the duties of acquiescence and of impartiality, unless they participate in the war as co-belligerents. While the "duty of acquiescence" requires a neutral to acquiesce in certain repressive measures taken by the belligerent against neutral merchantmen under international law, the "duty of

---

[77] Giulio Bartolini, "The Law of Neutrality and the Russian/Ukrainian Conflict: Looking at State Practice", *EJIL Talk!*, 11 April 2023, at https://www.ejiltalk.org/the-law-of-neutrality-and-the-russian-ukrainian-conflict-looking-at-state-practice/.

[78] For arguments that providing military assistance to Ukraine as such may violate the law of neutrality, see, e.g., Kevin Jon Heller, "The Legality of Weapons Transfer to Ukraine under International Law", *Journal of International Humanitarian Legal Studies*, Vol. 13 (2022), p. 263; Raul (Pete) Pedrozo, "Ukraine Symposium – Is the Law of Neutrality Dead?", Lieber Institute, West Point, 31 May 2022, at https://lieber.westpoint.edu/is-law-of-neutrality-dead/. Switzerland has adopted a policy of rejecting the provision of war materials either to Russia or to Ukraine out of consideration of the law of neutrality. Le Conseil federal (Confédération suisse), *Clarté et orientation de la politique de neutralité: Rapport du Conseil federal en réponse au postulat 22.3385 de la Commission de politique extérieure du Conseil des États du 11 avril 2022*, le 26 octobre 2022, p. 21. For arguments that such assistance would not violate the law of neutrality, see the many articles cited in the notes that follow.

[79] For different arguments on this issue, see infra note 114.

[80] See, generally, Robert W. Tucker, *The Law of War and Neutrality at Sea* (U.S. G.P.O., 1957), pp. 202–258; A.R. Thomas and James C. Duncan (eds.), "Annotated Supplement to The Commander's Handbook on the Law of Naval Operations", *U.S. Naval War College International Law Studies*, Vol. 73 (1999), p. 367, n. 12; U.S. Navy, *The Commander's Handbook on the Law of Naval Operations*, NWP 1-14M, Edition March 2022, para. 7.2; Dietrich Schindler, "Transformations in the Law of Neutrality since 1945", in Astrid J.M. Delissen and Gerard J. Tanja (eds.), *Humanitarian Law of Armed Conflict: Challenges Ahead, Essays in Honour of Frits Kalshoven* (Nijhoff, 1991), pp. 379–380; James Upcher, *Neutrality in Contemporary International Law* (Oxford U.P., 2020), pp. 70–124, 246–258. There are some variations in the explanation of the content of the neutrality obligations among materials and authors.

The War in Ukraine Under International Law: Its Use of Force and... 21

impartiality" obligates neutral States to fulfill their duties and to exercise their rights in an equal manner toward all belligerents. Together with the duty of impartiality, and of equal importance, the neutral State has a "duty of abstention" and a "duty of prevention". The former is to abstain from furnishing belligerents with certain goods or services, such as warships, munitions or war materials. The latter is to prevent the commission of certain acts by anyone within its jurisdiction, such as to prevent the use of neutral ports and waters as a base of operations.

Such traditional neutrality law was destined to be affected by the post-World War I movement toward outlawing war. Treating an aggressor State and its victim State impartially is not only conceptually incompatible with the outlawing of war, but it could also result in tacitly favoring an aggressor State. As a result, the argument arose that deviations from neutrality law were permissible.[81]

Such possibilities were discussed by Hersch Lauterpacht in the name of "qualified neutrality", which allows deviations from the traditional "absolute neutrality". According to Lauterpacht, the adoption of the Treaty for the Renunciation of War in 1928 and the Charter of the United Nations in 1945 allowed neutral States to deny the right of aggressor States to exact from neutrals a full measure of impartiality. Neutral States could, for example, implement economic sanctions as a discriminatory measure against aggressor States while remaining neutral.[82] Qualified neutrality is also called "non-belligerency/non-belligerence".[83]

---

[81] For instance, Schindler argues that third States can respond to the victim of aggression in any way (i.e., any posture ranging from strict neutrality to direct participation in the armed conflict on the side of the victim) such that the dualism neutrality-belligerency has thereby been abolished, and neutrality has become purely optional. Schindler, "Transformations in the Law of Neutrality since 1945", supra note 80, p. 373. See also Andrea Gioia, "Neutrality and Non-Belligerency", in Harry H.G. Post (ed.), *International Economic Law and Armed Conflict* (Nijhoff, 1994), pp. 76–82; Andrew Clapham, *War* (Oxford U.P., 2021), p. 72. On the other hand, there are also theories that the general law of neutrality has not been revoked by the UN Charter, arguing, for example, that if a neutral State renders support to the victim of aggression, this is contrary to the law of neutrality, and that reprisals taken against the State supporting the victim of aggression are admissible under the law of neutrality. Michael Bothe, "The Law of Neutrality", in Dieter Fleck (ed.), *The Handbook of International Humanitarian Law*, 3rd ed. (Oxford U.P., 2013), pp. 552, 558–559; Luca Ferro and Nele Verlinden, "Neutrality during Armed Conflicts: A Coherent Approach to Third-State Support for Warring Parties", *Chinese Journal of International Law*, Vol. 17, No. 1 (March 2018), pp. 33–35.

[82] H. Lauterpacht (ed.), *Oppenheim's International Law*, Vol. II (Disputes, War and Neutrality), 7th ed. (Longmans, 1952), pp. 217, 221, 648–649. See also Hersch Lauterpacht, "Memorandum on the Principles of International Law Governing the Question of Aid to the Allies by the United States, 15 January 1941", in Elihu Lauterpacht (ed.), *International Law Being the Collected Papers by Hersch Lauterpacht*, Vol. 5 (Disputes, War and Neutrality) (Cambridge U.P., 2004), pp. 645–658. Qualified neutrality in fulfilment of existing treaty obligations previous to the war (e.g., provision of troops and arms by a neutral State to one belligerent) was also practiced in the past. Ibid., p. 647; Lauterpacht (ed.), *Oppenheim's International law*, Vol. II, above, pp. 663–665.

[83] See, e.g., UK Ministry of Defence, *The Manual of the Law of Armed Conflict*, supra note 76, p. 19, para. 1.42.1; Gioia, "Neutrality and Non-Belligerency", supra note 81, pp. 76, 110; Lauterpacht (ed.), *Oppenheim's International law*, Vol. II, supra note 82, p. 649; Natalino Ronzitti, "Italy's Non-Belligerency during the Iraqi War", in Maurizio Ragazzi (ed.), *International*

With the obligations of the UN member States laid down in the UN Charter[84] as well as the priority of the obligations under the Charter over obligations under "any other international agreement",[85] it became increasingly difficult to maintain the law of neutrality.[86] It was said that the system of collective security, if it functioned effectively, simply would leave no room for neutrality.[87]

At the same time, in practice, during the Cold War era with its sharp and tense East-West confrontation, the Security Council never determined the existence of an act of aggression in the technical sense under Article 39 of the UN Charter. This meant that there was no authentic way of distinguishing between the aggressor and the victim States. There has also been State practice of "applying" the law of neutrality, and many take the view that the law of neutrality has survived the UN Charter.[88]

Overall, the law of neutrality is in a "chaotic state",[89] but perhaps because of this, Lauterpacht's concept of "qualified neutrality" is of interest in that neutrality law is not completely rejected, nor is its traditional formulation applied in its entirety.[90]

Responsibility Today: Essays in Memory of Oscar Schachter (Brill, 2005), p. 198. For discussions distinguishing between non-belligerency and qualified neutrality, see Raphaël van Steenberghe, "Military Assistance to Ukraine: Enquiring the Need for Any Legal Justification under International Law", *Journal of Conflict and Security Law*, Vol. 28, No. 2 (Summer 2023), pp. 239–241.

[84] The relevant obligations include the obligation to give the United Nations every assistance in any action it takes in accordance with the Charter and to refrain from giving assistance to any State against which the United Nations is taking preventive or enforcement action (Art. 2(5)) as well as the obligation to take actions required by the Security Council for the maintenance of international peace and security (Art. 48).

[85] UN Charter, Art. 103. Here, "other international agreement[s]" include the Hague Convention V respecting the Rights and Duties of Neutral Powers and Persons in Case of War on Land of 1907 and the Hague Convention XIII concerning the Rights and Duties of Neutral Powers in Naval War of 1907. Russia, Ukraine and the USA are all parties to both Conventions.

[86] This does not necessarily apply to the Treaty for the Renunciation of War, which does not contain any provisions for the enforcement of its principal obligation to renounce war. Cf. Lauterpacht (ed.), *Oppenheim's International law*, Vol. II, supra note 82, p. 643.

[87] Paul Seger, "The Law of Neutrality", in Andrew Clapham and Paola Gaeta (eds.), *The Oxford Handbook of International Law in Armed Conflict* (Oxford U.P., 2014), pp. 261–262.

[88] See, e.g., David Turns, "Cyber War and the Law of Neutrality", in Nicholas Tsagourias and Russell Buchan (eds.), *Research Handbook on International Law and Cyberspace* (Edward Elgar, 2015), pp. 389–391; Upcher, *Neutrality in Contemporary International Law*, supra note 80, pp. 34–36.

[89] Gioia, "Neutrality and Non-Belligerency", supra note 81, p. 51.

[90] That there can be a status which is neither at war nor neutral in relation to the belligerent is also recognized in the 1949 Geneva Conventions and the 1977 Additional Protocol I thereto. Along with the term "neutral Power/State", such expressions as "non-belligerent Power" and "State not a Party to the conflict" are used in Articles 4B(2) and 122 of the Third Geneva Convention relative to the Treatment of Prisoners of War, and in Articles 19, 22(2)(a), 31, 39(1), and 64(1) and (3) of Additional Protocol I. In the drafting of the Additional Protocol, the ICRC initially proposed the phrase "State not a Party to the conflict" for those cases where "neutral State" would have been used, because there are situations where a State not a Party to the conflict is not neutral in the technical and traditional sense. However, there were objections that the concept of neutrality was

The War in Ukraine Under International Law: Its Use of Force and... 23

Indeed, references to qualified neutrality are actually found in military manuals of major countries, including the United States[91] and the United Kingdom.[92] There are also some instances of relevant State practice.[93]

3.1.2 Qualified Neutrality Today

The question is: on what conditions, if any, could such a qualified neutrality status be permitted?[94] Conceptually, if the Security Council identifies one belligerent as an

---

still valid and valuable. As a result, both were written side by side as "neutral or other State not Party to the conflict". Michael Bothe, Karl Josef Partsch, and Waldemar A. Solf, *New Rules for Victims of Armed Conflicts: Commentary on the Two 1977 Protocols Additional to the Geneva Conventions of 1949*, 2nd ed. (Nijhoff, 2013), p. 113.

[91] The US Law of War Manual states that:

> The United States has taken the position that certain duties of neutral States may be inapplicable under the doctrine of qualified neutrality.
>
> The law of neutrality has traditionally required neutral States to observe a strict impartiality between parties to a conflict, regardless of which State was viewed as the aggressor in the armed conflict. However, after treaties outlawed war as a matter of national policy, it was argued that neutral States could discriminate in favor of States that were victims of wars of aggression. Thus, before its entry into World War II, the United States adopted a position of 'qualified neutrality' in which neutral States had the right to support belligerent States that had been the victim of flagrant and illegal wars of aggression.

General Counsel of the [US] Department of Defense, *Department of Defense: Law of War* [hereinafter cited as "*US Law of War Manual*"] (DOD, June 2015, updated December 2016), pp. 952–953, para. 15.2.2 (entitled "Qualified Neutrality"). However, it adds that "[t]his position was controversial" and acknowledges that there were many international lawyers who did not share the view of Attorney General Jackson who justified the US status (qualified neutrality) before entering World War II. Ibid., p. 953, n. 39. See also Edwin Borchard, "War, Neutrality and Non-Belligerency", *American Journal of International Law*, Vol. 35, No. 4 (October 1941), pp. 618–625.

[92] The UK Manual of the Law of Armed Conflict notes that:

> Traditionally, the law [of neutrality] has incorporated the principle of non-participation in armed conflict and also impartiality in certain dealings with the belligerents.
>
> In numerous conflicts, including the two World Wars, some non-belligerent states departed from a strict interpretation of the impartiality principle in certain respects, whether by taking non-violent discriminatory measures against states seen as having unlawfully resorted to force, or by giving extensive support to one side. Certain terms, such as 'qualified neutrality' and 'non-belligerence' have been used to describe a status which, while departing from certain traditional neutral duties, was still based on avoidance of active participation in hostilities.

UK Ministry of Defence, *The Manual of the Law of Armed Conflict,* supra note 76, p. 19, paras. 1.42, 1.42.1.

[93] During the Iraq war of 2003, Italy made a non-belligerency declaration. Ronzitti, "Italy's Non-Belligerency during the Iraqi War", supra note 83, p. 201.

[94] Upcher rejects the argument for qualified neutrality by stating that while the prohibition of the threat or use of force in international law has had profound effects on the status of neutrality, it has

aggressor State, there would be no major problem with a third State providing military assistance to the victim of the aggression. However, if the Security Council does not make such a determination, it is difficult to answer whether third States could choose to take the status of qualified neutrality at their own determination and discretion.

Hersch Lauterpacht and Christopher Greenwood argue that a neutral State can choose to remain neutral or, on the basis of the right of collective self-defense,[95] adopt a position of qualified neutrality and assist whichever side it regards as the victim of aggression, even without any Security Council determination.[96] Their argument appears to flow logically from the fact that third States could support the victim of aggression by force through collective self-defense, so it should be legal to support them by lesser means not involving the use of armed force[97] (*a majore ad minus*). However, this argument seems conceptually flawed in that self-defense is something to be invoked to justify the otherwise unlawful *use of force*, not the use of non-forcible measures.[98] It is also factually weak as far as the Ukraine case is

---

not led to the acceptance of an optional theory of neutrality or of a concept of non-belligerency in international law. Upcher, *Neutrality in Contemporary International Law,* supra note 80, p. 37. See also Jeremy K. Davis, "'You Mean They Can Bomb Us?': Addressing the Impact of Neutrality Law on Defense Cooperation", *Lawfare*, 2 November 2020, at https://www.lawfareblog.com/you-mean-they-can-bomb-us-addressing-impact-neutrality-law-defense-cooperation.

[95] Other commentators justifying military assistance to Ukraine based on collective self-defense include Alexander Wentker, "At War: When Do States Supporting Ukraine or Russia become Parties to the Conflict and What Would that Mean?", *EJIL: Talk!*, 14 March 2022, at https://www.ejiltalk.org/at-war-when-do-states-supporting-ukraine-or-russia-become-parties-to-the-conflict-and-what-would-that-mean/.

[96] Greenwood, "The Relationship between *ius ad bellum* and *ius in bello*", supra note 76, p. 230; Lauterpacht (ed.), *Oppenheim's International Law*, Vol. II, supra note 82, pp. 221, 651. There is a slight difference in their arguments. While Greenwood argues that where the Security Council identifies the aggressor State, the law of neutrality can have no place (p. 230), Lauterpacht holds that even in such a case, a third State may choose neutrality (including qualified neutrality) and maintain it, as long as no decision on military sanctions is taken (pp. 648–650). A conspicuous example where military assistance was provided solely on the basis of the decision of the State concerned can be found in the provision of arms by France, the Soviet Union and others to Iraq in the Iran-Iraq war, where no determination of the aggressor State was made by the Security Council and both sides of the war claimed a right of self-defense. Upcher, *Neutrality in Contemporary International Law*, supra note 80, p. 81; Gioia, "Neutrality and Non-Belligerency", supra note 81, pp. 68, 82–83.

[97] See Markus Krajewski, "Neither Neutral nor Party to the Conflict?: On the Legal Assessment of Arms Supplies to Ukraine", *Völkerrechtsblog*, 9 March 2022, at https://voelkerrechtsblog.org/neither-neutral-nor-party-to-the-conflict/. One might possibly argue that a breach of obligations *erga omnes* (prohibition of aggression) could be invoked to justify "violations" of neutrality law (duty of impartiality) as countermeasures. However, the question remains whether a State *other than the injured State* can take countermeasures against the State that is responsible for a violation of obligations *erga omnes*. See Articles on State Responsibility, Article 54. See also Masahiko Asada, "Definition and Legal Justification of Sanctions", in Masahiko Asada (ed.), *Economic Sanctions under International Law and Practice* (Routledge, 2020), pp. 16–17.

[98] van Steenberghe, "Military Assistance to Ukraine", supra note 83, p. 238.

The War in Ukraine Under International Law: Its Use of Force and... 25

concerned, as no States have expressly invoked collective self-defense in justifying military assistance given to Ukraine.[99]

On the other hand, it appears persuasive to argue that, from the standpoint of the UN collective security system and consistent with preventing the expansion of international conflict, qualified neutrality should be limited to cases where there is a Security Council determination of an aggressor State.[100] In addition, according to von Heinegg, third States assisting one belligerent against another have avoided explicitly invoking the right of (collective) self-defense; the fact that non-belligerents endeavored in many cases to conceal their assistance indicates that they did not base their conduct on relevant *opinio juris*.[101]

How, then, should we specifically analyze the military support from NATO countries rendered to Ukraine? As the war in Ukraine was initiated by Russia, a permanent member of the Security Council, the Security Council could not adopt a resolution substantively determining anything about the war. Even though there was no determination by the Security Council, the UN General Assembly in an emergency special session adopted a resolution, by an overwhelming majority, deploring "the aggression by the Russian Federation against Ukraine".

A finding of the occurrence of an act of aggression and the identity of the aggressor by the General Assembly in cases where the Security Council is paralyzed due to a veto cast by one of its permanent members arguably can be considered to have a legal effect. While General Assembly resolutions are normally not "legally binding" on UN member States, determinations of this kind can produce a certain legal effect.[102] Such findings by the General Assembly could thus justify States'

---

[99] Ibid., p. 235; Christian Schaller, "When Aid or Assistance in the Use of Force Turns into an Indirect Use of Force", *Journal on the Use of Force and International Law*, Vol. 10, No. 2 (2023), pp. 181, 185. Stefan Talmon argues that one reason for States assisting Ukraine not invoking collective self-defense might be that it would have made them "co-belligerents" of Ukraine in the latter's armed conflict with Russia. Stefan Talmon, "The Provision of Arms to the Victim of Armed Aggression: The Case of Ukraine", Bonn Research Papers on Public International Law, Paper No. 20/2022, 6 April 2022, p. 6, at https://papers.ssrn.com/sol3/papers.cfm?abstract_id=4077084.

[100] Davis, "'You Mean They Can Bomb Us?'", supra note 94; Wolff Heintschel von Heinegg, "Neutrality in the War against Ukraine", Lieber Institute, West Point, 1 March 2022, at https://lieber.westpoint.edu/neutrality-in-the-war-against-ukraine/. However, von Heinegg also states that the Ukrainian situation is a "game changer"—referring to the aggressor State itself preventing the enforcement mechanism from functioning, the Russian military operations being apparent acts of aggression, and an overwhelming number of States condemning the Russian attacks as violations of international law. He, accordingly, concludes that the many States supplying Ukraine with military equipment are not acting contrary to the law of neutrality. Ibid.

[101] Wolff Heintschel von Heinegg, "'Benevolent' Third States in International Armed Conflicts: The Myth of the Irrelevance of the Law of Neutrality", in Michael N. Schmitt and Jelena Pejic (eds.), *International Law and Armed Conflict: Exploring the Faultlines, Essays in Honour of Yoram Dinstein* (Nijhoff, 2007), pp. 552–556.

[102] A finding of aggression would also give rise to the obligations set out in Article 41 of the Articles on State Responsibility to cooperate to bring to an end any serious breach of an obligation arising under a peremptory norm of general international law (positive obligation), and not to recognize as lawful a situation created by such a breach and not to render aid or assistance in maintaining that situation (negative obligation).

deviation from certain neutrality obligations.[103] Accordingly, States can point to the General Assembly finding of aggression committed by Russia in its Resolution ES-11/1 as a justification for the provision of war materials to Ukraine.

3.2 Relationship Between Military Assistance and Belligerent Status

Another question that may arise is whether military assistance brings the donor State to the status of a co-belligerent[104] and could thus possibly justify Russia taking military action against such a State under certain circumstances.[105] In this connection, Russia clarified as early as in March 2022 that it would consider any country a participant in the armed conflict between Russia and Ukraine if the country imposed a no-fly zone over Ukraine[106] or allowed Ukrainian military aircraft to use its airfields for the use of force against Russia.[107]

With regard to the former (NATO-established no-fly zone[108]), if it were imposed, it would mean that NATO forces could intercept Russian aircraft flying over Ukraine

---

[103] After discussing the right of the UN member States to resort to discriminatory action against the aggressor State while maintaining their formal status of neutrality, Lauterpacht states that "[t]his is so in particular in cases in which the inability of the Security Council to take a decision, either on the question of aggression or on the means to suppress it, is followed by a recommendation of the General Assembly giving expression to the general sense of the United Nations on the subject". Lauterpacht (ed.), *Oppenheim's International Law*, Vol. II, supra note 82, p. 652.

[104] In the *Nicaragua* judgment, the ICJ held that the "provision of weapons" may constitute the "use of force". However, it was in the context of "assistance to rebels", and the context in that case is different from the State-to-State assistance in the Ukraine case. *Military and Paramilitary Activities in and against Nicaragua (Nicaragua v. United States of America)*, supra note 8, pp. 103–104, para. 195.

[105] It is said that a State becoming a party to an international armed conflict does not automatically mean that other parties can use force against it, and that every instance of use of force must be assessed against the prohibition of the use of force. Wentker, "At War: When Do States Supporting Ukraine or Russia become Parties to the Conflict and What Would that Mean?", supra note 95.

[106] "Ukraine No-Fly Zone Would Mean Participation in Conflict: Putin", *Aljazeera*, 5 March 2022, at https://www.aljazeera.com/news/2022/3/5/ukraine-no-fly-zone-would-mean-participation-in-conflict-putin.

[107] "Russia Warns Countries against Hosting Ukraine Military Aircraft", *Defense Post*, 6 March 2022, at https://www.thedefensepost.com/2022/03/06/russia-warns-hosting-ukraine-aircraft/.

[108] A no-fly zone is a restricted area over which certain aircraft are not permitted to fly, and offending aircraft may be shot down. In this connection, Ukrainian President Zelenskyy has called upon NATO and its members to declare a no-fly zone over Ukraine in order to stop Russia's air strikes against Ukraine. However, NATO members have ruled out declaring such a zone due to a fear of escalating the conflict, including the possibility of a direct clash between Russia and NATO members. Bernardo de Miguel, "What is a No-Fly Zone?: The Option that Russia Would Consider a Declaration of War by the West", *El Pais*, 7 March 2022, at https://english.elpais.com/international/2022-03-07/what-is-a-no-fly-zone-the-option-that-russia-would-consider-a-declaration-of-war-by-the-west.html.

The War in Ukraine Under International Law: Its Use of Force and... 27

attempting to bomb the country. Therefore, even though declaring a no-fly zone alone would not immediately render the relevant NATO countries as belligerents in relation to Russia, it could in effect create such a situation if interceptions were actually carried out.

Speaking of Russia's latter argument (hosting of Ukraine's military aircraft), it would be awkward if a party to an international armed conflict is not allowed to attack States assisting the contesting party by providing bases for the latter's military operations. This is because that may effectively mean that the latter party will have an absolute protection by securing a sanctuary that is completely immune from any enemy counterattacks. Additionally, there is some relevant State practice supporting such considerations. In the 2003 Iraq war, the United States noted that States would be its "co-belligerents" if they "allow their territories to be used as a base for [combat] operations".[109]

In this connection, it may be recalled that Article 3 (f) of the "Definition of Aggression" of 1974 provides that, if a State allows another State to use its territory for perpetrating an act of aggression against a third State, the territorial State *itself* will be assessed as having committed an act of aggression.[110] Military assistance in the form of allowing Ukrainian military aircraft to use NATO airfields may be deemed something similar to what is envisaged in the above provision.

However, the above provision is quite an exceptional and even somewhat illogical rule in that it legally *equates* one State's act of assistance (allowing the use of the territory) with another State's primary act (act of aggression). Therefore, it can be considered a special rule for an extremely serious illegal act of aggression.[111] In any event, in the current situation Ukraine is not an aggressor State but rather the victim of an aggression; hence, military assistance by NATO countries would not be assistance to an aggressor State even if such assistance involved the hosting of Ukraine's military aircraft.[112] To that extent, the above provision of the "Definition of Aggression" is not relevant here.

A more general rule on the provision of assistance to other States and the status of the assisting State can be found in Article 16 of the Articles on State Responsibility. It provides that "[a] State which aids or assists another State in the commission of an

---

[109] Alexander Wentker, "At War? Party Status and the War in Ukraine", *Leiden Journal of International Law*, Vol. 36 (2023), p. 655. However, Kuwait, one of the named States, denied the underlying factual allegations, though not the potential legal consequences thereof. Ibid., p. 655.

[110] UN Doc. A/RES/3314(XXIX), supra note 48, Annex, Art. 3 (f).

[111] In fact, the ILC stated in its Commentaries to Draft Articles on State Responsibility adopted in 1978 that it would be "inadmissible . . . to generalize the idea of such equivalence" as is found in Article 3 (f) of the Definition of Aggression. *Yearbook of the International Law Commission, 1978*, Vol. II, Pt. 2, pp. 103–104, Article 27, Commentary, para. 16.

[112] Article 3 (f) of the Definition of Aggression and Article 16 of the Articles on State Responsibility would apply to Belarus because it has provided Russia with a base for aggression. The emergency special session of the UN General Assembly's resolution deploring Russia's aggression also "[d] eplores the involvement of Belarus in [Russia's] unlawful use of force against Ukraine". UN Doc. A/RES/ES-11/1, supra note 13, para. 10.

internationally wrongful act by the latter is internationally responsible *for doing so*" (emphasis added), if certain conditions are met.[113] As the italicized phrase above indicates, unlike Article 3 (f) of the "Definition of Aggression", this provision does not equate the act of the assisting State with that of the assisted State.

Moreover, the Articles on State Responsibility essentially deal with "internationally wrongful acts", so Article 16 provides for the illegality of assistance in the commission of an internationally wrongful act. As noted above, Ukraine is the victim and not the aggressor in the current conflict, so this Article does not appear to apply, either.

Fundamentally, a possible change in status from neutral to belligerent is not dependent on the legality or illegality of the acts concerned. In other words, neither an act assisting illegal conduct nor an act violating neutrality obligations automatically results in an assisting or violating neutral State becoming a belligerent.[114]

Rather, whether a State is a neutral or a belligerent is, it seems, basically a matter to be determined under the law of armed conflict.[115] When a State become a party to an armed conflict, the law of armed conflict begins to apply. In other words, if the

---

[113] The conditions are: first, the assisting State aids another State with the knowledge of the circumstances of the internationally wrongful act; and second, the act would be internationally wrongful if committed by the assisting State.

[114] Lauterpacht, *Oppenheim's International Law*, Vol. II, supra note 82, p. 752; Bothe, "The Law of Neutrality", supra note 81, pp. 558–559; Wentker, "At War: When Do States Supporting Ukraine or Russia become Parties to the Conflict and What Would that Mean?", supra note 95; Stephen P. Mulligan, "International Neutrality Law and U.S. Military Assistance to Ukraine", Congressional Research Service, LSB10735, 26 April 2022, pp. 2, 3; *US Law of War Manual*, supra note 91, para. 15.4.1; Upcher, *Neutrality in Contemporary International Law*, supra note 80, pp. 57–63. See also Kai Ambos, "Will a State Supplying Weapons to Ukraine Become a Party to the Conflict and Thus Be Exposed to Countermeasures?", *EJIL: Talk!* , 2 March 2022, at https://www.ejiltalk.org/will-a-state-supplying-weapons-to-ukraine-become-a-party-to-the-conflict-and-thus-be-exposed-to-coun termeasures/. On the other hand, according to Bradley and Goldsmith, systematic or significant violations of obligations under the law of neutrality can make a State a co-belligerent. Curtis A. Bradley and Jack L. Goldsmith, "Congressional Authorization and the War on Terrorism", *Harvard Law Review*, Vol. 118, No. 7 (May 2005), pp. 2112–2113. However, this view has been criticized as "incorrect". Rebecca Ingber, "Co-Belligerency", *Yale Journal of International Law*, Vol. 42, No. 1 (Winter 2017), pp. 92–93.

[115] For a similar view, see Michael N. Schmitt, "Providing Arms and Materiel to Ukraine: Neutrality, Co-Belligerency, and the Use of Force", Lieber Institute, West Point, 7 March 2022, at https://lieber.westpoint.edu/ukraine-neutrality-co-belligerency-use-of-force/. Hathaway and Shapiro also maintain that "States would become parties to the international armed conflict between Russia and Ukraine if, and only if, they resort to armed force against Russia". Oona A. Hathaway and Scott Shapiro, "Supplying Arms to Ukraine Is not an Act of War", *Just Security*, 12 March 2022, at https://www.justsecurity.org/80661/supplying-arms-to-ukraine-is-not-an-act-of-war/. The ICRC is also of the view that if the conditions for the applicability of international humanitarian law are met, the entity will become a party to the armed conflict, be it an international armed conflict or a non-international armed conflict. International Committee of the Red Cross, *International Humanitarian Law and the Challenges of Contemporary Armed Conflicts*, 32nd International Conference of the Red Cross and Red Crescent, Geneva, 8–10 December 2015, p. 22.

requirements for the application of the law of armed conflict to a State are met, the State concerned should be considered a party to the armed conflict (a belligerent).

From this perspective, it is important to know the point of commencement of the application of the rules on the law of armed conflict (i.e., the point of commencement of an armed conflict),[116] except those applicable to neutral States or in peacetime.[117] Such a point of commencement can be found in Common Article 2 (1) of the 1949 Geneva Conventions (providing that the Conventions "apply to all cases of declared war or of any other armed conflict") and the Commentary to it by the International Committee of the Red Cross (ICRC).

According to the Commentary, which has also been relied on in the same context by the International Criminal Court in its *Lubanga* judgment,[118] "armed conflict" as referred to in Common Article 2 (1) of the Geneva Conventions is defined as "[a]ny difference arising between two States and leading to the intervention of armed forces. . . . It makes no difference how long the conflict lasts, or how much slaughter takes place".[119] The ICRC's Commentary to Article 1 (3) of the 1977 Additional Protocol to the Geneva Conventions, referring to the latter Conventions' Common Article 2 for the Protocol's scope of application, makes a similar statement. It maintains that humanitarian law covers "any dispute between two States involving the use of their armed forces. Neither the duration of the conflict, nor its intensity, play a role".[120] So did the International Criminal Tribunal for the former Yugoslavia (ICTY) in the *Tadic* case.[121] With all this in mind, it would follow that merely

---

[116] Masahiko Asada, "The Concept of 'Armed Conflict' in International Armed Conflict", in Mary-Ellen O'Connell (ed.), *What is War: An Investigation in the Wake of 9/11* (Nijhoff, 2012), pp. 53–59; idem, "The Intensity Element in the Concept of International Armed Conflict under International Humanitarian Law: A Dissenting Opinion to the International Law Association's Use of Force Committee Report", *Taiwanese Yearbook of International Law*, Vol. 2 (2016), pp. 119–157, esp. pp. 124–133. The latter article is a complete version of the author's original paper along with some additions; it had been shortened in the former book chapter due to disagreements in content with the editor.

[117] Such rules can be found, for instance, in Article 122 of the 1949 Third Geneva Convention and Article 83 of the 1977 Additional Protocol I.

[118] ICC, Case No. ICC-01/04-01/06 (*The Prosecutor v. Lubanga*), Decision on the Confirmation of Charges, Pre-Trial Chamber I, 29 January 2007, paras. 206–207.

[119] Jean S. Pictet (ed.), *Geneva Convention for the Amelioration of the Condition of the Wounded and Sick in Armed Forces in the Field: Commentary* (ICRC, 1952), p. 32. According to the ICRC's new Commentaries, "[a]n armed conflict can arise when one State unilaterally uses armed force against another State even if the latter does not or cannot respond by military means". ICRC, *Commentary on the Third Geneva Convention: Convention (III) relative to the Treatment of Prisoners of War* (Cambridge U.P., 2021), p. 94, paras. 255–256.

[120] Yves Sandoz et al. (eds.), *Commentary on the Additional Protocols of 8 June 1977 to the Geneva Conventions of 12 August 1949* (Nijhoff, 1987), p. 40, paras. 61–62.

[121] ICTY, Case No. IT-94-1-AR72 (*The Prosecutor v. Tadic*), Decision on the Defence Motion for Interlocutory Appeal on Jurisdiction, Appeals Chamber, supra note 75, p. 54, para. 70, which states that "an armed conflict exists whenever there is a resort to armed force between States".

providing military assistance, such as war materials, would not render the assisting State a belligerent.[122]

Then, one might ask: isn't it legally permissible for a belligerent to use force to eliminate military assistance by a neutral State? In general terms, it can be stated that if acts of a neutral State are in breach of its neutrality obligations, international law provides for countermeasures to induce that State to return to compliance with its obligations. According to Article 50 of the Articles on State Responsibility, however, countermeasures must not affect the obligation to refrain from the threat or use of force as embodied in the UN Charter. Thus, even if there has been a breach of the obligation of neutrality, the State affected by the breach may not take countermeasures using force (except in self-defense). This restriction would prevent a belligerent from using force to eliminate military assistance. It would therefore be unlikely, at least from a legal perspective, that the assisting neutral State would become involved in the armed conflict through its provision of assistance.

Furthermore, the above scenario assumes that qualified neutrality is a violation of the law of neutrality and the affected State takes countermeasures. If qualified neutrality is permissible under international law, as we assume here, no breach of neutrality law and thus no legal problem would arise in providing military assistance to the victim of aggression, particularly when the aggressor State is determined by the Security Council (or by the General Assembly in the case of the Council's dysfunction due to the casting of a veto). In fact, in relation to the War in Ukraine, no State, including Russia, has expressed the view that military assistance is a breach of the obligation of impartiality.[123] Thus, it would be *a fortiori* unlikely that the assisting State would become a party to the conflict as a result of its assistance.

While, according to the ICRC's Commentaries, it is basically the "intervention" or "involvement" of the armed forces of a State that makes the latter a party to the armed conflict, the key question is what kind of intervention or involvement would be sufficient in this regard. In fact, there are some nuanced views on this point, including regarding the joint planning or decision-making of military operations or targeting. For instance, it has sometimes been suggested that supporting a belligerent will make the supporting State a party to the conflict when the latter State is involved in the joint planning of combat operation or the decisions on specific targeting.[124] As

---

[122] Moreover, it is said that even if a neutral State uses force (in self-defense) to defend its neutrality and is engaged in hostilities with one of the parties to the conflict, this does not make the neutral State a belligerent. See Bothe, "The Law of Neutrality", supra note 81, p. 558; Peter Hostettler and Olivia Danai, "Neutrality in Air Warfare", in Rüdiger Wolfrum (ed.), *The Max Planck Encyclopedia of Public International Law*, Vol. VII (Oxford U.P., 2012), p. 635, para. 8; idem, "Neutrality in Land Warfare", in ibid., p. 640, para. 12; Christine Chinkin, *Third Parties in International Law* (Clarendon, 1993), p. 308.

[123] van Steenberghe, supra note 83, pp. 232, 241, 242.

[124] Schmitt acknowledges that the mere provision of arms and other materiel support to Ukraine's armed forces does not, standing alone, make the supporting States become parties to an international armed conflict with Russia. However, he also argues that supporting a belligerent will make the supporting State a party to the conflict when the latter State is involved in the joint planning and provisioning of another State's combat operation to the extent that it would trigger an international

it is said that international law does not contain any specific rules for identifying parties to the conflict,[125] perhaps except for most obvious cases, it is desirable to clarify the law in this respect.

In this connection, the war in Ukraine may be providing important State practice not only on what is permissible for neutral States in relation to neutrality or qualified neutrality but also on, as a conceptually and legally separate question, what makes them parties to the conflict. For example, the US restraints on the provision of missiles with a range that could easily reach Russia, and its request for assurances that such weapons would not be used in attacks on the Russian territory,[126] as well as its restraints on the provision of information only for "situational awareness" and not extending to "targeting intelligence",[127] may be seen in this light. However, as these restraints may well be strongly influenced by political considerations (i.e., wanting not to be drawn into a war with Russia),[128] as well as by the personal character of the Russian leadership, we should be cautious about over-emphasizing the State practice in the war in Ukraine for purposes of stating what international law would be in general terms.

---

armed conflict if conducted alone by the supporting State. Schmitt, "Providing Arms and Materiel to Ukraine", supra note 115. Milanovic also puts forward an analogous argument by saying that while supplying information does not make the assisting State a participant in the conflict, actually making decisions or specific suggestions on what targets should be struck, when and how, is "a material step further". Marko Milanovic, "The United States and Allies Sharing Intelligence with Ukraine", *EJIL: Talk!*, 9 May 2022, at https://www.ejiltalk.org/the-united-states-and-allies-sharing-intelligence-with-ukraine/. See also Alexander Wentker, "At War: When Do States Supporting Ukraine or Russia become Parties to the Conflict and What Would that Mean?", supra note 95.

[125] Wentker, "At War? Party Status and the War in Ukraine", supra note 109, pp. 647, 649–652.

[126] The United States is said to have provided Ukraine with the HIMARS advanced rocket system (which has a maximum range of 300 km) with a range limited to 70–80 km, and on condition that it would not be used to attack Russian territory. *Nihon Keizai Shimbun*, 5 October 2022. These restraints seem to have been somewhat modified later. In October 2023, the US government announced that it had provided Ukraine with long-range ATACMS missiles, with a range of 165 km; but the commitment not to employ these missiles to target Russian territory reportedly remains unchanged. *Yomiuri Shimbun*, 19 October 2023.

[127] Natasha Bertrand and Katie Bo Lillis, "US Officials Say Biden Administration Is Sharing Intelligence with Ukraine at a 'Frenetic' Pace after Republicans Criticize Efforts", *CNN Politics*, 4 March 2022, at https://edition.cnn.com/2022/03/04/politics/us-ukraine-intelligence/index.html. For somewhat conflicting information provided later, see Ryan Morgan, "Officials Say Ukraine Reliant on US Targeting Data to Carry out Strikes: Report", *Atlas News*, 9 February 2023.at https://theatlasnews.co/conflict/2023/02/09/officials-say-ukraine-reliant-on-us-targeting-data-to-carry-out-strikes-report/.

[128] This may well also apply to the Russian side.

4 Conclusion

The Russian invasion of Ukraine and the many atrocities that followed have led to a discourse on the uselessness of international law. However, such a discourse is no more constructive than a discourse on the uselessness of criminal law pointing to the constant occurrence of murder. We should instead focus on how to respond to this unprecedented crisis in the rule of law and what to do with it in order to avoid its recurrence.

It is not hyperbolic to claim that the ways in which the international community addresses the war in Ukraine will determine the future of the rule of law. The international community must not become a society in which overt acts of aggression and unimaginable atrocities of war crimes become permissible if a major power with nuclear weapons so wishes. 95 years since the outlawry of war by the Kellogg-Briand Pact and 78 years since the prohibition of the use of force by the UN Charter, these essential culminations of human wisdom must never be allowed to erode.

In this context, it is noteworthy that Russia is still, at least in part, attempting to justify its actions by reference to international law. The international community must continue to point out that most of Russia's claims are factually incorrect and/or groundless under international law principles. At the same time, this tragic situation offers the international community a chance to develop some of the unresolved or underdeveloped aspects of international law that could be relevant in the future.

Use of Force by Russia and *jus ad bellum*

Tatsuya Abe

Abstract The war in Ukraine is another case of the use of force by Russia and its predecessor the Soviet Union (the USSR) in the territory of another State, though its impacts are more significant than those of other cases. Since the adoption of the UN Charter that established the prohibition of the use of force, the USSR and Russia has used force in Hungary, Czechoslovakia, Afghanistan, Tajikistan, Georgia, Crimea, Syria, and Kazakhstan. This article conducts critical analysis of legal justifications demonstrated by the USSR and Russia and reaches a conclusion that in most cases their military actions were in violation of international law. The discussion also reveals that their use of force has two objectives—the maintenance of areas under their influence and the protection of Russian nationals in the former Soviet States—and that in order to achieve these objectives, they have attempted to expand the scope of exceptions to the prohibition on the use of force, though these attempts, not unique to them, have been unsuccessful.

1 Introduction

On 24 February 2022, Russia began a large-scale cross-border "special military operation" against neighboring Ukraine.[1] No matter what it was called, this was a use of force prohibited by Article 2, para. 4 of the Charter of the United Nations

---

This is an updated and English translated version of the original article "Use of Force by Russia and *jus ad bellum*", in Masahiko Asada and Dai Tamada (eds.), *The War in Ukraine, International Law and International Political Economics* (Toshindo, 2023), pp. 38–65 (in Japanese).

---

[1] Address by the President of the Russian Federation, 24 February 2022; UN Doc. S/2022/154, 24 February 2022, p. 6. See also UN Doc. S/2022/363, 5 May 2022, Annex, pp. 2–3, para. 5.

T. Abe (✉)
Aoyama Gakuin University, Tokyo, Japan
e-mail: t12891@aoyamagakuin.jp

© The Author(s), under exclusive license to Springer Nature Singapore Pte Ltd. 2024
M. Asada, D. Tamada (eds.), *The War in Ukraine and International Law*,
https://doi.org/10.1007/978-981-97-2504-5_2

(UN) and customary international law.[2] While Russia attempted to justify this use of force based on the right of self-defence,[3] most States have not supported Russia's argument but criticized Russia for a blatant violation of international law.[4] The UN Security Council should have responded to this situation; however, it became dysfunctional due to a veto cast by Russia itself.[5] As a consequence, the UN General Assembly held an emergency special session in accordance with the Uniting for Peace Resolution and adopted the Resolution "Aggression against Ukraine" by an overwhelming majority.[6] The international community is now facing a very serious

---

[2] Albania described this operation as a "domestic nickname and the new Russian definition for aggression" (UN Doc. S/PV.8988, 7 March 2022, p. 8 (Albania)). In its order in the Allegations of Genocide under the Genocide Convention case, the International Court of Justice put forward a general formulation as follows: "any military operation . . . inevitably causes loss of life, mental and bodily harm, and damage to property and to the environment" (*Allegations of Genocide under the Convention on the Prevention and Punishment of the Crime of Genocide (Ukraine v. Russian Federation), Provisional Measures, Order of 16 March 2022, I.C.J. Reports 2022*, p. 228, para. 74).

[3] UN Doc. S/2022/154, 24 February 2022, p. 6; UN Doc. A/ES-11/PV.1, 28 February 2022, p. 8 (Russia).

[4] UN Doc. S/PV.8979, 25 February 2022, pp. 2 (United States), 4 (United Kingdom), 5 (Mexico), 5 (Brazil), 8 (Norway), 8–9 (Ireland), 9–10 (Ghana), 11 (Kenya); UN Doc. A/ES-11/PV.1, 28 February 2022, pp. 11 (European Union), 12–13 (Denmark on behalf of eight Nordic-Baltic countries), 15 (Georgia), 19 (Austria), 20 (Switzerland), 22 (Panama on behalf of Costa Rica and the Dominican Republic), 23 (Bulgaria), 24 (Italy), 28 (Singapore); UN Doc. A/ES-11/PV.2, 28 February 2022, pp. 1 (Uruguay), 2 (Slovakia), 3 (Belgium), 4 (Netherlands), 7 (Slovenia), 9 (Ireland), 10 (Japan), 11 (Mexico), 16 (Greece), 17 (Peru), 18 (Guatemala); UN Doc. A/ES-11/PV.3, 1 March 2022, pp. 4 (Suriname), 5 (Brunei), 8 (Australia), 9 (Jamaica), 10 (Luxembourg), 14 (Spain), 15 (Belize), 16 (Gabon), 18 (Samoa), 18 (Philippines), 18 (Cabo Verde), 19 (Hungary), 20 (Malta); UN Doc. A/ES-11/PV.4, 1 March 2022, pp. 1 (Andorra), 3 (Moldova), 4 (Grenada), 5 (Republic of Korea), 6 (Trinidad and Tobago), 9 (Argentine), 11 (Niger), 13 (Romania), 13 (Montenegro), 14 (San Marino), 15 (Cyprus), 17 (North Macedonia), 15–16 (Portugal); UN Doc. A/ES-11/PV.5, 2 March 2022, pp. 2 (Myanmar), 3 (Djibouti).

[5] A draft resolution (UN Doc. S/2022/155, 25 February 2022) was rejected by eleven in favor, one against (Russia), and three abstentions (China, India, and United Arab Emirates) (UN Doc. S/PV.8979, 25 February 2022, p. 6).

[6] UN Doc. A/RES/ES-11/1, 2 March 2022. A draft resolution (UN Doc. A/ES-11/L.1, 1 March 2022) was adopted with 141 in favor, five against, and 35 abstentions (UN Doc. A/ES-11/PV.5, 2 March 2022, pp. 14–15). The resolution includes noticeable paragraphs relevant to the prohibition of the use of force, such as recalling the obligation of all States under Article 2 of the Charter (preamble para. 2); recalling also its resolution 2625 (XXV) (the Declaration on Principles of International Law concerning Friendly Relations and Cooperation among States in accordance with the Charter of the United Nations) (preamble para. 6); recalling further its resolution 3314 (XXIX) of 14 December 1974 (Definition of Aggression) (preamble para. 7); condemning the 24 February 2022 declaration by the Russian Federation of a "special military operation" in Ukraine (preamble para. 10); reaffirming that no territorial acquisition resulting from the threat or use of force shall be recognized as legal (preamble para. 11); recognizing that the military operations of the Russian Federation inside the sovereign territory of Ukraine are on a scale that the international community has not seen in Europe in decades (preamble para. 13); deplores in the strongest terms the aggression by the Russian Federation against Ukraine in violation of Article 2 (4) of the Charter (operative para. 2); demands that the Russian Federation immediately cease its use of force against Ukraine and to refrain from any further unlawful threat or use of force against any Member State

Use of Force by Russia and *jus ad bellum*

crisis of an all-out use of force by a sovereign State against another, which reminds us of a situation that happened in the era before the Kellogg-Briand Pact. This is "one of the greatest challenges ever to the international order", as described by the UN Secretary-General,[7] which cannot be acceptable to the international community after more than 75 years have passed since the use of force was prohibited by the UN Charter. This military conflict remains ongoing at the time of writing.

Having noted that this is another case of the use of force by Russia in the territory of another State, though its impacts are more significant than those of other cases, the author will outline similar cases involving the USSR and Russia since the adoption of the UN Charter that established the prohibition of the use of force (Sect. 2) and analyze their legal justifications from the perspective of *jus ad bellum* (Sect. 3).

2 Use of Force by the USSR and Russia

2.1 Cases and Legal Justifications

Irrespective of legality, the USSR/Russia has used force in the territory of another State depending on the situations and occasions since 1945, when the UN Charter entered into force. The widely recognized cases and the legal justifications adopted by the USSR/Russia are listed in the Table 1.

2.2 Features

The table suggests four features as follows. First and foremost, the States in which the USSR/Russia used force are limited to those that were under their influence. They were the socialist States in East Europe and neighboring Afghanistan during the Cold War and the former Soviet Union States and Syria after the end of the Cold War. Second, the USSR/Russia used force upon request of the territorial State in several cases, including those where collective self-defence was invoked. This indicates that the use of force was not carried out against the will of the territorial State. On the contrary, the present case of Ukraine is the second case where Russia used force in the territory of the "attacked State" based on collective self-defence after the use of force in the border dispute between Tajikistan and Afghanistan. Third, the protection of Russian nationals was the most important agenda in the

---

(operative para. 3); demands that the Russian Federation immediately, completely, and unconditionally withdraw all of its military forces from the territory of Ukraine within its internationally recognized borders (operative para. 4); deplores the involvement of Belarus in this unlawful use of force against Ukraine, and calls upon it to abide by its international obligations (operative para. 10).

[7]United Nations, 5 April 2022, at https://www.youtube.com/watch?v=YHN43mEWza8.

Table 1 List of cases where the USSR/Russia used force in the territory of another State

Justifications	Alleged cases where the territorial State made a request		Cases where the territorial State made no request		
	Military assistance on request	Collective self-defence	Collective self-defence	Individual self-defence	Individual self-defence (Protection of nationals abroad)
Hungary in 1956	X				
Czechoslovakia in 1968	X				
Afghanistan in 1979	X				
Tajikistan in 1993 (border dispute between Tajikistan and Afghanistan)	X				
Afghanistan in 1993 (border dispute between Tajikistan and Afghanistan)			X		
Georgia in 2008[a]				X	X
Crimea in Ukraine in 2014[b]	X				?
Syria in 2015	X				
Kazakhstan in 2022	X				
Ukraine in 2022			X	X	?
Donetsk and Luhansk regions in Ukraine in 2022	?	X			

[a] The deployment of Russian forces in Georgia for peace-keeping purposes was allowed based on Article 3, para. 1, the Agreement on Principles of Settlement of the Georgian–Ossetian Conflict, 24 June 1992 (https://peacemaker.un.org/sites/peacemaker.un.org/files/GE%20RU_920624_AgreemenOnPrinciplesOfSettlementGeorgianOssetianConflict.pdf) and para. 2 (b), the Cease-Fire and Separation-of-Forces Agreement, 14 May 1994 (UN Doc. S/1994/583, 17 May 1994, Annex I)
[b] The station of the Russian Black Sea Fleet in Crimea was allowed by a bilateral treaty with Ukraine (Partition Treaty on the Status and Conditions of the Black Sea Fleet, 28 May 1997, Article 8, para. 4: "Military units may in their locations and movements implement protection measures in accordance with the procedure established in the Armed Forces Federation, in cooperation with the competent authorities of Ukraine".)

recent three cases in the former Soviet Union States. Under Article 61, para. 2 of the 1993 Constitution of Russia, the Russian government is obliged to protect its nationals abroad. Last but not least, in most of the cases, the justifications used by the USSR/Russia were rejected by other States. Both justifications and criticisms in the previous cases were sometimes repeated in subsequent cases. To put it

Use of Force by Russia and *jus ad bellum*

differently, the international community has failed to prevent similar cases of the use of force by the USSR and Russia.

3 Critical Analysis of Legal Justifications

3.1 Cases Where the Territorial State Allegedly Made a Request

The USSR/Russia has claimed that the territorial States made requests for assistance in many cases. Two justifications are possible: collective self-defence and military assistance on request (or intervention by invitation). In theory, they are completely different justifications. On the one hand, the former allows the use of force against the attacking State not only in the territory of the attacked (territorial) State but also in the territory of the attacking State and the area beyond national jurisdiction. On the other hand, the latter permits the use of force only in the territory of the inviting State. It cannot justify the use of force against the third State. However, in practice, it is not easy to make a distinction between these two justifications.[8] In fact, the USSR relied on both justifications in two cases.[9]

(1) Collective self-defence

Collective self-defence is the justification to use force under Article 51 of the UN Charter and customary international law. When an armed attack by a State against another State happens, the third State can use force against the attacking State. In its Nicaragua case judgment, the International Court of Justice (ICJ) clarified the declaration and request of the attacked State as requirements for collective self-defence in addition to those for individual self-defence such as the occurrence of an armed attack, necessity, and proportionality.[10]

(a) Previous cases

In two cases during the Cold War, the USSR used force in the territory of the "attacked State" upon its request. However, the USSR was strongly criticized for abusing collective self-defence. In the case of Czechoslovakia in 1968, the USSR

---

[8] Christine Gray, *International Law and the Use of Force* (Fourth edition, Oxford University Press, Oxford, 2018), p. 177.

[9] Gray and Henderson discussed the use of force in Czechoslovakia and Afghanistan in 1968 and 1979 as examples of both collective self defence and intervention by invitation (Gray, supra note 8, pp. 93, 96–97, 183, 187; Christian Henderson, *The Use of Force and International Law* (Second edition, Cambridge University Press, Cambridge, 2024), pp. 336, 448, 474–475). It was in the judgment of the Nicaragua case in 1986 that the International Court of Justice (ICJ) clarified the request of the attacked State as one of the requirements for collective self-defence.

[10] *Military and Paramilitary Activities in and against Nicaragua (Nicaragua v. United States of America), Merits, Judgment, I.C.J. Reports 1986*, pp. 103–105, paras. 195 and 199.

argued that it sent its troops to Czechoslovakia upon request of the government of the latter and based on the right of individual and collective self-defence.[11] On the contrary, Czechoslovakia itself not only considered the action of the USSR to be illegal[12] but also denied its "request" to the USSR as such.[13] Other States thus condemned the USSR.[14] In the case of Afghanistan in 1979, the USSR claimed that the request of the Afghan government and the decision of the USSR were fully consistent with the right of individual and collective self-defence stipulated in the UN Charter.[15] However, it must be observed that the USSR deployed its armed forces in the territory of Afghanistan before the request.[16] Commentators are also of the view that a valid request was not present[17] and that it was unclear—or even doubtful—whether an armed attack by a foreign State against the territorial State occurred in both cases.[18]

(b) **Case of Ukraine**

Russia referred to the request of the "Donetsk People's Republic" and the "Luhansk People's Republic" and invoked collective self-defence.[19] This would be Russia's appeal of fulfilling one of the requirements for collective self-defence. However, it is very difficult to accept this argument. The statehood of two "people's republics" was extremely questionable.[20] Only when Russia recognized both "republics" as a State

---

[11] UN Doc. S/8759, 21 August 1968; UN Doc. S/PV.1441, 21 August 1968, pp. 7–8, paras. 75, 90 and 93 (USSR).

[12] UN Doc. S/PV.1441, 21 August 1968, pp. 13–14, paras. 137–140 (Czechoslovakia).

[13] UN Doc. S/PV.1445, 24 August 1968, p. 17, para. 161 (Czechoslovakia).

[14] UN Doc. S/PV.1441, 21 August 1968, p. 17, para. 162 (United States), p. 18, para. 171 (Canada), p. 19, para. 185 (Denmark); UN Doc. S/PV.1442, 22 August 1968, p. 1, para. 7 (Ethiopia), p. 9, para. 88 (United Kingdom); UN Doc. S/PV.1443, 22 August 1968, p. 2, para. 18 (Senegal).

[15] UN Doc. S/PV.2185, 5 January 1980, pp. 2–3, paras. 13, 16, 17 (USSR); UN Doc. S/PV.2186, 5 January 1980, p. 3, paras. 17 and 19 (USSR).

[16] UN Doc. S/PV.2185, 5 January 1980, p. 8, para. 76 (Pakistan).

[17] Gray, supra note 8, p. 187; George Nolte and Janina Barkholdt, "The Soviet Intervention in Afghanistan—1979–80", in Tom Ruys and Olivier Corten with Alexandra Hofer (eds.), *The Use of Force in International Law: A Case-Based Approach* (Oxford University Press, Oxford, 2018), p. 303.

[18] Olivier Corten, *The Law Against War* (Second edition, Hart Publishing, Oxford, 2021), pp. 452–453. Gerhard Hafner, "The Intervention in Czechoslovakia—1968", in Tom Ruys and Olivier Corten with Alexandra Hofer (eds.), *The Use of Force in International Law: A Case-Based Approach* (Oxford University Press, Oxford, 2018), pp. 154–155. If armed attack does not occur, the third State cannot invoke collective self-defence but must rely on intervention by invitation. Ambiguity in the facts might induce the third State to put forward two justifications in case.

[19] UN Doc. S/2022/154, 24 February 2022, p. 6 ("The People's Republics of Donbass appealed to Russia for help".); UN Doc. A/76/740–S/2022/179, 7 March 2022, Annex III and Annex IV.

[20] Claus Kreß, "The Ukraine War and the Prohibition of the Use of Force in International Law", *Occasional Paper Series*, No. 13 (2022), Torkel Opsahl Academic EPublisher at https://www.toaep.org/ops-pdf/13-kress/, pp. 7–8; Tamas Hoffmann, "War or Peace? - International Legal Issues concerning the Use of Force in the Russia-Ukraine Conflict", *Hungarian Journal of Legal Studies*, vol. 63 (2022), pp. 212–214; Olivier Corten and Vaios Koutroulis, "The 2022 Russian intervention

Use of Force by Russia and *jus ad bellum*

and concluded a bilateral "treaty" did they obtain the nominal status of "State," which could be entitled to make a request to Russia, as mentioned by many States at the meetings of the UN Security Council and General Assembly.[21] Contrary to the previous cases where the representativeness of the government was doubtful, in the case of Ukraine, the statehood itself is highly problematic. In its Resolution "Aggression against Ukraine", the UN General Assembly special emergency session "[d]eplores the 21 February 2022 decision by the Russian Federation related to the status of certain areas of the Donetsk and Luhansk regions of Ukraine as a violation of the territorial integrity and sovereignty of Ukraine and inconsistent with the principles of the Charter" (operative para. 5) and "[d]emands that the Russian Federation immediately and unconditionally reverse the decision related to the status of certain areas of the Donetsk and Luhansk regions of Ukraine" (operative para. 6). The Donetsk and Luhansk regions were not deprived of internal self-determination. It was not established that serious violations of human rights or acts of genocide took place.[22] The recognition of the State endorsing the separation of both "republics" from Ukraine constitutes a violation of the principle of non-intervention and thus has no legal effect. Since they have no status as an attacked "State", the request requirement by the attacked State and declaration thereof cannot be met. Furthermore, other requirements for the occurrence of an armed attack, that is, necessity and proportionality, are also not met. These points will be discussed later.

(2) **Military assistance on request**

Military assistance on request refers to "direct military assistance by the sending of armed forces by one State to another State upon the latter's request".[23] This concept—also known as "intervention by invitation"—is one of the justifications for a State to use force in the territory of another State. This concept is not only

---

[21] UN Doc. S/PV.8970, 21 February 2022, pp. 3 (United States), 6 (United Kingdom), 7 (Ireland), 8 (Kenya), 10 (Gabon), 10 (Norway), 13 (Ukraine); UN Doc. S/PV.8974, 23 February 2022, pp. 6 (Ireland), 7 (Norway); UN Doc. A/ES-11/PV.1, 28 February 2022, pp. 6 (Ukraine), 15 (Georgia), 19 (Austria); UN Doc. A/ES-11/PV.2, 28 February 2022, pp. 1 (Uruguay), 4–5 (Fiji), 8 (Turkey), 21 (Chile); UN Doc. A/ES-11/PV.3, 1 March 2022, pp. 1 (Colombia), 19 (Hungary); UN Doc. A/ES-11/PV.4, 1 March 2022, p. 5 (Republic of Korea); UN Doc. A/ES-11/PV.5, 2 March 2022, p. 24 (Turkey).

[22] James A. Green, Christian Henderson, and Tom Ruys, "Editorial: Russia's attack on Ukraine and the jus ad bellum", *Journal on the Use of Force and International Law*, vol. 9 (2022), p. 18. See also Chapter 'The War in Ukraine Under International Law: Its Use of Force and Armed Conflict Aspects' of this volume.

[23] Institute of International Law, Resolution on Military Assistance on Request, 8 September 2011, Article 1 (a).

widely supported in academia[24] but also often invoked in practice.[25] Military assistance on request is lawful as long as the request is valid. Having relied on Article 20, ILC Articles on the State Responsibility, and the commentary thereof,[26] commentators have identified elements for determining the validity of the request, such as the request from the government; the explicit, actual, and prior expression of request based on free will; and the limited use of force within the purposes and scope of the request.[27]

(a) **Previous cases**

The validity of the request was highly questionable in the cases during the Cold War. In the case of Hungary in 1956, the USSR argued that Hungary took military measures to suppress the anti-revolutionary groups and thus "appealed to the Government of the Soviet Union for assistance".[28] However, other States condemned the USSR by pointing out that the "request" was made by the puppet group installed after Russia's military intervention.[29] Commentators have taken virtually the same position.[30] In the cases of Czechoslovakia and Afghanistan in 1968 and 1979, even if they could be understood as examples of military assistance on request, other States expressed doubts, as illustrated above. Several international law scholars have also referred to them as the abuse of justification because the request of Czechoslovakia was not made or at least forced, and the request of

---

[24] Elihu Lauterpacht, "Intervention by Invitation", *International and Comparative Law Quarterly*, vol. 7 (1958), p. 103; Christopher Joyner, "The United States Action in Grenada: Reflections on the Lawfulness of the Invasion", *American Journal of International Law*, vol. 78 (1984), p. 138; Antonio Tanca, *Foreign Armed Intervention in Internal Conflict* (Martinus Nijhoff, Dordrecht/ Boston/London, 1993), p. 19; Russell Buchan and Nicholas Tsagourias, "The Crisis in Crimea and the Principle of Non-Intervention", *International Community Law Review*, vol. 19 (2017), p. 182; Corten, supra note 18, p. 248.

[25] See George Nolte, "Intervention by Invitation", in Rüdiger Wolfrum (ed.), *Max Planck Encyclopedia of Public International Law, VI* (Oxford University Press, Oxford, 2012), pp. 282–285, paras. 2–13; Seyfullah Hasar, *State Consent to Foreign Military Intervention during Civil Wars* (Brill, Leiden, 2022), pp. 182–272.

[26] "... the consent of the State must be valid in international law, clearly established, really expressed (which precludes merely presumed consent), internationally attributable to the State and anterior to the commission of the act to which it refers. Moreover, consent can be invoked as precluding the wrongfulness of an act by another State only within the limits which the State expressing the consent intends with respect to its scope and duration". (*Yearbook of the International Law Commission, 1979*, Volume II (Part Two), p. 112).

[27] Ibid., pp. 112–113; Henderson, supra note 9, pp. 473–475, 480; Corten, supra note 18, pp. 263–274.

[28] UN Doc. S/PV.746, 28 October 1956, p. 4, para. 20 (USSR).

[29] Ibid., p. 15, para. 90 (France); UN Doc. A/PV.564, 4 November 1956, p. 4, para. 43 (Peru). p. 7, para. 72 (United States).

[30] Yoran Dinstein, *War, Aggression and Self-Defence* (Sixth edition, Cambridge University Press, Cambridge, 2017), p. 127; Corten, supra note 18, pp. 261, 265.

Afghanistan was subsequently made by the puppet government installed by the USSR.[31]

On the contrary, there were different responses to the cases after the end of the Cold War. In the case of the Tajikistan-Afghanistan border dispute in 1993, the Russian forces that were lawfully stationed in Tajikistan, even after the fall of the USSR,[32] patrolled the border area upon request by Tajikistan.[33] In the case of Syria in 2015, Russia conducted airstrikes in response to the request by the Assad regime for military assistance with a view to eliminating terrorist organizations in Syria.[34] In the case of Kazakhstan in 2022, the Collective Security Treaty Organization (CSTO) decided to send its peacekeeping forces to Kazakhstan in light of the threat to domestic order and sovereignty of Kazakhstan caused by external aggression upon request by the President of Kazakhstan in accordance with Article 4[35] of the Collective Security Treaty.[36] These are the non-problematic cases. However, the legitimacy of the requesting actor was strongly criticized in the case of Crimea in 2014.

Russia claimed that the "Prime Minister" of the Crimea Autonomous Republic requested the President of Russia to provide assistance to restore peace in Crimea and that the President of Ukraine, Yanukovych, expressed his support.[37] However, the United States denied the validity of the request from "subregional authorities".[38] Commentators have been critical of Russia's argument because a request cannot be

---

[31] Dinstein, supra note 30, pp. 127–128; Gray, supra note 8, pp. 96–97; Henderson, supra note 9, pp. 474–475; Erika de Wet, *Military Assistance on Request and the Use of Force* (Oxford University Press, Oxford, 2020), p. 167, footnote 103; Corten, supra note 18, pp. 261–262, 265–266.

[32] Christopher Le Mon, "Unilateral Intervention by Invitation in Civil Wars: The Effective Control Test Tested", *New York University Journal of International Law and Politics*, vol. 35 (2003), p. 787. See also UN Doc. S/24725, 28 October 1992, p. 2; Article 3, Treaty on Friendship, Cooperation and Mutual Assistance between Russia and Tajikistan of 25 May 1993 (Hamrokhon Zarifi (ed.), *Tajikistan Diplomacy: The past and the present I* (Irfon, 2009), p. 69).

[33] UN Doc. S/26241, 5 August 1993, p. 1. cf. UN Doc. S/26092, 16 July 1993, Annex, p. 2; UN Doc. S/26110, 19 July 1993, Annex, p. 2.

[34] UN Doc. S/2015/792, 15 October 2015, Annex, p. 2.

[35] The original Article 4 limited the scope of aggressor to "any state or a group of states" and had no mention about the request of the victim member State (Treaty on Collective Security, Tashkent, 15 May 1992, *United Nations Treaty Series*, Volume 1894, I-32307). However, the amended text deleted the limited scope of aggressor, inserted the text "(armed attack menacing to safety, stability, territorial integrity and sovereignty)" after the term "aggression" and added the request of the member State who suffered aggression as an explicit requirement (Protocol Amending the Treaty on Collective Security, Moscow, 10 December 2010).

[36] The Statement by Nikol Pashinyan, the Chairman of the CSTO Collective Security Council - Prime Minister of the Republic of Armenia, 6 January 2022, at https://en.odkb-csto.org/news/news_odkb/zayavlenie-predsedatelya-soveta-kollektivnoy-bezopasnosti-odkb-premer-ministra-respubliki-armeniya-n/#loaded; Foreign Ministry statement on the CSTO Collective Security Council's decision to send CSTO Collective Peacekeeping Forces to the Republic of Kazakhstan, 6 January 2021.

[37] UN Doc. S/PV.7124, 1 March 2014, p. 5 (Russia).

[38] UN Doc. S/PV.7125, 3 March 2014, p. 5 (United States).

made by a regional authority but by a State or a government under international law.[39]

Russia also referred to a letter addressed from the President of Ukraine, Yanukovych, to the President of Russia, Putin, dated 1 March 2014, in which Russia was requested to send its armed forces to "restore law and order, peace and stability and to protect people of Ukraine".[40] In response, Ukraine asserted that Yanukovych was no longer a legitimate President and his request addressed to the President of Russia was not "an official request of Ukraine because Yanukovych left the capital and failed to fulfill his official duties as the head of State, and the Parliament established this "legal fact" and appointed an Acting President.[41] While the motion to dismiss failed to gain the number of affirmative votes necessary to meet the requirement under the Constitution of Ukraine,[42] the United Kingdom expressed difficulty in finding legitimacy in the pronouncements of the former leader,[43] and the United States cast doubt about the legitimacy of the President because Yanukovych fled the city and left the seat of the presidency vacant.[44] In academia, commentators have expressed critical views on Russia's arguments for the following reasons. Yanukovych had left Ukraine and lost effective control;[45] despite that the Parliament did not gain the required number of votes in favor of his removal, he was no longer effectively acting as the President of Ukraine;[46] he did not enjoy significant international recognition;[47] even if he remained the lawful President, it was doubtful whether the request was given freely, and its scope was too broad and

---

[39] James Green, "The Annexation of Crimea: Russia, Passportisation and the Protection of Nationals Revisited", *Journal of the Use of Force and International Law*, vol. 1 (2014), p. 7; Veronika Bílková, "The Use of Force by the Russian Federation in Crimea", *Zeitschrift für ausländisches öffentliches Recht und Völkerrecht (ZaöRV)*, vol. 75 (2015), pp. 40–41; Buchan and Tsagourias, supra note 24, p. 185.

[40] UN Doc. S/2014/146, 3 March 2014, Annex, p. 2; UN Doc. S/PV.7125, 3 March 2014, pp. 3–4 (Russia).

[41] UN Doc. S/2014/152, 5 March 2014.

[42] Bílková, supra note 39, p. 41.

[43] UN Doc. S/PV.7125, 3 March 2014, p. 7 (United Kingdom).

[44] Ibid., p. 18 (United States).

[45] Christian Marxsen, "The Crimea Crisis: An International Law Perspective", *Zeitschrift für ausländisches öffentliches Recht und Völkerrecht (ZaöRV)*, vol. 74 (2014), p. 379; Peter Olson, "The Lawfulness of Russian Use of Force in Crimea", *Military Law and Law of War Review*, vol. 53 (2014), pp. 31–32; Thomas Grant, "Current Developments: Annexation of Crimea", *American Journal of International Law*, vol. 109 (2015), p. 82; Olivier Corten, "The Russian Intervention in the Ukrainian Crisis: Was Jus Contra Bellum Confirmed rather than Weakened", *Journal on the Use of Force and International Law*, vol. 2 (2015), p. 32; Buchan and Tsagourias, supra note 24, p. 183. See also Mary Ellen O'Connell, "The Crisis in Ukraine—2014", in Tom Ruys and Olivier Corten with Alexandra Hofer (eds.), *The Use of Force in International Law: A Case-Based Approach* (Oxford University Press, Oxford, 2018), p. 866; Henderson, supra note 9, p. 455.

[46] Green, supra note 39, p. 7; Marissa Mastroianni, "Russia Running Rogue: How the Legal Justifications for Russian Intervention in Georgia and Ukraine Relate to the U.N. Legal Order", *Seton Hall Law Review*, vol. 46 (2016), p. 651.

[47] Bílková, supra note 39, p. 42; Buchan and Tsagourias, supra note 24, pp. 183–184.

Use of Force by Russia and *jus ad bellum*

indeterminate;[48] Article 85 of the 1996 Constitution of Ukraine empowers the Parliament to "approve decisions on admitting units of armed forces of other states on to the territory of Ukraine";[49] even assuming that Yanukovych's request was valid, the use of force by Russia was beyond the scope of the request;[50] and the intervention by Russia was not aimed at restoring the Yanukovych regime.[51] Yanukovych also later expressed regret about his request for Russia to intervene in Crimea.[52]

(b) Case of Ukraine

While the requests of the "Donetsk People's Republic" and "Luhansk People's Republic" should be regarded as a requirement for collective self-defence, it is theoretically possible to understand them in the context of military assistance upon request. However, the situation surrounding this case was far less likely to endorse the reliance on this justification. As indicated above, it is difficult to consider both "Republics" as States. The requests were not made in advance because the armed conflict between the government and the pro-Russian insurgents was ongoing before the use of force by Russia.[53] Russia was using force not only in the territory of two "Republics" but also against the other part of the territory of Ukraine.[54] In light of these points, it is obvious that the use of force by Russia cannot be justified based on military assistance upon request.[55] While the requests of the "Donetsk People's Republic" and "Luhansk People's Republic" could be understood as those of the rebels, the ICJ denied the intervention by the third party upon request of the opposition groups.[56]

3.2   Cases Where the Territorial State Made No Request

After the fall of the USSR, cases where the territorial State made no request have been witnessed. Since the "invasion . . . by the armed forces of a State of the territory of another State" constitutes aggression under Article 3 (a) of the Definition of

---

[48] Ibid., p. 184.

[49] Bílková, supra note 39, p. 41.

[50] Ibid., p. 42; Mastroianni, supra note 46, p. 651; Juergen Bering, "The Prohibition of Annexation: Lessons from Crimea", *New York University Journal of International Law and Politics*, vol. 49 (2017), p. 765.

[51] Marxsen, supra note 45, p. 379.

[52] Olson, supra note 45, p. 32; Bílková, supra note 39, p. 40.

[53] Terry Gill, "The Jus ad Bellum and Russia's 'Special Military Operation' in Ukraine", *Journal of International Peacekeeping*, vol. 25 (2022), p. 125.

[54] Corten and Koutroulis, supra note 20, p. 1008.

[55] Green, Henderson and Ruys, supra note 22, pp. 22–23.

[56] *Military and Paramilitary Activities in and against Nicaragua (Nicaragua v. United States of America)*, supra note 10, p. 126, para. 246.

Aggression and thus unlawful use of force, use of force in the territory of another State without its request requires sound justification to preclude wrongfulness. In this context, Russia explicitly invoked individual and collective self-defence. It seems that Russia also relied on the protection of nationals abroad, though it remains within the scope of individual self-defence. In academia, other possible justifications, such as the theory of humanitarian intervention and the use of force to assist the right of self-determination, have been discussed.

(1) **Collective self-defence**

If the requirements for collective self-defence are met, the use of force in the territory of the attacking State—the invasion by the armed forces of the territory of another State, the bombardment or the use of weapons against the territory of another State and so on—can legally be justified.

(a) **Previous case**

In the case of the border dispute between Tajikistan and Afghanistan in 1993, collective self-defence under the regional security treaty was invoked. In response to the attacks by the Tajik opposition groups,[57] Kazakhstan, Kyrgyzstan, Russia, Tajikistan, and Uzbekistan decided to provide "emergency supplementary assistance, including military assistance" in accordance with the Treaty on Collective Security and "in implementation of the right of individual and collective self-defence under Article 51 of the Charter of the United Nations".[58] Afghanistan claimed that the Commonwealth of Independent States' armed forces were deployed on the border of Afghanistan and that massive attacks on Afghan villages took place.[59] A lack of negative response from Russia and other States is an indication that they used force in and against the territory of Afghanistan.

(b) **Case of Ukraine**

Russia justified its use of force against Ukraine based on collective self-defence requested by the "Donetsk People's Republic" and the "Luhansk People's Republic".[60] The use of force by Russia in the territory of Ukraine might be justified if Ukraine carried out an armed attack and the other requirements for collective self-defence were met. However, unlike the previous case, the requirements for the occurrence of an armed attack, that is, necessity and proportionality, were not fulfilled.[61] Moreover, as discussed above, the statehood of the two requesting

---

[57] UN Doc. S/26091, 16 July 1993, Annex, p. 2; UN Doc. S/26092, 16 July 1993, Annex, pp. 2–3. It must be noted that the armed attack was carried out by the Tajik rebels—non-State actors—who had their bases in Afghanistan. In this regard, Afghanistan strongly rejected the allegations of Russia and Tajikistan that "the Tajik refugees are trained and armed in Afghanistan and sent to Tajikistan for destructive activities" (UN Doc. S/26145, 22 July 1993, p. 2).

[58] UN Doc. S/26290, 11 August 1993, Annex III, p. 6.

[59] UN Doc. S/26145, 22 July 1993, pp. 2–3.

[60] See footnote 19.

[61] Hoffmann, supra note 20, p. 215.

Use of Force by Russia and *jus ad bellum* 45

"Republics" is extremely doubtful. It is thus difficult to invoke collective self-defence to justify Russia's use of force.

(2) Individual self-defence

Individual self-defence is also a justification for the use of force under Article 51 of the UN Charter and customary international law. If there is an armed attack and the requirements of necessity and proportionality[62] are met, and when a victim State is a UN member, a report is submitted to the UN Security Council, the use of force by the victim State will be justified by individual self-defence. The ICJ confirmed individual self-defence in response to armed attacks not only against its own territory but also against its warship on high seas.[63] In academia, it is accepted that individual self-defence extends to the protection of nationals abroad.[64]

(a) Previous cases

In the case of Georgia in 2008, Russia relied on "its inherent right to self-defence enshrined in Article 51 of the Charter of the United Nations".[65] Russia referred to armed attacks not only "against the servicemen of the Russian Federation deployed in the territory of Georgia on legitimate grounds but also against citizens of the Russian Federation" and considered them as "illegal use of military force against the Russian Federation".[66]

Regarding individual self-defence in response to an armed attack against the Russian military personnel, at the normative level, there is almost no doubt that a State has the right of individual self-defence to protect its troops deployed in a foreign State under international law.[67] However, at the factual level, Georgia and Russia criticized each other for attacking first, and the Independent International Fact-Finding Mission was not able to reach a definitive conclusion in this regard.[68] Despite that, scholars have argued that Russia's use of force was illegal in light of

---

[62] *Military and Paramilitary Activities in and against Nicaragua (Nicaragua v. United States of America)*, supra note 10, p. 103, paras. 194–195.

[63] *Oil Platforms (Islamic Republic of Iran v. United States of America), Judgment, I.C.J. Reports 2003*, p. 195, para. 72.

[64] Humphrey Waldock, "The Regulation of the Use of Force by Individual States in International Law", *Recueil des Cours*, vol. 81 (1952), p. 467; Derek Bowett, *Self-Defence in International Law* (Manchester University Press, Manchester, 1958), pp. 87–105; Derek Bowett, "The Use of Force for the Protection of Nationals Abroad", in Antonio Cassese (ed.), *The Current Legal Regulation of the Use of Force* (Martinus Nijhoff, Dordrecht, 1986), p. 39, pp. 40–46; Christopher Greenwood, "Self Defence", in Rüdiger Wolfrum (ed.), *Max Planck Encyclopedia of Public International Law, IX* (Oxford University Press, Oxford, 2012), p. 113, para. 108.

[65] UN Doc. S/2008/545, 11 August 2008, p. 1.

[66] Ibid.

[67] Christine Gray, "The Conflict in Georgia—2008", in Tom Ruys and Oliver Corten with Alexandra Hofer (eds.), *The Use of Force in International Law: A Case-Based Approach* (Oxford University Press, Oxford), pp. 719 and 724.

[68] Report of the Independent International Fact-Finding Mission on the Conflict in Georgia (2009), Vol. II, p. 252. However, the Mission was not able to confirm a large-scale presence of the Russian

other requirements for individual self-defence such as proportionality and necessity. For the United States, Russia's reaction "goes far beyond any reasonable measure" required to protect its peacekeepers.[69] The United Kingdom indicated, "[t]hose actions have gone beyond any reasonable, proportionate response".[70] Croatia argued that Russia's actions "go far beyond the role of a peacekeeper as foreseen in the 1992 armistice agreement".[71] Panama condemned "the entirely disproportionate, and therefore illegitimate, use of force by the Russian Federation with the stated aim of protecting its ... peacekeeping forces".[72] The Independent International Fact-Finding Mission indicated that the subsequent military operations deeper into Georgia went "far beyond the reasonable limits of defence".[73] Commentators have also expressed the same opinions.[74]

Regarding individual self-defence in response to an armed attack against Russian citizens, international law scholars have long discussed the general question of whether the use of force to protect nationals abroad can be justified by individual self-defence.[75] A negative position has been put forward by those who do not equate the attack against nationals with that against the State.[76] The Independent International Fact-Finding Mission took this position.[77] However, except for Georgia,[78] no State raised this point. Rather, a lack of proportionality and necessity was also used to criticize the argument of Russia that there was an attack against the Russians in Georgia.[79] In academia, despite the different positions on the general question above,[80] it has been shared that Russia's argument was not acceptable for three

---

armed forces in South Ossetia in advance of the Georgian offensive (Report of the Independent International Fact-Finding Mission on the Conflict in Georgia (2009), Vol. I, p. 23).

[69] UN Doc. S/PV.5953, 10 August 2008, p. 6 (United States).

[70] Ibid., p. 11 (United Kingdom).

[71] Ibid., p. 13 (Croatia).

[72] Ibid., p. 15 (Panama).

[73] Report of the Independent International Fact-Finding Mission on the Conflict in Georgia (2009), Vol. I, p. 24.

[74] Mastroianni, supra note 46, p. 637; Henderson, supra note 9, pp. 331–332; Gray, supra note 67, p. 726.

[75] See Tom Ruys, "The Protection of Nationals' Doctrine Revisited", *Journal of Conflict and Security Law*, vol. 13 (2008), pp. 235–236; Gray, supra note 67, pp. 722–723.

[76] Albrecht Randelzhofer and Georg Nolte, "Article 51", in Bruno Simma et al. (eds.), *The Charter of the United Nations: A Commentary* (Third edition. Oxford University Press, Oxford, 2012), p. 1413; Marxsen, supra note 45, p. 374.

[77] Report of the Independent International Fact-Finding Mission on the Conflict in Georgia (2009), Vol. II, pp. 287–288. See also Report of the Independent International Fact-Finding Mission on the Conflict in Georgia (2009), Vol. I, pp. 24–25.

[78] Report of the Independent International Fact-Finding Mission on the Conflict in Georgia (2009), Vol. II, p. 187.

[79] UN Doc. S/PV.5953, 10 August 2008, p. 15 (Panama).

[80] For affirmative positions, see Robert Chatham, "Defense of Nationals Abroad: The Legitimacy of Russia's Invasion of Georgia", *Florida Journal of International Law*, vol. 23 (2011), pp. 88–90. For a critical position, see Green, supra note 39, p. 4.

reasons. Russia's use of force was not proportional to the purpose for protecting its nationals.[81] The circumstance did not endorse the necessity to use force.[82] It was far from self-evident that there was a "genuine connection"—a requirement clarified by the ICJ in its Nottebohm case[83]—between Russia and the relevant individuals who recently received a Russian passport.[84]

In the case of Crimea in 2014, Russia did not invoke individual self-defence.[85] While it mentioned "threat against the lives of Russian citizens, our compatriots",[86] "ongoing threats of violence by ultranationalists against the security, lives and legitimate interests of Russians and all Russian-speaking peoples",[87] and "threat posed to Russian citizens, our compatriots",[88] it did not even claim the armed attack against its territory or the Russian armed forces that were lawfully stationed in Crimea. Other States stressed that "no evidence of violence against Russian or pro-Russian communities" was reported and that "[n]o one is threatening the Russian-speaking populations".[89] In academia, no matter what Russia argued, commentators have rejected the use of force based on individual self-defence to protect Russian nationals for several reasons. No prior armed attack by Ukraine occurred.[90] There was a lack of proportionality and necessity.[91] Despite no threat to the lives of Russian nationals, the military actions were not limited to those necessary to protect nationals.[92] The passportization policy did not meet the requirement of "real and effective" nationality.[93]

---

[81] Green, supra note 39, p. 9; Chatham, supra note 80, p. 99; Mastroianni, supra note 46, p. 637.

[82] Chatham, supra note 80, pp. 98–99; Russell Buchan and Nicholas Tsagourias, *Regulating Use of Force in International Law: Stability and Change* (Edward Elgar Publishing, 2021), p. 52.

[83] *Nottebohm Case (second phase), Judgment of April 6th, 1955, I.C.J. Reports 1955*, p. 23.

[84] Green, supra note 39, p. 4; Mastroianni, supra note 46, pp. 636–637. See also Report of the Independent International Fact-Finding Mission on the Conflict in Georgia (2009), Vol. I, p. 18; Report of the Independent International Fact-Finding Mission on the Conflict in Georgia (2009), Vol. II, pp. 288–289. While Russia claimed that it used force to stop the genocidal acts by Georgia against the Ossetians, there was distinction between the Ossetians and the Russians (Report of the Independent International Fact-Finding Mission on the Conflict in Georgia (2009), Vol. II, p. 221). It would thus be difficult to understand the genocidal acts by Georgia in the context of the protection of Russian nationals abroad.

[85] Corten, supra note 45, p. 32.

[86] UN Doc. S/PV.7124, 1 March 2014, p. 5 (Russia).

[87] UN Doc. S/PV.7125, 3 March 2014, p. 3 (Russia).

[88] Ibid., p. 3 (Russia).

[89] Ibid., pp. 4 (United States), 6 (France).

[90] Green, supra note 39, p. 8; Mastroianni, supra note 46, p. 649.

[91] Green, supra note 39, pp. 8–9; Olson, supra note 45, pp. 36–37; Buchan and Tsagourias, supra note 82, p. 53.

[92] Olson, supra note 45, pp. 35–36; Bílková, supra note 39, p. 47; Bering, supra note 50, pp. 766–767.

[93] Green, supra note 39, pp. 7–8. See also Buchan and Tsagourias, supra note 24, p. 188; Buchan and Tsagourias, supra note 82, p. 53.

(b) Case of Ukraine

Russia invoked individual self-defence as well.[94] It stressed the threat to itself rather than the armed attack against itself. The case of Ukraine is quite different from that of Georgia in this regard. According to Russia, the NATO countries' so-called policy of containment of Russia is "a real threat not just to our interests, but to the very existence of our State and its sovereignty".[95] Moreover, Russia was not able to "feel safe, develop and exist with a constant threat emanating from the territory of present-day Ukraine".[96] However, the ICJ is not satisfied with a simple threat but requires an "armed attack" that constitutes a grave form of the use of force.[97] In this case, no armed attack of NATO or Ukraine happened.[98] Even if pre-emptive self-defence against the imminent armed attack is permitted, no imminent armed attack of NATO or Ukraine existed.[99] No evidence for the development of biological weapons was demonstrated by Russia, too.[100] Regarding the requirements of necessity and proportionality, the prevention of "threat" seems to be insufficient to meet the necessity, and it would be very difficult to evaluate the proportionality between "threat" and the use of force. Therefore, the use of force by Russia cannot be justified by individual self-defence.[101]

Russia further referred to individual self-defence to protect nationals abroad and pointed out damage and genocide against the Russians in this context. According to the President of Russia, the purpose of a special military operation is "to protect people who have been subjected to abuse and genocide by the Kiev regime for eight years".[102] Unlike the case of Georgia, the "people" may mean the "Russians" who received a Russian passport through the passportization policy. However, it is quite

---

[94] Address by the President of the Russian Federation, 24 February 2022; UN Doc. S/2022/154, 24 February 2022, p. 6. See also UN Doc. S/2022/363, 5 May 2022, Annex, pp. 2–3, para. 5.

[95] UN Doc. S/2022/154, 24 February 2022, p. 5.

[96] Ibid., p. 6.

[97] *Military and Paramilitary Activities in and against Nicaragua (Nicaragua v. United States of America),* supra note 10, p. 101, para. 91; *Oil Platforms(Islamic Republic of Iran v. United States of America),* supra note 63, p. 187, para. 51.

[98] Gill, supra note 53, pp. 124–125. See also Chapter 'The War in Ukraine Under International Law: Its Use of Force and Armed Conflict Aspects' of this volume.

[99] Gill, supra note 53, pp. 124–125; Hoffmann, supra note 20, pp. 211–212; Aman McLeod and Catherine Archibald, "Putin's Version of History and Claims of Provocation: An International Law Perspective on Russia's Justifications for the Ukraine War", *University of Detroit Mercy Law Review*, vol. 100 (2023), p. 510.

[100] While the UN Security Council and the Biological Weapons Convention Consultative Meeting held discussions upon request by Russia, Russia, on the one hand, and the United States and Ukraine, on the other hand, maintained their own views (UN Doc. S/PV.8991, 11 March 2022; UN Doc. S/PV.8999, 19 March 2022; Biological Weapons Convention – Formal Consultative Meeting: Documents, at https://meetings.unoda.org/section/bwc-fcm-2022-documents/). Hoffmann, supra note 20, pp. 211–212.

[101] Green, Henderson and Ruys, supra note 22, pp. 8–14.

[102] UN Doc. S/2022/154, 24 February 2022, p. 6.

Use of Force by Russia and *jus ad bellum*

doubtful whether there was the abuse of human rights against the Russians that would constitute an armed attack against Russia.[103] Even if there was, Russia used force against areas that may not have been threatened, and the passportization policy itself was very controversial. Therefore, it is difficult to justify the use of force based on individual self-defence.[104]

(3) Protection of nationals abroad without reference to individual self-defence?

In academia, it is argued that the limited use of force for the protection of nationals abroad is allowed under customary international law.[105] However, the question of whether this is established as justification under international law should be carefully examined. The UN Charter does not explicitly include it. It is unclear whether State practice endorses it or not. Moreover, the risk of abuse may be high because they rely on more subjective judgment than the requirements for individual self-defence.

(a) Previous cases

In the case of Georgia in 2008, Russia explicitly invoked individual self-defence.[106] The discussion on the protection of nationals abroad under customary international law is thus irrelevant.[107] In the case of Crimea in 2014, it is unclear whether Russia invoked this justification or not.[108] In academia, irrespective of Russia's position, the use of force based on this justification has been rejected. It has been pointed out that no threat to the lives of Russian nationals existed in Crimea,[109] and even if it existed, Russia used force beyond the purpose of protecting its nationals.[110]

---

[103] Henderson, supra note 9, pp. 326–327.

[104] Green, Henderson and Ruys, supra note 22, pp. 14–16. See also Hoffmann, supra note 20, pp. 215–216. Apart from their normativity and validity, justifications of Russia have varied depending on the understanding of individuals who received a Russian passport. If they are Russians as claimed by Russia, the protection of nationals abroad is relevant. If they remain Ukrainians as indicated by Ukraine, the humanitarian intervention theory offers justification. See also Chapter 'The War in Ukraine Under International Law: Its Use of Force and Armed Conflict Aspects' of this volume.

[105] Albrecht Randelzhofer and Olivier Dörr, "Article 2 (4)", in Bruno Simma et al. (eds.), *The Charter of the United Nations: A Commentary* (third edition, Oxford University Press, Oxford, 2012), p. 228; Olivier Dörr, "Use of Force, Prohibition of", in Rüdiger Wolfrum (ed.), *Max Planck Encyclopedia of Public International Law X* (Oxford University Press, Oxford, 2012), p. 617. For a negative position, see Grant, supra note 45, p. 80.

[106] Corten, supra note 45, p. 32.

[107] One author assumed that a State is allowed to use force for the protection of nationals abroad without reliance on (individual) self-defence and reached a negative conclusion for the same reasons as the use of force for the same purpose based on (individual) self-defence, such as a lack of proportionality and denial of recognition of the people of Russian origins as the lawful "Russians" (Mastroianni, supra note 46, pp. 637–638).

[108] Corten, supra note 45, pp. 31–32.

[109] Marxsen, supra note 45, p. 374; Buchan and Tsagourias, supra note 24, pp. 187–188.

[110] Bering, supra note 50, pp. 766–767.

(b) Case of Ukraine

Like in the case of Georgia, Russia has explicitly relied on individual self-defence. Thus, customary rule on the use of force to protect nationals abroad has no relevance. While this is for the sake of discussion, the conclusion will not change. The use of force by Russia constitutes a violation of international law. As indicated, it is highly doubtful whether there was an imminent threat—including genocide[111]—against the "Russians" in the territory of Ukraine.[112] If there was no imminent threat, the use of force has no objective, and the will or ability of the territorial State does not matter.

(4) Theory of humanitarian intervention?

There has been much debate over the issue of whether the so-called humanitarian intervention theory—the use of force to protect local populations in the territory of another State from genocide and serious abuse of human rights—is established under international law. Belgium justified the airstrikes during the Kosovo crisis in 1999 based on this theory.[113] The United Kingdom also relied on this theory when it used force in response to the use of chemical weapons in Syria in 2018.[114] However, these are rare cases. In other cases, virtually no State has explicitly invoked this theory until today.[115] Rather, a certain number of States have consistently raised strong objections to the use of force based on this theory.[116] In academia, the

---

[111] Ukraine requested the ICJ to indicate provisional measures including those to protect its rights "not to be subjected to another State's military operations on its territory based on a brazen abuse of Article I of the Genocide Convention" (*Allegations of Genocide under the Convention on the Prevention and Punishment of the Crime of Genocide (Ukraine v. Russian Federation)*, supra note 2, p. 224, para. 52).

[112] Gill, supra note 53, p. 125.

[113] CR 99/15, 10 May 1999, pp. 16–17 (Ergec).

[114] United Kingdom, Policy paper, Syria action – UK government legal position, 14 April 2018, at https://www.gov.uk/government/publications/syria-action-uk-government-legal-position/syria-action-uk-government-legal-position; UN Doc. S/PV.8233, 14 April 2018, pp. 7, 25 (United Kingdom); OPCW Doc. EC-M-58/NAT.4, 16 April 2018 (United Kingdom), p. 3. See also Policy paper, Chemical weapon use by Syrian regime: UK government legal position, Published 29 August 2013, at https://assets.publishing.service.gov.uk/government/uploads/system/uploads/attachment_data/file/235098/Chemical-weapon-use-by-Syrian-regime-UK-government-legal-position.pdf.

[115] Hoffmann, supra note 20, p. 217. In the author's opinion, it is necessary to pay more attention to this fact when discussing the normativity of the humanitarian intervention theory.

[116] UN Doc. S/PV.8233, 14 April 2018, pp. 3 (Russia), 10 (China), 10 (Kazakhstan), 14 (Bolivia), 17 (Equatorial Guinea), 25 (Russia).

Use of Force by Russia and *jus ad bellum* 51

overwhelming majority of commentators have expressed their negative views.[117] A handful have supported it.[118]

(a) **Previous cases**

In the case of Georgia in 2008, while the Independent International Fact-Finding Mission examined the possibility of justifying the use of force by Russia based on the humanitarian intervention theory, it reached a negative conclusion, pointing out that this has been a highly controversial issue among commentators, that Russia has consistently and persistently objected to the humanitarian intervention theory in the context of NATO airstrikes in the Kosovo crisis, and that Russia has political and other interests in South Ossetia as a directly neighboring State.[119]

In the case of Crimea in 2014, analysis was conducted solely from an academic perspective. Having noted that the humanitarian intervention theory is a very controversial concept, that Russia took a negative position on it, that even if this theory exists, no serious human rights abuses have occurred, and that the scope and purpose of the use of force are beyond this theory, an international law scholar reached the conclusion that the use of force by Russia cannot be justified by this theory.[120]

(b) **Case of Ukraine**

As illustrated above, Russia argued that the purpose of the special military operation was "to protect people who have been subjected to abuse and genocide by the Kiev regime for eight years".[121] If the "people" are not the Russians abroad but the

---

[117]Bruno Simma, "NATO, the UN and the Use of Force: Legal Aspects", *European Journal of International Law*, vol. 10 (1999), p. 5; Richard Bilder, "Kosovo and the New Interventionism: Promise or Peril", *Journal of Transnational Law and Policy*, vol. 9 (1999), p. 153, p. 161; Louis Henkin, "Kosovo and the Law of 'Humanitarian Intervention'", *American Journal of International Law*, vol. 93 (1999), p. 825; Ian Brownlie, "International Law and the Use of Force by States Revisited", *Australian Yearbook of International Law*, vol. 21 (2000), pp. 34–35; Carsten Stahn, "Syria and the Semantics of Intervention, Aggression and Punishment: On Red Lines and Blurred Lines", *Journal of International Criminal Justice*, vol. 11 (2013), p. 965; Mika Hayashi, "Reacting to the Use of Chemical Weapons: Options for Third States", *Journal on Use of Force and International Law*, vol. 1 (2014), p. 116; Christian Henderson, "The UK Government's Legal Opinion on Forcible measures in Response to the Use of Chemical Weapons by the Syrian Government", *International and Comparative Law Quarterly*, vol. 64 (2015), pp. 183–192; O'Connell, supra note 45, p. 871; Anne Lagerwall, "Threats of and Actual Military Strikes Against Syria—2013 and 2017", in Tom Ruys and Olivier Corten with Alexandra Hofer (eds.), *The Use of Force in International Law: A Case-based Approach* (Cambridge University Press, Cambridge, 2018), p. 847; Corten, supra note 18, pp. 534–537; Agata Kleczkowska, "The Illegality of Humanitarian Intervention: The Case of the UK's Legal Position Concerning the 2018 Strikes in Syria", *Utrecht Journal of International and European Law*, vol. 35 (2020), p. 47.

[118]Christopher Greenwood, "Humanitarian Intervention: The Case of Kosovo", *Finnish Yearbook of International Law*, vol. 10 (1999), p. 170.

[119]Report of the Independent International Fact-Finding Mission on the Conflict in Georgia (2009), Vol. II, pp. 421–429.

[120]Bílková, supra note 39, pp. 47–49.

[121]UN Doc. S/2022/154, 24 February 2022, p. 6.

Ukrainians in Donetsk and Luhansk regions, Russia's argument is something like a humanitarian intervention theory. However, the humanitarian intervention theory cannot be invoked. It allows a State to use force against another State to save the nationals of the latter from the serious violation of human rights by the government of the same. The fact that Russia recognized the "Donetsk People's Republic" and the "Luhansk People's Republic" as a State is not compatible with this theory because the people in both "Republics" are no longer Ukrainians.[122] Even if this point could be put aside, it is difficult to justify Russia's use of force.[123] As with the case of Georgia, there was no evidence of the serious violation of human rights, including genocide.[124] It is not convincing that the special military operation was necessary to avoid preventing the abuse of human rights and that it was proportionate to this purpose.[125] The ICJ also expressed doubt as to whether the Genocide Convention authorizes a State Party to conduct unilateral use of force in the territory of another State for the purpose of preventing or punishing an alleged genocide.[126] Subsequently, Russia refrained the argument of something like a humanitarian intervention theory and relied only on self-defence.

(5) Use of force for assisting the right of self-determination?

In the past, there had been a heated discussion on the issue of whether the use of force to assist in exercising the right of self-determination was allowed under international law. However, it lost its significance because of the development of decolonization and the resolution of illegal occupation.[127] There has been almost no support for expanding the scope of this idea and covering contexts other than decolonization and illegal occupation.[128]

---

[122] See Chapter 'The War in Ukraine Under International Law: Its Use of Force and Armed Conflict Aspects' of this volume. For other States that do not recognize both "Republics" as a State, the argument of Russia should be understood as the humanitarian intervention theory, because the peoples in Donetsk and Luhansk regions remain Ukrainians. Ukraine seemed to refer the dispute to the ICJ under this understanding.

[123] Green, Henderson and Ruys, supra note 22, pp. 25–26.

[124] *Allegations of Genocide under the Convention on the Prevention and Punishment of the Crime of Genocide (Ukraine v. Russian Federation)*, supra note 2, p. 225, para. 59. McLeod and Archibald, supra note 99, p. 518; Hoffmann, supra note 20, p. 218; Kreß, supra note 20, p. 9. See also Chapter 'The War in Ukraine Under International Law: Its Use of Force and Armed Conflict Aspects' of this volume.

[125] Hoffmann, supra note 20, pp. 219–220.

[126] *Allegations of Genocide under the Convention on the Prevention and Punishment of the Crime of Genocide (Ukraine v. Russian Federation)*, supra note 2, p. 225, para. 59.

[127] Gray, supra note 8, p. 72.

[128] Bílková, supra note 39, p. 45; Gray, supra note 8, p. 73.

Use of Force by Russia and *jus ad bellum*

(a) **Previous cases**

In the case of Crimea in 2014, the international community witnessed its subsequent development. Crimea declared independence nearly a month after the use of force by Russia and then was incorporated into Russia based on a bilateral "treaty" with Russia. While it is unclear whether Russia included the assistance for the right of self-determination in its reasons for the use of force, commentators have opined that even if the use of force to assist the right of self-determination is allowed, Russia is not able to rely on this justification. It was not demonstrated that the people in Crimea suffered suppression or serious abuse of human rights from Ukraine.[129] It is difficult to say whether the people reached a decision freely when there was the use of force.[130] The situation where a decision to incorporate Crimea into Russia only ten days after the "declaration of independence" of the former raised doubt about whether Russia's use of force to assist the right of self-determination was in good faith.[131]

(b) **Case of Ukraine**

It is unclear whether Russia used force to assist its exercise of the right of self-determination. No explicit reference to it doing so exists. The background may be that Russia recognized two "Republics" as a State before the special military operation. As far as Donetsk and Luhansk were concerned, State recognition meant the complete exercise of the right of self-determination from the Russian perspective. There was a rapid development in the situation. The pro-Russia groups led the "referendums" in the "Donetsk People's Republic" and the "Luhansk People's Republic", as well as the Kherson and Zaporizhzhia regions. In light of its "results", the President of Russia signed "the treaties" on the accession of these areas to Russia.[132] In his statement at the ceremony for signature, the President of Russia mentioned the principle of equal rights and self-determination of peoples in Article 1 of the UN Charter.[133] From the viewpoint of Russia, its use of force assisted the people of these areas in "exercising" the right of self-determination, like Crimea. However, the UN General Assembly adopted the resolution titled "Territorial integrity of Ukraine: defending the principles of the Charter of the United Nations" by an overwhelming majority,[134] condemning the illegal so-called referendums and the attempted illegal annexation and declaring the invalidity of these actions.[135]

---

[129] Bílková, supra note 39, p. 45; Mastroianni, supra note 46, p. 653; Buchan and Tsagourias, supra note 24, p. 190.

[130] Grant, supra note 45, p. 85.

[131] Ibid., p. 86.

[132] President of Russia, Signing of treaties on accession of Donetsk and Lugansk people's republics and Zaporozhye and Kherson regions to Russia, 30 September 2022, at http://en.kremlin.ru/events/president/news/69465.

[133] Ibid.

[134] UN Doc. A/RES/ES-11/4, 12 October 2022. A draft resolution (UN Doc. A/ES-11/L.5, 7 October 2022) was adopted by 143 votes to five with 35 abstentions (UN Doc. A/ES-11/PV. 14, 12 October 2022, pp. 11–12).

[135] UN Doc. A/RES/ES-11/4, 12 October 2022, operative paras. 2 and 3.

4 Conclusion

This article discussed the use of force by the USSR/Russia from the perspective of *jus ad bellum*. It becomes clear that in most cases, the USSR and Russia did not demonstrate sound legal justifications and thus violated international law. This is also true in the ongoing case of Ukraine.[136] The author concludes this article with key general findings drawn from the discussion in the main part as follows:

First, the use of force by the USSR/Russia in the territory of another State has two objectives. One is to maintain the areas under its influence. This has not changed since the era of the Soviet Union. The other is to protect Russian nationals in the former Soviet States. This is a new issue for Russia that emerged from the fall of the USSR. To achieve these objectives, the USSR/Russia must justify its use of force as an exception to its prohibition. Here, the USSR/Russia attempted to expand the scope of exceptions. This is the second finding. In the era of the Soviet Union, it cooperated with the territorial State and its government to maintain the Soviet bloc by eliminating the opposition groups. The USSR relied on the request of the "government", which acted allegedly on behalf of the State, though this "government" apparently lacked legitimacy. The validity of the request was thus loosened. This was a questionable attempt to expand the scope of exceptions to the principle of the non-use of force. After the end of the Cold War, to achieve two purposes—the maintenance of the former Soviet bloc and the protection of nationals and ethnic Russians who remain in the former Soviet States—Russia has provided assistance to the opposition groups and these peoples by taking tricky measures, such as the recognition of a nominal entity as a State and the protection of nationals who become Russians through the passportization policy. This is a new but more controversial attempt to expand the scope of exceptions to the principle of the non-use of force.[137] Russia created nominal "Republics" and "Russians" and attempted to accommodate them in the existing justifications, such as collective or individual self-defence. However, it is quite obvious that the nominal "Republics" and "Russians" lack legal basis and cannot be accommodated in the existing justifications. It is thus very difficult to accept this attempt. Third, the USSR/Russia has not been the sole State that attempted to expand the scope of exceptions. It is a fact that other States—other permanent members of the UN Security Council in most cases—have also made the same attempts. At this critical juncture, we should recall the value of the most important rule of the international community as stipulated in Article 2, para. 4 of the UN Charter and make every effort to restore and revive this severely damaged rule under the UN Charter system.

---

[136] See also Chapters 'The War in Ukraine Under International Law: Its Use of Force and Armed Conflict Aspects' and 'Russia's War of Aggression Against Ukraine and the Crime of Aggression' of this volume.

[137] cf. Corten and Koutroulis, supra note 20, p. 1012.

Russia's War of Aggression Against Ukraine and the Crime of Aggression

Claus Kreß

Abstract A 'negative precedent' regarding the prosecution of the crime of aggression after Russia's aggression against Ukraine would be fundamentally detrimental to the international legal order. Yet, the hands of its Prosecutor are currently tied due to distinct limitations governing the International Criminal Court's exercise of jurisdiction over this crime. This state of affairs is reflective of the fact that the crime of aggression, while occupying the central place in the foundational trials of Nuremberg and Tokyo, has until today been hanging only by a thread in the firmament of international offences. Russia's aggression has exposed the gap in the international legal architecture and has hereby given rise to a renewed focus on the crime of aggression, including an intensive inter-governmental discussion about the establishment of a Special Tribunal for the Crime of Aggression. Irrespective of the outcome of this convoluted debate, the jurisdictional regime within the Statute of the International Criminal Court (ICC) should be harmonized by aligning the conditions for the exercise of jurisdiction over the crime of aggression with those relating to other core crimes so that the current gap regarding the prosecution of the crime of aggression by the ICC will be duly closed.

The text builds on and updates the Second Nuremberg Academy Lecture, held by the author on 4 May 2023 in Courtroom 600 of the Nuremberg Palace of Justice; https://www.nurembergacademy.org/events/nuremberg-academy-lecture-2023/. The author wishes to thank Fiona Abken for excellent research assistance and Astrid Reisinger Coracini and Sergey Vasiliev for several helpful suggestions for improving a draft version of this essay.

C. Kreß (✉)
Faculty of Law, University of Cologne, Cologne, Germany
e-mail: claus.kress@uni-koeln.de

© The Author(s), under exclusive license to Springer Nature Singapore Pte Ltd. 2024
M. Asada, D. Tamada (eds.), *The War in Ukraine and International Law*,
https://doi.org/10.1007/978-981-97-2504-5_3

1 Introduction

The following starting points of this analysis should not be controversial: In 2014, in Crimea, the Russian Federation began to violate the prohibition of the use of force to the detriment of Ukraine. On 24 February 2022, Russia escalated its course of action into a full-scale war of aggression, which is ongoing unabated at the time of writing. Russia's conduct *vis-à-vis* Ukraine thus constitutes a continuing act of aggression which, by its character, gravity and scale constitutes a manifest violation of the Charter of the United Nations.[1] Hereby, Russia has been fulfilling the State conduct element of the international consensus definition of the crime of aggression,[2] enshrined in Article 8 *bis* of the ICC Statute as a result of the diplomatic breakthrough at the first Review Conference on the ICC Statute, held in Kampala in the summer of 2010.[3] As consequence of their role in Russia's aggression, President Putin and some other members of the Russian leadership are under suspicion of having been committing the crime of aggression.[4]

Yet, the ICC cannot presently exercise its jurisdiction over this crime.[5] For, pursuant to Articles 15 *bis* and 15 *ter* of the ICC Statute,[6] crimes of aggression arising out of an act of aggression committed by or against a non-State-Party remain beyond the Court's reach, unless the UN Security Council refers the relevant situation to the ICC. In the situation of Ukraine, the ICC's exercise of jurisdiction over the crime of aggression would thus be dependent on a UN Security Council referral. But at least for as long as President Putin holds power, Russia would subject

---

[1] On the legal issues related to the prohibition of the use of force, see the chapter by Masahiko Asada in this volume; see also Claus Kreß, *The Ukraine War and the Prohibition of the Use of Force in International Law* (2022); see also James Green, Christian Henderson and Tom Ruys, "Russia's Attackon Ukraine and the *ius ad bellum*", 9 *Journal on the Use of Force and International Law* (2022), pp. 4–30.

[2] Claus Kreß, "The State Conduct Element", in C. Kreß and S. Barriga (eds.), *The Crime of Aggression: A Commentary*, vol. 1 (2017), pp. 412–564.

[3] Stefan Barriga, "Negotiating the Amendments on the Crime of Aggression", S. Barriga and C. Kreß (eds.), *The Travaux Préparatoires of the Crime of Aggression* (2011), pp. 3–57.

[4] For two early 'Model Indictments', see Open Society Justice Initiative, *Model Indictment for the Crime of Aggression Committed against Ukraine* (May 2022); Ryan Goodman and Rebecca Hamilton, "Model Indictment for Crime of Aggression against Ukraine: Prosecutor v. Vladimir Putin", *Just Security* (14.3.2022); https://www.justsecurity.org/80669/model-indictment-of-the-crime-of-aggression-against-ukraine-vladimir-putin/. This essay's focus is on Russia's aggression, but Belarus' active territorial involvement in this aggression must be mentioned as well because it also gives rise to the suspicion of the commission of crimes of aggression; for an international legal analysis of the conduct of the Belarussian State, see Alexander Wentker and Claus Kreß, "L'assistance d'États Tiers dans la Guerre d'Ukraine au Regard du Droit International", 68 *Annuaire Français de Droit International* (2022), pp. 173, 180.

[5] Statement of ICC Prosecutor, Karim A.A. Khan QC, on the Situation on Ukraine; https://www.icc-cpi.int/news/statement-icc-prosecutor-karim-aa-khan-qc-situation-ukraine-i-have-been-closely-following.

[6] Carrie McDougall, *The Crime of Aggression under the Rome Statute of the International Criminal Court* (2nd ed., 2021), pp. 258–352.

Russia's War of Aggression Against Ukraine and the Crime of Aggression 57

such a draft resolution to the same kind of abusive veto as it did with the Council's draft resolution of February 2022[7] which included a condemnation of Russia's aggression against Ukraine.

2 A Gap in the International Legal Architecture

To some, this state of affairs is not worrisome: One should be content, so they think, that the ICC can exercise its jurisdiction in Ukraine over genocide, crimes against humanity and war crimes. If seen in that light, the present situation regarding the crime of aggression, is a luxury problem[8] at best. In this essay, however, it is submitted that Russia's aggression against Ukraine has shed a bright light on a gap in the existing international legal architecture with respect to the crime of aggression. In order to make this point, it is not necessary to embrace the well-known statement in the Nuremberg Judgment that waging a crime of aggression is the 'supreme international crime'.[9] Instead, the following argument starts from the premise that the crime of aggression is not necessarily more heinous than genocide, crimes against humanity or war crimes committed systematically and on a large scale. The argument set out in this contribution does therefore not in any way belittle the enormous significance of the ongoing ICC investigation led by Prosecutor Khan which in 2023 resulted in an arrest warrant of historic importance against President Putin and in an arrest warrant against his commissioner for children's rights Lvova-Belova, to be followed by two further arrest warrants against Russian military commanders in 2024.[10] Instead, the argument is premised simply on the assertion that the crime of aggression is no less significant than the other crimes and that there may be occasions where it is crucial to prosecute the crime of aggression. It is submitted that Russia's war of aggression against Ukraine is such an occasion.

Certainly, the war of aggression against Ukraine violates that State's sovereignty and territorial integrity as well as the right of self-determination of the Ukrainian people.[11] And certainly, Russia's war of aggression has opened the floodgate, at a

---

[7] UN Doc. S/2022/155, 25.2.2022.

[8] Former Judge at the ICTY Wolfgang Schomburg spoke of a 'luxury problem' at a conference hold in February 2023 in Berlin; for a report on this conference, see Maurice Niccolò Uhlig, *Berliner Anwaltblatt* (June 2023), p. 229.

[9] International Military Tribunal (Nuremberg), 1.10.1946, 41 *American Journal of International Law* (1947), pp. 172, 186.

[10] ICC Press Release, 17.3.2023; https://www.icc-cpi.int/news/situation-ukraine-icc-judges-issue-arrest-warrants-against-vladimir-vladimirovich-putin-and#:~:text=Today%2C%2017%20March%202023%2C%20Pre,Ms%20Maria%20Alekseyevna%20Lvova%2DBelova; for a first analysis, see Sergey Vasiliev, "The International Criminal Court Goes all in: What now?", *EJIL:Talk!* (20.3.2023); https://www.ejiltalk.org/the-international-criminal-court-goes-all-in-what-now/; ICC Press Release, 5.3.2024; https://www.icc-cpi.int/news/situation-ukraine-icc-judges-issue-arrest-warrants-against-sergei-ivanovich-kobylash-and#:~:text=Today%2C%205%20March%202024%202C%20Pre,Kobylash%20and%20Mr%20Viktor%20Nikolayevich.

[11] On those protected values, see Kreß, note 2, pp. 419–420.

minimum, for the commission of horrendous war crimes.[12] But crucially, the legal wrong entailed in Russia's aggression does not end there: It includes all the infringements of fundamental rights of Ukrainians which Russia has caused without violating the international law of armed conflict. The law of international armed conflict provides not only the soldiers of the victim State, but also the soldiers fighting on the side of the aggressor State, with the liberty to kill enemy combatants.[13] The aggressor is also at liberty, under the law of armed conflict, to accept the possibility of unavoidable, non-excessive civilian deaths or injuries as a result of attacks directed against military objects. Countless losses of such kind have been inflicted upon Ukrainians by the Russian aggressor[14] and none of those amount to war crimes, crimes against humanity, or genocide. Only by prosecuting the crime of aggression can Russia's leadership be held criminally responsible for that vast part of the war's violence.

In more general terms, Frédéric Mégret has made the point that, for humanitarian reasons, the law on the conduct of hostilities 'launders' a very significant part of the violence in war which means that 'war represents a monstrous exception to the notion that all human beings have an inalienable right to life, security, bodily and psychological integrity, freedom of movement etc.'[15] Only the crime of aggression ensures the individual criminal responsibility of the leadership of the aggressor State for opening the floodgate to this monstrous exception. For this reason, it is deeply misleading to divide the four crimes under international law into three atrocity crimes on the one hand and the crime of aggression on the other. On the contrary, the crime of aggression is as much an atrocity crime as the other international crimes. The prohibition of aggression does not only protect the rather abstract value of State sovereignty, but also very concrete fundamental human rights of potentially countless human beings, who may suffer and die in a war of aggression.

All this is under threat when the international legal prohibition of aggression is at risk of erosion.[16] This is why a 'negative precedent' regarding the crime of aggression—that is a failure to institute proceedings for that crime—in connection with Russia's aggression against Ukraine, far from being a luxury problem, would be fundamentally detrimental to the international legal order. Robert Jackson, the U.-S. chief prosecutor at Nuremberg, had identified the danger of norm erosion after Germany's wars of aggression in all clarity. Hence, Jackson saw the acute need to

---

[12] In that respect, see only the reports of the Independent International Commission of Inquiry on Ukraine, as established by the UN Human Rights Council on 4.3.2022; https://www.ohchr.org/en/hr-bodies/hrc/iicihr-ukraine/index.

[13] For a recent criticism of this position, see Chile Eboe Osuji, "Military Necessity and Aggression", 65 *German Yearbook of International Law* (2022), pp. 11–36.

[14] On some of those losses, see the August 2023 report by the Independent International Commission of Inquiry on Ukraine, UN Doc A/HCR/52/CRP.4, 29.8.2023, paras. 44–49; https://www.ohchr.org/sites/default/files/2023-08/A_HRC_52_CRP.4_En%20%28003%29.pdf.

[15] Frédéric Mégret, "What is the Specific Evil of Aggression?", in Kreß and Barriga, note 2, vol. 2, p. 1398, pp. 1420–1424, 1432.

[16] On this risk, see Kreß, note 1, pp. 9–11.

activate what we would today call the expressive function of international criminal law. In his opening speech in Nuremberg, Jackson made the following pronouncement:

> The ultimate step in avoiding periodic wars, which are inevitable in a system of international lawlessness, is to make statesmen responsible to law. And let me make clear that while this is first applied against German aggressors, the law includes, and if it is to serve a useful purpose it must condemn, aggression by other nations, including those which sit here now in judgment.[17]

The pronouncement of this Nuremberg promise constitutes a shining moment of true United States leadership in international criminal justice.[18] Jackson's promise remains at the core of Nuremberg's legacy. In view of Russia's war of aggression against Ukraine, it should resonate more loudly and strongly than ever since the entry into force of the UN Charter.

3 The Politics Behind the Gap

The question is why aggression had experienced 'a decline from the leading and central crime at Nuremberg and Tokyo to one that only barely made it into the Rome Statute'[19] and why we are left with a gap in the international legal architecture concerning this crime even after the activation of the Kampala amendments.

One important reason is that the prohibition of the use of force soon turned out to be surrounded by a grey area of genuine legal uncertainty which is reflective of deep-seated policy differences among States.[20] This made it a real challenge to generalize the precedents of Nuremberg and Tokyo. This challenge had been foreshadowed by Britain's Foreign Minister Austen Chamberlain in 1927 when he informed the House of Commons of his view that a definition of aggression would amount to 'a trap to the innocent'.[21] But after lengthy negotiations at the global level, including States Parties to the ICC Statute and Non-State Parties alike, a definition of the crime of aggression was agreed upon at the Kampala Review Conference and enshrined in Article 8 *bis* ICC Statute. This definition contains the so-called threshold clause, which requires an act of aggression by a State, which 'by its character, gravity and scale constitutes a manifest violation of the Charter of the United Nations'. This

---

[17] Opening Speech by the Chief Prosecutor of the United States, reprinted in *Trial of Major German War Criminals by the International Military Tribunal Sitting at Nuremberg Germany* (William S. Hein & Co., 2001), p. 45.

[18] Claus Kreß, "A Plea for True U.S. Leadership in International Criminal Justice", *Articles of War*, 7.5.2021; https://lieber.westpoint.edu/plea-true-u-s-leadership-international-criminal-justice/.

[19] Mégret, note 15, p. 1399.

[20] Claus Kreß, "On the Principle of Non-Use of Force in Current International Law", *Just Security*, 30.9.2019; https://www.justsecurity.org/66372/on-the-principle-of-non-use-of-force-in-current-international-law/.

[21] House of Commons, *Hansard* (24.11.1927), col. 2105.

requirement makes it plain that the preference of a significant number of delegations, to progressively develop the meaning of the State conduct element of the crime so as to align it with the prohibition of the use of force in its most rigorous understanding, has not prevailed. To the contrary, the formulation of Article 8 *bis* is as modest as the definition of a crime under international law should be and, accordingly, it stays clear of the above-mentioned grey area of genuine legal uncertainty. Instead, it allows for an interpretation in conformity with existing customary international law, as it should be the case with respect to a crime under international law.[22] China's Kampala representative Zhou Lulu has thus rightly observed that 'the threshold clause reflects customary international law and distinguishes appropriately between illegal international acts and international crimes.[23]

This suggests that there is another part of the truth to the fact that the governments of those nations that sat in judgment in Nuremberg have in the meantime turned away from the daunting task of delivering on their Nuremberg promise. As it has recently been written in relation to the United States: 'We fight war crimes, but have forgotten the crime of war'.[24] When it comes to the question of independent legal scrutiny of the decision to use military force, not only the Soviet Union and now Russia, but also the three Western powers that sat in judgment in Nuremberg have adopted a position of resistance that has aptly been called sovereigntist.[25] None other than Benjamin B. Ferencz has described this sovereigntist mindset in the following way:

> The vital ingredient that was really lacking was the political will of a few major powers that persisted in their refusal to accept rational international controls over the use of military force.[26]

In the course of the negotiations, this lack of political will was mostly veiled by legal arguments. The two most important arguments, neither of which is convincing, were the assertion of a Security Council monopoly on the initiation of proceedings for the crime of aggression, and the treatment of the crime of aggression like a new crime in the ICC Statute for the purposes of setting out the conditions for the ICC's exercise of jurisdiction over it.[27] As the Coalition for International Criminal Justice recalled in a statement of April 2023:

---

[22] For a detailed account, see Kreß, note 2, pp. 526–536; for a different view, see Carrie McDougall, *The Crime of Aggression under the Rome Statute of the International Criminal Court* (2nd ed., 2021), pp. 168–200.

[23] Zhou Lulu, 'China', in Kreß/Barriga, note 2, pp. 1131, 1133. Russia's Kampala delegates Gennady Kuzmin and Igor Panin also even voiced explicit agreement with the definition enshrined in Article 8 *bis*: 'Russia is satisfied with the outcome of the Review Conference with regard to the definition of the crime of aggression'; in Kreß and Barriga, note 2, p. 1264.

[24] Samuel Moyn, *Humane: How the United States Abandoned War and Reinvented War* (2021), p. 9.

[25] Gerry Simpson, "'Stop Calling it Aggression: War as Crime", 61 *Current Legal Problems* (2008), pp. 191, 219.

[26] Benjamin B. Ferencz, "The Long Journey to Kampala: A Personal Memoir", Kreß and Barrriga, note 2, pp. 1501, 1512.

[27] Claus Kreß and Leonie von Holtzendorff, "The Kampala Compromise on the Crime of Aggression", 8 *Journal of International Criminal Justice* (2010), pp. 1179–1217.

> The majority of State Parties from Africa, Latin America and Europe opposed this position. Nevertheless, the Kampala Conference ultimately gave way to the debilitating conditions regarding the crime of aggression, although they were undoubtedly understood as being driven by self-interest of larger powers.[28]

The sidelining of the crime of aggression by the major powers during the ICC negotiations was significantly facilitated by the stance that an important part of the international human rights movement had long taken regarding the question of war. By and large, this movement had accepted the idea that the killing by an aggressor during the conduct of hostilities is no violation of human rights and not the business of human rights organizations if in conformity with the permissive rules of the law of international armed conflict. In addition, organizations with a moral authority as important as Amnesty International and Human Rights Watch had adopted the policy not to comment on the conformity of military action with the *ius contra bellum*. Instead of fully recognizing that aggression opens the floodgate to a monstrous exception to fundamental human rights irrespective of the commission of war crimes, the international human rights movement had come to see aggression primarily as an offense against State sovereignty as such.[29] This paved the way for a mindset that scholars would later conceptualize through a narrow notion of atrocity crime that embraces genocide, crimes against humanity and war crimes, but excludes the crime of aggression.[30]

When international criminal justice experienced its revival in the 1990s, this approach took a firm hold in much of the non-governmental discourse community and this had tangible consequences: While civil society played a decisive role in the creation of the ICC Statute, it did not exert sufficient public pressure to remind the major powers of Jackson's Nuremberg promise.[31] And in the meantime, France, Great Britain and the U.S., and quite a few other States, happily embraced the concept of atrocity crime as a most welcome rhetorical device to continue sidelining the crime of aggression. As a result, even after the activation of the ICC's jurisdiction over the crime of aggression as from 17 July 2018[32] the prevailing concern was to humanize war rather than to outlaw it. Here are five examples that reflect this persistently prevailing mindset:

In 2019, Turkey conducted its massive military operation 'Peace Spring' in Syria: Although there was a very serious possibility that this use of force fulfilled the State conduct element of the crime of aggression, this crime was not a salient issue in the

---

[28]Coalition for International Criminal Justice, "States Parties Should Strengthen the ICC's Ability to Prosecute Aggression", *CICJ Statement No. 3* (27.4.2023), p. 1; https://cicj.eu/statement-3/.

[29]Mégret, note 15, pp. 1424–1428.

[30]For an influential essay, see David Scheffer, "Genocide and Atrocity Crimes", 1 *Genocide Studies and Prevention* (2006), pp. 229–250.

[31]Noah Weisbord, "Civil Society", in Kreß and Barriga, note 2, pp. 1310–1355.

[32]Claus Kreß, "On the Activation of ICC Jurisdiction over the Crime of Aggression", 16 *Journal of International Criminal Justice* (2018), pp. 1–18.

discourse among governments.[33] Second, in 2021, the European Union chose to simply ignore that crime on the day of international criminal justice. High Representative Borrell stated as follows:

> Every 17th of July we commemorate the historic adoption of the Rome Statute of the International Criminal Court in 1998, as an important moment to reflect on the importance of fighting impunity and bringing justice to the victims of the most serious crimes: genocide, war crimes and crimes against humanity[34] – full stop.

Third, in May 2022, the European Union adopted an amendment of its Regulation on Eurojust.

This amendment extended Eurojust's scope of action with respect to genocide, crimes against humanity and war crimes. The crime of aggression, however, was left out.[35] Fourth, in August 2022, the International Law Commission adopted, on first reading, its Draft Articles on immunity of State officials from foreign criminal jurisdiction. Its draft article 7 recognizes the non-applicability of functional immunity in proceedings for genocide, crimes against humanity and war crimes, but not in those for the crime of aggression.[36] And fifth, most governments, apart from the Ukrainian, kept silent about the crime of aggression even for months after the UN General Assembly had properly characterized Russia's unlawful use of force against Ukraine as an aggression. In view of all this, it was difficult, even in the summer of 2022, to disagree with the assessment that 'aggression belongs to, but is hanging by a thread in the firmament of international offences'.[37]

4 The Renewed Focus on the Crime of Aggression

In the meantime, however, the picture has begun to change: Already in 2018, the UN Human Rights Committee laid an important doctrinal ground for such a change. In its General Comment 36, it stated: 'State Parties engaged in acts of aggression as defined in international law resulting in deprivation of life, violate *ipso facto* article

---

[33] Claus Kreß, "A Collective Failure to Prevent Turkey's Operation 'Peace Spring' and NATO's Silence on International Law", *EJIL:Talk!*, 14.10.2019; https://www.ejiltalk.org/a-collective-failure-to-prevent-turkeys-operation-peace-spring-and-natos-silence-on-international-law/.

[34] European Union, "Day of International Criminal Justice: Declaration by the High Representative Josep Borrell on behalf of the European Union", Press Release, 16.7.2021; https://www.consilium.europa.eu/en/press/press-releases/2021/07/16/day-of-international-criminal-justice-declaration-by-the-high-representative-josep-borrell-on-behalf-of-the-european-union/.

[35] Regulation (EU) 2022/838 of the European Parliament and of the Council of 30.5.2022, *Official Journal of the European Union*, 31.5.2022, L 148/4, Art. 1.

[36] Report of the International Law Commission, Seventy-third session (18 April-3 June and 4 July-5 August 2022), UN Doc A/77/10, p. 191 (para. 68).

[37] Mégret, note 15, p. 1399.

Russia's War of Aggression Against Ukraine and the Crime of Aggression 63

6 of the Covenant.'[38] The significance of this statement can hardly be overstated: Hereby, the Human Rights Committee has rightly claimed a space for the human rights conscience to address by its own distinct normative voice all the war violence inflicted by an aggressor State.[39]

After 24 February 2022, Philippe Sands was the first to raise the issue of the crime of aggression in public: 'Why not create a dedicated international criminal tribunal to investigate Putin and his acolytes for the crime of aggression?', he asked, and he recalled: 'After all, it was a Soviet jurist, Aaron Trainin, who did much of the legwork to bring crimes against peace into international law.' 'Let Putin reap the legacy of Nuremberg', so Sands concluded.[40] His call, which was taken up soon thereafter at a meeting at Chatham House,[41] resonated powerfully with the victims of Russia's aggression and was immediately embraced by the head of Ukraine's diplomacy. After all, Dmytro Kuleba, now Ukraine's Minister of Foreign Affairs and an international lawyer, had written a paper at the National University of Kviv on the Declaration of St James, of January 1942, a catalyst for Nuremberg.[42] Leading voices of Ukraine's civil society soon lent their emphatic support, among them Oleksandra Matviychuk from the Centre for Civil Liberties, one of the recipients of the Nobel Peace Prize.[43]

Soon thereafter, parliamentarians worldwide began to raise their voices. One Parliamentary Assembly after the other (and, notably, also Parliamentarians for Global Action[44]) addressed the issue of the crime of aggression.[45] The culmination of this series of public pronouncements was Resolution 2482 of the Council of

---

[38] UN Human Rights Committee, "General Comment No. 36, Article 6: right to life"; UN Doc CCPR/C/GC/36, 30.10.2018, para. 70.

[39] Claus Kreß, "A Reply to Judge Eboe-Osuji", 65 *German Yearbook of International Law* (2022), pp. 37, 47–51.

[40] Philippe Sands, "Putin's Use of Military Force is a Crime of Aggression", *Financial Times* (28.2.2022). Soviet scholar Aron Trainin had coined the term 'crimes against peace', that is the name under which the crime of aggression entered the international scene in Nuremberg; on the Soviet Union's contribution to the Nuremberg trial, see Francine Hirsch, *Soviet Judgment at Nuremberg. A New History of the International Military Tribunal after World War II* (2020).

[41] For references, see Independent International Commission of Inquiry, note 14, p. 156 (paras. 928–929).

[42] The author is grateful to Judge Mykola Gnatovskyy for sharing this information with him.

[43] See, e.g., "The Appeal of Human Rights Defender Oleksandra Matviischuk to the Secretary-General of the United Nations", 28.9.2022, op. para. 3; https://ccl.org.ua/en/claims/the-appeal-of-human-rights-defender-oleksandra-matviichuk-to-the-secretary-general-of-the-united-nations/.

[44] 12th Consultative Assembly of Parliamentarians on the International Criminal Court and the Rule of Law (CAP-ICC), 43rd Annual Forum of Parliamentarians for Global Action, "Plan of Action on the Universality and Effectiveness of, and political support for, the Rome Statute system against impunity", 4-5.11.2022 (National Congress of Argentina, Buenos Aires); https://www.pgaction.org/pdf/2022/buenos-aires-poa-2022-en.pdf.

[45] For an exhaustive list of references, see Independent International Commission of Inquiry, note 14, p. 155 (para. 926 (note 625).

Europe's Parliamentary Assembly.[46] This resolution, adopted by unanimity, demands that the Russian and Belarusian political and military leaders concerned 'should be identified and prosecuted for the crime of aggression'.[47] The Assembly cited General Comment 36 of the UN Human Rights Committee and stated as follows: 'Without their decision to wage this war of aggression against Ukraine, the atrocities that flow from it as well as all the destruction, death and damage resulting from lawful acts of war would not have occurred.'[48] In its report of August 2023, the UN Independent International Commission of Inquiry on Ukraine also devoted an elaborate and important passage to the crime of aggression[49] and recognized that the international criminal justice response to Russia's war of aggression against Ukraine must include accountability for crimes of aggression. The Commission states as follows:

> Should the investigations result in trials against lead perpetrators based on genocide, crimes against humanity or war crimes, it may be argued that evidence relating to acts of aggression can be taken into account during the judicial proceedings, both as context of the crimes and as an aggravating circumstance. (...) However, this course of action will not fully reflect the gravity of the crime of aggression as such, which is a separate crime, different from the three other crimes. No other existing international court can adjudicate allegations of the crime of aggression in the current context of Ukraine.[50]

As of lately, there also seems to be a growing interest in ensuring accountability for the crime of aggression within the NGO Coalition for the ICC. The Open Society Justice Initiative, for example, has been an active participant in the debate for quite some while.[51]

This 'renewed focus on the crime of aggression', as ICC Prosecutor Khan has called it,[52] was powerful enough to spill over to the governmental level. Liechtenstein and the Baltic States took the lead[53] and subsequently more and more governments took up the issue of the crime of aggression. In October of 2022, the UN General Assembly for the first time explicitly mentioned the activation of the ICC's

---

[46] Parliamentary Assembly of the Council of Europe, 'Legal and human rights aspects of the Russian Federation's aggression against Ukraine', Resolution 2842 (2023), 26.1.2023; https://pace.coe.int/en/files/31620/html.

[47] *Ibid.*, para. 4.

[48] *Ibid.*

[49] Independent International Commission of Inquiry, note 14, pp. 155–160 (paras. 922–946).

[50] *Ibid.*, p. 155 (paras. 924–925).

[51] See above in note 4.

[52] Karim A.A. Khan, Prosecutor of the International Criminal Court, Statement made on 5 December 2022 at the opening plenary of the 21st session of the Assembly of States Parties, para. 21; https://asp.icc-cpi.int/sites/asp/files/2022-12/ASP21-STMT-PROS-ENG.pdf.

[53] For references, see Independent International Commission of Inquiry, note 14, p. 155 (para. 926, note 625); see also Gabija Grigaité-Daugirdé, "The Lithuanian Case for an International Special Tribunal for the Crime of Aggression Against Ukraine", *Just Security* (1.6.2023); https://www.justsecurity.org/86766/the-lithuanian-case-for-an-international-special-tribunal-for-the-crime-of-aggression-against-ukraine/.

jurisdiction over the crime of aggression.[54] Only a little later, the European Council declared that the prosecution of the crime of aggression is of concern to the international community as a whole.[55] In February of 2023, the European Council followed suit and endorsed the setting up of the International Center for the Prosecution of the Crime of Aggression[56] against Ukraine.[57] And in March of 2023, the U.S. has added its voice to the growing chorus. In an address delivered in Washington, Ambassador-at-Large for Global Criminal Justice Beth van Schaack recalled the United States' 'leading role in prosecuting the crime of aggression at Nuremberg'. She recognized that this is 'a critical moment in history' and she confirmed that 'there are compelling reasons for why the crime of aggression must be prosecuted'.[58] With the U.S. appearance on the public scene, it had become abundantly clear that the new momentum concerning the crime of aggression had an effect even on the attitude of some of those governments that had for decades adopted a position of sovereigntist resistance. In that regard, however, the key question remains whether one is witnessing a genuine change of position, one that truly embraces Jackson's call for a consistent, non-selective application the Nuremberg precedent on crimes against peace.

5   Reform Paths

5.1   The Most Principled Path: Amending the ICC Statute

As a matter of principle, the best way to close the existing gap would be to do it directly in the ICC Statute as proposed, most notably, by Prosecutor Khan.[59] The ICC, the only permanent international criminal court—and one with a credible universal orientation—is the most legitimate judicial institution to deliver on Nuremberg's fundamental promise.[60] It has been asked whether the principle of

---

[54] UN Doc A/77/L.7, 26.10.2022, para. 25.

[55] European Council Meeting (15.12.2022) – Conclusions, EUCO 34/22, CO EUR 29, CONCL 7, para. 8; https://www.consilium.europa.eu/media/60872/2022-12-15-euco-conclusions-en.pdf.

[56] For the website of the ICPA, see https://www.eurojust.europa.eu/international-centre-for-the-prosecution-of-the-crime-of-aggression-against-ukraine.

[57] Special Meeting of the European Council (9.2.2023) – Conclusions, EUCO 1/23, CO EUR 1, CONCL 1, para. 4; https://data.consilium.europa.eu/doc/document/ST-1-2023-INIT/en/pdf.

[58] Ambassador Beth van Schaack's Remarks on the U.S. Proposal to Prosecute Russian Crimes of Aggression (27.3.2023); https://www.state.gov/ambassador-van-schaacks-remarks/.

[59] Khan, note 52: 'When we recognize that there is a gap in that architecture, in my view, we should try to address it through the Rome Statute (...).' For the same view, see Claus Kress/Stephan Hobe/Angelika Nussberger, "The Ukraine War and the Crime of Aggression: How to Fill the Gaps in the International Legal System", *Just Security*, 23.1.2023; https://www.justsecurity.org/84783/the-ukraine-war-and-the-crime-of-aggression-how-to-fill-the-gaps-in-the-international-legal-system/.

[60] Independent International Commission of Inquiry, note 14, p. 155 (para. 923).

retroactivity in criminal law could stand in the way of eliminating limitations on the Court's exercise of jurisdiction over the crime of aggression with retroactive effect to Russia's war aggression against Ukraine.[61] But the principle only concerns the substantive criminal law[62] and the conduct of the relevant Russian leaders in question was criminalized under customary international law long before 2014. Yet, the necessary reform of the ICC Statute raises a number of legal and policy issues[63] and at the time of writing it seems that decision-makers do not regard an amendment of the ICC Statute as fast enough a solution to the immediate challenge: the war of aggression against Ukraine.

5.2 A Special Tribunal for the Crime of Aggression Against Ukraine

Therefore, considerable attention has been given and continues to be given to the establishment of a Special Tribunal for the Crime of Aggression against Ukraine.[64]

---

[61] Independent International Commission of Inquiry, note 14, p. 158 (para. 938).

[62] Claus Kreß, "Nulla poena nullum crimen sine lege", A. Peters (ed.), *Max Planck Enclycopedia of Public International Law*, para. 20 (February 2010); https://opil.ouplaw.com/display/10.1093/law:epil/9780199231690/law-9780199231690-e854.

[63] Astrid Reisinger-Coracini, "Is Amending the Rome Statute the Panacea Against Perceived Selectivity and Impunity for the Crime of Aggression Against Ukraine?", *Just Security*, 21.3.2023; https://www.justsecurity.org/85593/is-amending-the-rome-statute-the-panacea-against-perceived-selectivity-and-impunity-for-the-crime-of-aggression-committed-against-ukraine/; Fiona Abken and Paulina Rob, "Amending the Amendment: In Search of an Adequate Procedure for a Revision of the Jurisdictional Regime for the Crime of Aggression in the Rome Statute", *EJIL:Talk!* (13.1.2023); https://www.ejiltalk.org/amending-the-amendment-in-search-of-an-adequate-proce dure-for-a-revision-of-the-jurisdictional-regime-for-the-crime-of-aggression-in-the-rome-statute/.

[64] For scholarly contributions, see Advisory Committee on Public International Law, *Challenges in prosecuting the crime of aggression: jurisdiction and immunities*, Advisory report no. 40 (12.9.2022); https://www.advisorycommitteeinternationallaw.nl/publications/advisory-reports/2022/09/12/challenges-in-prosecuting-the-crime-of-aggression-jurisdiction-and-immuni ties; Kai Ambos, "A Ukraine Special Tribunal with Legitimacy Problems?", *Verfassungsblog* (6.1.2023); https://verfassungsblog.de/a-ukraine-special-tribunal-with-legitimacy-problems/; Gleb Bogush and Sergei Golubok, "Why the World Needs a Special Tribunal to Prosecute Russia's Aggression Against Ukraine", *The Moscow Times* (26.6.2023); https://www.themoscowtimes. com/2023/06/23/why-the-world-needs-a-special-tribunal-to-prosecute-russias-aggression-against-ukraine-a81606; Annegret Hartig, "Ein Aggressionstribunal für die Ukraine?", *Deutsche Richterzeitung* (2022), pp. 368–371; Olivier Corten and Vaios Koutroulis, "Tribunal for the crime of aggression against Ukraine – a legal assessment", In-depth Analysis Requested by the DROI Subcommittee of the European Parliament (December 2022); https://www.europarl.europa. eu/RegData/etudes/IDAN/2022/702574/EXPO_IDA(2022)702574_EN.pdf; Tom Dannenbaum, "A Special Tribunal for the Crime of Aggression?", 20 *Journal of International Criminal Justice* (2022), pp. 859–873; Oona Hathaway, "A Crime in Search of a Court", *Foreign Affairs* (19.5.2022); Kevin Jon Heller, "Options for Prosecuting Russian Aggression Against Ukraine, A Critical Analysis", *Journal of Genocide Research* (2022), pp. 1–24; Patryk Labuda, "Countering

Russia's War of Aggression Against Ukraine and the Crime of Aggression 67

The idea had first been put forward in a statement which was published after the above-mentioned Chatham House meeting and which has been signed by a significant number of international experts and personalities.[65] In the meantime, the process has been taken over by governments: At the time of writing, no less than 40 States have joined a so-called Core Group in support of Ukraine's call for the establishment of such a tribunal which builds the forum of an ongoing inter-governmental conversation conducted behind closed doors.

5.2.1 On Two Policy Objections

It is worth addressing two arguments which challenge the very idea of a special tribunal. The first argument is that a special tribunal could weaken the ICC. But there are weighty considerations speaking against that concern: The ICC would continue to carry out its important work with respect to allegations of war crimes, crimes against humanity and genocide. A special tribunal would do no more than to complement this work with respect to the crime of aggression.[66] The special tribunal would serve precisely the same overarching goal as the ICC, that is to ensure the most comprehensive accountability possible for crimes under international law. Experienced practitioners have long suggested ways, such as the establishment of a liaison office, to allow the ICC and a special tribunal to coordinate their work and to thereby create useful synergies instead of causing friction.[67] Again, the ICC is the

---

Imperialism in International Law: Examining the Special Tribunal for Aggression against Ukraine Through a Post-Colonial Eastern European Lens", 49 *Yale Journal of International Law* (2023) (forthcoming); Flavia Lattanzi, Quale tribunale per I crimini russi in Ucrainia? Le proposte di Lattanzi, *Formiche.net* (20.2.2023); Carrie McDougall, "The Imperative of Prosecuting Crimes of Aggression Against Ukraine", 28 *Journal of Conflict & Security Law* (2023), pp. 208–230; Anne Peters and Robert Spendel, "Ein Sondertribunal zur Aggression gegen die Ukraine? Ja.", *Vereinte Nationen* (2023), p. 74; Carmen Queseda Alcalá, "El Crimen del Agresión contra Ucrania, un Crimen Cierto, con Enjuiciamiento Incierto, 46 *Revista Electrónica de Estudios Internacioanles* (2023); Jennifer Trahan, "The Need for an International Criminal on the Crime of Aggression Regarding the Situation in Ukraine", 46 *Fordham International Law Journal* (2023), pp. 671–690.

[65] Statement Calling for the Creation of a Special Tribunal for the Punishment of the Crime of Aggression Against Ukraine; https://gordonandsarahbrown.com/wp-content/uploads/2022/03/Combined-Statement-and-Declaration.pdf.

[66] Independent International Commission of Inquiry, note 14, p. 158 (para. 937).

[67] Astrid Reisinger Coracini, "The Case for Creating a Special Tribunal to Prosecute the Crime of Aggression Against Ukraine (Part II): Jurisdiction and Composition", *Just Security* (23.9.2022); https://www.justsecurity.org/83201/tribunal-crime-of-aggression-part-two/; David Scheffer, "Forging a Cooperative Relationship Between International Criminal Court and a Special Tribunal for the Crime of Aggression Against Ukraine", *Just Security* (25.10.2022); https://www.justsecurity.org/83757/forging-a-cooperative-relationship-between-intl-crim-court-and-a-special-tribunal-for-russian-aggression-against-ukraine/; Carrie McDougall, "The Proposed Special Tribunal for Crimes of Aggression Against Ukraine Should be Viewed as an Accountability Partner, Not a Competitor: Should the Tribunal be established, the ICC Should Cooperate With It to the Greatest Extent Possible", *ICC Forum* (13.9.2023); https://iccforum.com/decentralized-accountability#McDougall;

most important pillar of the existing global system for the prosecution of crimes under international law. But the work of the ICC will invariably need to be complemented by additional judicial activity.[68] Which kind of additional activity will differ in each situation. As Judges Higgins, Kooijmans, and Buergenthal, wrote in their memorable separate opinion in the ICJ's 2002 Arrest Warrant Case:

> The international consensus that the perpetrators of international crimes should not go unpunished is being advanced by a flexible strategy in which newly established international criminal tribunals, treaty obligations and national courts all have their part to play.[69]

The second counter-argument is that proceedings before a special tribunal for the situation of Ukraine would constitute selective justice.[70] This argument is central: Selectivity in international criminal justice undermines its legitimacy. Selectivity must therefore be reduced. With respect to the special tribunal, the argument of selectivity has been made with respect both to the past and to the future. It carries far lesser weight with respect to the past. Most regrettably, there were indeed a number of serious violations of the prohibition of the use of force in the past where investigations into possible crimes of aggression would have been warranted: Iraq's use of force against Kuwait in 1990, Uganda's use of force against the Democratic Republic of Congo as from September 1998, the use of force by the United States and United Kingdom-led Coalition of the Willing against Iraq in 2003 and Turkey's use of force in Syria in 2019. Yet, at every historic turning point in the history of international criminal justice so far, decision-makers were faced with past failures. Had those failures of the past posed an insurmountable obstacle to taking action for the future, there would have been neither Nuremberg and Tokyo, nor the International Tribunals for the former Yugoslavia (ICTY) and Rwanda (ICTR), nor the ICC. Failures of the past with respect to the crime of aggression should therefore not prevent decision-makers from doing the right thing today for the future. And even less so in view of Russia's aggression against Ukraine, which, taking all relevant factors into account, constitutes a violation of the prohibition of the use of force of unprecedented seriousness.

The issue of selectivity weighs heavily, however, if one looks to the future. Today, Russia's leadership benefits from jurisdictional constraints that have resulted not only from its own preferences, but, as mentioned above, also from the sovereigntist resistance of three major Western powers to a principled jurisdictional

---

for the specific legal issue of double jeopardy, see Gaiane Nuridzhanian and Carrie McDougall, "On Double Jeopardy, the ICC, and the Special Tribunal for the Crime of Aggression", *Just Security*, 18.1.2024; https://www.justsecurity.org/91314/on-double-jeopardy-the-icc-and-the-special-tribu nal-for-the-crime-of-aggression/.

[68] Independent International Commission of Inquiry, note 14, pp. 158–159 (para. 940).

[69] ICJ, Case Concerning the Arrest Warrant of 11 April 2000 (Democratic Republic of the Congo v. Belgium), Judgment of 14 February 2002, Joint Separate Opinion of Judges Higgins, Koijmans and Buergenthal, *I.C.J. Reports* 2002, pp. 63, 78 (para. 51).

[70] Luis Moreno Ocampo, "Ending Selective Justice for the International Crime of Aggression", *Just Security* (31.1.2023); https://www.justsecurity.org/84949/ending-selective-justice-for-the-interna tional-crime-of-aggression/.

regime in the ICC Statute. This begs a burning question of legitimacy: Is the creation of a special tribunal for the war of aggression against Ukraine perhaps meant by those powers to remain an event as isolated as Nuremberg and Tokyo have remained to date? But asking this question should not be the end of the matter. It should rather embolden governments to show true leadership. If they decide to establish a special tribunal, they should conceive of it as an imperfect instrument of transition, as a stepping stone towards a genuine embrace of Nuremberg's promise through a more principled jurisdictional regime in the ICC Statute. Such an effect would certainly not be without precedent. It may suffice to remember how the ICTY and the ICTR, both special international criminal tribunals, helped prepare the ground for the ICC's jurisdiction over genocide, crimes against humanity and war crimes.[71] Germany's Foreign Minister Annalena Baerbock publicly recognized the need for principled action in her important speech delivered at the Hague Academy of International Law in January 2023. Minister Baerbock was as sensitive to the question of selectivity in international criminal justice as one should be. But she did not rule out a special tribunal for the war of aggression against Ukraine. Instead, she suggested that the establishment of such a tribunal should be the first track of a two-track strategy. The second and more time-consuming track would have to be, she said, the amendment of the ICC Statute with respect to the crime of aggression.[72] While, as already mentioned above, it would be preferable, to solve the problem on the single-track approach of amending the ICC Statute, Minister Baerbock's proposed two track-approach nevertheless constitutes a principled path. The following statement of the UN Independent International Commission of Inquiry on Ukraine gently points in the same direction:

> A process aimed at amending the Rome Statute in parallel with the setting up (sic!) a new tribunal would demonstrate that the current conflict in Ukraine has shown "the jurisdictional gap" in the International Criminal Court Statute and that the international community is now seeking to fill it, based on a two-pronged approach.[73]

5.2.2 On the Question of Format

In April 2023, the Foreign Ministers of the G7 came forward in favor of an internationalized Ukrainian tribunal as their format of choice: 'We support', they said, 'the creation of an internationalized tribunal based in Ukraine's judicial

---

[71] Claus Kreß, "The International Criminal Court as a Turning Point in the History of International Criminal Justice", in A. Cassese (ed.), *The Oxford Companion of International Criminal Justice* (2009), pp. 143–159.

[72] Speech by Federal Foreign Minister Annalena Baerbock in The Hague, "Strengthening International Law in Times of Crisis" (16.1.2023); https://www.auswaertiges-amt.de/en/newsroom/news/strengthening-international-law-in-times-of-crisis/2573492.

[73] Independent International Commission of Inquiry, note 14, p. 159 (para. 940).

70   C. Kreß

system'.[74] Almost at the same time, thirteen European and non-European States issued a joint statement in favor of an international tribunal.[75] The latter is in line with the unanimous call of the Parliamentary Assembly of the Council of Europe.[76] In the abstract, none of the two formats is inherently superior to the other and the choice must rather be made in light of the circumstances and needs of the given situation. In her Washington address, Ambassador van Schaack gave essentially two reasons why the U.S. favors a tribunal based in Ukraine's judicial system. She said that such a court would provide the 'clearest path to establishing a new Tribunal, maximizing our chances of achieving meaningful accountability'.[77] None of these arguments is, however, convincing.[78] In fact, both of them are rather astonishing.

First of all, creating an internationalized tribunal in Ukraine's legal system is by no means the clearest path available. On the contrary, it remains unclear to date, what precisely the international elements of a Ukrainian tribunal should be. The only thing that is reasonably clear is that the internationalization of a Ukrainian tribunal would have to be meaningful. Otherwise, such a tribunal would become an all too easy target of charges of politicization. However, a meaningful internationalization of a Ukrainian tribunal would require this State to change its constitution.[79] Even if somehow practicable despite the imposition of martial law, this approach would cost a lot of precious time in a situation where time is of the essence. This is one important reason why Ukraine does not favor the option of an internationalized Ukrainian tribunal.[80] It is rather odd to speak of a 'clearest path' under such

---

[74] G7 Japan 2023, Foreign Minister's Communiqué (18.4.2023) Karuizawa, Nagano; https://www.mofa.go.jp/files/100492731.pdf.

[75] Joint Statement by Belgium, Costa Rica, Czech Republik, Estonia, Guatemala, Latvia, Liechtenstein, Lithuania, Luxemburg, Marshall Islands, North-Macedonia, and Poland on the accountability for the crime of aggression committed on the territory of Ukraine (17.4.2023); https://un.mfa.ee/joint-statement-on-the-accountability-for-the-crime-of-aggression-committed-on-the-territory-of-ukraine/.

[76] Parliamentary Assembly of the Council of Europe, note 46, para. 6.

[77] Ambassador Beth van Schaack's Remarks, note 58.

[78] For two further critical analyses of the U.S. position, see Rebecca Hamilton, "An Assessment of the United States' New Position on an Aggression Tribunal for Ukraine", *Just Security* (29.3.2023); https://asp.icc-cpi.int/sites/asp/files/2022-12/ASP21-STMT-PROS-ENG.pdf.; Jennifer Trahan, "Don't be Fooled by U.S. Smoke and Mirrors on the Crime of Aggression. Weak Proposals Carry the Risk of Weak Results", *Just Security* (14.4.2023); https://www.justsecurity.org/85986/dont-be-fooled-by-u-s-smoke-and-mirrors-on-the-crime-of-aggression/.

[79] Alexander Komarov and Oona Hathaway, "Ukraine's Constitutional Constraints: How Achieve Accountability for the Crime of Aggression?", *Just Security* (5.4.2022); https://www.justsecurity.org/80958/ukraines-constitutional-constraints-how-to-achieve-accountability-for-the-crime-of-aggression/.

[80] In January 2024, President Zelenskyy has reiterated his call for a "Special International Tribunal for the Crime of Aggression against Ukraine"; Joint Statement by the President of the Republic of Lithuania, H. E. Mr Gitanas Nauseda, and the President of Ukraine, H.E. Mr Volodymyr Zelenskyy (10.1.2024); https://www.president.gov.ua/en/news/spilna-zayava-prezidenta-ukrayini-volodimira-zelenskogo-i-pr-88193; perhaps the clearest pronouncement of President Zelenskyy's against an internationalized Ukrainian tribunal can be found in "The Speech by Volodymyr Zelenskyy to

circumstances. At the time of writing, consideration is being given within the Core Group to the question whether the constitutional challenge that the original proposal faces can be overcome by a transfer of Ukraine's most important proceedings[81] for the crime of aggression to one recipient State[82] or to a group of recipient States. Such State(s) could then establish a multinational tribunal for the purpose of conducting the proceedings thus received. At this stage, too little is known outside the Core Group to offer a considered opinion about the viability of such a model. But the fact alone, that the conversation on such a model is ongoing at the time of writing, suggests that the path leading to such a solution is not particularly straight-forward either.

Moreover, an internationalized Ukrainian tribunal, in whatever form, does not maximize the chances for meaningful accountability: First, accountability will be all the more meaningful, both for the Ukrainians and for the defense of the essence of the international legal order, the more comprehensively it reaches up to those allegedly most responsible including those forming the Russian troika. Yet, the Judgment of the International Court of Justice (ICJ) in the Arrest Warrant Case and the relevant *obiter dictum* therein,[83] the judgment rendered by the Special Court for Sierra Leone in the case against Charles Taylor,[84] the judgment issued by the ICC in the case against Al-Bashir,[85] which was followed in the ICC's decision on the arrest warrant against Putin,[86] as well as Draft Article 3 on immunity of State officials from foreign criminal jurisdiction, as adopted in 2022 on first reading by the ILC,[87] make it more likely that the judges of a future special tribunal will pierce

---

representatives of the public, political and expert circles of the Kingdom of the Netherlands and international institutions based in The Hague" (4.5.2023); https://www.president.gov.ua/en/news/promova-prezidenta-ukrayini-volodimira-zelenskogo-u-generaln-74001. In this speech President Zelenskyy states: 'But only one institution is capable of responding to the original crime: the crime of aggression. A Tribunal! Not something hybrid that can formally close the topic ... Not some compromise that will allow politicians to say that the case is allegedly done ... But a true, full-fledged tribunal. True and full justice.'

[81] The transfer of criminal proceedings has received a detailed international treaty regulation in The European Convention on the Transfer of Proceedings in Criminal Matters of 15 May 1972, *European Treaty Series* No 73.

[82] For a more recent example, see Art. 5 (2) and Art. 6 of the Agreement between the Kingdom of the Netherlands and Ukraine on International Legal Cooperation regarding Crimes connected with the Downing of Malaysia Airlines Flight MH on 17 July 2014; https://www.eerstekamer.nl/behandeling/20170707/verdrag_tussen_het_koninkrijk_der/document3/f=/vkmvd36xqxwj.pdf.

[83] ICJ, *Case Concerning the Arrest Warrant of 11 April 2000 (Democratic Republic of the Congo v. Belgium)*, Judgment of 14 February 2002, pp. 3, 24 (para. 58), 25 (para. 61).

[84] SCSL, *Prosecutor v. Charles Ghankay Taylor, Decision on Immunity from Jurisdiction*, 31 May 2004, SCSL-2003-01-I, 31 May 2004, para. 52.

[85] ICC, *Prosecutor v. Omar Hassan Ahmad Al Bashir, Judgement in the Jordan Referral re Al-Bashir Appeal*, ICC-02/05-01/09 OA 2, 6 May 2019, para. 114 in conjunction with para. 2.

[86] For the reference, see note 10.

[87] Report of the International Law Commission, note 36, p. 190 (para. 68).

the veil of personal immunities[88] with respect to members of the Russian troika before a genuinely international criminal court than before an internationalized Ukrainian tribunal.[89]

In addition, the ILC's above-mentioned[90] exclusion of the crime of aggression from the list of crimes in Draft Article 7 of its immunity project, as adopted on first reading, adds to the risk that judges of a tribunal based in Ukraine's legal system might also grant functional immunity.[91] This would reduce the chances for 'meaningful accountability' to close to zero because the great majority of the suspects will be Russian officials who acted in that capacity. In that context, it is striking how strongly the United States has rejected Draft Article 7 in its most recent statement *vis-à-vis* the ILC[92] and how firmly France has, at the same occasion, opposed the inclusion of the crime of aggression in the list of crimes contained in this Draft Article.[93] It remains a mystery, how these positions can be reconciled with the view

---

[88] On the concept of personal immunity in international law, see Claus Kreß, "Art. 98", in K. Ambos (ed.), *Rome Statute of the International Criminal Court: Article-by-Article Commentary* (4th ed., 2022), pp. 2626–2627 (para. 84).

[89] The topic of personal immunities is perhaps the single most intricate legal issue in connection with the conversation about the establishment of a special tribunal. This question cannot receive a detailed treatment within the limited space of this essay. The two central questions are, first, whether there exists at all an exception from the customary international personal immunity in proceedings for crimes under international law, and, second, if such an exception exists, whether it exists in all international criminal proceedings, only in certain international proceedings or in certain international and also exceptionally in national criminal proceedings. The relevant scholarly literature on these questions has been rapidly growing in parallel to the inter-governmental discourse. Apart from the pieces mentioned in note 64, see, above all, Rosanne van Alebeek, Larissa van den Herik, and Cedric Ryngaert, "Prosecuting Russian Officials for the crime of aggression: what about immunities?", 4 *European Convention of Human Rights Law Review* (2023), pp. 115–132; Open Society Justice Initiative, *Immunities and a Special Tribunal for the Crime of Aggression against Ukraine* (February 2023); https://www.justiceinitiative.org/publications/immunities-and-a-special-tribunal-for-the-crime-of-aggression-against-ukraine; André de Hoogh, "Personal Immunities Redux Before a Special Tribunal for Prosecuting Russian Crimes of Aggression: Resistance is Futile, *EJIL:Talk!* (5.1.2024); https://www.ejiltalk.org/personal-immunities-redux-before-a-special-tribunal-for-prose cuting-russian-crimes-of-aggression-resistance-is-futile/; Chile Eboe-Osuji, "International Law Rejects Immunity for International Crimes – Full Stop", 21 *Journal of International Criminal Justice* (2023), pp. 461–485; Astrid Reisinger Coracini and Jennifer Trahan, "Special Tribunal to Prosecute the Crime of Aggression Against Ukraine (Part IV): On the Non-Applicability of Personal Immunities", *Just Security* (8.11.2022); https://www.justsecurity.org/84017/the-case-for-creating-a-special-tribunal-to-prosecute-the-crime-of-aggression-committed-against-ukraine-part-vi-on-the-non-applicability-of-personal-immunities/; for this author's position, see Kreß, note 88, pp. 2639–2653 (paras. 114–130).

[90] See above text accompanying note 35.

[91] On the concept of functional immunity in international law, see Kreß, note 88, p. 2601 (para. 22).

[92] Comments from the United States on the International Law Commission's Draft Articles on Criminal Immunity of States Officials As Adopted by the Commission in 2022 on First Reading, pp. 9–10; https://legal.un.org/ilc/sessions/75/pdfs/english/iso_us.pdf.

[93] Commentaires et observations de la République Française relatifs aux projets d'articles de la Commission de Droit International sur « l'immunité de juridiction pénale étrangère des représentants de l'État », para. 36; https://legal.un.org/ilc/sessions/75/pdfs/french/iso_france.pdf.

of those same two States that an internationalized Ukrainian special tribunal constitutes the preferable format and maximizes the chances for 'meaningful accountability'.[94]

The question of 'meaningful accountability' has yet another dimension, and here again a genuinely international solution offers a clear advantage: As was pointed out above, the crime of aggression, because of its distinct history, today only 'hangs by a thread in the firmament of international crimes'.[95] Hence, at this historic juncture, the strongest possible message is needed to confirm that the crime of aggression is a crime under international law as much as genocide, crimes against humanity and war crimes. Yet, the establishment of an internationalized Ukrainian tribunal would fail to send out a message of such a strength: The institutional design would not clearly convey the international character of the crime of aggression and would emphasize Ukraine's national interest in prosecuting it as the immediate victim rather than that of the international community as a whole. Hence, to heed Ukraine's call for the establishment of a truly international tribunal for the crime of aggression would not only be a welcome deference to this country's democratic choice and, notably, to a demand voiced by a group of courageous Russian dissident international criminal and human right lawyers.[96] It would also be the most plausible way to translate into institutional design what the G7 States themselves have explicitly recognized: that proceedings for the crime of aggression are in the interest of the international community as a whole.[97]

---

[94] For Ukraine's detailed explanation as to why functional immunity does not apply in proceedings for crimes under international law, including those for the crime of aggression, see Comments and observations of Ukraine in relation to Draft Article 7 of the Draft Articles on Immunity of State officials from foreign criminal jurisdiction; https://legal.un.org/ilc/sessions/75/pdfs/english/iso_ukraine.pdf; for the concurring position of this author, see Kreß, note 88, pp. 2601–2626 (paras. 23–83).

[95] See above text accompanying note 37.

[96] Gleb Bogush and Sergey Vasiliev, "Russian International and Human Rights Lawyers' Statement on Accountability", *Just Security* (12.6.2023); The Brussels Declaration: https://www.justsecurity.org/86911/the-brussels-declaration-russian-international-and-human-rights-lawyers-statement-on-accountability/.

[97] Of course, there are means to internationalize a tribunal anchored in the Ukrainian system in a manner that would move the expressive force of such a tribunal closer in the desirable direction: Those include an explicit reference of the crime's international character and its definition in Art. 8 *bis* of the ICC Statute, strong international features in terms of its prosecution service and the composition of the benches, and ideally also an endorsement of the tribunals' establishment by the UN General Assembly.

While severable options have been put forward in that respect,[98] the preferable path to establish a truly international tribunal would be to set it up on the basis of an agreement between the UN and Ukraine, negotiated on behalf of the UN by its Secretary-General and at the request of the General Assembly.[99] Doubts have been expressed about the power of the General Assembly to get involved. These doubts are however ill-founded:[100] In its 1962 Advisory Opinion in 'Certain Expenses', the ICJ has set out the functions and powers conferred on the General Assembly to exercise its secondary responsibility for the maintenance of international peace and security, taking into account both the text of the UN Charter and the practice subsequent to its adoption including that under the 'Uniting for Peace' umbrella.[101] The Court explicitly recognized that those functions and powers are not confined to the making of recommendations and that they are not merely hortatory. The Court found that only coercive action is within the exclusive realm of the Security Council.[102] But the request to the UN Secretary-General to conclude an agreement with a State on the establishment of an international tribunal for the exercise of jurisdiction over crimes under international law does not involve coercive action. That was confirmed by no lesser body than the Security Council itself in relation to the establishment of the Special Court for Sierra Leone. For in that case, the Council acted under Chapter VI, rather than Chapter VII, when it requested the Secretary-General to conclude the relevant agreement with Sierra Leone to establish a special international criminal tribunal exercising jurisdiction over crimes under international

---

[98] For a reference to the 'London-model' underlying the Nuremberg International Military Tribunal, see the statement referred to in note 65; on regional alternatives, see Corten and Koutroulis, note 64, pp. 18–19.

[99] The preference for an involvement of the UN General Assembly in the establishment of the special tribunal was voiced by the group of States referred to above in note 75; the model is set out in greater detail in "Yale Club Round Table: A Special Tribunal for the Crime of Aggression Recommended by the UN General Assembly?" (22.6.2022), Annex to the letter dated 12 August 2022 from the representatives of Latvia, Liechtenstein, and Ukraine, to the United Nations addressed to the Secretary-General; UN Doc A/ES-11/7-S/2022/616, 17.7.2022; Ukraine Task Force of the Global Accountability Network, *Proposal for a Resolution by the United Nations General Assembly and Accompanying Proposal for a Statute of a Special Tribunal for the Crime of Aggression* (7.9.2022).

[100] For two succinct analyses, see Hans Corell, "A Special Tribunal for Ukraine – The Role for the U.N. General Assembly", *Just Security* (14.2.2023); https://www.justsecurity.org/85116/a-special-tribunal-for-ukraine-on-the-crime-of-aggression-the-role-of-the-u-n-general-assembly/; Oona Hathaway, Maggie Mills, and Heather Zimmerman, "The Legal Authority to Create a Special Tribunal for the Crime of Aggression Upon the Request of the UN General Assembly, *Just Security* (5.5.2023); https://www.justsecurity.org/86450/the-legal-authority-to-create-a-special-tribunal-to-try-the-crime-of-aggression-upon-the-request-of-the-un-general-assembly/; for a detailed analysis, see Carsten Stahn, "From 'United for Peace' to 'United for Justice': Reflections of the Power of the United Nations General Assembly to Create Criminal Tribunals or to Make Referrals to the ICC", 55 *Case Western Reserve Journal of International Law* (2023), pp. 251–286.

[101] UN Doc A/RES/377 (V)), 3.11.1950; in that respect, see, in particular, Corell, note 99.

[102] ICJ, *Certain Expenses of the United Nations (Article 17, Paragraph 2, of the United Nations Charter)*, Advisory Opinion of 20 July 1962, I.C.J. Reports 1962, pp. 151, 163.

law.[103] It is difficult to avoid the impression that one is once again confronted with the old strategy of conceiling a lack of political will behind a veil of legal doubt. By way of historical comparison, it is interesting to recall that in 1946 the intended precedent on crimes against peace did involve a strong element of novelty. But then, Sir Hartley Shawcross, the British Chief Prosecutor, confidently exclaimed: 'If this be an innovation, it is an innovation which we are prepared to defend and justify.'[104]

The second argument against an international tribunal refers to an alleged skepticism among those States that are often, but somewhat simplistically, grouped together under the umbrella term 'Global South'. Because of this skepticism, so the argument goes, the necessary majority in the UN General Assembly is unlikely to emerge. At first sight, this argument sounds benign because it indicates a concern for the position of States belonging to the 'Global South'. But suspicion sets in when this argument is advanced by major powers from the 'Global North', and this before a serious and sincere engagement with the 'Global South' on the issue in question has taken place. This author is not in a position to speak on behalf of anybody in the 'Global South'. But he may perhaps be allowed to make the following five observations: First, many States from the 'Global South' were driving forces for the inclusion of the crime of aggression in the ICC Statute in Rome.[105] Subsequently, a majority of those States supported the activation of the ICC's jurisdiction over the crime of aggression on the basis of a stronger and more principled jurisdictional regime in Kampala. This suggests that at least most of the States in question are, as a matter of principle, favorably disposed to the international adjudication of the crime of aggression. For example, after the Kampala Review Conference two leading Brazilian negotiators stated as follows:

> The Brazilian delegation strongly advocated for the need to define the crime of aggression. This position reflects Brazil's long-standing commitment to international law and, specifically, to the primacy of multilateral rules on the use of force. The adoption of the definition of the crime of aggression strengthens the Court, fulfils an obligation undertaken by the world community in Rome in 1998 and helps ensure a more just, safe and equitable international order.[106]

Against this background, it is far from obvious why the establishment of a special international tribunal should be in the interest of the 'Global North' only. Second, it is not at all far-fetched to see Ukraine's resistance against Russia's aggression and its embrace of international law in support of its cause through a(n Eastern European) post-colonial lens, not altogether different from the one often adopted within the

---

[103] UN Doc S/RES/1315 (2000), 14.8.2000, in particular op. para.

[104] Sir Hartley Shawcross, *Nuremberg Trial Proceedings*, vol. 3, Twelfth Day, Tuesday, 4 December 1945, Morning Session http://avalon.law.yale.edu/imt/12-04-45.asp.

[105] Namira Negm, 'Egypt', in Kreß and Barriga, note 2, pp. 1300–1301.

[106] Marcel Biato and Marcelo Böhlke, 'Brazil', in Kreß and Barriga, note 2, pp. 1117, 1129–1130.

'Global South'.[107] Third, on 23 February 2023, 141 UN Member States recognized the need to ensure accountability for the most serious crimes under international law committed on the territory of Ukraine.[108] Fourth, among the thirteen States that issued a joint statement in support of an international criminal tribunal there are three States from the 'Global South'.[109] Fifth, eminent personalities from the 'Global South', such as the former ICC President Eboe Osuji[110] and the former ICTY Chief prosecutor Richard Goldstone,[111] have voiced their support for the establishment of an international tribunal. It is also noteworthy in that context that the former UN Secretary-General Ban-Ki Moon has voiced a strong preference for establishing an international tribunal at the request of the UN General Assembly.[112] Taken together, all this is to suggest that negative speculations regarding the position of the 'Global South', when put forward by the G7, might well have been calculated to preempt a serious and sincere engagement with the States concerned on the question of the establishment of a special international criminal tribunal.

The most plausible explanation for this avoidance strategy might be that an earnest engagement with the 'Global South' about the establishment of a special tribunal would have had to include a credible answer to the question, formulated above, as to how those who now plead for the establishment of such a tribunal for the war of aggression against Ukraine intend to deal with similar aggressions in the future. Those thirteen States that have issued the joint statement in support of the establishment of a special international criminal tribunal have given the right answer: They have reaffirmed 'their commitment to harmonize the jurisdiction of the Rome Statute over its four crimes in order to allow the International Criminal Court to prosecute the crime of aggression in similar future situations'.[113] However, the same commitment by the G7 is conspicuously missing. This suggests that the support of some G7 States for the establishment of a special tribunal remains overshadowed by a cloud of illegitimacy.

---

[107] For an elaborate exposition of this point, see Labuda, note 64; for such a regional perspective, see also Patrycja Grzebyk, "Crime of Aggression Against Ukraine: The Role of Regional Customary Law", 21 *Journal of International Criminal Justice* (2023), pp. 435–459.

[108] UN Doc A/RES/ES-11/6, 2.3.2023, op. para. 9.

[109] For the list of States, see note 75.

[110] Chile Eboe-Osuji, Letter to Editor: On So-Called Selectivity and a Tribunal for Aggression Against Ukraine', *Just Security* (10.2.2023); https://www.justsecurity.org/85060/letter-to-editor-on-so-called-selectivity-and-a-tribunal-for-aggression-in-ukraine/.

[111] Note 65.

[112] Ban Ki-moon, 'The Path to international tribunal on aggression against Ukraine must run through UNGA', *The Djakarta Post* (20.4.2023); https://www.thejakartapost.com/opin ion/2023/04/20/the-path-to-international-tribunal-on-aggression-in-ukraine-must-run-through-unga.html.

[113] Note 75.

6 A Look Ahead

It is currently impossible to predict the outcome of the inter-governmental conversation over the establishment of a Special Tribunal for the Crime of Aggression against Ukraine. At the time of writing, a bilateral agreement between Ukraine and the Council of Europe constitutes a possible legal basis under serious consideration.[114] Whether or not a special tribunal will eventually become a reality, States Parties to the ICC are urgently called upon to close the gap in the international legal architecture against aggression within the ICC Statute.

In that regard, it is encouraging to note that a Group of Friends, favorably disposed to working toward such a principled solution, was formed last year, and that a first elaborate text proposal has been submitted for consideration by the Group of Friends by a group of independent experts.[115] It is imperative that European States which, at the time of writing, form the large majority of this group reach out to States from the other world regions to reinvigorate their interest in the subject-matter. This will require a dedicated diplomatic effort, given the disappointment caused to many of those States in the course of the negotiations before and in Kampala and later in New York that have resulted in the legal regime currently governing the ICC's exercise of jurisdiction over the crime of aggression. This disappointment is apparent from the statement that one of South Africa's leading delegates made after Kampala:

> The major weakness is, of course, the fact that (…) Non-State Parties (…) will be able to commit aggression with a sense of impunity, and this reflection of realpolitik may result in a very slow process of ratification and acceptance.[116]

Yet, the issue at stake is of such a significance for the future world order that it is worth every effort: This is a moment in time, when the prohibition of aggression is at risk of erosion and when tensions between different world regions are being strongly felt. At such a juncture, it would be particularly welcome to send out the message that in today's multipolar world dedicated co-operation across the 'Global North' and the 'Global South' is not only possible, but also capable of reconsolidating the international legal order at its core. A cross-regional diplomatic effort, yielding the harmonization of the conditions, under which the ICC may exercise its jurisdiction over all four crimes under international, would send out precisely this message.

---

[114] Council of Europe, CM/Del/Dec(2024)1497/10.2, 30.4.2004; https://search.coe.int/cm/pages/result_details.aspx?objectid=0900001680af831c.

[115] For an introduction of this proposal, which was worked out under the auspices of the Global Institute for the Crime of Aggression (https://crimeofaggression.info), see Jennifer Trahan, "Amending the Kampala Amendments: A Proposal to Harmonize the ICC's Jurisdiction", *Opinio Iuris* (2.10.2023); https://opiniojuris.org/2023/10/02/amending-the-kampala-amendments-a-proposal-to-harmonize-the-iccs-jurisdiction/; for an overview over the options, see Astrid Reisinger Coracini, "One Regime to Rule Them All. Harmonizing the Exercise of Jurisdiction over Crimes Within the Jurisdiction of the International Criminal Law", in C. Stahn (ed.), *The International Criminal Court in its Third Decade: Reflecting on Law and Practices* (2023), pp. 527–561.

[116] André Stemmet, 'South Africa', in Kreß and Barriga, note 2, pp. 1271, 1282.

Ultimately, an important responsibility will also lie with France, Great Britain, and the United States: After the Second World War, they, together with the Soviet Union, set the foundational precedent for the crime of aggression at Nuremberg. Lately, however, they have insisted most strongly, from inside the Rome Statute system and from the outside, on the imposition of legal restraints that debilitate the Court's exercise of jurisdiction over the crime of aggression and that cannot be characterized as anything other than as the embodiment of a double-standard in the existing international legal architecture. May it be recalled that the U.S. Ambassador van Schaack has observed that Russia's war of aggression against Ukraine has brought the world to a 'critical moment in history'.[117] The Ambassador is right, but it would be worth recognizing that such a moment calls for true leadership not only on the military front, but also in the field of international criminal justice.[118] The three major powers in question would rise to the critical moment in history that the world is facing, if they were to overcome their long-standing sovereigntist resistance to a principled jurisdictional regime for the crime of aggression in the ICC Statute.

---

[117] Ambassador Beth van Schaack, note 58.

[118] Kreß, note 18.

War in Ukraine and the International Court of Justice: Provisional Measures and the Third-Party Right to Intervene in Proceedings

Dai Tamada

Abstract At the time of writing, the war in Ukraine was the subject of ICJ proceedings in the *Allegations of Genocide* case. As the case title suggests, however, the key issue before the ICJ is not Russia's use of force, but the question of genocide. Restrictions on its jurisdiction have led to the ICJ facing a serious dilemma between, on the one hand, having to meet unprecedented high levels of expectation and political pressure to stop Russia's military action and, on the other, inherent legal constraints in maintaining its judicial character. This article elucidates how the ICJ has overcome procedural hurdles, including the requirements for provisional measures and intervention, to reach conclusions in favour of Ukraine. It also highlights the procedural challenges arising from the acrobatic reasoning adopted by the ICJ in the present case.

1 Introduction

Russia initiated its full-scale military action against Ukraine on 24 February 2022 and shortly after that, on 26 February 2022, Ukraine filed an Application[1] to the ICJ claiming *inter alia* the non-existence of genocide in Ukraine and the lack of legal basis for Russia's military action under the Genocide Convention,[2] giving rise to the *Allegations of Genocide* case.[3] Ukraine also filed a Request for provisional measures for the immediate suspension of military action.[4] As at 3 December 2023, the case had gone through the provisional measures phase (Order on 16 March 2022;

---

[1] Application Instituting Proceedings filed in the Registry of the Court on 26 February 2022 (hereinafter 'Application').

[2] Convention on the Prevention and Punishment of the Crime of Genocide 1948, 78 U.N.T.S. 277.

[3] *Allegations of Genocide under the Convention on the Prevention and Punishment of the Crime of Genocide (Ukraine v. Russian Federation: 32 States intervening)*.

[4] Request for the Indication of Provisional Measures Submitted by Ukraine (hereinafter 'Request').

D. Tamada (✉)
Graduate School of Law, Kyoto University, Kyoto, Japan
e-mail: tamada@law.kyoto-u.ac.jp

© The Author(s), under exclusive license to Springer Nature Singapore Pte Ltd. 2024
M. Asada, D. Tamada (eds.), *The War in Ukraine and International Law*,
https://doi.org/10.1007/978-981-97-2504-5_4

hereinafter 'Order 2022') and the intervention phase (Order on 5 June 2023; hereinafter 'Order 2023').

This case is characterised by its jurisdictional aspects: namely, the limited scope for the Court to establish its jurisdiction under Article IX of the Genocide Convention. This means that Ukraine cannot directly claim a breach of the prohibition of the use of force under Article 2 (4) of the UN Charter and other relevant rules of international law. To overcome this hurdle, Ukraine argues that, since genocide has never occurred in Donbas, "Russia has no lawful basis to take action in and against Ukraine for the purpose of preventing and punishing any purported genocide" (Application 4 [3]). In this case, one of the most crucial, yet thorny, questions is how Russia's use of force may be regulated by the Genocide Convention, which, at first glance, contains no prohibition of the use of force.

It is necessary to refer to the terminology in this article. First, to avoid prejudging the substantive law evaluation, this article uses the term 'military action' to describe the war in Ukraine, notwithstanding other terms employed by other parties, such as 'special military operation' (Russia), 'full-scale invasion against Ukraine' (Ukraine),[5] 'aggression' (the UN General Assembly),[6] 'invasion' (EU),[7] and 'the unlawful, unjustified, and unprovoked invasion' (OAS).[8] Second, the term 'allegation(s)' is of tremendous importance in the context of the case before the ICJ.[9] However, this article uses the term 'allegation' as a neutral term, equivalent to the unilateral expression of opinions, irrespective of whether they are sufficiently substantiated. Ukraine has used terms such as 'false and offensive allegations',[10] 'falsity of allegations of genocide', 'false allegations of genocide', 'falsely claimed [. . .] genocide', 'false and pretextual allegations of genocide', and 'unsupported allegations of "horror and genocide"' (Application 2, 4 [2], 10 [16], 10 [17]). It

---

[5] Application 10 [16].

[6] A/RES/ES-11/1, para. 2.

[7] 'EU response to Russia's invasion of Ukraine', available at https://www.consilium.europa.eu/en/policies/eu-response-ukraine-invasion/. The EU also uses the term 'brutal war of aggression' here.

[8] OAS, Declaration 'The Situation in Ukraine': the Declarating States (i.e., OAS members) strongly condemn the "unlawful, unjustified, and unprovoked invasion of Ukraine by the Russian Federation and call for the immediate withdrawal of the military presence and the cessation of any further military actions in that country." 'OAS Member States Condemn Russian Attack on Ukraine' (25 February 2022), available at https://usoas.usmission.gov/oas-member-states-condemn-russian-attack-on-ukraine/.

[9] Ukraine stated that it "considers it important that the official name of the present case include a reference to 'allegations'." Application 2.

[10] E.g., 'Statement of the Ministry of Foreign Affairs of Ukraine on Russia's False and Offensive Allegations of Genocide As a Pretext For Its Unlawful Military Aggression' (26 February 2022), available at https://mfa.gov.ua/en/news/zayava-mzs-ukrayini-shchodo-nepravdivih-ta-obrazlivih-zvinuvachen-rosiyi-v-genocidi-yak-privodu-dlya-yiyi-protipravnoyi-vijskovoyi-agresiyi.

War in Ukraine and the International Court of Justice:... 81

follows that the term 'allegation', without any adjective, should be used as a neutral term.[11]

2 Order of Provisional Measures (16 March 2022)

2.1 Summary of the Order

In its Request, Ukraine asked the ICJ to indicate provisional measures to the effect *inter alia* that "[t]he Russian Federation shall immediately suspend the military operations [...]" (Request [5]; Order 2022 [14]). The ICJ found that all the requirements for indicating provisional measures were satisfied, as follows. First, as to the *prima facie* jurisdiction, the ICJ affirmed the fact that Russia argued that it took its military action to 'stop a genocide' (Order 2022 [37]-[41]), while Ukraine denied Russia's argument (ibid. [42]). Based on this fact, the ICJ concluded that the existence of a dispute was *prima facie* established (ibid. [47]). Second, as to the plausibility requirement, the ICJ concluded that Ukraine had a "plausible right not to be subjected to military operations by the Russian Federation for the purpose of preventing and punishing an alleged genocide in the territory of Ukraine" (ibid. [60]). Third, with regard to the link between the rights whose protection is sought and the provisional measures being requested, the ICJ found that the first two provisional measures sought by Ukraine are aimed at preserving the plausible right of Ukraine, thus satisfying the link requirement. As to the third and fourth provisional measures, the ICJ found that, by their nature, no link is required (ibid. [63]). Fourth, with respect to the requirement of risk of irreparable prejudice, the ICJ took into account matters including large-scale loss of life, mental and bodily harm, and damage to property and to the environment (ibid. [74]), to conclude that "disregard of the right deemed plausible by the Court [...] could cause irreparable prejudice to this right and that there is urgency" (ibid. [77]). Lastly, exercising its power under Article 75 (2) of the Rules of Court to indicate measures that are, in whole or in part, other than those requested, the ICJ found that the measures need not be identical to those requested by Ukraine (ibid. [79]-[80]). In addition, the ICJ indicated a measure directed to both Parties and aimed at ensuring the non-aggravation of the dispute (ibid. [82]) while declining to indicate a measure directing Russia to submit a report to the ICJ (ibid. [83]).

In the operative paragraphs, the ICJ indicated the following provisional measures: (1) "Russia shall immediately suspend the military operations that it commenced on 24 February 2022 in the territory of Ukraine" (13-2; against: Vice-President Gevorgian; Judge Xue); (2) "Russia shall ensure that any military or irregular

---

[11] If 'allegation' is understood as an unsubstantiated opinion, it presupposes the lack of evidence. As the ICJ stated that it found no "evidence substantiating the allegation of the Russian Federation" (Order 2022 [59]), the term 'allegation' should be thought neutral.

82 D. Tamada

armed units which may be directed or supported by it, as well as any organizations and persons which may be subject to its control or direction, take no steps in furtherance of the military operations referred to in point (1) above" (13-2; against: Vice-President Gevorgian; Judge Xue); (3) "Both Parties shall refrain from any action which might aggravate or extend the dispute before the Court or make it more difficult to resolve" (15-0) (Order 2022 [86]).

2.2 Non-Appearance of Russia

First of all, the question arises as to whether Russia's non-appearance in the oral proceedings had any impact on the ICJ's finding. On the one hand, Russia's position was carefully examined by the ICJ. Shortly after the oral proceedings (held on 7 March 2022), Russia filed a document substantially containing an objection to the Court's jurisdiction (Order 2022 [15]-[16]).[12] The ICJ positively evaluated this submission and decided to "take account of the document [...] to the extent that it finds this appropriate in discharging its duties" (ibid. [22]). In this sense, there was no unfair treatment of Russia's position. On the other hand, as was pointed out by the ICJ, the non-appearance of a party has a "negative impact on the sound administration of justice, as it deprives the Court of assistance that a party could have provided to it" (ibid. [21]). In the present case, Russia's non-appearance actually brought about a 'negative impact', to the effect that, since Russia did not submit any *evidence* of genocide, the ICJ concluded that it "[was] not in possession of *evidence* substantiating the allegation [of genocide]" (emphasis added. ibid. [59]). However, it is doubtful whether Russia could provide any 'evidence' of genocide in Donbas, even if it had appeared before the Court. Though Russia has long asserted the occurrence of genocide, with the suggestion of genocidal intent,[13] it has never substantiated it, nor made public any 'evidence'.[14] Therefore, it is reasonable to conclude that it is unlikely that Russia's appearance at the oral proceedings stage would have resulted in a different conclusion on the part of the ICJ.

---

[12] 'Document (with annexes) from the Russian Federation setting out its position regarding the alleged "lack of jurisdiction" of the Court in the case (7 March 2022)' (hereinafter 'Document') comprises: i) Russia's objection to the Court's jurisdiction; ii) a letter by Russia submitted to the UN Secretary-General; and iii) an Address by the President of Russia (24 February 2022) (hereinafter the '2022 Putin Address'). As is evident from the title, the first part of the Document is substantially an objection to the jurisdiction of the Court.

[13] According to Judge Robinson, the Investigative Committee of Russia found in 2014 that: the "top political and military leadership of Ukraine, the Armed Forces of Ukraine, the National Guard of Ukraine and the 'Right Sector' gave *orders to completely destroy* specifically Russian-speaking population living on the territory of the Donetsk and Luhansk republics." (emphasis added) Sep Op Robinson 2022 [8].

[14] On many occasions, including the Document of 7 March 2022, Russia had the opportunity to submit 'evidence' of genocide to the ICJ, relating *inter alia* to the criminal proceedings conducted in Russia (Order 2022 [37]).

2.3 Formulation of a Single Dispute

Ukraine originally asserted three disputes: i) a factual dispute (namely, whether genocide has occurred in the sense of Article II); ii) a legal dispute (namely, whether Russia has any lawful basis to take military action to prevent and punish genocide under Article I); and iii) a further dispute (namely, whether Russia may take military steps unilaterally under Article VIII) (Request 4 [11]). However, Ukraine eventually integrated these into a single dispute,[15] as adopted by the ICJ (Order 2022 [45]):

> The statements [...] of the Parties indicate a divergence of views [i.e., a dispute] as to whether certain acts allegedly committed by Ukraine in the Luhansk and Donetsk regions amount to genocide in violation of its obligations under the Genocide Convention, as well as whether the use of force by the Russian Federation for the stated purpose of preventing and punishing alleged genocide is a measure that can be taken in fulfilment of the obligation to prevent and punish genocide contained in Article I of the Convention [...] (ibid. [45]).

Here, the ICJ admitted, albeit *prima facie*, the existence of *a* dispute (i.e., 'a divergence of views')[16] composed of *two* elements,[17] corresponding to the first two disputes (namely, factual and legal) in Ukraine's original claim. This formulation is quite important. First, as was suggested by Russia's Document, there was doubt as to the existence of the second dispute (Document [20]). The ICJ's formulation could set aside such doubt by finding *a* dispute to exist. Second, if isolated, the second element (i.e., the legal dispute) would have made it more difficult for Ukraine's claim to satisfy some of the requirements for provisional measures.

2.4 Plausible Right of Ukraine

One of the most difficult hurdles for Ukraine was the plausibility requirement (that is to say, that a right claimed must exist at least plausibly) because the Genocide Convention does not explicitly refer to any 'right' of Ukraine. For its part, the ICJ eventually admitted the "plausible right [of Ukraine] not to be subjected to military operations by the Russian Federation for the purpose of preventing and punishing an alleged genocide in the territory of Ukraine" (Order 2022 [60]). This finding requires some examination. First, although it was not made clear from which provision of the

---

[15] Ukraine argued that "the parties' dispute over first, the existence of acts of genocide, and second, Russia's claim to legal authority to take military action in and against Ukraine to punish and prevent such alleged genocide, is *a dispute* that concerns the interpretation, application or fulfilment of the Genocide Convention." (emphasis added) (Request 4 [11]).

[16] It seems that the term 'a divergence of views' (Order 2022 [45]), rather than 'dispute', was used by the ICJ to avoid suggesting the definitive existence of a 'dispute' at this phase of the procedure.

[17] Judge Robinson pointed out that "a dispute, properly characterized, may have more than one element, and indeed, a case may have more than one dispute". Sep Op Robinson 2022 [5].

Table 1 Structure of the ICJ's interpretation (Order 2022 [56]-[60])

	Article	Content	Consideration
Main article	I	Obligation to prevent genocide	To be implemented in *good faith*, taking into account *other parts* [56].
Other parts	VIII	Call upon the competent organs	Other means (e.g., bilateral engagement or exchanges within a regional organisation) may be taken, within the 'limits permitted by international law' [57]
	IX	Submission of dispute to the ICJ	
	Preamble	Reference to the 'spirit and aims' of the UN[a]	Article 1 of the UN Charter: 'to maintain international peace and security' [58]; no authorisation of unilateral use of force [59].

[a] Preamble of the Genocide Convention: "[h]aving considered the declaration [. . .] that genocide is a crime under international law, contrary to *the spirit and aims of the United Nations* [. . .]." (emphasis added)

Convention this 'plausible right' arose,[18] it must be understood that it was from Article I (i.e., the obligation to prevent and punish genocide) (ibid. [56]).[19] Second, in its finding, the ICJ relied on the good faith principle (ibid.). This means that the 'plausible right', admitted by the ICJ, follows Ukraine's argument that it has a "right under Article I to good faith performance of the Convention by any State party" (CR 2022/5, 65 [29] Mr. Koh). Third, in clarifying the good faith implementation of the obligation under Article I, the ICJ took into account: i) Articles VIII and IX of the Convention which suggest that, if a Contracting Party takes means other than those stipulated in two articles, it must be taken 'within the limits permitted by international law' (Order 2022 [57]); and ii) the Preamble of the Convention which refers to the 'spirits and aims of the United Nations', as set out in Article 1 of the UN Charter (ibid. [58]). Fourth, as the highlight of its interpretation, the ICJ, through the Preamble of the Genocide Convention, incorporated the principles of the UN (reflected in Article 1 of the UN Charter) into Article I of the Convention, to conclude that "it is doubtful that the Convention, in light of its object and purpose, authorizes a Contracting Party's unilateral use of force" (ibid. [59]). This finding suggests that, at the merits phase, the ICJ is likely to establish a good faith review standard with regard to the obligation under Article I, to integrate pivotal articles of the UN Charter (e.g., Article 2 (4) and possibly Article 51) into the interpretation of Article I of the Genocide Convention (Table 1).

---

[18] Judge Bennouna observed that: "[t]he Court must also be able to found this alleged plausible right on *one of the provisions* of the Genocide Convention which the Russian Federation is said to *have breached*. The Court clearly failed in this task; it did not identify the *rights* of Ukraine under the Convention [. . .]." (emphasis added) Decl Bennouna 2022 [6].

[19] The ICJ stated that the Contracting Parties must implement "this obligation [to prevent and to punish the crime of genocide under Article I] in good faith". See also, Sep Op Robinson 2022 [25]-[27].

2.5 Criterion of Plausibility

The criterion of 'plausibility' has been alternating between two tests in the Court's jurisprudence. First, plausibility was first required in the *Belgium v. Senegal* case, in which the ICJ applied the *legal* plausibility test, to the effect that a 'possible interpretation' of a provision satisfies the plausibility requirement.[20] Second, in the *Ukraine v. Russia* case, the ICJ applied the *factual* plausibility test, in the sense that the claim of the applicant State must be grounded in evidence.[21] Third, after the *Ukraine v. Russia* case, the ICJ's approach has been mixed.[22] In the present case, the ICJ maintained its mixed approach in line with recent jurisprudence. On the one hand, the ICJ has stated that it "can only take a decision on the Applicant's *claims* if the case proceeds to the merits" (emphasis added. Order 2022 [59]), thus suggesting the exclusion of the *factual* plausibility test. Further, the ICJ has stated that "it is doubtful that the Convention [. . .] authorizes a Contracting Party's unilateral use of force" (Order 2022 [59]). As the Court hints at a 'possible interpretation' of Article I of the Genocide Convention, this suggests the adoption of the *legal* plausibility test. On the other hand, the Court appears to rely also on the *factual* plausibility test. First, insofar as the Court refers to no "*evidence* substantiating the allegation [of genocide]" (emphasis added. Ibid.), it seems to rely on the *factual* plausibility test. Second, when the ICJ casts doubt on the legality of the 'unilateral use of force' under the Genocide Convention (ibid.), this hints at the *legal* plausibility test. However, considering the well-known fact that Russia has *unilaterally* used force against Ukraine (Order 2022 [18]), the ICJ's finding may be understood as adopting the *factual* plausibility test. Overall, the ICJ has adopted the mixed approach to the plausibility requirement by alternating between the *legal* and *factual* plausibility tests. Therefore, it seems undeniable that, insofar as the ICJ strays, albeit partially, into *factual* plausibility territory, it risks prejudging a subsequent merits decision.[23]

---

[20] *Questions relating to the Obligation to Prosecute or Extradite (Belgium v. Senegal)*, Provisional Measures, Order, [2009] ICJ Rep 152 [60]. In the present case, Judge Robinson has adopted the *legal* plausibility test (i.e., 'possible interpretation' test). Sep Op Robinson 2022 [2].

[21] The ICJ has stated that "Ukraine has not put before the Court *evidence* which affords a sufficient basis to find it plausible that these elements [of intention or knowledge] are present" (emphasis added). *Application of the International Convention for the Suppression of the Financing of Terrorism and of the International Convention on the Elimination of All Forms of Racial Discrimination (Ukraine v. Russian Federation)*, Provisional Measures, Order, [2012] ICJ Rep 131–132 [75].

[22] E.g., *Application of the Convention on the Prevention and Punishment of the Crime of Genocide (The Gambia v. Myanmar)*, Provisional Measures, Order, [2020] ICJ Rep 23 [56].

[23] Judge Xue observed that the 2022 Order (paras. 56–59) 'prejudges the merits of the case'. Decl Xue 2022 [6].

2.6 Repercussions for Humanitarian Intervention

Correlative to some plausible *right* on the part of Ukraine (Order 2022 [59]), there must exist some plausible *obligation* on the part of Russia under Article I of the Convention, namely, an obligation to refrain from resorting to the use of force in the territory of another State for the purpose of preventing or punishing an alleged genocide. This would suggest that Article I of the Genocide Convention, at least plausibly, prohibits humanitarian intervention.[24] This understanding inevitably casts doubt on the legality, *inter alia*, of NATO's bombardment against Yugoslavia in 1999, insofar as it was carried out to prevent genocide in Kosovo.[25] To avoid such repercussion, the ICJ referred to two factors that may distinguish Donbas from Kosovo: i) the non-presentation of 'evidence' on the part of Russia; and ii) the 'unilateral' use of force by Russia (Order 2022 [59]). Here, conversely, the ICJ suggests that a *multilateral*, or at least *plurilateral*, use of force in the territory of another State for the purpose of preventing or punishing alleged genocide, sufficiently substantiated by *evidence*, is not necessarily prohibited by the Genocide Convention. At the merits phase, should it arise, the ICJ will have the opportunity to fully explore the legal issues at play. On the other hand, if the Court were to flexibly interpret Article I of the Convention in favour of Ukraine, this could have a boomerang effect on Kosovo, as well as on US policy on humanitarian intervention.[26]

2.7 Measures Other Than Those Requested

Ukraine had requested, *inter alia*, a measure to the effect that Russia "shall immediately suspend the military operations commenced on 24 February 2022 *that have as their stated purpose and objective the prevention and punishment of a claimed genocide in the Luhansk and Donetsk oblasts of Ukraine*" (emphasis added. Order 2022 [5]). The first measure indicated by the ICJ omitted the emphasised part of

---

[24] Judge Xue correctly pointed out that "Ukraine's claim ultimately boils down to the very question whether recourse to use of force is permitted under international law in case of genocide." Decl Xue 2022 [4]. Later, Judge Xue also observed that the purpose of intervention of many States was to obtain the finding of the Court that the "Convention does not authorize or require – or indeed that the Convention *prohibits* – uses of force to prevent and punish genocidal acts" (emphasis added). Diss Op Xue 2023 [24].

[25] Belgium justified its use of force on the basis of 'humanitarian intervention', by observing that NATO's intervention "is an armed humanitarian intervention, compatible with Article 2, paragraph 4, of the Charter." *Legality of Use of Force (Yugoslavia v. Belgium)*, Provisional Measures, CR 99/15 (10 May 1999), p. 12. However, Judge Nolte observed that the 'stated' purpose of NATO's bombardment had not been the prevention of genocide. Decl Nolte 2022 [3], [6].

[26] William Schabas, "Preventing Genocide and the Ukraine/Russia case", *EJIL Talk!* (March 10, 2022), https://www.ejiltalk.org/preventing-genocide-and-the-ukraine-russia-case/.

War in Ukraine and the International Court of Justice:... 87

Ukraine's request (ibid. [86 (1)]), thus covering all aspects of the 'military operations' of Russia, regardless of their purpose and objective. Even though this decision is justified as an exercise of the ICJ's power to indicate a measure different to that requested (Order 2022 [79]),[27] it merits careful review. First, it seems that the ICJ attempted to deny Russia's claim that it had pursued military operations, not to prevent and punish genocide, but to exercise the right of self-defence.[28] Second, the ICJ appears to have considered the factual consequences caused by the full-scale and ongoing military action by Russia (Order 2022 [74]-[76]).[29] In this context, notably, the ICJ referred to the 'irreparable consequences' generated by the disregard of rights,[30] in addition to the "irreparable prejudice [...] to rights" (Order 2022 [65]). This suggests that, when it examined 'risk', the ICJ broadly considered the factual consequences of the disregard of the right, namely the actual 'harm' and 'material damage' at the factual level (ibid. [74]-[75]).[31]

Although the foregoing may be the reason behind operative paragraph (1), questions remain unanswered. First, a measure to order Russia to suspend all use of force goes beyond the context of preventing and punishing genocide and, consequently, lacks a *link* with the plausible right of Ukraine not to be subjected to military operations on the part of Russia "for the purpose of preventing and punishing an alleged genocide" (Order 2022 [60]).[32] Second, the ICJ itself had denied such a far-reaching measure pertaining to the use of force. In the *Bosnian Genocide* case, with regard to the request for provisional measures to cease the military activities of the Respondent,[33] the ICJ stated that:

> the Court [...] ought not to indicate measures for the protection of any disputed rights other than those which might ultimately form the basis of a judgment in the exercise of [the] jurisdiction; whereas accordingly the Court will confine its examination of the measures

---

[27] Article 75 (2) of the Rules of Court: "Court may indicate measures that are in whole or in part other than those requested [...]".

[28] The ICJ was aware that the dispute in the present case "falls within the ambit of more than one treaty", including the UN Charter (Order 2022 [46]).

[29] The ICJ mentioned the 'widespread damage' in Ukraine as a 'well-known' fact and stated that it was "accurately aware of the extent of the human tragedy" (Order 2022 [17]).

[30] In recent cases, the ICJ has referred to 'irreparable consequences' as being an element of the risk requirement. *Alleged Violations of the 1955 Treaty of Amity, Economic Relations, and Consular Rights (Islamic Republic of Iran v. United States of America)*, Provisional Measures, Order, [2018] ICJ Rep 645 [77]; *Application of the Convention on the Prevention and Punishment of the Crime of Genocide (The Gambia v. Myanmar)*, Provisional Measures, Order, [2020] ICJ Rep 24 [64].

[31] Judge Robinson suggests that the expansion of the scope of the measure is based on the ICJ's consideration of the 'patent irreparable harm' caused by the military action of Russia. Sep Op Robinson 2022 [31].

[32] Andreas Kulick, "Provisional Measures after *Ukraine v Russia* (2022)", *Journal of International Dispute Settlement*, vol. 13 (2022), pp. 328, 334. Judge Xue pointed out the lack of a link in this case. Decl Xue 2022 [1]-[2].

[33] *Application of the Convention on the Prevention and Punishment of the Crime of Genocide (Bosnia and Herzegovina v. Yugoslavia (Serbia and Montenegro))*, Provisional Measures, Order, [1993] ICJ Rep 8 [3].

requested, and of the grounds asserted for the request for such measures, to those which fall within the scope of the Genocide Convention.[34]

If compared to this restrained approach, the ICJ's measure in the present case is an undesirable precedent of excessively expanding the scope of the measure that is likely to disturb the establishment of consistent jurisprudence.

2.8 Measure Addressed to Both Parties

In operative paragraph (3), the ICJ indicated the measure: "*[b]oth Parties* shall refrain from any action which might aggravate or extend the dispute [. . .]" (emphasis added). Although this finding has provoked criticism,[35] there can be justifications. First, as the scope of the 'dispute' was already expanded in operative paragraph (1), it is reasonable that the ICJ orders *both parties to that dispute* to refrain from aggravating or extending it. Second, as the armed conflict became full-scale between the two States, it was not effective, in securing the implementation of the first two measures, to order only Russia to stop the aggravation and extension of the dispute.[36] It can be concluded that the ICJ had to balance: i) the expansion of the scope of the dispute in the first two measures, reflecting the widespread armed conflict between the two States; against ii) the third measure to restrain aggravating acts on the part of both States in that conflict. In this sense, the ICJ took a realistic approach, taking into consideration the urgent need for stopping the ongoing full-scale military action by Russia.

2.9 No Measure of Reporting

The ICJ rejected Ukraine's request for a measure of reporting (Order 2022 [83]), without any further explanation.[37] Before this case, on 21 December 2020, the ICJ had revised its Resolution to establish a new procedure for the measure of reporting, aimed at monitoring the implementation of measures indicated.[38]

---

[34] [1993] ICJ Rep 19 [35].

[35] Judge Robinson observed that the measure "should have been directed solely to the Russian Federation." Sep Op Robinson 2022 [33].

[36] Judge Xue posed the question as to how, in the context of an armed conflict, the first two measures can be "meaningfully and effectively implemented by only one Party to the conflict." Decl Xue 2022 [6].

[37] Judge Robinson observed that "it would have been advantageous for the Court to examine periodic reports by Russia on its implementation of the provisional measures and to make appropriate orders." Sep Op Robinson 2022 [33].

[38] Article 11 (i) of the Resolution concerning the Internal Judicial Practice of the Court (adopted by the Court on 21 December 2020): "Where the Court indicates provisional measures, it *shall* elect

War in Ukraine and the International Court of Justice:...

Table 2 Recent cases relating to the measure of reporting

Date	Cases	Decisions and reasonings
23/1/ 2020	*The Gambia v. Myanmar*	A measure of reporting: the ICJ "has the power, reflected in Article 78 of the Rules of Court,[a] to request the parties to provide information on any matter connected with the implementation of any provisional measures it has indicated. In view of the *specific provisional measures* it has decided to indicate, the Court considers that Myanmar must submit a report to the Court on all measures taken to give effect to this Order [...] (emphasis added)."[b]
7/12/ 2021	*Armenia v. Azerbaijan*	The request was rejected for unspecified reasons.[c]
7/12/ 2021	*Azerbaijan v. Armenia*	The request was rejected for unspecified reasons.[d]
16/3/ 2022	*Ukraine v. Russia*	The request was rejected for unspecified reasons (Order 2022 [83]).
22/2/ 2023	*Armenia v. Azerbaijan*	No request. No measure of reporting.
22/2/ 2023	*Azerbaijan v. Armenia*	No request. No measure of reporting.
16/11/ 2023	*Canada and the Netherlands v. Syria*	The request was implicitly rejected for unspecified reasons.[e]
17/11/ 2023	*Armenia v. Azerbaijan*	A measure of reporting: "In view of the specific provisional measures it has decided to indicate, and in light of the undertakings made by the Agent of Azerbaijan at the public hearing [...], the Court considers that Azerbaijan must submit a report to the Court on the steps taken to give effect to the provisional measures indicated and to the undertakings made by the Agent of Azerbaijan."[f]

[a] Article 78: "The Court may request information from the parties on any matter connected with the implementation of any provisional measures it has indicated"
[b] *Application of the Convention on the Prevention and Punishment of the Crime of Genocide (The Gambia v. Myanmar)*, Provisional Measures, Order, [2020] ICJ Rep 29 [82]
[c] *Application of the International Convention on the Elimination of All Forms of Racial Discrimination (Armenia v. Azerbaijan)*, Provisional Measures, Order, [2021] ICJ Rep 392 [95]
[d] *Application of the International Convention on the Elimination of All Forms of Racial Discrimination (Azerbaijan v. Armenia)*, Provisional Measures, Order, [2021] ICJ Rep 430 [73]
[e] *Application of the Convention against Torture and Other Cruel, Inhuman or Degrading Treatment or Punishment (Canada and the Netherlands v. Syrian Arab Republic)*, Provisional Measures, Order, [2023] ICJ Rep [83]
[f] *Application of the International Convention on the Elimination of All Forms of Racial Discrimination (Armenia v. Azerbaijan)*, Provisional Measures, Order, [2023] ICJ Rep [71]

The precedents listed in Table 2 show that a requirement for the measure of reporting has yet to be established. When it comes to ordering reporting measures, court practice seems to indicates a qualitative difference between, on the one hand,

---

three judges to form an ad hoc committee which will assist the Court in monitoring the implementation of provisional measures" (emphasis added).

measures that impose due diligence, obligations of prevention or obligations arising from respondent state commitments and, on the other, measures ordering the cessation of a particular act. The *Allegations of Genocide* case may be classified as falling within the latter category.

3 Order of Intervention (5 June 2023)

After the submission of Ukraine's Memorial (1 July 2022), 33 States successively filed declarations of intervention to the ICJ under Article 63(2) of the ICJ Statute. As Canada and the Netherlands jointly submitted a declaration, there were 32 declarations in total. Russia filed objections to the admissibility of those declarations (Order 2023 [22]). In its Order of 5 June 2023, the ICJ finally allowed 32 States, except the US, to intervene in the preliminary objections phase.

3.1 Summary of the Order

The Order can be summarised as follows. First, the ICJ found that all declarations satisfied formal requirements[39] (Order 2023 [40]). Second, the ICJ rejected all Russian objections: a) as to the objection based on the alleged intention behind the declarations, the ICJ stated that the motivation of intervention is not relevant to the admissibility of a declaration (ibid. [44]); b) as to the objection based on an alleged infringement of the equality of the Parties and the good administration of justice, the ICJ stated that the intervention under Article 63 means the submission of observations by non-Parties and, thus, does not infringe the principles of equality of the parties or the good administration of justice (ibid. [53]); c) as to the objection based on an alleged abuse of process, the ICJ stated that there are 'no exceptional circumstances' for rendering the declarations inadmissible (ibid. [59]); d) as to the objection based on the alleged inadmissibility of the declarations at the preliminary objections stage, the ICJ stated that Article 63 of the Statute and Article 82 of the Rules do not restrict the right of intervention to a particular phase of the proceedings, or to a certain type of provision in a convention (ibid. [63]); e) as to the objection based on the argument that the declarations presuppose the Court's jurisdiction and the admissibility of Ukraine's Application, the ICJ stated that it will only take into account the elements relevant to determining jurisdiction (ibid. [74]); f) as to the objection based on the argument that intervention cannot concern the construction of

---

[39] Article 82(2) of Rules of the Court: 'The declaration shall [. . .] contain: (a) particulars of the basis on which the declarant State considers itself a party to the convention; (b) identification of the particular provisions of the convention the construction of which it considers to be in question; (c) a statement of the construction of those provisions for which it contends; (d) a list of the documents in support, which documents shall be attached'.

compromissory clauses such as Article IX of the Genocide Convention, the ICJ stated that compromissory clauses may be the subject-matter of an intervention under Article 63 of the Statute (ibid. [79]); and g) as to the objection alleging that the declarations go beyond the construction of the Genocide Convention, the ICJ stated that it will not consider matters other than the construction of provisions, and that references to other rules and principles of international law outside the Convention will only be considered under Article 31(3)(c) of the Vienna Convention on the Law of Treaties (ibid. [84]). Third, with regard to the joint declaration of Canada and the Netherlands, the ICJ stated that relevant provisions do not prohibit this (ibid. [88]). Fourth, Russia contended that, as a result of the US reservation to Article IX of the Convention,[40] the US declaration was inadmissible. The ICJ stated that the US, even if a party to the Convention, has no legal interest in the construction of Article IX and, therefore, its declaration is inadmissible (ibid. [95]).

In the operative paragraphs, the ICJ: (1) decided that the declarations of intervention under Article 63 of the Statute submitted by 32 States are admissible at the preliminary objections stage of the proceedings in so far as they concern the construction of Article IX and other provisions of the Genocide Convention that are relevant for the determination of the jurisdiction of the Court (14-1; against: Judge Xue); (2) decided that the declaration of intervention under Article 63 of the Statute submitted by the US is inadmissible in so far as it concerns the preliminary objections stage of the proceedings (15-0); and (3) fixed 5 July 2023 as the time-limit for the filing [. . .] of the written observations referred to in Article 86, paragraph 1, of the Rules of Court (14-1; against: Judge Xue).

3.2 Mass and Individual Intervention

First and foremost, this case is characterised by "active collaboration in litigation strategy",[41] that has the purpose of pursuing common political interests in ICJ litigation (Decl Gevorgian 2023 [2]). Before submitting intervention declarations, more than 40 States had expressed their intention to support Ukraine in ICJ

---

[40]The US reservation to Article IX: "That with reference to Article IX of the Convention, before any dispute to which the United States is a party may be submitted to the jurisdiction of the International Court of Justice under this article, the specific consent of the United States is required in each case" (Order 2023 [94]).

[41] *Whaling in the Antarctic (Australia v. Japan)*, Declaration of Intervention of New Zealand, Order (6 February 2013), Decl Judge Owada, [2013] ICJ Rep 12 [5]. In the present case, Russia refers to this as a "collective strategy of supporting the Applicant against the Respondent" (Order 2023 [54]).

proceedings in two joint statements (22 May 2022[42] and 13 July 2022[43]). Thereafter, 33 States separately submitted declarations of intervention.[44] This litigation strategy has two aspects: *mass* and *individual*. First, a *mass* submission of declarations has the following effects: i) to create a visible impression that many States are actually supporting Ukraine in international litigation, and ii) to exert political pressure on the judiciary to be on the side of Ukraine.[45] Second, the *individual* submission of declarations by individual States has the following effects: i) provide individual States with an opportunity to make public their own detailed legal positions against Russia; ii) force Russia to listen repeatedly to views against its military action; and iii) avoid wasting time in assimilating a variety of positions of States into a certain number of declarations. In light of the foregoing, the individual submission of declarations is more effective than the joint declaration of 33 States. Consequently, in order to avoid delays in court proceedings, all declarations relied on Article 63,[46] rather than Article 62. This is because Article 63 admits the 'right' of intervention without subjecting this to severe ICJ scrutiny.

3.3 Intervention Under Article 63

In a series of cases, including that under review, the ICJ has gradually clarified the characteristics of intervention under Article 63 of the Statute, namely: i) it is admitted as an 'exercise of a right' of a State party to a convention in question (Order 2023 [26]); ii) the intervening State can only submit observations on the

---

[42] Joint statement on Ukraine's application against Russia at the International Court of Justice (20 May 2022) by 41 States and the EU. In this statement, the parties expressed their "joint intention to explore all options to support Ukraine in its efforts before the ICJ and to consider a possible intervention in these proceedings", https://www.esteri.it/en/sala_stampa/archivionotizie/comunicati/2022/05/joint-statement-on-ukraines-application-against-russia-at-the-international-court-of-justice/.

[43] Joint statement on supporting Ukraine in its proceeding at the International Court of Justice (13 July 2022) by 43 States and the EU. It is stated that "[i]t is in the interest of all States Parties to the Genocide Convention, and more broadly of the international community as a whole, that the Convention not be misused or abused. That is why the signatories of the present declaration which are Parties to the Genocide Convention intend to intervene in these proceedings", https://ec.europa.eu/commission/presscorner/detail/en/statement_22_4509.

[44] On 17 August 2022, the EU furnished the Court with relevant information in this case, in accordance with Article 34 (2) of the Statute and Article 69 (2) of the Rules. ICJ Press Release No. 2022/29 (18 August 2022).

[45] Vice-President Gevorgian stated that, being *en masse* and publicly available, the declarations generate a "significant amount of political pressure on judges to decide this case in a particular way [i.e., in favour of Ukraine]." Decl Gevorgian 2023 [9]. Judge Xue echoed this point by stating that the intervening States' strategy "would certainly lend strong political support to the Applicant and at the same time exert political pressure on the Court to entertain the case." Decl Xue 2023 [28].

[46] Article 63(2) of the Statute: "[e]very state so notified has the right to intervene in the proceedings; but if it uses this right, the construction given by the judgment will be equally binding upon it."

Table 3 Cases of intervention under Article 63 of the Statute

Cases	Intervenors	Conclusions
1923 *Wimbledon*	Poland	**Admissible**
1951 *Haya de la Torre*	Cuba	**Admissible**
1984 *Nicaragua*	El Salvador	Inadmissible
1995 *Request Para. 63*	Australia, Micronesia, the Marshall Islands, the Solomon Islands, and Samoa	Inadmissible
2013 *Whaling*	New Zealand	**Admissible**
2023 *Allegations of Genocide*	33 States	**Admissible (32 States)**

construction of the convention in question (ibid. [44], [49]); iii) it 'does not become a party to the proceedings' (ibid. [49]); iv) the 'legal interest' of the declarant State in the construction of the convention 'is presumed by virtue of its status as a party thereto' (ibid. [27]). In total, Article 63 provides the 'right' to any contracting Party to a convention to intervene as a non-party to the proceedings, to submit its observations on the interpretation of that convention (Table 3).

3.4 Intervention Under Article 62

Unlike Article 63 of the Statute, Article 62 requires on the part of a State seeking to intervene an "interest of a legal nature."[47] There have been two positions on the possibility of Article 62 intervention with regard to the Genocide Convention. On the one hand, it is argued that, as each contracting party to the Genocide Convention is entitled to invoke the State responsibility of another for a breach of an obligation *erga omnes partes* (i.e., public interest litigation), this legal standing satisfies the requirement of 'interest' under Article 62.[48] On the other hand, many others have counterargued that: i) while Article 63 purports to protect the collective interests of the contracting parties of a treaty, Article 62 aims to protect the 'private interest' of the State seeking to intervene;[49] ii) standing and 'interest' under Article 62 are two

---

[47] Article 62(1): "Should a state consider that it has an interest of a legal nature which may be affected by the decision in the case, it may submit a request to the Court to be permitted to intervene."

[48] Giorgio Gaja, "The Protection of General Interests in the International Community", *Recueil des Cours*, vol. 364 (2011), p. 119.

[49] Béatrice Bonafé, "The collective dimension of bilateral litigation: The Ukraine v. Russia case before the ICJ", *Question of International Law: Zoom-out*, vol. 96 (2022), p. 33. It is also argued that intervention under Article 62 "remains predominantly bilateral". Paula Wojcikiewicz Almeida, "International Procedural Regulation in the Common Interest: The Role of Third-Party Intervention and Amicus Curiae before the ICJ", *The Law and Practice of International Courts and Tribunals*, vol. 18 (2019), p. 169.

different notions;[50] iii) the rationale of standing on the basis of an obligation *erga omnes partes* (i.e., there must be at least one State to claim a breach) is different to that of Article 62 (i.e., addition of more states to ongoing proceedings).[51] With regard to this debate, it is useful to recall that in the *Rohingya Genocide* case, the ICJ referred to the 'right', albeit plausible, of each Party to the Genocide Convention in the following terms:

> there is a correlation between the rights of members of groups [Rohingya] protected under the Genocide Convention, the obligations incumbent on States parties [Myanmar] thereto, and *the right of any State party* [The Gambia] *to seek compliance therewith by another State party* (emphasis added).[52]

Even if the 'interest of a legal nature' under Article 62 must be 'particularized',[53] the individualised 'right' of each contracting party, recognised by the ICJ, seems to satisfy the requirement of 'interest of a legal nature' under Article 62.

3.5 Equality of the Parties

The fact that 33 States sought to intervene gave rise to questions as to the inequality between the litigating Parties (Order 2023 [47]). However, this argument was summarily and categorically dismissed by the ICJ, for the following reasons: i) the *non-party* intervention under Article 63 of the Statute does 'not affect the equality of the parties to the dispute' (ibid. [49])[54] and ii) the ICJ cannot limit the number of intervening States, since intervention is a matter of 'right[s]' under Article 63 (ibid. [50]). This means that the Statute and the Rules neither regulate nor prohibit mass or one-sided intervention and, consequently, intervening States may present observations, whether favourable to the applicant or respondent State.[55] This is exactly what

---

[50] Christine Chinkin, *Third Parties in International Law* (Clarendon Press, 1993), p. 160; Matina Papadaki, "Substantive and Procedural Rules in International Adjudication: Exploring their Interaction in Intervention before the International Court of Justice", in Hélène Ruiz Fabri (ed.), *International Law and Litigation: A Look into Procedure* (Nomos, 2019), p. 61.

[51] Brian McGarry, "A rush to judgment? The wobbly bridge from judicial standing to intervention in ICJ proceedings", *QIL, Zoom-in*, vol. 100 (2023), p. 18; Brian McGarry, "Obligations *Erga Omnes (Partes)* and the Participation of Third States in Inter-State Litigation", *The Law and Practice of International Courts and Tribunals*, vol. 22 (2023), p. 298.

[52] *Application of the Convention on the Prevention and Punishment of the Crime of Genocide (The Gambia v. Myanmar)*, Provisional Measures, Order, [2020] ICJ Rep 20 [52].

[53] McGarry, *supra* note 58 (obligations *erga omnes*), pp. 298–299.

[54] The ICJ relied on the *Whaling* case. *Whaling in the Antarctic (Australia v. Japan)*, Declaration of Intervention of New Zealand, Order [2013] ICJ Rep 9 [18].

[55] This understanding makes it difficult to agree with Judge Xue's observation that the intervening States should be 'neutral and objective' to the litigating parties. Decl Xue 2023 [15].

we witnessed in the *Whaling* case.[56] However, when compared to the Japan's position in that case, a heavier burden seems to be imposed on Russia, since the declarations of 33 States were successively submitted in a relatively short period and, consequently, Russia had to defend itself against written submissions 'at once' (Decl Gevorgian 2023 [3]). As pointed out by Judge Xue, this fact "should not be taken lightly and treated as a normal situation of intervention under Article 63" (Decl Xue 2023 [28]).[57] Against this backdrop, the ICJ attempted to mitigate the significance of these issues by taking into consideration the good administration of justice, as we shall see below.

3.6 Good Administration of Justice

In addition to party equality, the ICJ has taken into consideration the wider notion of the sound administration of justice, which comprises the following elements: i) procedural efficiency;[58] ii) the equality of parties;[59] iii) the protection of the respective rights of the parties;[60] and iv) the interest of justice.[61]

---

[56] Dai Tamada, "Unfavourable but Unavoidable Procedures: Procedural Aspects of the Whaling Case", in Malgosia Fitzmaurice and Dai Tamada (eds.), *Whaling in the Antarctic: Significance and Implications of the ICJ Judgment* (Brill, Nijhoff, 2016), pp. 163–192.

[57] It was argued that "[t]here is indeed a fear that any expansion of procedural rules would open the floodgates and expose the ICJ to an uncontrolled number of subjects, which could compromise its function of settling bilateral disputes by undermining party equality and the efficient management of proceedings". Paula Wojcikiewicz Almeida, "Enhancing ICJ Procedures in Order to Promote Fundamental Values: Overcoming the Prevailing Tension between Bilateralism and Community Interests", in Massimo Iovane et al. (eds.), *The Protection of General Interests in Contemporary International Law* (2021), p. 262.

[58] It is said that the sound administration of justice may be taken into account by the ICJ to exercise "functions of judicial administration for the purposes of hastening the proceedings." Hironobu Sakai, "*La Bonne Administration de la Justice* in the Incidental Proceedings of the International Court of Justice", *Japanese Yearbook of International Law*, vol. 55 (2012), p. 121.

[59] It has been argued that the fair administration of justice includes the principle of equality of the parties (Decl Gevorgian 2023 [4]). *Judgments of the Administrative Tribunal of the ILO upon Complaints Made against UNESCO*, Advisory Opinion (23 October 1956) [1956] ICJ Rep 86: "[t]he principle of equality of the parties follows from the requirements of good administration of justice."

[60] The sound administration of justice is considered for "protecting the respective rights of the parties to the case from the abuse of the right to intervene by a third party." Sakai, *supra* note 65, p. 120.

[61] The sound administration of justice aims to protect not only parties' interests, but also the interest of 'justice' itself. This means that "hearing from [a lot of] parties other than the principal ones may be in the interest of the best possible outcome." Caterina Milo, "What is good for the administration of justice? Considerations in light of the practice on third-party participation", *QIL, Zoom-in*, vol. 100 (2023), p. 33.

In the present case, some procedural issues went beyond the scope of party equality, as the ICJ relied on the notion of the sound administration of justice. First, the timing for the submission of declarations is relatively flexible under the Rules.[62] The ICJ received 23 declarations up to 31 October 2022 and, on that day, fixed the time limit for any further declarations, by stating that the "interest of the sound administration of justice and procedural efficiency would be advanced if any State [...] would file its declaration not later than 15 December 2022" (Order 2023 [20]). By this, the ICJ attempted to strike a balance between the flexible time limit and the likely burden on Russia of having to respond to declarations, as well as possible procedural delays. Second, a further question was whether oral proceedings should be held. When a respondent State opposes the admissibility of declarations of intervention, the ICJ is required to 'hear' the declaring States and the litigating parties.[63] Despite Russia's request for oral proceedings, however, the ICJ decided to 'hear' the parties by only accepting written submissions (Order 2023 [22]-[23]). Although, in principle, it is desirable to hold oral proceedings,[64] the ICJ decided not to, probably considering the likely procedural delays and any consequential inequality between the litigating parties (Decl Gevorgian 2023 [3]). The foregoing demonstrates the ICJ's attempt to mitigate potential risks concerning party inequality, by taking into consideration the interests of the good administration of justice.

3.7 Regulation of Procedural Abuse

A more substantive problem arising from the mass and one-sided declarations of intervention, is the fact that they referred to issues other than interpretation and jurisdiction issues. It should be recalled that in the *Whaling* case, the ICJ stated that intervention under Article 63:

---

[62] Article 82 (1) of the Rules only provides that the declaration must be submitted "as soon as possible" and "not later than the date fixed for the opening of the oral proceedings." Judge Bhandari observed that, if the requirement (i.e., 'as soon as possible') was not applied strictly, the ongoing submission of declarations "could place great strain on the Court's time and resources, not to mention the procedure in a case" (Decl Bhandari 2023 [5]).

[63] Article 84 (2) of Rules: "[i]f [...] an objection is filed to an application for permission to intervene, or to the admissibility of a declaration of intervention, the Court shall *hear* the State seeking to intervene and the parties before deciding" (emphasis added). However, the Court is not required to 'hear' the declaring State through oral proceedings.

[64] In the *Nicaragua* case, the ICJ did not hold oral proceedings on the declaration of intervention of El Salvador. On this point, several Judges argued that "it would have been more in accordance with judicial propriety if the Court had granted a hearing to the State seeking to intervene, and had not decided only on the basis of the written communications." Separate Opinion of Judges Ruda, Mosler, Ago, Sir Robert Jennings and Lacharrière [1984] ICJ Rep 219 [4].

War in Ukraine and the International Court of Justice:... 97

is limited to submitting observations on the construction of the convention in question and does not allow the intervenor, which does not become a party to the proceedings, to deal with *any other aspect* of the case before the Court (emphasis added).[65]

If strictly understood, the declaring States are prohibited from expressing any aspect other than the interpretation of Article IX of the Genocide Convention in the present phase of the case. However, all declarations went beyond that limit since they referred to: i) the application of Article IX (i.e., whether a dispute exists or not);[66] ii) Russia's non-compliance with provisional measures;[67] iii) the facts of the case; iv) political statements;[68] and v) legal allegations against Russia[69] (Decl Gevorgian 2023 [8]; Decl Xue 2023 [11]). In response, the ICJ merely stated that it would only take into account the "elements relevant to determining jurisdiction" (Order 2023 [74]) and that it "will not consider" other elements (Order 2023 [84]).

However, several issues remain unsettled. First, as the ICJ has uploaded all the declarations on its website, the political purpose of the declaring States to make their opinions public has already been realised. Second, such publication, with references to a wide range of topics, brought about a "significant amount of political pressure on judges to decide this case in a particular way [i.e., in favour of Ukraine]" (Decl Gevorgian 2023 [9]). Third, the intervening States would be allowed to deal with the merits of the case and, by this, may be afforded 'two hearings' to present their views on the merits (Decl Xue 2023 [10], [29]).

It is worth noting that the ICJ has enacted regulations in similar cases. First, by relying on *forum prorogatum*, many States have submitted Applications to unilaterally publicise their positions vis-à-vis Respondent States, without having any jurisdictional basis for doing so. To prevent abuses of procedure, the ICJ enacted a new rule.[70] Second, in provisional measure requests, a number of States would frequently refer to jurisdiction and merits issues. To discourage this, the ICJ introduced a new provision by way of a Practice Direction.[71] A similar enactment will be needed to prevent abuse of the intervention procedure under Article 63 of the Statute.

---

[65] *Whaling in the Antarctic (Australia v. Japan)*, Declaration of Intervention of New Zealand, Order, [2013] ICJ Rep 9 [18].

[66] Germany [30]; Lichtenstein [18]; and Portugal [31].

[67] Estonia [10]; Spain [8]; Ireland [8]; Latvia [9]; Malta [8]; Poland [8]; Slovakia [10]; Slovenia [8]; and Sweden [10].

[68] Norway [16]; Lithuania [16], [20]; New Zealand [11]; and Poland [36].

[69] Lithuania [16] and New Zealand [11].

[70] Article 38(5) of the Rules of Court: "[w]hen the applicant State proposes to found the jurisdiction of the Court upon a consent thereto yet to be given or manifested by the State against which such application is made, the application shall be transmitted to that State. It shall not however be entered in the General List, nor any action be taken in the proceedings, unless and until the State against which such application is made consents to the Court's jurisdiction for the purposes of the case."

[71] Practice Direction XI: "In the oral pleadings on requests for the indication of provisional measures parties should limit themselves to *what is relevant to the criteria for the indication of provisional measures* as stipulated in the Statute, Rules and jurisprudence of the Court. They should not enter into the merits of the case beyond what is strictly necessary for that purpose" (emphasis added).

3.8 Abuse of Process

With regard to Russia's objection concerning abuse of process, the ICJ rejected this simply because there were "no exceptional circumstances" that would render the declarations of intervention inadmissible (Order 2023 [59]). As the ICJ did not clarify what may constitute 'exceptional circumstances', its finding cannot escape the criticism that the "circumstances of the present case are indeed 'exceptional'" (Decl Gevorgian 2023 [7]). Here, it seems useful to compare the notion of abuse of process and that of abuse of rights.[72] In the *Iranian Assets* case, the ICJ rejected the US objection concerning 'abuse of rights', by stating that:

> The Court could only accept the abuse of rights defence in this instance if it were demonstrated by [the US], on the basis of compelling evidence, that [Iran] seeks to exercise rights conferred on it by the Treaty of Amity for *purposes* other than those for which the rights at issue were established, and that it was doing so to the *detriment* of [the US] (emphasis added).[73]

According to the ICJ, there must be two elements to prove abuse of rights: i) the abusive purpose of exercising rights, and ii) the detriment of the respondent State. In the present case, however, the ICJ has stated that the purpose (i.e., motivation) of the intervention cannot be taken into consideration (Order 2023 [44], [58]). This means that, insofar as the declaring States present, at least formally, their legal interpretations of the Genocide Convention, it is quite difficult to establish by 'compelling evidence' that some abusive purpose may be at play. Behind this argument there seems to be the ICJ's basic stance not to interrogate the real and political intentions behind recourse to ICJ proceedings, as this would open 'Pandora's box' (Del Gevorgian 2023 [7]).

3.9 Intervention at the Preliminary Objections Phase

The ICJ allowed intervention at the preliminary objections phase,[74] on the ground that this is not excluded by Article 63 (2) of the Statute which allows intervention 'in

---

[72] As Article 63 admits the 'right' of intervention, 'abuse of process' may be regarded as 'abuse of right' in the context of the intervention procedure. In this case, in its attempt to establish 'abuse of process', Russia referred to two elements – purpose and harm – which are similar to those of 'abuse of rights' (Order 2023 [54]).

[73] *Certain Iranian Assets (Islamic Republic of Iran v. United States)*, Judgment (30 March 2023) [2023] ICJ Rep [93].

[74] This position is supported by scholars. MN Shaw (ed.), *Rosenne's Law and Practice of the International Court 1920-2015* (5th ed., Brill/Nijhoff, 2016), p. 1533; Arina Miron and Christine Chinkin, "Article 63", in Andreas Zimmermann et al. (eds.), *The Statute of the International Court of Justice: A Commentary* (3rd ed., OUP, 2019), p. 1763 (fn. 46).

the proceedings' (Order 2023 [63]; Decl Bhandari 2023 [2]).[75] Prior to this case, the ICJ had never admitted declarations at such an early stage of proceedings. An issue is that the ICJ had found *inadmissible* the declaration of intervention of El Salvador (Article 63) in the jurisdiction phase of the *Nicaragua* case, by stating that:

> the Declaration [...] addresses itself also in effect to matters, including the construction of conventions, which presuppose that the Court has jurisdiction to entertain the dispute [...] and that Nicaragua's Application [...] is admissible.[76]

In this finding of the ICJ, it is not clear whether the intervention at the jurisdiction phase is, in principle, admissible. In 2023, the ICJ interpreted it as follows:

> El Salvador [...] failed to identify the provisions of any convention the interpretation of which, in its view, would be in question at the stage of the proceedings concerning [the jurisdiction and the admissibility]. Moreover, this declaration referred to conventions that could only concern the merits of the case' (Order 2023 [65]).

The ICJ in 2023 understood that El Salvador's declaration was rejected because it had not identified the provisions to be discussed at the jurisdiction phase. Judge Xue criticised this understanding on the ground that El Salvador had referred to Article 36 of the ICJ Statute and other legal instruments in question at the jurisdictional phase (Decl Xue 2023 [8]). It is true that El Salvador had referred to Article 36 of the Statute, as well as to a variety of treaties in relation to the ICJ's jurisdiction. However, the problem was that El Salvador had failed to identify specific provisions of the convention in question at the jurisdiction phase,[77] thus failing to satisfy the requirement under the Rules.[78] In the case under review, the fact that all declaring States expressly referred to Article IX of the Genocide Convention distinguishes their position from that of El Salvador.

3.10 Reservation and Intervention

The ICJ found the US declaration inadmissible because of the US's reservation to Article IX. In the *Legality of Use of Force* cases, the ICJ rejected Yugoslavia's

---

[75] Under Article 63 (2) of the Statute ('construction given by the judgment'), intervention is not permissible in the provisional measures phase.

[76] *Military and Paramilitary Activities in and against Nicaragua (Nicaragua v. United States of America)*, Declaration of Intervention of the Republic of El Salvador, Order, [1984] ICJ Rep 216 [2].

[77] Bonafé observes that the "declaration of El Salvador was pretty ambiguous: it made only a vague reference to the existence of multilateral conventions and it did not indicate which provisions had to be interpreted nor which interpretation was supported by El Salvador." Bonafé, *supra* note 56, p. 37.

[78] Article 82 (2) of the Rules of Court requires: (b) identification of the particular provisions of the convention the construction of which it considers to be in question; and (c) a statement of the construction of those provisions for which it contends.

provisional measures requests against Spain[79] and the US,[80] because of their reservations to Article IX. This suggests that the ICJ presupposed the validity of the two reservations, on the basis of no objection on the part of Yugoslavia.[81] Thereafter, Spain withdrew its reservation,[82] while the US maintained it. In the *Armed Activities* case, the ICJ clearly admitted that the Article IX reservation was valid.[83] As a result, the US remains a contracting party to the Genocide Convention notwithstanding its reservation to Article IX. Consequently, insofar as contracting parties may intervene "provided that they are bound by the provision in question" (Order 2023 [96]),[84] it follows therefore that the US has no 'legal interest' in the construction of Article IX, and thus its declaration was inadmissible. On the other hand, as was suggested by the ICJ (ibid. [98]), the US will be allowed to intervene in the merits phase in which substantive provisions other than Article IX will be interpreted. What is more, it should be noted that the US attaches a further reservation, as well as five other 'understandings', to the Genocide Convention.[85]

3.11 Interim Conclusions

This case exhibits new aspects and functions of the intervention procedure.

First, the present case illustrates the "collective interest that prompted the declarations of intervention."[86] In other words, the intervention procedure is used by States to protect their common and collective interests.[87] On this point, however, it

---

[79] The ICJ concluded that, because of the reservation, Article IX "manifestly does not constitute a basis of jurisdiction in the present case, even prima facie" and ordered that the "case be removed from the List." *Legality of Use of Force (Yugoslavia v. Spain)*, Provisional Measures, Order (2 June 1999) [1999] ICJ Rep 772 [33], 774 [40] (2).

[80] *Legality of Use of Force (Yugoslavia v. United States of America)*, Provisional Measures, Order (2 June 1999), [1999] ICJ Rep 924 [25], 926 [34] (2).

[81] The ICJ stated that "Yugoslavia did not object to Spain's reservation to Article IX" and that "the said reservation had the effect of excluding that Article from the provisions of the Convention in force between the Parties." [1999] ICJ Rep 772 [32].

[82] Spain withdrew its reservation on 24 September 2009. https://treaties.un.org/pages/ViewDetails. aspx?src=IND&mtdsg_no=IV-1&chapter=4&clang=_en#EndDec.

[83] *Armed Activities on the Territory of the Congo (New Application: 2002) (Democratic Republic of the Congo v. Rwanda)*, Jurisdiction and Admissibility, Judgment, [2006] ICJ Rep 32 [67].

[84] Prior to Order 2023, Bonafé had stated that the "third State must be bound by the provisions the Court has to interpret." Bonafé, *supra* note 56, p. 33.

[85] The US reservation (2): "That nothing in the Convention requires or authorizes legislation or other action by the United States of America prohibited by the Constitution of the United States as interpreted by the United States."

[86] Bonafé, *supra* note 56, p. 27.

[87] It is said that the new strategy of intervention "shows the interest of the international community and civil society for increasingly using such procedural tool as a way to enhance the protection of collective values." Gian Maria Farnelli and Alessandra Sardu, "Third-party participation in

must be remembered that many States are paying close attention to this case, because of its *jus ad bellum* dimension, in addition to the core issue of genocide. This becomes clear if compared to the *Rohingya Genocide* case in which seven States (Canada, Denmark, France, Germany, the Netherlands, the United Kingdom, and the Maldives), much fewer than 33 States, had filed declarations of intervention,[88] even though the subject-matter of the dispute directly related to genocide.

Second, the present case clarifies, again, that Article 63 intervention operates as a loophole, to the effect that it opens the door: i) at the preliminary objections phase; ii) for an unlimited number of Contracting Parties to a multilateral treaty; iii) to individually submit their declarations of intervention; iv) to openly support one of the litigating States; and v) to touch upon a wide range of issues, including merits, evidence, facts, and the application of specific provisions. In other words, Article 63 does not prevent States from pursuing political goals within ICJ litigation to widely express support or criticism against other States.

Third, to narrow this loophole, the ICJ should reformulate the intervention procedure into something akin to the situation with *amicus curiae* briefs.[89] For example, it seems possible to skip 'hear[ing]' the observations of intervenors who are not 'Parties' to a case, even where a construction on the part of the ICJ would be binding on the former. If States would like to engage more deeply in proceedings, the following remain open to them: i) party intervention under Article 62, which requires a jurisdictional link; and ii) non-party intervention under Article 62, which does not require a jurisdictional rink. The ICJ should further reformulate the intervention procedure to deal with multilateralised disputes in future.

4 Potential Impacts of ICJ Litigation

4.1 Denial of Russia's Claims

Although the scope of the present case is strictly limited to the Genocide Convention (Order 2022 [19]), its impact will go beyond that, to the effect that it ends up rejecting Russia's claims aimed at justifying its military action: i) humanitarian intervention: prevention of genocide in Donbas;[90] ii) individual self-defence:

---

international adjudication: Recent trends and ongoing issues", *Zoom in, Question of International Law*, vol. 100 (2023), p. 2.

[88] ICJ Press Release No. 2023/68 (16 November 2023).

[89] Almeida observed that "*[a]mici curiae* would also be important in order to avoid possible delays to the judicial proceedings in case of multiple interveners, that is, whenever multiple states decide to intervene in a case in which the construction of a multilateral convention is at issue." Almeida, *supra* note 64, p. 257.

[90] The 2022 Putin Address stated that "[w]e had to stop that atrocity, that genocide of the millions of people who live there [in Donbas]" and that the "purpose of this [special military] operation is to

prevention of Ukraine's attempt to join NATO, which constitutes a threat to Russia;[91] and iii) collective self-defence: genocide in Donbas entitled two oblasts to independence as an exercise of remedial secession (i.e., DPR and LNR),[92] recognised by Russia as States,[93] which respectively concluded the Treaty with Russia[94] (ratified on 22 February 2022),[95] and, lastly, Russia resorts to military action in accordance with these treaties.[96] If, in the present case, the ICJ were to deny the occurrence of genocide in Donbas, this mere finding would automatically deny Russia's claims i) and iii), because they presuppose the occurrence of genocide in Donbas. On the other hand, an ICJ finding as to the absence of genocide would not suffice for denying Russia's claim ii) as this does not presuppose the occurrence of genocide. Furthermore, there remains a significant issue that, even if the ICJ were to order Russia to cease its military action on the basis of the Genocide Convention, this finding would not supersede Russia's justification based on self-defence,[97] due to the primacy of the UN Charter (Article 103).

4.2 Objective of ICJ Litigation

It is highly unlikely that Russia would comply with any ICJ decision ordering its withdrawal from Ukrainian territory. What is more, it is most likely that Russia would veto any attempt for a UN Security Council resolution aimed at enforcing

---

protect people who, for eight years now, have been facing humiliation and genocide perpetrated by the Kiev regime."

[91] The 2022 Putin Address referred to 'fundamental threats' by the 'eastward expansion of NATO' and stated that "[i]t is not only a very real threat to our interests but to the very existence of our state and to its sovereignty."

[92] The 2022 Putin Address stated that "[i]t is their aspirations, the feelings and pain of these people [in Donbas] that were the main motivating force behind our decision to recognise the independence of the Donbass people's republics."

[93] Signing of documents recognising Donetsk and Lugansk People's Republics, available at http://en.kremlin.ru/events/president/news/67829.

[94] The Treaty of Friendship, Cooperation and Mutual Assistance between the Russian Federation and the Donetsk People's Republic and the Treaty of Friendship, Cooperation and Mutual Assistance between the Russian Federation and the Lugansk People's Republic. Ibid.

[95] President signed Federal Law On Ratifying the Treaty of Friendship, Cooperation and Mutual Assistance Between the Russian Federation and the Lugansk People's Republic, available at http://en.kremlin.ru/events/president/news/67834.

[96] The 2022 Putin Address stated that "in accordance with Article 51 (Chapter VII) of the UN Charter [...] and in execution of the treaties of friendship and mutual assistance with [DPR and LPR], I made a decision to carry out a special military operation."

[97] Judge Robinson clearly pointed out that "[t]he right of self-defence recognized in Article 51 is inherent in every State and cannot be overridden by any pronouncement the Court may make as to the consistency of Russia's military operation with the Genocide Convention." Sep Op Robinson 2022 [32].

such an ICJ decision.[98] If this speculation is borne out by events, this case would illustrate the special objective of this ICJ litigation, other than the enforcement of an ICJ decision itself.

First, this case is part of Ukraine's 'lawfare' litigation strategy[99] to utilise international courts and tribunals for the legal counteroffensive against Russia. Its purpose appears to be to obtain authoritative findings in favour of Ukraine, which, cumulatively, are likely to a greater impact on restricting Russia's activities in the international arena. In this sense, this strategy is similar to Mauritius's so-called 'legal Statecraft' to successively use a variety of means aimed at reaching direct negotiations with the UK Government on the Chagos Archipelago issue.[100]

Second, ICJ litigation will help Ukraine to strengthen its own position. On the one hand, the discussion about the war in Ukraine, from a *jus ad bellum* viewpoint, would soon reach an impasse between arguments for the use of force and self-defence, and the involvement of the UN Security Council resulting in Russia's veto. However, this is nothing other than following Russia's claims, which were fabricated just a few days before the commencement of its military action. On the other hand, an ICJ decision would eventually enhance Ukraine's claim that the real dispute between the two State is not about the use of force but about Russia's allegation of genocide in Donbas.[101]

Third, the ICJ's findings are expected to bear considerable political impacts on stakeholders in the Russia-Ukraine war, to the effect that they would: i) enable Western countries already participating in sanctions against Russia to maintain public support for financially and militarily supporting Ukraine; ii) persuade States in the so-called Global South currently not participating in sanctions against Russia, to support Ukraine and to join the sanctions against Russia; iii) make the Russian population aware of the adverse international climate surrounding Russia, and lead to their war-weariness; and iv) would bring Ukraine to a better legal position in eventual ceasefire negotiations with Russia. From the foregoing, it is necessary to evaluate the effectiveness of the ICJ decision in light of various considerations beyond those of a strictly legal nature.

---

[98] Kulick considers that this "dispute thus painfully demonstrates the frustrating limits of international law and international adjudication." Kulick, *supra* note 33, p. 340.

[99] Ukraine characterises its litigation activities against Russia as 'lawfare', referring to cases before the ICJ, the UNCLOS tribunals, and investor-State arbitration. 'Law Confrontation with Russian Federation: Lawfare', https://lawfare.gov.ua/.

[100] Douglas Guilfoyle, "Litigation as Statecraft: Small States and the Law of the Sea", *British Yearbook of International Law* (advance article) (2023), p. 3, available at https://doi.org/10.1093/bybil/brad009.

[101] Judge Robinson correctly observed that "the real issue in the case is not the use of force, as argued by Russia... [but the]... allegation by Russia that Ukraine was carrying out acts that constituted genocide under the Genocide Convention and Ukraine's denial of that allegation." Sep Op Robinson 2022 [13].

5 Conclusions

This case is characterised by the political circumstances surrounding the ICJ, namely the ongoing full-scale military action by Russia, a permanent member of the UN Security Council. As the Security Council is paralysed by the realities of veto prerogatives, great expectations have been placed on the ICJ to maintain and restore international peace and security in place of the Security Council. There is no doubt that, as one of the 'principal organs' of the United Nations (Article 7 of the UN Charter), the ICJ has "responsibilities in the international peace and security" (Order 2022 [18]),[102] and, by performing them, it can play its part in upholding those responsibilities it shares with the UN Security Council, particularly at a time that the latter is at an impasse. On the other hand, the ICJ, being a *judicial* organ, cannot distort its judicial character. In this respect, this case illustrates the dilemma between the international expectations on the ICJ to fulfil broader peace and security responsibilities and the restraints of its judicial function.

Because of international concern about peace and security arising from the war in Ukraine, considerable political pressure has been placed on the ICJ[103] by Ukraine[104] and intervening States.[105] On the one hand, it is not unusual for the ICJ to be exposed to political pressure on the part of stakeholders; the ICJ has never been immune to this. Furthermore, the political motivation of States, as a source of pressure, is not a matter to be regulated by the ICJ. It is futile for the ICJ to attempt to regulate the exercise of State rights to intervene in proceedings, in order to prohibit politically motivated attempts to intervene. On the other hand, the risk remains that the greater the pressure States place on the ICJ, the greater the chances for States to obtain favourable judicial outcomes. Evidently, this impairs the Court's authority and prestige as an objective, fair, and just arbiter. As a court of law, the ICJ is required to also maintain the *appearance* that it cannot be swayed by political pressure. To maintain this, the ICJ should seek to reformulate its own rules of procedure, as discussed in this chapter (Sects. 3.7 and 3.11).

---

[102] The ICJ had referred to its "responsibilities in the maintenance of international peace and security." *Legality of Use of Force (Serbia and Montenegro v. Belgium)*, Provisional Measures, Order, [1999] ICJ Rep 132 [18].

[103] Judge ad hoc Daudet observed that "many people placed their hopes in the voice of international law that the World Court would carry. I believe that this Order will meet their legitimate expectations." Decl Daudet 2022 [9].

[104] In a symbolic manner, Ukraine argued that "the whole world is looking to you [the ICJ] for guidance and leadership. Once you have fulfilled your role, these other [international] bodies can fulfil theirs" (CR 2022/5, 62 [19] Mr. Koh) and that "the world awaits your actions" (CR 2022/5, 68 [42] Mr. Koh).

[105] Judge Gevorgian observed that the publication of many intervention declarations on the ICJ website brought a "significant amount of political pressure on judges." Decl Gevorgian 2023 [9]. Similarly, Judge Xue referred to the "political pressure on the Court to entertain the case." Diss Op Xue 2023 [28].

6 Postscript

On 2 February 2024, the ICJ rendered the preliminary objections Judgment.[106] Although the ICJ affirmed its jurisdiction on the first aspect of the dispute (i.e., whether 'there is no credible evidence that Ukraine is responsible for committing genocide in violation of the Genocide Convention in the Donetsk and Luhansk oblasts of Ukraine'), it finally denied its jurisdiction *ratione materiae* on the second aspect of the dispute (i.e., whether Russia's 'use of force' and 'recognition of the independence' of two 'Republics' violate Articles I and IV of the Genocide Convention). This means that, at the merits phase, the ICJ does not touch upon the aspects of the dispute arising from the recognition of independence and the use of force by Russia. However, the prospective ICJ Judgment on the merits will not lose its value. First, the ICJ's finding on whether the genocide occurred in Ukraine (or whether there is such an evidence) will bring a significant implication to deny a large part of the Russia's justifications of its military action. Second, as the ICJ did not revoke the provisional measures Order, there remains a legally binding Order, which has obliged Russia to 'immediately suspend the military operations'. This means that the ICJ, at the merits phase, will be able to find that Russia, by not suspending its military action, has breached this legal obligation.[107] This finding of unlawfulness on the part of Russia will enable or make it easier for Western countries to move on to the next stage of procedure to confiscate the Russian assets, frozen in their financial organs.

---

[106] *Allegations of Genocide under the Convention on the Prevention and Punishment of the Crime of Genocide (Ukraine v. Russian Federation: 32 States intervening)*, Preliminary Objections, Judgment of 2 February 2024.

[107] It is worth referring to another case between Ukraine and Russia. *Application of the International Convention for the Suppression of the Financing of Terrorism and of the International Convention on the Elimination of All Forms of Racial Discrimination (Ukraine v. Russian Federation)*, Judgment (31 January 2024). In this Judgment, the ICJ concluded that Russia 'has violated its obligation [of the provisional measures Order] to refrain from any action which might aggravate or extend the dispute' ([2024] ICJ Rep [404] (6)). As to the remaining biding force of the provisional measures Order 2022, see Dai Tamada, "Still Valid: Provisional Measures in Ukraine v. Russia (Allegations of Genocide)", EJIL: Talk! (15 March 2024).

Part II
Economic Aspects

Economic Sanctions Against Russia: Questions of Legality and Legitimacy

Mika Hayashi and Akihiro Yamaguchi

Abstract Despite the apparent aggression by Russia against Ukraine, the legality of the autonomous ('non-UN') economic sanctions against Russia remains uncertain. Measures adopted as sanctions are generally assumed to be lawful by those states imposing such sanctions. The same sanctions are denounced as illegal by Russia and also by a number of other states. The question of legitimacy of these sanctions is also divisive. As the main criticism of these sanctions pertains to their 'unilateral' nature, an initial response to such criticism is to attempt to present sanctions as actually being collective UN sanctions. However, assimilating autonomous economic sanctions to collective sanctions under UN auspices is an untenable argument. Another justification proposed is labelling the sanctions as so-called 'third-party countermeasures.' However, there is no evidence that states imposing sanctions against Russia rely on such legal justification. This mirrors the current, inconclusive status of the right of third parties to take countermeasures.

1 Introduction

The economic sanctions against Russia since the start of the war against Ukraine in February 2022 are neither authorised, mandated nor recommended by the United Nations (UN) Security Council. Such 'non-UN' sanctions are referred to in this article as 'autonomous' sanctions. The emphasis in the legal literature on the

---

The views expressed in this chapter are solely those of the authors, and do not represent the views of NIDS or the Ministry of Defense.

M. Hayashi (✉)
Graduate School of International Cooperation Studies, Kobe University, Kobe, Japan
e-mail: nmika@kobe-u.ac.jp

A. Yamaguchi
Graduate School of International Cooperation Studies, Kobe University, Kobe, Japan

Cyber Security Division, Policy Studies Department National Institute for Defense Studies, Tokyo, Japan
e-mail: yamaguchi-aki@nids.go.jp

© The Author(s), under exclusive license to Springer Nature Singapore Pte Ltd. 2024
M. Asada, D. Tamada (eds.), *The War in Ukraine and International Law*,
https://doi.org/10.1007/978-981-97-2504-5_5

preferred term 'autonomous,' rather than unilateral,[1] is undoubtedly due to such economic sanctions being autonomous of any collective decisions of the UN Security Council.[2] The question as to the legality of such sanctions is divisive. Measures adopted as sanctions are generally assumed to be lawful by those states and groups of states[3] imposing such sanctions. The same sanctions are denounced as illegal by Russia. Not much detail is given beyond these general positions by either side. Against this backdrop, this article explores the legal justification for economic sanctions imposed against Russia.

States imposing economic sanctions against Russia purportedly do so in response to Russian aggression against Ukraine, but the fact of aggression is often twisted or even refuted by Russia. Because of this, some may deem it unnecessary to ask imposing states to justify their actions. Nevertheless, while sanctions pursuant to UN Security Council decisions enjoy a strong sense of legitimacy, autonomous economic sanctions outside the ambit of the UN Security Council are generally seen with some suspicion. Legitimacy questions aside, it is also entirely possible for a particular measure that is part of a sanctions package to be attacked as unlawful in a court of law.[4] There is therefore a point in examining the justifications for such sanctions, as questions of, both, legality and legitimacy.

As becomes apparent from these introductory remarks, this article deals with the terms 'legality' and 'legitimacy' as distinguishable inter se. 'Legitimacy' is a term characterised by semantic complexity; if claimed by one side to a dispute, the claim of legitimacy inevitably invites criticism as biased. The strength of such a claim and criticisms against it, is determined, at least in part, by the number of states siding with, or distancing themselves from, either.[5] In this article the term 'legitimacy' denotes the wide acceptance within the international community of a state's action as

---

[1] Masahiko Asada, "Definition and Legal Justification of Sanctions" in Masahiko Asada (ed.), *Economic Sanctions in International Law and Practice* (2020), pp. 10–11.

[2] European Union (EU) restrictive measures, albeit collectively decided and implemented by multiple (EU member) states, remain 'autonomous' economic sanctions when decided without UN Security Council involvement or endorsement, and are treated as such in this article.

[3] The main two actors that currently impose economic sanctions against Russia are the United States and a group of states in the form of the EU. For the sake of simplicity, the present authors use the term 'state' or 'states' whenever referring to these two types of entities instead of 'a state or a group of states' or 'states and groups of states'.

[4] Targeted corporations have in fact tried to claim that measures targeting them were unlawful, for instance, in the General Court and the Court of Justice of the EU. An example of a lawsuit by Rosneft as a result of sanctions regarding the 2014 annexation of Crimea is examined in Michel Erpelding, "L'annexion de la Crimée devant les juges," 63 *Annuaire français de droit international* (2017), pp. 104–107; Mika Hayashi, "Russia: the Crimea Question and Autonomous Sanctions", in Masahiko Asada (ed.), *Economic Sanctions in International Law and Practice* (2020), pp. 233–234. For a more recent example, see, e.g., Arrêt du Tribunal (grande chambre) du 27 juillet 2022. *RT France contre Conseil de l'Union européenne*, Case T-125/22.

[5] 141 states in the UN General Assembly were in favour of adopting a resolution condemning Russian aggression against Ukraine. U.N. Doc. A/ES-11/1 (2 March 2022). See the United Nations Meeting Coverage and Press Releases, "General Assembly Overwhelmingly Adopts Resolution Demanding Russian Federation Immediately End Illegal Use of Force in Ukraine, Withdraw All

politically rational and morally sound. The term 'legality' pertains to formal conformity with international law. Political legitimacy, as defined above, may encompass the dimension of legality alongside other considerations. However, the legitimacy of a state's action does not automatically resolve the legality of that action. When an action, though perceived as politically legitimate, presents doubts as to its legality, it gives rise to fundamental questions concerning whether and in what manner international law endorses such an action. In the context of the current economic sanctions against Russia, even though the sanctions are politically legitimate, certain measures within the context of such sanctions may not comply with certain rules of specific agreements or general international law.

Following an overview of autonomous sanctions taken against Russia since February 2022, illustrated by EU sanctions packages (Sect. 2), this article first presents the opposition of views between the states imposing sanctions and, on the receiving end, Russia (Sect. 3). An examination of the justifications for such autonomous economic sanctions follows (Sect. 4).

2   Overview of Economic Sanctions Against Russia

The term 'economic sanctions' broadly covers all non-military, "coercive measures taken against the will of a target state or entity."[6] Concretely, these are measures that inflict trade, or other types of, damage "with the aim of putting pressure on the target state or persons for convincing it or them to act or not act in a certain manner."[7] An embargo of goods against a target state is a typical economic sanction. Economic sanctions can also take the form of travel bans and asset freezes aimed at specific individuals. In the present case, the Russian president is a target of a US asset freeze,[8] and the US president is a target of a travel ban by Russia.[9] Entities such as corporations can also be targets of an asset freeze.

Individual states are not the only actors that adopt economic sanctions autonomously. The European Union (EU) and other regional organisations do so, too. The EU is in fact a leading actor in economic sanctions against Russia.

Troops", https://press.un.org/en/2022/ga12407.doc.htm (2 March 2022). All internet sources cited in this chapter were last accessed in August 2023, save for a few, more recent updates.

[6] Asada (n 1), p. 5.

[7] Jean-Marc Thouvenin, "History of Implementation of Sanctions" in Masahiko Asada (ed.), *Economic Sanctions in International Law and Practice* (2020), p. 89.

[8] Press Statement by the US Department of State, "Imposing Sanctions on President Putin and Three Other Senior Russian Officials", https://www.state.gov/imposing-sanctions-on-president-putin-and-three-other-senior-russian-officials/ (25 February 2022).

[9] Заявление МИД России о персональных санкциях в отношении представителей руководства США и связанных с ними лиц [Russian Foreign Ministry's statement concerning personal sanctions on US senior officials and affiliated persons], https://mid.ru/ru/foreign_policy/news/1804365/ (15 March 2022).

2.1 Example of the Sanctions Packages by the EU

The EU adopted a series of economic sanctions, which it then incrementally expanded and strengthened in ten additional phases by the summer of 2023.[10] Following Russia's recognition of the unilateral declaration of independence of the Donetsk and Luhansk regions in eastern Ukraine, the EU decided on 23 February 2022 to impose the first package of economic sanctions. The main components of the first package were restrictions on entry into the EU and freezing of assets located in the EU. These restrictions were imposed on 351 members of the Russian State Duma who had voted in favour of recognising the independence of Donetsk and Luhansk. The same or similar sanctions were also imposed on high-profile individuals and entities, including government members, senior military officers, businesspersons and banks.

The second package of targeted sanctions on 25 February 2022 added the incumbent President and the Foreign Minister of the Russian Federation, among other individuals and entities, to the sanctions list. At the same time, the visa policy was changed so that diplomats and related groups from Russia, as well as certain businesspersons, no longer had privileged access to the EU. Together, the total number of names on the sanctions list rose to 654 individuals and 52 entities. The second package also included sectoral economic sanctions in the financial, energy, defence and aerospace sectors and industries. The third package, announced on 28 February and 2 March 2022, among other measures, placed a ban on entering EU airspace and access to EU airports by Russian carriers of all kinds, excluded key Russian banks from the SWIFT system, and added more persons and entities to the sanctions list. 'Oligarchs' and oil and financial conglomerates that were believed to be close to President Vladimir Putin, were the main targets of this sanctions package.

After the announcement of a compliance package regarding the previous sanctions, the fourth package, announced on 15 March 2022, further expanded the sanctions regime to include a ban on all transactions with certain Russian state-owned companies; a ban on imports of iron and steel products from Russia; a ban on exports of luxury goods to Russia; and a ban on new investment in the Russian energy industry. More oligarchs and businesspersons linked to the Kremlin were also added to the sanctions list. The fifth package, announced on 8 April 2022, included a ban on imports of all forms of Russian coal. Cement, rubber products, wood, and other goods that generated significant revenue for Russia also came under this package's import ban.

The sixth package of sanctions, announced in June 2022, included oil import restrictions. The package was followed by the seventh, 'maintenance and alignment' package in July 2022, which included, among other things, the import ban of all gold originating from Russia as well as a targeted export ban of goods and technologies that could contribute to Russia's military and technological improvements or the

---

[10]The main information in this section can be found at the following well-organised EU webpage: "Sanctions adopted following Russia's military aggression against Ukraine", https://finance.ec.europa.eu/eu-and-world/sanctions-restrictive-measures/sanctions-adopted-following-russias-military-aggression-against-ukraine_en (last updated on 6 February 2024).

development of Russia's military and security sector. This package also prohibited Russian vessels from accessing EU ports to prevent the circumvention of sanctions.

The eighth package in October 2022 reinforced existing sanctions by adding yet more import and export restrictions. The target sanctions were further reinforced, targeting political decision-makers, oligarchs, senior military officials and others. This sanctions package also widened the scope of services that cannot be provided to the government of Russia or legal persons established in Russia. The ninth package saw the addition of close to 200 names to the listing of target sanctions. More export bans were introduced to restrict the export of sensitive dual-use and advanced technologies that contribute to Russia's military capabilities and technological enhancement.

These restrictions on the export of sensitive dual-use and advanced technologies were further strengthened in February 2023 in the tenth package of sanctions. Additional export bans were also introduced on goods that can be easily redirected to the use in the ongoing war, such as radars, electric generators and certain types of vehicles. The eleventh package of sanctions followed in June 2023. In light of the amount of Western military supplies that reportedly end up in Russia, new trade measures and transport measures were introduced aimed at reducing the circumvention of sanctions. The latest package as of this writing, the twelfth package, has once again broadened the scope of embargoes, including a ban on the importation of diamonds and liquified petroleum gas (LPG). Additional asset freezing measures in this package target, inter alia, those individuals who organised the so-called 'elections' in the occupied territories of Ukraine. The EU has also taken stronger steps to prevent the circumvention of sanctions in addition to the measures decided in the previous, eleventh sanctions package. Exporters are required to contractually prohibit the re-export of military and aviation-related goods to Russia.

2.2 Some Notable Features

Compared to the autonomous sanctions imposed on Russia at the time of the 2014 annexation of Crimea,[11] sanctions imposed since February 2022 are striking in two ways. First, there is greater solidarity in the international community than in the period between 2014 and 2022: some states that were reluctant to impose sanctions in 2014 for the sake of Crimea[12] have participated more actively in the current sanctions. Second, current sanctions also target a far wider range of economic sectors and entities. The EU sanctions regime outlined in the foregoing exemplifies this.

Within the sanctions packages that were implemented because of the invasion of Ukraine, there were also a series of sanctions against specific issues accompanying

---

[11] For an outline of autonomous sanctions at the time of the 2014 annexation of Crimea, see Alexandra Hofer, "The 'Curiouser and Curiouser' Legal Nature of Non-UN Sanctions: The Case of the US Sanctions against Russia," 23(1) *Journal of Conflict and Security Law* (2018), pp. 75–104; Hayashi (n 4), pp. 225–231.

[12] For a description of such states, see Hayashi (n 4), pp. 229–231.

or related to the invasion. For example, the EU prohibited a few Russian media outlets from broadcasting and reporting within the EU as part of its sanctions, because "in order to justify and support its aggression against Ukraine, the Russian Federation has engaged in continuous and concerted propaganda actions targeted at civil society in the Union and neighbouring countries, gravely distorting and manipulating facts."[13] Following the discovery of a number of civilian corpses in Bucha, near Kyiv, targeted sanctions for atrocities committed by the Russian military forces were further decided.[14] The EU and other states have also adopted sanctions against Belarus for its involvement in the aggression.[15]

To sum up, major features of current economic sanctions against Russia is the extensive range of measures taken and the wide participation in such efforts. The extensiveness of measures means sanctions packages include measures of varying legal nature. For a legal evaluation, therefore, the initial step would be dividing hostile yet lawful measures of retorsion on the one hand, and measures that in some way infringe legal rules on the other.[16]

3 Views of the States on the Legality of Economic Sanctions Against Russia

States that impose economic sanctions against Russia consider such sanctions lawful (Sect. 3.1), while the target state, Russia, considers these unlawful (Sect. 3.2).

3.1 Economic Sanctions from the Perspective of Imposing States

States imposing sanctions do not actively declare the bases of the legality of each and every measure they include in their sanctions packages (Sect. 3.1.1). Nevertheless, they are abundantly clear about the cause of these sanctions: they are reactions to the unacceptable conduct of Russia in light of the UN Charter and general international law (Sect. 3.1.2).

---

[13] Council Regulation (EU) 2022/350 of 1 March 2022 amending Regulation (EU) No 833/2014 concerning restrictive measures in view of Russia's actions destabilising the situation in Ukraine, preamble (7).

[14] Council Implementing Regulation (EU) 2022/878 of 3 June 2022 implementing Regulation (EU) No 269/2014 concerning restrictive measures in respect of actions undermining or threatening the territorial integrity, sovereignty and independence of Ukraine.

[15] E.g., Council Regulation (EU) 2022/355 of 2 March 2022 amending Regulation (EC) No 765/2006 concerning restrictive measures in view of the situation in Belarus, preamble (3).

[16] See Sect. 4.3.1.

3.1.1 On the Legality of Individual Measures

On the part of the states imposing economic sanctions, there seems to be a lack of interest in discussing the legality of individual measures within autonomous sanctions packages against Russia. This may be strategic thinking on their part to foreclose discussion, lest any legality assertions be questioned. In any case, the compatibility of measures adopted as sanctions against Russia with international law is rarely explained in detail by imposing states.

The EU holds the view that its measures that constitute autonomous sanctions generally conform with both its internal regulations and international law. In its 'Guidelines on the Implementation and Evaluation of Restrictive Measures (Sanctions)',[17] the EU expresses its commitment that "[t]he introduction and implementation of restrictive measures must always be in accordance with international law."[18] However, these guidelines do mention, albeit briefly, that the compatibility of such restrictive measures with relevant WTO agreements may be of concern. The guidelines acknowledge that where restrictive measures on trade and services fall outside the scope of relevant security exceptions (Article XXI of GATT, and Article XIV *bis* of GATS), they must meet the requirements of the relevant general exceptions: Article XX of GATT and Article XIV of GATS, respectively.[19] In light of this, the guidelines further acknowledge that "[i]f EU measures are in conflict with the international obligations of the Union or its Member States, a common approach for dealing with such conflicts may have to be developed."[20] However, the official EU webpage on current economic sanctions against Russia does not refer to such possible conflicts with international law; it merely declares that all EU sanctions are: "fully compliant with obligations under international law,"[21] without shedding any further light on how this is so.

Similarly, the position of the United States (US) on the legality of its own measures is not expressed in any detail. In a 2014 press briefing of the US State Department after the annexation of Crimea, a journalist querying US sanctions against Russia suggested "that people who put the sanctions together didn't have this [possible incompatibility with the WTO rules] as a concern."[22] The US general

---

[17] Guidelines on Implementation and Evaluation of Restrictive Measures (Sanctions) in the Framework of the EU Common Foreign and Security Policy (4 May 2018), available at the EU webpage titled "How and When the EU Adopts Sanctions", https://www.consilium.europa.eu/en/policies/sanctions/ (last updated 7 October 2023).

[18] *Ibid.*, para. 9.

[19] *Ibid.*, para. 11.

[20] *Ibid.*, para. 12.

[21] See Section "Do EU sanctions fall under international law?" at EU webpage titled "EU Sanctions against Russia Explained", https://www.consilium.europa.eu/en/policies/sanctions/restrictive-measures-against-russia-over-ukraine/sanctions-against-russia-explained/ (last updated 26 June 2023).

[22] US Department of State, Daily Press Briefing, https://2009-2017.state.gov/r/pa/prs/dpb/2014/09/231529.htm (12 September 2014). The journalist's suggestion, cast rhetorically, was neither denied nor confirmed by the State Department spokesperson. The incident is recounted in Takuhei Yamada, "Keizai Seisai no Houteki Kiritsu (2-Kan) – Tai Roshia Seisai no Kentou" [Legal Regulations of the Economic Sanctions, part 2: Examination of the Sanctions against Russia] (in Japanese), 54(1) *Ryukoku Hogaku* (2021), pp. 198–199.

position regarding autonomous economic sanctions is that they are indeed lawful, as, for instance, numerous US statements made in the United Nations indicate.[23]

In sum, the states that impose autonomous sanctions against Russia appear to demonstrate little concern regarding the legality of their sanctions.

3.1.2 On Violations of International Law on the Part of Russia

In contrast to scarce pronouncements over the legality of their own sanctions, the same states are vocal and loud in their assessment of the legality of Russia's conduct in relation to Ukraine: namely, that Russian aggression is illegal. Imposing states make it equally clear that this violation of international law is the very reason for imposing autonomous economic sanctions against Russia. While economic sanctions against Russia are not collectively organised under any international institution, there is a common, shared understanding among imposing states regarding the illegality of Russian conduct.

A few statements on the part of such states suffice to demonstrate the importance given to their assessment of the legality of Russian conduct. When economic sanctions were announced by the US as an immediate response to Russia's recognition of the independence of Donetsk and Luhansk in eastern Ukraine, the US condemned this recognition in the following terms: "Russia's decision is yet another example of President Putin's flagrant disrespect for international law and norms."[24] Russia's invasion of Ukraine, that followed the recognition of the two breakaway regions, was a straightforward 'aggression', 'invasion' or 'war' for other states, too, when they elaborated their reasons for imposing autonomous economic sanctions. 'Aggression', 'invasion' and 'war' are terms that need no further explanation: they are all examples of the use of force prohibited under the UN Charter and general international law. Moreover, the states that imposed sanctions would very often add qualifications such as 'illegal' and 'unjustified' to these terms, undoubtedly to stress their legal characterisation of the root cause of their sanctions: Russia's "unprovoked aggression,"[25] "unprovoked and unjustified military aggression,"[26] "full-scale

---

[23] For a convenient collection of US statements in the UN, see Alexandra Hofer, "The Developed/ Developing Divide on Unilateral Coercive Measures: Legitimate Enforcement or Illegitimate Intervention?", 16 *Chinese Journal of International Law* (2017), p. 175, p. 199.

[24] US Department of State, "Kremlin Decision on Eastern Ukraine", https://www.state.gov/kremlin-decision-on-eastern-ukraine/ (21 February 2022).

[25] "Fact Sheet: Joined by Allies and Partners, the United States Imposes Devastating Costs on Russia", https://www.whitehouse.gov/briefing-room/statements-releases/2022/02/24/fact-sheet-joined-by-allies-and-partners-the-united-states-imposes-devastating-costs-on-russia/ (24 February 2022).

[26] "European Council Conclusions on Russia's unprovoked and unjustified military aggression against Ukraine", https://www.consilium.europa.eu/en/press/press-releases/2022/02/24/european-council-conclusions-24-february-2022/ (24 February 2022).

invasion,"[27] "illegal invasion of Ukraine,"[28] and "illegal war against Ukraine"[29] are typical phrases found in their condemnations. These terms were also present in the statement adopted during the 2023 Hiroshima G7 summit where G7 leaders, including Japan's, emphatically condemned the manifest violation of the UN Charter.[30] The stress in many statements is that economic sanctions against Russia were motivated by violations of international law: "Russia's attack on Ukraine is also an attack on democracy, on international law, on human rights, and on freedom."[31] Economic sanctions against Russia are, to sum up, meant to "weaken this war of aggression, which is against international law, and to make clear that we do not tolerate in any way the breach of international rules."[32]

3.2 Economic Sanctions from the Russian Perspective

For Russia which presents its war against Ukraine as a "special military operation" with its own pretexts,[33] there is no legitimacy in the sanctions (Sect. 3.2.1). Though relatively little is said about the legality of individual measures, Russia's narrative on sanctions as a whole is consistent: they are unilateral and illegal (Sect. 3.2.2).

3.2.1 On the Legitimacy of the Sanctions

When referring to economic sanctions, Russia admits little or no connection between its invasion of Ukraine and current sanctions. Instead, it systematically presents

---

[27] Foreign and Commonwealth Office, "Foreign Secretary imposes UK's most punishing sanctions to inflict maximum and lasting pain on Russia", https://www.gov.uk/government/news/foreign-secretary-imposes-uks-most-punishing-sanctions-to-inflict-maximum-and-lasting-pain-on-russia (24 February 2022).

[28] *Ibid.*

[29] Australian Foreign Ministry, "Additional sanctions in response to Russia's invasion", https://www.foreignminister.gov.au/minister/marise-payne/media-release/additional-sanctions-response-russias-invasion (4 May 2022).

[30] "G7 Leaders' Statement on Ukraine", https://www.mofa.go.jp/files/100506474.pdf (19 May 2023).

[31] Canadian Office of the Prime Minister, "Canada announces additional measures to support Ukraine", https://www.pm.gc.ca/en/news/news-releases/2022/02/24/canada-announces-additional-measures-support-ukraine (24 February 2022).

[32] Remark by the German Foreign Minister on 17 May 2022, cited in "Geschlossenes Vorgehen gegen Putins Krieg in der Ukraine: Welche Sanktionen sind in Kraft?", https://www.auswaertiges-amt.de/de/aussenpolitik/eu-sanktionen-russland/2515304 (4 June 2022) (translated by the present authors).

[33] For more details about the Russian pretext for the invasion of Ukraine, see Chapters "The War in Ukraine Under International Law: Its Use of Force and Armed Conflict Aspects" and "Use of Force by Russia and *jus ad bellum*" of this volume.

these sanctions in an alternative context: search for power and dominance by the West. For example, in a statement accompanying a counter-sanction, claimed to be in response to "a series of unprecedented sanctions that prohibit, among other things, entry to the United States for top officials of the Russian Federation,"[34] Russia explains that its measure is "the inevitable result of the extreme Russophobic policy of the current US Administration"[35] rather than resulting from the invasion of Ukraine by Russia. Many public statements made by President Vladimir Putin since February 2022 also promote this narrative. In these statements, not once is the war against Ukraine mentioned as a trigger or context of economic sanctions. In one of his public appearances in June 2022, President Putin deplored that "some Western states" have "the irrepressible urge to punish, to economically crush anyone who does not fit with the mainstream, does not want to blindly obey."[36] Having mentioned Yugoslavia, Syria, Libya and Iraq as examples of western bullying, Putin then went on to state that: "[t]his is the nature of the current round of Russophobia in the West, and the insane sanctions against Russia."[37] The same characterisation of the current economic sanctions was later repeated in the 2022 Eastern Economic Forum,

> [...] the pandemic has given way to new challenges, global ones that are threatening the world as a whole. I am referring to the Western sanctions frenzy and the open and aggressive attempts to force the Western mode of behaviour on other countries, to extinguish their sovereignty and to bend them to its will. In fact, there is nothing unusual in that: this policy has been pursued by the "collective West" for decades.[38]

In short, in relation to economic sanctions, the invasion of Ukraine is neither here nor there for Russia.

3.2.2 'Unilateral and Illegal' Economic Sanctions

In his speech to the UN General Assembly in September 2022, the Russian Foreign Minister, Sergey Lavrov, described the economic sanctions as "illegal and unilateral.[39] The combination of the terms 'illegal' and 'unilateral' is a formulation that Russia employs regularly in, both, multilateral[40] and bilateral settings[41] when referring to the current economic sanctions against it. In these instances, presumably,

---

[34] See n 9, Foreign Ministry's Statement concerning Personal Sanctions on US Senior Officials and Affiliated Persons, https://mid.ru/en/foreign_policy/news/1804365/ (15 March 2022).

[35] *Ibid.*

[36] St Petersburg International Economic Forum, Plenary Session, http://en.kremlin.ru/events/president/news/68669 (17 June 2022).

[37] *Ibid.*

[38] Eastern Economic Forum, Plenary Session, http://en.kremlin.ru/events/president/news/69299 (7 September 2022).

[39] "Russia had 'no choice' but to launch 'special military operation' in Ukraine, Lavrov tells UN", *UN News*, https://news.un.org/en/story/2022/09/1127881 (24 September 2022).

[40] *Ibid.*

[41] E.g., "Illegal unilateral sanctions by unfriendly states against Russia", in Russia-Kazakhstan talks: Excerpts from the transcript, http://government.ru/en/news/45564/ (30 May 2022).

it is the legality of the entirety of economic sanctions which is disputed, for no detail is given. When so-called 'counter-sanctions' are enacted by Russia, accompanying explanations also repeat these assessments regarding sanctions packages as a whole. For instance, Russia claims that "the European Union has been carrying on with its policy of imposing unilateral sanctions. Illegitimate in terms of international law, these actions go hand in hand with unprecedented anti-Russia rhetoric."[42] The latest round of EU sanctions[43] is also denounced in its entirety as illegal and unilateral: "On June 23, EU countries passed the 11th package of sanctions against Russia. We believe that these actions by the EU are illegitimate, and that they undermine international law prerogatives of the UN Security Council."[44]

It is to be noted that Russia is not in complete isolation in criticising sanctions in this manner. China's view on these sanctions, and the bases for its criticism, are quite similar. Since February 2022, whenever asked about economic sanctions against Russia, the spokespersons of the Chinese Foreign Ministry have essentially repeated the position that these are "unilateral sanctions that lack the basis of international law"[45] and "unilateral sanctions [...] that have no basis in international law or mandate from the Security Council."[46] Very similar views were expressed by states that voted against the draft resolution of the General Assembly condemning Russian aggression against Ukraine,[47] and abstaining states.[48] Some of the states in favour of the draft resolution also distanced themselves from sanctions without a Security Council mandate[49] or even went so far as to label them illegal.[50]

---

[42] Foreign Ministry's Statement on Russia's Response to the European Union's Decisions on Sanctions, https://mid.ru/en/foreign_policy/news/1828901/ (7 September 2022). The phrase "illegitimate *in terms of international law*" (emphasis added) indicates the legal assessment of the sanctions as illegal.

[43] See Sect. 2.1.

[44] Foreign Ministry's Statement on Retaliatory Measures regarding the EU's Eleventh Package of Anti-Russia Sanctions, https://mid.ru/en/foreign_policy/news/1891827/ (23 June 2023). Regarding the meaning of the term 'illegitimate' in the statement, see n 42.

[45] E.g., Foreign Ministry Spokesperson Wang Wenbin's Regular Press Conference, https://www.fmprc.gov.cn/eng/xwfw_665399/s2510_665401/202202/t20220228_10646378.html (28 February 2022).

[46] E.g., Foreign Ministry Spokesperson Zhao Lijian's Regular Press Conference, https://www.fmprc.gov.cn/mfa_eng/xwfw_665399/s2510_665401/2511_665403/202206/t20220629_1071220 9.html (29 June 2022).

[47] "Eritrea opposes all forms of unilateral sanctions and deems them illegal and counterproductive." U.N. Doc. A/ES-11/PV.5 (2 March 2022), p. 19 (Eritrea).

[48] "The imposition of sanctions and unilateral coercive measures are direct aggressions against peoples [...]", U.N. Doc. A/ES-11/PV15 (14 November 2022), p. 18 (Nicaragua).

[49] "Türkiye supports sanctions if they are mandated by the Security Council", U.N. Doc. A/77/PV.11 (23 September 2022), p. 48 (Türkiye).

[50] "We support all efforts to reduce the economic impact of this crisis, but we do not believe that the best way is to adopt unilateral and selective sanctions that are inconsistent with international law", U.N. Doc. A/77/PV.4 (20 September 2022), p. 10 (Brazil); "[...] all sanctions, other than those approved by the Security Council as part of its actions to preserve peace and security, are illegitimate and contrary to international law", U.N. Doc. A/77/ PV.5 (20 September 2022), p. 16 (Peru).

In addition, Russia is generally hostile towards autonomous sanctions. Its general hostility towards such sanctions is consistent with its criticism of current sanctions against it: the legality of autonomous sanctions is refuted on account of their being unilateral. In a joint statement issued by Russia and China in February 2022, the two expressed their opposition to "power politics, bullying, unilateral sanctions, and extraterritorial application of jurisdiction, as well as the abuse of export control policies" in the context of criticising "attempts to substitute universally recognized formats and mechanisms that are consistent with international law for rules elaborated in private by certain nations or blocs of nations."[51] This echoes earlier concerns expressed in a 2016 joint declaration: "[I]mposition of unilateral coercive measures not based on international law, also known as 'unilateral sanctions'" was criticised as "the practice of double standards or imposition by some States of their will on other States," and was incompatible with "good faith implementation of generally recognized principles and rules of international law."[52] The 2016 joint declaration further clarified that such unilateral sanctions "can defeat the objects and purposes of measures imposed by the Security Council, and undermine their integrity and effectiveness."[53] This may in fact be the most important issue for Russia and China, both being permanent members of the Security Council. Autonomous sanctions are unilateral measures that bypass Security Council oversight.

In short, in these declarations, autonomous economic sanctions are criticised for being unilateral and coercive. The latter element of criticism—that autonomous sanctions constitute illegal economic coercion—is a frequent criticism examined in literature in light of the principle of non-intervention.[54] However, this element is much less prominent than the former element in Russian denunciations of current economic sanctions.[55] Therefore, in the section that follows, the present authors continue to deal with the most persistent element of Russian criticisms against the current sanctions: unilateralism.

---

[51] Joint Statement of the Russian Federation and the People's Republic of China on the International Relations Entering a New Era and the Global Sustainable Development, http://en.kremlin.ru/supplement/5770 (4 February 2022).

[52] Declaration of the Russian Federation and the People's Republic of China on the Promotion of International Law, https://www.mid.ru/en/foreign_policy/news/1530748/ (25 June 2016), and https://www.fmprc.gov.cn/eng/wjdt_665385/2649_665393/201608/t20160801_679466.html (25 June 2016).

[53] *Ibid.*

[54] Natalino Ronzitti, "Coercive Diplomacy, Sanctions and International Law", in Natalino Ronzitti (ed.), *Sanctions as Instruments of Coercive Diplomacy: An International Law Perspective* (2016), pp. 1–9; Jean-Marc Thouvenin, "Sanctions économiques et droit international", 57 *Droits* (2013), pp. 161–175; Nigel White, "Shades of Grey: Autonomous Sanctions in the International Legal Order", in Surya Subedi (ed.), *Unilateral Sanctions in International Law* (2021), pp. 79–82; Daniel H. Joyner, "International Legal Limits on the Ability of States to Lawfully Impose International Economic/Financial Sanctions", in Ali Z. Marossi and Marisa R. Bassett (eds.), *Economic Sanctions under International Law: Unilateralism, Multilateralism, Legitimacy, and Consequences* (2015), pp. 83–93.

[55] See Sect. 3.2.1.

4 Autonomous (Non-UN) Sanctions and Their Justifications

4.1 Two Approaches

If there is anything fundamentally amiss with autonomous economic sanctions, it is that there is no apparent and established legality in such sanctions. On the one hand, prominent commentators conclude that such economic sanctions are not expressly prohibited in international law,[56] while on the other, that neither is there some specific and accepted rule endorsing the right of individual states to impose economic sanctions on other states.[57] Many commentators are weary of endorsing some perceived right to adopt autonomous economic sanctions,[58] especially when economic measures by a powerful state against a small state can easily be economic coercion. Against this background, the literature that examines the legality of economic sanctions generally comprises the following two potential approaches to justifications: collective sanctions under the auspices of the UN or countermeasures by individual states.[59] The outline of the two approaches follows.

In light of the history of sanctions in international law, when there was neither an international organisation nor any form of centralisation in the international community, the only measure that could be called a sanction against an illegal action by some state was a unilateral measure of 'self-help' by a victim state. As the international community became more organised, self-help measures by victim states and collective sanctions—typically decided by international organisations—against the illegal actions of states, became two distinct legal concepts. On the one hand, self-help measures by individual states may be justified and as such remain legitimate

---

[56] Olivier Corten et al., *Critical Introduction to International Law* (2017), p. 161; Thouvenin (n 54), pp. 171–172.

[57] There is "no unilateral form of autonomous sanctioning power belonging to states," and autonomous sanctions are simply "unlawful acts of coercion." White (n 54), p. 80 (though such sanctions may still be justified as third-party countermeasures (*Ibid.*)).

[58] Alexandra Hofer, "The Proportionality of Unilateral 'Targeted' Sanctions: Whose Interests Should Count?", 89(3–4) *Nordic Journal of International Law* (2020), p. 410, footnote 52; Devika Hovell, "Unfinished Business of International Law: The Questionable Legality of Autonomous Sanctions", 113 *AJIL Unbound* (2019), p. 144.

[59] Ronzitti (n 54), pp. 9–14; Alexandra Hofer, "Unilateral Sanctions as a Challenge to the Law of State Responsibility", in Charlotte Beaucillon (ed.), *Research Handbook on Unilateral and Extraterritorial Sanctions* (2021), pp. 186–189; White (n 54), pp. 64–67. In addition, in the context of Russia's aggression against Ukraine, a number of authors discuss the right to collective self-defence as another possible legal basis to justify economic sanctions that are otherwise unjustified. Matthias Goldmann, "Hot War and Cold Freezes: Targeting Russian Central Bank Assets", *VerfassungsBlog*, https://verfassungsblog.de/hot-war-and-cold-freezes/ (28 February 2022); Valentin von Stosch, "Targeting the Assets of the Russian Central Bank: Self-Defense as (Another) Avenue?", *Völkerrechtsblog*, https://voelkerrechtsblog.org/targeting-the-assets-of-the-russian-central-bank/ (22 April 2024). See, more generally, Russell Buchan, "Non-Forcible Measures and the Law of Self-Defence", 72(1) *International and Comparative Law Quarterly* (2023), especially pp. 17–19.

means/countermeasures: an illegal measure against a wrongdoing state, which, when a number of conditions are satisfied, is justified. In that sense, countermeasures are legally permissible, and are considered legitimate even when unilaterally decided and imposed; they are a measure carried out in accordance with secondary rules in the law of state responsibility. An injured state's right to take countermeasures is well-established in international law.[60]

At the other end of the spectrum, so-called sanctions decided by the UN Security Council are also considered legitimate and legal. Such sanctions are decided by the Security Council in light of "the existence of any threat to the peace, breach of the peace, or act of aggression."[61] Economic sanctions decided by the Security Council are lawful so long as these are consistent with its powers as established by the UN Charter and accepted by UN member states. In fact, when UN member states adopt economic sanctions pursuant to some binding Security Council resolution, they are exonerated from the legal consequences of conflict between their obligations to enforce such resolutions and their obligations under any other international agreement.[62] It is also apparent that economic sanctions decided by the Security Council obtain the kind of political legitimacy that unilateral sanctions lack.

Autonomous economic sanctions, such as those under review in this article, appear to possess neither:[63] that is to say, they are not legitimate or legal in the way the UN sanctions are, and they are not legitimate or legal in the way countermeasures are, either. The legitimacy of UN sanctions derives from the collective nature of deliberations and decision-making within an international organisation. Their legality derives from the way the UN Charter formulates the powers of the Security Council. Countermeasures may be accepted as actions within the law and legitimate by the international community, even though such measures are unilaterally decided. Autonomous economic sanctions do not appear to be akin to either type of measures. On the one hand, autonomous economic sanctions are not enacted pursuant to Security Council resolutions demanding such measures, while, on the other, they are often enacted by states other than victim states and, therefore, outside the sense of the term 'injured states' entitled to take countermeasures within the context of the law on state responsibility.

Against this backdrop and the ambiguity surrounding questions of legality and legitimacy, the default position could well be that current autonomous actions against Russia are "unilateral and illegal,"[64] unless it could be persuasively argued that they are lawful and legitimate. The literature outlined above suggests that there

---

[60] E.g. *Gabčíkovo-Nagymaros Project (Hungary/Slovakia)* (25 September 1997), paras. 82–84.

[61] Art. 39, UN Charter. The threat to the peace and the breach of the peace determined by the Security Council may or may not involve violations of international law. When they do, measures decided by the Security Council are collective sanctions, in the narrow sense of the term 'sanction.' Asada (n 1), p. 4.

[62] Art. 103, UN Charter.

[63] See White (n 54), pp. 66–67.

[64] See Sect. 3.2.2.

are two approaches at play. As it was shown previously, the main component of Russian objections is that measures adopted as economic sanctions are unilateral.[65] The former approach to counter such objections, accordingly, is to show that measures are not as unilateral as they may appear. The present authors will refer to this approach as an assimilation of autonomous economic sanctions to UN sanctions. The latter approach is to accept the unilateral character of the economic sanctions, but to argue that certain categories of unilateral measures are permissible in exceptional circumstances. While the basic idea is that of countermeasures, in the present context, the latter approach would still need to grapple with the issue of 'third-party' countermeasures.

4.2 Assimilation of Autonomous Economic Sanctions to UN (Collective) Sanctions

As described earlier, the main component of Russian objections towards autonomous sanctions against it is that they are unilateral. One logical way to counter such objections is to demonstrate that such sanctions are not as unilateral as they are made to appear. In other words, the attempt is to present these sanctions as collective sanctions of the UN, by scrutinising what is said and done in the UN. An idea in line with this approach, for example, is to turn to a vetoed Security Council resolution, that is, "the 'near-decision' of the Security Council" or "an 'almost adopted' decision of the UN Security Council"[66] as potential justification of autonomous economic sanctions.

Another study that takes up this approach zooms in on adopted resolutions even when these are not expressly about economic sanctions; it discusses two resolutions in two different cases, in an attempt to show that sanctions in these instances were in fact 'collective' sanctions—sanctions based on the international authority of the UN—and not unilateral: the Security Council resolution against Argentina regarding the Falkland Islands (Islas Malvinas) (1982) and the General Assembly resolution regarding the military intervention in Afghanistan (1980).[67] In the former case, when

---

[65] See Sect. 3.2.2.

[66] Jean-Marc Thouvenin, "Articulating UN Sanctions with Unilateral Restrictive Measures", in Charlotte Beaucillon (ed.), *Research Handbook on Unilateral and Extraterritorial Sanctions* (2021), p. 162. In exploring this idea, Thouvenin does recognise that "it goes without saying that an 'almost adopted' decision of the UN Security Council cannot have the same legal effect as an adopted decision." (*Ibid.*)

[67] Paola Gaeta, Jorge E. Viñuales and Salvatore Zappalà (eds.), *Cassese's International Law* (2020), p. 307. Note that the economic sanctions in both of these cases are treated as autonomous sanctions by the majority of authors, and not collective sanctions as is argued by these writers. E.g., Christian Tams, *Enforcing Obligations* Erga Omnes *in International Law* (2005), pp. 215–216 (measures against Argentina); Thouvenin (n 7), p. 88 (measures against Afghanistan) and p. 89 (measures against Argentina); Martin Dawidowicz, *Third-Party Countermeasures in International Law* (2017), pp. 127–132 (measures against Afghanistan) and pp. 140–149 (measures against Argentina).

Argentina started its military operations regarding the Falkland Islands, the UN Security Council adopted a resolution that determined these actions to be "a breach of the peace,"[68] demanding the withdrawal of the Argentinian armed forces.[69] About a week later, the EC member states not only suspended their export of arms and other military materials to Argentina, but also decided to implement a general import ban from Argentina.[70] The contention of the study mentioned in the foregoing is that the resolution in question, Resolution 502, "can be considered *sufficient international authority* for imposing economic sanctions on that country [Argentina]."[71]

The discussion of the economic sanctions in the latter case[72] regarding the invasion of Afghanistan follows a similar characterisation, albeit in relation to a General Assembly resolution,

> In the case of Afghanistan, the resolution adopted by the UN General Assembly by a very large majority, on 14 January 1980 (resolution ES-6/2), "deploring" the "armed intervention in Afghanistan as being contrary to the fundamental principle of respect for sovereignty, territorial integrity and political independence of States" (the USSR, however, was not named), *can be regarded as warranting* the economic sanctions taken by individual States or a group of States.[73]

Assimilating autonomous economic sanctions to collective sanctions can be quite attractive to individual states and groups of states that impose economic sanctions. However, there is an apparent problem. In the two cases in support of this approach, the resolutions cited do not refer to any economic sanctions. Even so, states that opted for economic sanctions could certainly claim, if criticised, that the political legitimacy of such sanctions flows from relevant resolutions. Nevertheless, is it right to claim in terms of the law that these sanctions are collective sanctions, just like UN sanctions expressly provided for by the wording of resolutions?[74] It would be tantamount to a claim that a resolution which recommends trade restrictions and a resolution which does not do so have identical legal effects on trade restrictions

---

[68] U.N. Doc. S/RES/502 (3 April 1982).

[69] *Ibid.*, operative paragraph 2.

[70] Canada and Australia also adopted similar economic sanctions against Argentina, though not mentioned in Gaeta et al. (n 67), p. 307. For more detailed descriptions of the case, see Tams (n 67), pp. 215–216 and Dawidowicz (n 67), pp. 140–149.

[71] Gaeta et al. (n 67), p. 307, (emphasis added).

[72] For a more detailed description of the case, e.g. Dawidowicz (n 67), pp. 127–132.

[73] Gaeta et al. (n 67), p. 307, (emphasis added).

[74] Well-known examples of resolutions which are explicitly about economic sanctions include the resolution establishing economic sanctions against Iraq in 1990, stating "all States shall prevent: (a) The import into their territories of all commodities and products" from specific states (U.N. Doc. S/RES/661 (6 August 1990)) and the resolution establishing an arms embargo against Libya in 2011, stating "all Member States shall immediately take the necessary measures to prevent the direct or indirect supply, sale or transfer" of "arms and related materiel of all types" (U.N. Doc. S/RES/1970 (26 February 2011)). For a short list of typical examples, see Thouvenin (n 7), pp. 86–87.

imposed by UN member states. This, the present authors assert, is taking too much out of a resolution that is silent with respect to economic sanctions.

With this issue of law in mind, let us leave the Falkland Islands and Afghanistan, and examine the resolutions of our case at hand: the Russian invasion of Ukraine. The Security Council has yet to adopt any resolution condemning the Russian invasion of Ukraine,[75] let alone adopt one demanding the implementation of economic sanctions. There are, however, General Assembly resolutions that are relevant to the case at hand. The first resolution adopted in an emergency session of the General Assembly after the start of the invasion deplored "in the strongest terms the aggression by the Russian Federation against Ukraine in violation of Article 2 (4) of the Charter."[76]

There is certainly a technical issue when examining the chronology. While the first resolution condemning the Russian invasion was adopted on 2 March 2022,[77] many states and the EU had announced their economic sanctions against Russia prior to that. Thus, to claim that those initial rounds of economic sanctions had been based on, and subsequent to, a resolution is factually false. That being said, the determination that there was aggression in breach of the most fundamental rule of the UN Charter was made beyond any doubt by the resolution in question, and was supported by a very large majority of states.[78] While this does not turn autonomous sanctions into collective sanctions, those UN member states that have imposed economic sanctions against Russia could seek to rely on this resolution as a source of political legitimacy in their attempts to justify their actions.

There remains a question to be considered: if particular measures within sanctions packages are criticised as illegal, are General Assembly resolutions that condemn Russian aggression but which fall short of recommending sanctions, capable of offering justification for such measures? The answer seems to be no, on two accounts. First, in the case of conflict between the UN Charter obligations and obligations under any other international agreement, "obligations under the present Charter shall prevail."[79] However, General Assembly resolutions are generally hortative in nature and do not impose obligations on UN member states. Consequently, no normative conflict arises between obligations flowing from an international agreement and the contents of UN General Assembly resolutions, and therefore not even the prospect of this type of exoneration comes into play. Second, and more importantly, the General Assembly resolutions in question do not even contemplate, let alone recommend, sanctions. Recall a similar characteristic in the

---

[75] The draft resolution which "deplores in the strongest terms the Russian Federation's aggression against Ukraine in violation of Article 2, paragraph 4 of the United Nations Charter" (U.N. Doc. S/2022/155 (February 2022))—vetoed by Russia—was not adopted in the event. The Security Council resolution regarding the Falkland Islands (U.N. Doc. S/RES/502 (3 April 1982))—spearheaded by the United Kingdom—was successfully adopted.

[76] U.N. Doc. A/ES-11/1 (2 March 2022).

[77] *Ibid.*

[78] See n 5.

[79] Art. 103, UN Charter.

two resolutions discussed earlier: one concerning the Falkland Islands by the Security Council and the other concerning Afghanistan by the General Assembly. Neither the term 'economic sanctions' nor analogous terms appear in these resolutions. It was the same with the General Assembly resolution of 2 March 2022 condemning the Russian invasion. There was no explicit recommendation or mention of trade restrictions or travel bans for UN member states to implement. While isolated remarks mentioning economic sanctions were made during deliberations, this neither generated discussion on sanctions nor led to any conclusion about sanctions: a few states referred to the economic measures they had taken so far,[80] while others were critical of sanctions not mandated by the Security Council.[81] Mentions of economic sanctions continued to be absent from subsequent General Assembly resolutions which, nevertheless, continued to condemn Russian aggression.[82]

In light of these observations, it is submitted that the General Assembly resolutions pertaining to Russian aggression cannot justify any particular measure, within a sanctions package, that is illegal. A remedy would need to be found on some other grounds. This is among the reasons for the next section on the examination of countermeasures.

4.3 Autonomous Economic Sanctions as 'Third-Party Countermeasures'

The latter approach to the question of legitimacy and legality of autonomous sanctions is in sharp contrast to the former approach: namely, the acceptance of the unilateral character of such measures. It is to claim that these sanctions, even when involving illegal actions (Sect. 4.3.1), amount to 'countermeasures' taken in response to violations of international law. In addition, in the case of sanctions against Russia, it is necessary to discuss a particular type of countermeasures: 'third-party' countermeasures (Sect. 4.3.2).

4.3.1 Legality of Individual Measures Against Russia

In theory, any sanctions packages against Russia can be divided into acts that are not prohibited under international law, that is, they are within the discretion of states, and acts that are prohibited under international law. As an example of the former, airspace closures and travel bans are measures within the discretion of states and

---

[80] U.N. Doc. A/ES-11/PV.1 (28 February 2022).

[81] See n 47–50, Sect. 3.2.

[82] See, notably, U.N. Doc. A/RES/ES-11/2 (24 March 2022) and U.N. Doc. A/ES-11/5 (14 November 2022).

Economic Sanctions Against Russia: Questions of Legality and Legitimacy 127

do not involve violations of international rules, unless some applicable international agreements state otherwise. These unfriendly but lawful measures are known as retorsion, and, by definition, need no justification for their legality. In contrast, there are other measures that, again in theory, may violate international rules. It is for this latter group of measures that a justification, in the form of countermeasures, is needed.

It should be noted that while it is far from straightforward to indicate that a measure in the sanctions packages bears clear and uncontested illegality, potential candidates may be identified in the field of trade. Trade restrictions on certain goods and services may deprive Russia, as WTO member, of the Most-Favoured-Nation (MFN) treatment it enjoys within the WTO, and may constitute violations of, among other things, Article 1 of GATT. In fact, the Russian ambassador to the WTO has claimed that restrictions targeting Russian companies are illegal measures in contravention of WTO rules.[83] However, as the EU notes in its sanctions guidelines mentioned earlier, trade restrictions may be permissible under GATT if they fall within its security exceptions (e.g. GATT Article XXI) or general exceptions (e.g. GATT Article XX).[84]

Another type of measure, frequently discussed in relation to current economic sanctions that may violate international law is the freezing of the assets of the Russian Central Bank as well as the assets of the incumbent president and ministers. It has been pointed out that the freezing of assets of the Russian Central Bank violates the rules of immunity and inviolability.[85] Several scholarly works indeed view that freezing bank accounts belonging to foreign state organs, including central banks, in the general context of economic sanctions contravenes international rules governing the immunity and inviolability of foreign states.[86] However, as immunity rules have historically functioned to shield such assets from judicial jurisdiction in the context of court proceedings on foreign soil, it is not immediately clear whether these rules also apply to asset freezes in the context of economic sanctions as

---

[83] Bryce Baschuk, "Russia Lashes Out at the WTO for 'Illegal' Trade Curbs", *Bloomberg News*, https://www.bloomberg.com/news/newsletters/2023-03-08/supply-chain-latest-russia-blasts-the-west-for-illegal-trade-curbs (8 March 2023). The same evaluation is reportedly shared by President Putin. "Putin instructs government to assess actions taken against Russia in WTO", *Reuters*, https://www.reuters.com/world/putin-instructs-government-assess-actions-taken-against-russia-wto-2022-05-20/ (20 May 2022).

[84] For more detailed analyses of WTO security exceptions, see Chapters "Trade Sanctions Against Russia and Their WTO Consistency: Focusing on Justification Under National Security Exceptions" and "WTO Dispute Settlement and Trade Sanctions as Permissible Third-Party Countermeasures Under Customary International Law" of this volume.

[85] For a focused analysis of Russian Central Bank and oligarch assets, see the next chapter of this volume.

[86] Jean-Marc Thouvenin and Victor Grandaubert, "The Material Scope of State Immunity from Execution", in Tom Ruys, Nicolas Angelet and Luca Ferro (eds.), *The Cambridge Handbook of Immunities and International Law* (2019), pp. 250–252; Emanuel Castellarin, "Le gel des avoirs d'une banque centrale étrangère comme réaction décentralisée à un fait internationalement illicite : rétorsion ou contremesure ?", 25 *Annuaire de La Haye de Droit International* (2012), pp. 8–19.

executive actions unrelated to court proceedings.[87] Indeed, many states that impose sanctions resort to asset freezes, occasionally freezing the assets of central banks without showing much concern about the lawfulness of such measures.[88] In the present case under examination, in alignment with other like-minded states, the EU initiated the freezing of assets, encompassing those of the Russian Central Bank worth approximately EUR 300 billion.[89] Yet, in a striking contrast to a high profile legal consideration in a case of confiscation, it is not clear whether there were considerations of the potential legal risks of this asset freeze. The target state, Russia, also seems much less vocal about its legal position on this asset freeze than it is, for example, about WTO-related trade restrictions.

In contrast, taking a further step—going from a temporary freezing of an asset to its confiscation—raises a number of legal concerns, not just for lawyers but also for the states imposing such sanctions. The plan that raised these concerns pertains to confiscating assets and either transferring them directly, or using the revenue they generate, to finance Ukraine's reconstruction.[90] Initially, both the EU and the US publicly acknowledged that there were legal and political obstacles to such

---

[87] Ruys observes that while regulations governing state immunity necessitate a link with judicial proceedings, the concept of inviolability does not uniformly demand such a connection. Nonetheless, he confirms the absence of customary law that generally grants inviolability to a state's foreign assets, except in the case of specific state assets such as diplomatic property. Tom Ruys, "Immunity, Inviolability and Countermeasures – a Closer Look at Non-UN Targeted Sanctions", in Tom Ruys, Nicolas Angelet and Luca Ferro (eds.), *The Cambridge Handbook of Immunities and International Law* (2019), pp. 670–710. See also Ingrid (Wuerth) Brunk, "Does Foreign Sovereign Immunity Apply to Sanctions on Central Banks?", *Lawfare*, https://www.lawfaremedia.org/article/does-foreign-sovereign-immunity-apply-sanctions-central-banks (7 March 2022). Conversely, notable criticism arises from the ambiguity surrounding the demarcation between judicial and executive actions, coupled with the inapplicability of customary immunity rules to executive measures, even in the absence of judicial scrutiny. Such discrimination could be perceived as absurd. Daniel Franchini, "Ukraine Symposium – Seizure of Russian State Assets: State Immunity and Countermeasures", *Articles of War* (Lieber Institute), https://lieber.westpoint.edu/seizure-russian-state-assets-state-immunity-countermeasures/ (8 March 2023); Menno T. Kamminga, "Confiscating Russia's Frozen Central Bank Assets: A Permissible Third-Party Countermeasure?", 70-(1) *Netherlands International Law Review* (2023), p. 6. The difference between these views may be, after all, whether conventional laws on immunity and inviolability with limited scopes imply or exclude a customary rule of a more general scope. This divergence of opinion can be seen in the respective statements of parties to the dispute in ICJ proceedings on *Questions relating to the Seizure and Detention of Certain Documents and Data (Timor-Leste v. Australia)*. See Ruys (2019) cited earlier in this note, pp. 681–683, 699–700.

[88] Ruys (n 87), pp. 674–675; Ingrid W. Brunk, "Central Bank Immunity, Sanctions, and Sovereign Wealth Funds", 91 *George Washington Law Review* (2023), pp. 1632–1634.

[89] Statement by President von der Leyen on Russian Accountability and the Use of Russian Frozen Assets, https://ec.europa.eu/commission/presscorner/detail/en/statement_22_7307 (30 November 2022).

[90] Eamonn Noonan, "Confiscating Russian Sovereign Assets to Fund Ukraine's Reconstruction: Mission Impossible?", *European Parliamentary Research Service*, https://www.europarl.europa.eu/thinktank/en/document/EPRS_ATA(2022)738180 (25 October 2022).

Economic Sanctions Against Russia: Questions of Legality and Legitimacy

measures: such concerns were promptly picked up by the media[91] including legal blogs.[92] The US position has evolved, however, and as of this writing, it considers that confiscation of Russian sovereign assets is "justifiable" under international law.[93] European states are reportedly still sceptical, and therefore cautious towards the confiscation.[94]

In addition, the asset freeze of the incumbent Head of State and the foreign minister touches upon yet another aspect of the controversy. The targeted assets in question are the overseas personal assets of President Putin, Foreign Minister Lavrov and others.[95] Whether an executive measure, unrelated to a judicial proceeding, that freezes a personal bank account and other types of personal assets of an incumbent Head of State or an incumbent foreign minister violates the rules of immunity also remains unclear. Again, the literature is divided in its assessment of the relevant 2001 resolution of the *Institut de droit international*,[96] and of the current status of the applicable rules.[97]

---

[91] Paola Tamma, "Ballsy EU Commission moves to make Russia pay for Ukraine", *Politico*, https://www.politico.eu/article/brussels-to-go-after-russian-frozen-foreign-reserves/ (21 June 2023).

[92] Scott R. Anderson and Chemène Keitner, "The Legal Challenges Presented by Seizing Frozen Russian Assets", *Lawfare*, https://www.lawfaremedia.org/article/legal-challenges-presented-seizing-frozen-russian-assets (26 May 2022); Robert Currie, "Seizing Russian Assets: Canada has the Spirit of International Law on its Side", *Opinion* (World Refugee & Migration Council), https://wrmcouncil.org/news/opinion/seizing-russian-assets-canada-has-the-spirit-of-international-law-on-its-side/ (5 July 2022); Anton Moiseienko, International Lawyers Project, and Spotlight on Corruption, "Frozen Russian Assets and the Reconstruction of Ukraine: Legal Options", *World Refugee & Migration Council Research Paper*, https://www.wrmcouncil.org/wp-content/uploads/2022/07/Frozen-Russian-Assets-Ukraine-Legal-Options-Report-WRMC-July2022.pdf (July 2022); Anton Moiseienko, "Politics, Not Law, Is Key to Confiscating Russian Central Bank Assets", *Just Security*, https://www.justsecurity.org/82712/politics-not-law-is-key-to-confiscating-russian-central-bank-assets/ (17 August 2022).

[93] The reported remark of the US Secretary of the Treasury is "I believe that based on international law and other factors that outright seizure of the assets is justifiable." Christopher Condon, "Yellen Says G-7 Can Borrow Against Russian Assets", *Bloomberg News*, https://news.bloomberglaw.com/banking-law/yellen-says-g-7-can-borrow-against-income-of-russian-assets (26 April 2024). See also Ingrid (Wuerth) Brunk, "The Controversial REPO Act Is Now Law", *Lawfare*, https://www.lawfaremedia.org/article/the-controversial-repo-act-is-now-law (25 April 2024).

[94] Laura Gozzi, "EU moves to give profits from Russian assets to Ukraine", *BBC News*, https://www.bbc.com/news/articles/c4n1y9zz8ydo (9 May 2024); Philippe Escande, "Actifs russes gelés : « Les Européens ont arbitré avec le plus de prudence possible »", *Le Monde*, https://www.lemonde.fr/economie/article/2024/05/09/actifs-russes-geles-les-europeens-ont-arbitre-avec-le-plus-de-prudence-possible_6232337_3234.html (9 May 2024).

[95] E.g., US Department of the Treasury, "U.S. Treasury Imposes Sanctions on Russian Federation President Vladimir Putin and Minister of Foreign Affairs Sergei Lavrov", https://home.treasury.gov/news/press-releases/jy0610 (25 February 2022). On the same measure, see also a press statement by the U.S. Department of State (n 8).

[96] See sceptical views on the authority of Article 4 of the Resolution on the Immunities of Heads of State and Government of the *Institut*, e.g. in Hazel Fox, "The Resolution of the Institute of International Law on the Immunities of Heads of State and Government", 51 *International and Comparative Law Quarterly* (2002), p. 125; Ruys (n 87), pp. 694–695.

[97] Thouvenin (n 54), pp. 161–175; Joanne Foakes, *The Position of Heads of State and Senior Officials in International Law* (2014).

Be that as it may, for the purposes of this article, it suffices to show that the legality of certain measures in economic sanctions packages is less firmly established than it is generally assumed for the entire packages by states imposing such sanctions. Consequently, there is room, to discuss the justification for specific measures taken within the framework of autonomous economic sanctions against Russia. This brings us to the discussion on justifications provided by circumstances precluding wrongfulness, in particular, countermeasures.

4.3.2 Justification by 'Third-Party Countermeasures'

Although some of the economic and diplomatic measures discussed in the foregoing may potentially run counter to the rules agreed between Russia and the states that impose these sanctions, it has been argued that the latter may justify their actions by invoking their right to countermeasures under general international law.[98] Much commentary on the confiscation of the assets of the Russian Central Bank, for example, takes the position that even where an executive measure violates the rules of immunity and inviolability, it may be justified as countermeasures.[99]

Nonetheless, the acceptability of this legal justification within the international community needs re-examination for the following reason: the established customary rule is that an injured state is entitled to take countermeasures against a wrongdoing state.[100] Ukraine has been directly injured by the aggression on the part of Russia, while the US, the United Kingdom, EU member states and other states that have imposed sanctions are not. Article 42(b) of the Draft Articles on State Responsibility (ARSIWA)[101] by International Law Commission (ILC) extends the concept of 'injured state' eligible to take countermeasures by recognising that multiple states

---

[98] For a focused analysis of the justification of WTO-related measures as countermeasures, see Chapters "Trade Sanctions Against Russia and Their WTO Consistency: Focusing on Justification Under National Security Exceptions" and "WTO Dispute Settlement and Trade Sanctions as Permissible Third-Party Countermeasures Under Customary International Law" of this volume (n 84).

[99] E.g., Anderson and Keitner (n 92); Currie (n 92); Moiseienko et al (n 92); Moiseienko (n 92); Paul B. Stephan, "Seizing Russian Assets", 17(3) *Capital Markets Law Journal* (2022), pp. 285–286; Ingrid (Wuerth) Brunk, "Countermeasures and the Confiscation of Russian Central Bank Assets", *Lawfare*, https://www.lawfaremedia.org/article/countermeasures-and-the-confiscation-of-russian-central-bank-assets (3 May 2023); Paul R. Williams and Alexandra Koch, "Invoicing Russia for Ukraine's Recovery: The Complexities of Repurposing Frozen Russian Assets", *Opinio Juris*, http://opiniojuris.org/2023/05/12/invoicing-russia-for-ukraines-recovery-the-complexities-of-repurposing-frozen-russian-assets/ (12 May 2023).

[100] See Sect. 4.1. As a recent case where a state explicitly referred to countermeasures in response to violations of mutual obligations, see U.S. Department of State, "U.S. Countermeasures in Response to Russia's Violations of the New START Treaty", https://www.state.gov/u-s-countermeasures-in-response-to-russias-violations-of-the-new-start-treaty/ (1 June 2023).

[101] International Law Commission, "Draft Articles on Responsibility of States for Internationally Wrongful Acts, with Commentaries" [hereinafter ARSIWA], *Yearbook of the International Law Commission* (2001), vol. II, Part Two.

may be considered 'injured' when an obligation owed to "a group of States including that State, or the international community as a whole"[102] is violated. To qualify as an injured state, however, it is also required that the violation "specially affects that State" or "is of such a character as radically to change the position of all the other States to which the obligation is owed with respect to the further performance of the obligation."[103]

In the case under examination, the prohibition of aggression and other obligations under, among other things, international humanitarian law, which Russia has been accused of violating, are clearly of a so-called *erga omnes* nature, described as the first component of Article 42(b), cited above. However, it can neither be said that the states imposing sanctions have been specially affected by Russia's violations of these obligations nor that its violations have radically changed the position of these states regarding their further performance of these obligations. Accordingly, for the purpose of providing a legal justification to the economic sanctions' individual measures, this particular provision—or, rather, the customary law norm this draft provision is taken to mirror—is of limited use.

The ILC Draft Articles further provide that states other than an injured state may play a role in coaxing the wrongdoing state to discharge its responsibility in case of breaches of obligations protecting collective interests or obligations owed to the international community as a whole.[104] The viable claims these states may pursue in invoking responsibility are limited, and exhaustively listed.[105] Regarding the most important question, for the purposes of this article, namely, whether third parties are also entitled to take countermeasures, the ILC in its Draft Articles refrains from affirming this. The accompanying commentary attributes the reservation surrounding this issue to the fact that the evidence from state practice regarding the right of third-party countermeasures was "limited and rather embryonic."[106]

As a question of legal policy, advantages and disadvantages of establishing a right of a state other than an injured state to take countermeasures are apparent. Those in favour argue that it safeguards common interests in the international community.[107] Conversely, opponents are worried that the right of third-party countermeasures can justify unlawful actions arbitrarily undertaken by any state, free from control and oversight by international authorities: the risk of abuse is simply too great.[108] Setting aside this legal policy debate, several studies conducted after the 2001 ILC Draft Articles with a focus on state practice contend that the precedents involving the right of third-party countermeasures are no longer limited

---

[102] ARSIWA, Article 42(b).

[103] *Ibid.*

[104] ARSIWA, Article 48(1).

[105] ARSIWA, Article 48(2), and the commentary of this provision (para.11).

[106] ARSIWA, Article 54, and the commentary of this provision (para. 3).

[107] Dawidowicz (n 67), p. 3.

[108] Topical Summary of the Discussion Held in the Sixth Committee of the General Assembly during its Fifty-fifth Session, UN Doc. A/CN.4/513, paras. 174–175.

nor embryonic; this right has already been established.[109] In reaching this conclusion, such studies assess numerous instances involving autonomous sanctions, showcasing these as samples of third-party countermeasures.

However, the conclusion drawn from these case studies remains the subject of debate on several fronts. Despite the view that third-party countermeasures already represent widespread state practice, it has been observed, no doubt correctly, that autonomous economic sanctions against states violating *erga omnes* obligations have been implemented almost exclusively by the West.[110] This pattern is also evident in the current instance. Even in the face of blatant and full-scale aggression and of greater support on the part of states for current sanctions than of sanctions at the time of the annexation of Crimea, states imposing sanctions are predominantly member states of the North Atlantic Treaty Organization (NATO) and their allies.[111] It would be premature to assert that legal entitlement to autonomous sanctions is universally and unequivocally accepted, considering the persistent resistance and objection towards autonomous sanctions.[112] In the present case, too, there are states other than Russia that have deemed these sanctions illegal.[113]

Besides the tendency of states to impose autonomous sanctions with partisan inclinations and the opposition of certain states to this practice, the following question remains regarding the nature of this practice: do cases involving autonomous sanctions imply the right to implement third-party countermeasures? Even when a targeted state claims that imposed sanctions are illegal, as is the case with Russia which contends that these sanctions violate WTO law, the imposing states accused of such violations typically refrain from referring to their sanctions as countermeasures.[114] Admittedly, invoking countermeasures presupposes the illegality of sanctions; states are unlikely to be willing to admit that their sanctions are illegal.[115] Consequently, it may be argued that even in the absence of official state declarations labelling sanctions as countermeasures, the accumulation of cases involving autonomous sanctions can establish customary law regarding third-party countermeasures. The contention is that while states that take such action believe this to be lawful, some measures taken as autonomous sanctions are actually illegal and should be justified as countermeasures.[116] Meanwhile, others argue that the

---

[109] E.g., Tams (n 67), pp. 228–241; Dawidowicz (n 67), pp. 239–284.

[110] E.g. Erpelding (n 4), pp. 96–97.

[111] See the list of unfriendly countries and territories drawn up by Russia, that basically lists the states which imposed sanctions against Russia. "The Government approves the list of unfriendly countries and territories", http://government.ru/en/docs/44745/ (7 March 2022).

[112] Hofer (n 23), pp. 204–211.

[113] See n 45–50, Sect. 3.2.

[114] James Crawford, Third Report on State Responsibility, U.N. Doc. A/CN.4/507 and Add. 1–4, para. 396.

[115] Nonetheless, there are also examples of states explicitly invoking countermeasures in bilateral settings. E.g., U.S. Department of State, "U.S. Countermeasures in Response to Russia's Violations of the New START Treaty" (n 100).

[116] Dawidowicz (n 67), p. 252.

measures in question may be compatible with applicable rules.[117] This difference in legal assessment is inevitable because, as discussed earlier, the illegality of such measures is not clearly established.

Due to differing perspectives on the legal assessment of measures within autonomous sanctions, there is no consensus on whether the international community already recognises the right to third-party countermeasures.[118] In this context, the following remark by Focarelli provides valuable insight: preference for third-party countermeasures is "a 'self-fulfilling prophecy': the more we say that TPCs [third-party countermeasures] are lawful, the more it becomes likely that TPCs will be lawful because every relevant actor will think that this is what everybody 'objectively' supports."[119]

How can this discussion on third-party countermeasures contribute to clarifying the legality of autonomous sanctions imposed on Russia? On the one hand, were we to embrace the right of third parties to take countermeasures, the current sanctions against Russia could be evaluated as third-party countermeasures, in that states, other than the injured state, including the US, the United Kingdom and EU member states have all vehemently condemned Russian aggression as a violation of international law, followed by implementing sanctions packages that include potentially illegal measures in response. It is indeed a model scenario for third-party countermeasures.

On the other hand, however, some facts of the case under examination militate against such a position. On occasions where states imposing sanctions had identified legal concerns associated with particular measures, they have refrained from adopting such potentially illegal measures. This cautious approach was witnessed concerning the confiscation of frozen assets of specific entities, as discussed earlier. In theory, such caution towards potential illegality is redundant, if a state intends to justify any such measures as countermeasures.

To sum up, there is scholarly tendency towards justifying economic sanctions against Russia, including asset confiscation, by reference to the notion of third-party countermeasures.[120] This suggests that the 'self-fulfilling prophecy' in the remark of

---

[117]Ruys (n 87), pp. 708–709; Brunk (n 88), pp. 14–23.

[118]Hofer points out that "[t]he debate is, therefore, methodological as it concerns a discussion on how State practice should be analyzed and interpreted." Hofer (n 11), pp. 97–98. See also Tom Ruys, "Sanctions, Retortions and Countermeasures: Concepts and International Legal Framework", in Larissa van den Herik (ed.), *Research Handbook on UN Sanctions and International Law* (2017), pp. 46–48.

[119]Carlo Focarelli, "Zoom In: International Law and Third-Party Countermeasures in the Age of Global Instant Communication", 29 *Questions of International Law* (2016), pp. 23–24.

[120]In order to justify sanctions against Russia as third-party countermeasures, further examination is necessary. Established countermeasures have a few requirements to fulfil, and third-party countermeasures are likely to be—though not established, since the concept itself is not unequivocally established—also subject to the same requirements. The confiscation of assets and their use to compensate Ukraine seem unable to satisfy the following requirements of countermeasures: countermeasures are "taken with a view to procuring the cessation of and reparation for the internationally wrongful act and not by way of punishment"; "they are temporary in character

Focarelli is indeed gaining momentum. However, as head-on and persistent objections to the legality of autonomous sanctions cannot be ignored, and as no straightforward claims of countermeasures have been made by sanctioning states, it cannot definitively be asserted that the prophecy is now fulfilled.

5 Conclusion

Russia's official pretext for the invasion of Ukraine is that it is simply a 'special military operation,' which, presumably, also means Russia should not be a target of economic sanctions in the first place. Against this background, one is tempted to retort that economic sanctions against Russia equally constitute a 'special economic operation' that need no justification. Nevertheless, justifications to autonomous economic sanctions matter. Concretely, the legality of measures within sanctions packages would be a crucial question in any legal proceedings, if the complainant were to contend that they are illegal. The legitimacy of sanctions, in addition to the question of legality, also matters, not least because the effectiveness of many measures rests on removing all scope for evasion. It rests on solidarity in the international community. If these sanctions were to be seen as lacking legitimacy or legality, it would simply be harder to convince reluctant states to join in on these efforts. For these reasons, this article has explored two potential justifications for autonomous economic sanctions.

As the main criticism of economic sanctions against Russia pertains to their 'autonomous' and 'unilateral' nature, an initial response to such criticism is to attempt to present sanctions as actually being collective sanctions. However, assimilating autonomous economic sanctions to collective sanctions under UN auspices is an argument not without its weaknesses. One cannot accept the proposition that a General Assembly resolution says, in equal measure, both what it expressly states and what it omits to state. While the General Assembly resolutions condemning the Russian invasion of Ukraine can be a limited source of political legitimacy for autonomous sanctions, on their own strength such resolutions are incapable of transforming autonomous sanctions into collective sanctions.

A subsequent response to such criticism could be to accept the unilateral character of such sanctions, but to seek to justify these as third-party countermeasures. This exercise is complex, for there is a need to identify individual measures violating some international rule, that may nevertheless be justified as countermeasures on the

---

and must be as far as possible reversible in their effects in terms of future legal relations between the two States." ARSIWA, the introductory commentary to Chapter II of Part Three (para. 6). See Anderson and Keitner (n 92); Brunk, (n 99); Claus Kreß, "Russia's Aggression Against Ukraine - The Question of Reparation", *Luther Lecture*, 1:14:47-1:16:20, https://www.youtube.com/watch?v=vocxEc0UQcw (March 2023). But see Anton Moiseienko, "The Freezing and Confiscation of Foreign Central Bank Assets: How Far Can Sanctions Go?" (17 April 2023), available at SSRN: https://ssrn.com/abstract=4420459, pp. 38–44.

part of third parties. In the present case, there is no clear evidence that states imposing sanctions against Russia consider any of their measures to be third-party countermeasures. Furthermore, as is the case with the ambiguity present in many examples of autonomous economic sanctions, whether contemporary international law establishes the right of third parties to countermeasures remains controversial.

Freezing, Confiscation and Management of the Assets of the Russian Central Bank and the Oligarchs: Legality and Possibility Under International Law

Kazuhiro Nakatani

Abstract As the most powerful measure of economic sanctions against Russia which invaded Ukraine, the Western States froze the assets of the Russian Central Bank and the Oligarchs which are situated in their States. This article attempts to clarify the legality of the freezing, confiscation, and management of assets under international law. The freezing of assets is a legal countermeasure against aggression. Confiscation is lawful only if certain conditions are satisfied. Management is a realistic option which avoids the legal risks which might arise from confiscation.

1 Preface

In response to the Russian aggression against Ukraine, Western States have imposed a series of financial sanctions against Russia.[1] Among the various financial measures, the author sheds light on the measures targeting the assets of the Russian Central Bank (Bank of Russia) and the Oligarchs (very rich and powerful people who support President Putin) which are situated in their countries, precisely because

---

[1] Japan has taken the following financial measures to: (1) prevent financing to Russia from the leading multilateral financial institutions, including IMF, the World Bank and the European Bank for Reconstruction and Development, (2) respond to sanctions evasion by Russia, including through digital assets, (3) restrict transactions with Russia's central bank, (4) impose sanctions that include the freezing of assets of persons related to the Government of Russia, including President Putin, and Russian business Oligarchs, (5) freeze assets of 11 Russian banks (Sberbank, Alfa-Bank, VEB.RF, Promsvyazbank, Bank Rossiya, VTB Bank, Sovcombank, Novicombank, Bank Otkritie, Credit Bank of Moscow and Russian Agricultural Bank [Rosselkhozbank]) and their subsidiaries in Japan, (6) join in with efforts to isolate Russia from the international financial system and the global economy such as excluding selected Russian banks from the SWIFT (Society for Worldwide Interbank Financial Telecommunication) messaging system, and (7) prohibit the issuance or transaction of new Russian sovereign debt in the primary and secondary market. Japan Stands with Ukraine, Website of the Prime Minister's Office, available at https://japan.kantei.go.jp/ongoingtopics/pdf/jp_stands_with_ukraine_eng.pdf.

K. Nakatani (✉)
Faculty of Law, Tokai University, Hiratsuka, Japan
e-mail: pacta@rapid.ocn.ne.jp

© The Author(s), under exclusive license to Springer Nature Singapore Pte Ltd. 2024
M. Asada, D. Tamada (eds.), *The War in Ukraine and International Law*,
https://doi.org/10.1007/978-981-97-2504-5_6

these measures can be the most powerful against Russia[2] and pose some complicated problems in international law. The legality of the following three measures under international law is analysed: freezing, confiscation, and management of assets.

The conclusions are as follows: First, freezing assets is a legal countermeasure against aggression, which is the most serious violation of international law. Second, confiscation is lawful only if certain conditions are satisfied. Third, management, distinct from the confiscation of frozen assets, is a realistic option which avoids legal risks which might arise from confiscation.

2 Freezing Assets of the Russian Central Bank and the Oligarchs

2.1 Japan

Western States have frozen the assets of the Russian Central Bank and the Oligarchs. Japan froze its assets under Articles 16 and 21 of the Foreign Exchange and Foreign Trade Act (Act No. 228 of 1949).

Article 16 paragraph 1 provides: 'When the competent minister finds it to be necessary in order for Japan to sincerely implement a treaty or any other international agreement that it has signed, when the competent minister finds it to be particularly necessary *in order for Japan to contribute to international efforts for international peace*, or when the cabinet decision referred to in Article 10, paragraph 1 is made, the competent minister may, pursuant to the provisions of the Cabinet Order, impose on a resident or non-resident that intends to make a payment from Japan to a foreign country or a resident that intends to make a payment to or receive a payment from a non-resident an obligation to obtain permission for making the payment or for making or receiving the payment, except when the payment to be made or received arises from a transaction or act on which an obligation to obtain permission or approval is imposed from the same perspective as mentioned above.' (*italics* added by author)

Article 21 paragraph 1 provides: ' When the Minister of Finance finds that, if a capital transaction (meaning the capital transaction prescribed in the preceding Article, and excluding one which falls within the category of specified capital transaction prescribed in Article 24, paragraph (1); the same applies in paragraph (1) of the following Article, Article 55-3, and Article 70, paragraph (1)) were conducted by a resident or a non-resident subject to no restrictions, it would cause

---

[2] It is remarkable that major Russian banks have been excluded from the SWIFT messaging system. But even if SWIFT is not available, Russian banks can resort to other means including China's CIPS (Cross-Border Interbank Payment System) or out of date facsimile to send money, although very inconvenient and time-consuming. Therefore it is an overstatement to say that the SWIFT sanction is financial nuclear weapons.

a situation in which Japan would be hindered from sincerely implementing a treaty or any other international agreement that it has signed or from *contributing to international efforts for international peace*, thereby making it difficult to achieve the purpose of this Act, or when the cabinet decision referred to in Article 10, paragraph (1) has been made, the minister may, pursuant to the provisions of Cabinet Order, impose on a resident or non-resident that intends to conduct the capital transaction an obligation to obtain permission for conducting the capital transaction.'[3] (*italics* added by author)

Pursuant to the Cabinet Order dated 1 March 2022 Japan, *in order to contribute to international efforts for international peace*, imposed restrictions on making or receiving payments and capital transactions to the Russian Central Bank.[4] This is the legal basis for freezing the Russian Central Bank's assets in Japan. As to the freezing assets of the Oligarchs, as of 27 January 2023, Japan has frozen the assets of 700 individuals and 207 entities. Most of the individuals were Oligarchs and government officials of the Russian Federation.[5]

2.2 The European Union

The European Union, Article 5a paragraph 4 of the Council Regulation (EU) 833/2014 concerning restrictive measures in respect of actions undermining or threatening the territorial integrity, sovereignty or independence of Ukraine, as amended by the Council Regulation (EU) 2022/394 of 9 March 2022 provides the freezing of the assets of the Russian Central Bank as follows: 'Transactions related to the management of reserves as well as of assets of the Central Bank of Russia, including transactions with any legal person, entity or body acting on behalf of, or at the direction of, the Central Bank of Russia, such as the Russian National Wealth Fund, are prohibited'.

It is noteworthy that the assets of the Russian National Wealth Fund, leading the Russian Sovereign Wealth Fund, were also frozen by the United States and the EU.

As for the assets of the Oligarchs, as of 27 January 2023 the EU has frozen the assets of almost 1800 individuals and entities.[6] Most of the individuals were Oligarchs.

---

[3] English translation is available at the Website of the Ministry of Finance. https://www.mof.go.jp/english/policy/international_policy/fdi/FEFTA.pdf.

[4] Announcement No. 81 of the Ministry of Foreign Affairs, *Official Daily Gazette,* 1 March 2023.

[5] Measures based on the Foreign Exchange and Foreign Trade Act regarding the situation surrounding Ukraine (26 May 2023), website of the Ministry of Foreign Affairs, available at https://www.mofa.go.jp/press/release/press4e_003267.html.

[6] EU Restrictive Measures against Russia over Ukraine (since 2014), website of the European Council/Council of the European Union, available at https://www.consilium.europa.eu/en/policies/sanctions/restrictive-measures-against-russia-over-ukraine/#economic.

Article 2 of the Council Regulation 269/2014 (EU) of 17 March 2014 provides: '1. All funds and economic resources belonging to, owned, held, or controlled by any natural or legal persons, entities, bodies, natural or legal persons, entities, or bodies associated with them, as listed in Annex I shall be frozen. 2. No funds or economic resources shall be made available, directly or indirectly, to or for the benefit of natural or legal persons, entities, or bodies, or natural or legal persons, entities, or bodies associated with them, as listed in Annex I.'

By the Council Regulation (EU) 2022/330 of 25 February 2022 amending the Council Regulation (EU) 269/2014, Annex 1 shall include '(a) natural persons responsible for, supporting or implementing actions or policies which undermine or threaten the territorial integrity, sovereignty and independence of Ukraine, or stability or security in Ukraine, or which obstruct the work of international organizations in Ukraine; (b) legal persons, entities or bodies supporting, materially or financially, actions which undermine or threaten the territorial integrity, sovereignty and independence of Ukraine; (c) legal persons, entities or bodies in Crimea or Sevastopol whose ownership has been transferred contrary to Ukrainian law, or legal persons, entities or bodies which have benefited from such a transfer; (d) natural or legal persons, entities or bodies supporting, materially or financially, or benefiting from Russian decision makers responsible for the annexation of Crimea or the destabilization of Ukraine; (e) natural or legal persons, entities or bodies conducting transactions with the separatist groups in the Donbas region of Ukraine; (f) natural or legal persons, entities or bodies supporting, materially or financially, or benefiting from the Government of the Russian Federation, which is responsible for the annexation of Crimea and the destabilization of Ukraine; or (g) leading businesspersons or legal persons, entities or bodies involved in economic sectors providing a substantial source of revenue to the Government of the Russian Federation, which is responsible for the annexation of Crimea and the destabilization of Ukraine, and natural or legal persons, entities or bodies associated with them.'

2.3 The United States

On 28 February 2022 the U.S. Department of the Treasury's Office of Foreign Assets Control (OFAC) prohibited the United States persons from engaging in transactions with the Central Bank of the Russian Federation, the National Wealth Fund of the Russian Federation, and the Ministry of Finance of the Russian Federation. This action effectively immobilises any assets of the Central Bank of the Russian Federation held in the United States or the United States persons, wherever located.[7]

---

[7]Treasury Prohibits Transactions with Central Bank of Russia and Imposes Sanctions on Key Sources of Russia's Wealth, Website of the US Department of Treasury, available at https://home.treasury.gov/news/press-releases/jy0612.

The Office of Foreign Assets Control (OPAC) Directive 4 under Executive Order 14024 provides: 'Pursuant to sections 1(a)(iv), 1(d), and 8 of Executive Order 14024, 'Blocking Property With Respect To Specified Harmful Foreign Activities of the Government of the Russian Federation' (the 'Order'), the Director of the Office of Foreign Assets Control has determined, in consultation with the Department of State, that the Central Bank of the Russian Federation, the National Wealth Fund of the Russian Federation, and the Ministry of Finance of the Russian Federation are political subdivisions, agencies, or instrumentalities of the Government of the Russian Federation, and that the following activities by a United States person are prohibited, except to the extent provided by law, or unless licensed or otherwise authorized by the Office of Foreign Assets Control: any transaction involving the Central Bank of the Russian Federation, the National Wealth Fund of the Russian Federation, or the Ministry of Finance of the Russian Federation, including any transfer of assets to such entities or any foreign exchange transaction for or on behalf of such entities.'[8]

As for the assets of Oligarchs, the United States has designated Oligarchs to the SDN list pursuant to Executive Order 14024 (15 April 2021) has frozen their assets.

Section 1 of the Executive Order states that all property and interests of the following persons are blocked and may not be transferred, paid, exported, or withdrawn. The persons include any person determined '(a)(ii) to be responsible for or complicit in, or to have directly or indirectly engaged or attempted to engage in, any of the following for or on behalf of, or for the benefit of, directly or indirectly, the Government of the Russian Federation: (F) activities that undermine the peace, security, political stability, or territorial integrity of the United States, its allies, or its partners' and '(vi) to have materially assisted, sponsored, or provided financial, material, or technological support for, or goods or services to or in support of: (A) any activity described in subsection (a)(ii) of this section'.

Searching the Specially Designated Nationals (SDN) list by Country,[9] as of 4 February 2023 1890 persons are found to be listed as 'nationality Russia' and most of them are considered to be the Oligarchs and high-level officials of the Russian Governments and their family members.

2.4   The International Reserves of the Russian Central Bank

As of 31 January 2022 the amount of international reserves of the Russian Central Bank was $ 630,207 million (foreign exchange reserves $ 497,951 million plus gold

---

[8] Directive 4 under the Executive Order 14024, Website of the Department of Treasury, available at https://home.treasury.gov/system/files/126/eo14024_directive_4_02282022.pdf.

[9] SDN List by Country. Website of the Ministry of Treasury, avalible at https://www.treasury.gov/ofac/downloads/ctrylst.txt.

$ 132,256 million).[10] Although the amount of frozen assets is not clear, according to the Russian Elites, Proxies, and Oligarchs (REPO) Task Force[11] Joint Statement on 29 June 2022 REPO members have immobilised about 300 billion US dollars' worth of Russian Central Bank assets and have blocked or frozen more than 30 billion US dollars' worth of sanctioned Russians' assets in financial accounts and economic resources.[12] On 30 November 2022 President von der Leyen of the European Commission said, 'We have blocked 300 billion euros of the Russian Central Bank reserves and we have frozen 19 billion euros of Russian Oligarchs' money'.[13] The breakdown of the reserves held by Russia's Central Bank as of 30 June 2021 is as follows: (1) By currency: euro 32.3%, gold 21.7%, US Dollar 16.4%, yuan 13.1%, sterling 6.4%, others 10%. (2) By Geography: monetary gold 21.7%, China 13.8%, France 12.2%, Japan 10.0%, Germany 9.5%, USA 6.6%, International Institutions 5.0%, UK 4.5%, Austria 3.0%, Canada 2.8%, others 10.7%.[14] According to the Joint Statement from the REPO Task Force released on 9 March 2023 members of the REPO Task Force successfully blocked or frozen more than $58 billion worth of sanctioned Russian assets in financial accounts and economic resources.[15]

2.5 Legality of Freezing Assets of the Russian Central Bank and the Oligarchs

Is it legal to freeze the assets of the Russian Central Bank and the Oligarchs under international law? Asset owners usually dispose of their assets. As a corollary of protecting the right to possess assets, the disposal of their own assets is considered to be established as customary international law. Freezing assets is a temporary restriction on this right; therefore, it is *per se* illegal. However, this measure can be justified

---

[10] Monthly Values, Website of the Bank of Russia, available at https://cbr.ru/eng/hd_base/mrrf/mrrf_m/.

[11] Australia, Canada, the European Commission, France, Germany, Japan, Italy the United Kingdom and the United States are the participants of the REPO Task Force.

[12] Russian Elites, Proxies, and Oligarchs (REPO) Task Force Joint Statement, Website of the US Department of the Treasury, available at https://home.treasury.gov/news/press-releases/jy0839#:~:text=The%20Russian%20Elites%2C%20Proxies%2C%20and,Russians%27%20access%20to%20the%20international.

[13] Statement by President von der Leyen on Russian Accountability and the Use of Russian Frozen Assets, Website of the European Commission (30 November 2022), available at https://ec.europa.eu/commission/presscorner/detail/en/statement_22_7307.

[14] Bank of Russia, *Bank of Russia Foreign Exchange and Gold Asset Management Report*, No.1 (61), 2022, p. 6, available at https://www.cbr.ru/Collection/Collection/File/39685/2022-01_res_en.pdf.

[15] Joint Statement from the REPO Task Force, Website of the U.S. Department of Treasury, available at https://home.treasury.gov/news/press-releases/jy1329.

when it pertains to one of the circumstances precluding wrongfulness, particularly countermeasures against an internationally wrongful act.

On countermeasures, Article 22 on the Articles on Responsibility of States for Internationally Wrongful Acts adopted by the International Law commission in 2001[16] provides: 'The wrongfulness of an act of a State not in conformity with an international obligation towards another State is precluded if and to the extent that the act constitutes a countermeasure taken against the latter State in accordance with chapter II of Part Three'.

It is fair and fit to State practice to consider that against violations of international obligations, *erga omnes,* violations of *jus cogens,* or international crimes of States, not only directly injured States but also other third States can take some economic sanctions against the wrongdoer.[17]

Remarkably, in the Russian aggression case, the United Nations General Assembly, in its Resolution ES-11/1 dated 2 March 2022 deplored the Russian Federation's aggression against Ukraine in violation of Article 2 (4) of the Charter (paragraph 2). With this resolution, fact-finding and evaluation of Russian brutality was given international authority by the General Assembly. Therefore, the criticism that economic sanctions against Russia, including freezing of assets, were made arbitrarily, is out of the mark. Necessity is another option for justifying the freezing of assets. Particularly, a State on the verge of default can temporarily restrict withdrawals from bank accounts. However, necessity does not directly relate to this case.

Freezing assets against Russia is also compatible with Article 48, paragraph 1 and Article 54 of the Articles on Responsibility of States for Internationally Wrongful Acts.

Article 48 paragraph 1 provides: 'Any State other than an injured State is entitled to invoke the responsibility of another State in accordance with paragraph 2 if: (a) the obligation breached is owed to a group of States including that State, and is established for the protection of a collective interest of the group; or (b) the obligation breached is owed to the international community as a whole.' Russian aggression satisfied both (a) and (b).

As the freezing assets is only a temporary suspension to dispose them, it satisfies the condition stipulated by Article 53, which provides: 'Countermeasures shall be terminated as soon as the responsible State has complied with its obligations under Part Two in relation to the internationally wrongful act'.

Although Article 50, paragraph 1, provides that countermeasures shall not affect: '(a) the obligation to refrain from the threat or use of force as embodied in the Charter of the United Nations; (b) obligations for the protection of fundamental human rights; (c) obligations of a humanitarian character prohibiting reprisals; and

---

[16]UN Doc. A/56/10.

[17]Kazuhiro Nakatani, 'Economic Sanctions and Compliance: Theoretical Aspects', *in* T.J. Schoenbaum, J. Nakagawa and L.C. Reif (ed.), *Trilateral Perspectives on International Legal Issues: From Theory into Practice* (Brill Nijhoff, 1998), pp. 347–364.

(d) other obligations under peremptory norms of general international law', the freezing assets do not violate any of the obligations.

Regarding the freezing of central banks' assets, their relationships with immunity enjoyed by them must be clarified.

Freezing assets falls under the category of pre-judgment measures of constraint and Article 18 of the United Nations Convention on Jurisdictional Immunities of States and Their Property provides: 'No pre-judgment measures of constraint, such as attachment or arrest, against property of a State may be taken in connection with a proceeding before a court of another State unless and except to the extent that: (a) the State has expressly consented to the taking of such measures as indicated: (i) by international agreement; (ii) by an arbitration agreement or in a written contract; or (iii) by a declaration before the court or by a written communication after a dispute between the parties has arisen; or (b) the State has allocated or earmarked property for the satisfaction of the claim which is the object of that proceeding.'

Despite this, freezing assets can be justified as a countermeasure against internationally wrongful acts, including aggression. Even if freezing is not compatible with immunity based on the pre-judgment measures of constraints, wrongfulness is precluded.

As central banks are political subdivisions, agencies, or instrumentalities of the government, and are intimately related to them, they can be targets of economic sanctions.

However, the situation of Oligarchs varies. For the freezing assets of the Oligarchs to be lawful under international law, *prima facie* basis of the nexus between the Oligarchs and Russian aggression must be proved. If Oligarchs contribute financially to the Russian government or its officials, the nexus is established and its assets can be the target of freezing.

State practices strengthen the legality of freezing assets as a countermeasure. There are many precedents in which States, although their subjective rights have not been directly injured, have frozen assets that are responsible for or related to serious violations of international law by the State. Some measures were not in accordance with United Nations Security Council Resolutions.

For example, Japan has frozen the assets of the following persons: (1) Former President Milosevic of the Federal Republic of Yugoslavia, his family members, and related government officials (10 persons since February 2001); (2) President Al-Assad of Syria and related persons and entities (59 persons and 35 entities since September 2011); and (3) persons directly related to the Russian annexation of Crimea, destabilisation of Eastern Ukraine, and the so-called incorporation of Eastern and Southern Parts of Ukraine (295 persons and 16 entities).[18] These measures have been taken 'in order for Japan to contribute to international efforts for international peace' (Articles 16 and 20 of the Foreign Exchange and Foreign

---

[18] Measures of freezing assets in force based on the Foreign Exchange and Foreign Trade Act (as of 2 February 2023), website of the Ministry of Finance, available at https://www.mof.go.jp/policy/international_policy/gaitame_kawase/gaitame/economic_sanctions/list.html.

Trade Act). The freezing of assets of responsible persons started as part of non-military enforcement measures in accordance with the United Nations Security Council Resolutions, which constitute an important part of smart sanctions. Although there are no Security Council Resolutions, they have been widely adopted as unilateral countermeasures.

The following are the precedents of the freezing of central banks' assets: (1) In 1979, the United States froze the assets of the Iranian Central Bank in response to hostage-taking.[19] (2) In accordance with the United Nations Security Council Resolution 1973, adopted on 17 March 2011 the Libyan Central Bank assets were frozen. The Libyan Central Bank was placed under the control of Muammar Gaddafi and his family and was a potential source of funding for his regime. The assets of the Libyan Investment Authority, leading the Libyan Sovereign Wealth Fund, were frozen for the same reasons. (3) In 2012, the United States and European Union froze the assets of the Iranian Central Bank in response to Iran's development of military nuclear technology.[20] (4) In 2011 and 2012, the United States and the European Union froze Syrian Central Bank assets in response to Syria's violation of human rights.[21]

(4) In 2019, the United States froze the assets of the Venezuelan Central Bank as a response to Venezuelan presidential crisis.[22] (5) In 2021, the United States froze the assets (approximately 7 billion USD) of the Afghan Central Bank (Da Afghanistan Bank) deposited in the Federal Reserve Bank of New York to prevent Taliban from withdrawing them.[23]

When the financial assets of foreign persons or entities are frozen, the State imposing the freezing must notify the Executive Board of the International Monetary Fund.

Paragraph 1 of the IMF Executive Board Decision No 144-(52/51) on 14 August 1952 provides: 'A member intending to impose restrictions on payments and transfers for current international transactions that are not authorised by Article VII, Section 3(b) or Article XIV, Section 2 of the Fund Agreement and that, in the judgment of the member, are solely related to the preservation of national or international security, should, whenever possible, notify the Fund before imposing such restrictions. Any member may obtain a decision from the fund prior to the imposition of such restrictions by indicating it in its notice, and the fund will act

---

[19] Executive Order 12170 (14 November 1979).

[20] Executive Order 13599 (5 February 2012) and Council Decision 2012/35/CFSP (27 February 2012).

[21] Executive Order 13582 (18 August 2011) and Council Regulation (EU) 168/2012 (27 February 2012).

[22] Executive Order 13884 (5 August 2019).

[23] Although the Treasury Department did not indicate the legal basis for the action, a former senior adviser to the director of OFAC suggested that there was sufficient authority under Executive Order Afghan 13268. Contemporary Practice of the United States (The United States Establishes Fund for the Afghan People from Frozen Afghan Central Bank Assets), 117 *American Journal of International Law*, p. 140, note 6.

promptly on its request. If any member intending to impose such restrictions finds that circumstances preclude advance notice to the fund, it should notify the fund as promptly as circumstances permit, but ordinarily not later than 30 days after imposing such restrictions. Each notice received in accordance with this decision was circulated immediately to the Executive Directors. Unless the Fund informs the member within 30 days after receiving notice that it is not satisfied that such restrictions are proposed solely to preserve such security, the member may assume that the fund has no objection to the imposition of the restrictions.'[24] Although an Executive Board can object to freezing, there is no such precedent.

Regarding the freezing assets of the Russian National Wealth Fund, it is important to mention that sovereign wealth funds, as opposed to central banks, usually enjoy neither immunity from jurisdiction before a court of another State nor immunity from execution, because Article 15, paragraph 1 of the United Nations Convention on Jurisdictional Immunities of States and Their Property provides that a State cannot invoke immunity from jurisdiction before a court of another State which is otherwise competent in a proceeding which relates to its participation in a company or other collective body, and portfolio investment of sovereign wealth funds comes under the category of participation.[25]

Freezing the assets of high-level officials of the Russian government, as opposed to Oligarchs, is easy to justify because they are directly accountable for the Russian Aggression.

3 Possibility of the Confiscation of the Frozen Assets

3.1 *The General Assembly Resolution ES-11/5*

On 14 November 2022 the General Assembly of the United Nations adopted Resolution ES-11/5 which provides in paragraph 2: '(The General Assembly) recognizes that the Russian Federation must be held to account for any violations of international law in or against Ukraine, including its aggression in violation of the Charter of the United Nations, as well as any violations of international humanitarian law and international human rights law, and that it must bear the legal consequences of all of its internationally wrongful acts, including making reparation for the injury, including any damage, caused by such acts'.

This Resolution applies the following general principle of State responsibility to the present case: 'The responsible State is under an obligation to make full reparation

---

[24] *Selected Decisions and Selected Documents of the International Monetary Fund* (42nd Issue, 31 December 2022), pp. 590–591.

[25] On this point, see Kazuhiro Nakatani, 'Sovereign Wealth Funds: Problems of International Law between Possessing and Recipient States', 2015-2 *International Review of Law* (electronic journal of the Qatar University), Volume (Special Issue on Sovereign Wealth Funds, March 2015), available at https://www.qscience.com/content/journals/10.5339/irl.2015.swf.7.

Freezing, Confiscation and Management of the Assets of the Russian... 147

for the injury caused by the internationally wrongful act'. (Article 31, Paragraph 1 of the Articles on the Responsibility of States for Internationally Wrongful Acts).

Article 36 paragraph 1 of the said Articles provides: 'The State responsible for an internationally wrongful act is under an obligation to compensate for the damage caused thereby, insofar as such damage is not made good by restitution'.

Consequently, Russia, which refuses to withdraw from Ukraine, is obligated to compensate for the damage caused by aggression.

3.2 The G7 Leaders Statement on Ukraine

Since the war, the compensation problem in the case of armed conflict/aggression has usually been dealt with through peace treaties. Should injured States wait for a peace treaty as an absolute requirement to receive compensation? The problem arising from waiting for a peace treaty is that Russia and/or Ukraine might fall into default due to long-term armed conflict which requires huge expenditures.

The G7 Leaders Statement on Ukraine adopted on 19 May 2023 at Hiroshima provides in paragraph 8 (Responsibility for Damage): 'we will continue to take measures available within our domestic frameworks to find, restrain, freeze, seize, and, *where appropriate, confiscate or forfeit* the assets of those individuals and entities that have been sanctioned in connection with Russia's aggression'[26] (*italics* added by the author). Remarkably, G7 States did not exclude the possibility of confiscating frozen assets.

3.3 The Canadian Law

Coming to the question of whether States can confiscate the Russian Central Bank's frown assets without waiting for peace treaties? What about Oligarchs' frozen assets?

There has already been some State practices concerning the confiscation of frozen Russian assets.

On 23 June 2022 the Senate of Canada passed Bill C-19 (An Act to implement certain provisions of the budget tabled in parliament on 7 April 2022 and other measures). Its Section 441, 5.6 provides as follows: 'After consulting with the Minister of Finance and the Minister of Foreign Affairs, the Minister may—at the times and in the manner, and on any terms and conditions, that the Minister considers appropriate—pay out of the Proceeds Account, as defined in section 2 of the Seized Property Management Act, amounts not exceeding the net proceeds from the

---

[26] G7 Leaders Statement on Ukraine, Website of the Ministry of Foreign Affairs of Japan, available at https://www.mofa.go.jp/mofaj/files/100506324.pdf.

disposition of property forfeited under section 5.4, but only for any of the following purposes: (a) the reconstruction of a foreign State adversely affected by a grave breach of international peace and security; (b) the restoration of international peace and security; and (c) the compensation of victims of a grave breach of international peace and security, gross and systematic human rights violations or acts of significant corruption.'[27]

3.4 The United States Law

On 22 December 2022 the U.S. Senate of the United States passed the Whitehouse-Graham-Rennet Amendment (SA6596) to the Consolidated Appropriations Act of 2023. Sec.1708 (a) provides, 'The Attorney General may transfer to the Secretary of State the proceeds of any covered forfeited property for use by the Secretary of State to aid Ukraine to remediate the harms of Russian aggression towards Ukraine. Any such transfer shall be considered foreign assistance under the Foreign Assistance Act of 1961 (22 U.S.C. 2151 et seq.), including for the purposes of making the administrative authorities available and implementing the reporting requirements contained in that Act.'[28]

Some frozen oligarch assets have already been confiscated by the US. On 3 February 2023 US Attorney General Merrick Garland, in a press conference with Ukrainian Prosecutor General Andriy Kostin, stated as follows: 'Congress has also given the Justice Department new authority to transfer certain assets we have seized from Russian Oligarchs from the rebuilding Ukraine. Today, I am announcing that I have authorised the first-ever transfer of forfeited Russian assets for use in Ukraine.' 'With my authorization today, the forfeited funds will next be transferred to the State Department to support the people of Ukraine'.[29] Kostin added: 'Today, we are witnessing the authorization of transfer of the confiscated assets in the amount of $5.4 million US dollars to the State Department for the purpose of rebuilding war ravaged Ukraine.'

3.5 Analysis

This problem should be analysed, taking into consideration the two elements of distinction: object (whether the confiscated asset is that of the Russian Central Bank

---

[27] https://www.parl.ca/DocumentViewer/en/44-1/bill/C-19/second-reading.

[28] H.R.2617-742.

[29] Attorney General Merrick Garland met with Ukrainian Prosecutor General Andriy Kostin, Website of the Department of Justice, available at https://www.justice.gov/opa/video/attorney-general-merrick-b-garland-met-ukrainian-prosecutor-general-andriy-kostin.

or that of Oligarchs) and purpose (whether the confiscation is for the recovery of Ukraine or for the compensation of the loss suffered by their corporations or persons). In addition, regarding the frozen assets of the Russian Central Bank, the extent to which the whole assets or only the proceeds can be confiscated is another problem, which will be considered in Sect. 4 (Possibility of the Management of the Frozen Assets).

There are six negative elements on the confiscation.

First, confiscation is usually in conflict with Article 53 of the Articles on Responsibility of States for Internationally Wrongful Acts, which provides: 'Countermeasures shall be terminated as soon as the responsible State has complied with its obligations under Part Two in relation to the internationally wrongful act'.

Second, confiscation by third States, whose subjective rights are not compromised, might cause unjust enrichment.

Third, regarding the confiscation of the Russian Central Bank's assets, Article 19 of the United Nations Convention on Jurisdictional Immunities of States and Their Property provides that no post-judgment measures of constraint, such as attachment, arrest, or execution, against the property of a State may be taken in connection with a proceeding before the court of another State. Although some property specifically in use or intended for use by the State for other than government non-commercial purposes can be target of post-judgment measures of constraint, Article 21 (c) provides that 'property of the central bank or other monetary authority of the State shall not be considered as such property[30]'.

Fourth, if a central bank has separate legal status from the State, an opinion against considering that the central bank is also accountable for the acts of the State might appear. According to the website of the Russian Central Bank, 'the Bank of Russia is not a body of State power, but its powers are, in effect, the functions of a body of State power, because their implementation implies the use of State enforcement', 'the State is not liable for the obligations of the Bank of Russia, and similarly, the Bank of Russia is not liable for the obligations of the State unless they have assumed such obligations or unless federal laws stipulate otherwise'.[31] However, as mentioned in Sect. 2.5, central banks are considered to be, or at least presumed to be,[32] political subdivisions, agencies, or instrumentalities of the government, even if they have their own legal personality.

---

[30] Article 19 of the Japanese Act on the Civil Jurisdiction of Japan with respect to Foreign States (Act No.24 of April 24, 2009) provides that foreign central banks have immunity from jurisdiction and execution. The English translation of the Act is available at https://www.japaneselawtranslation.go.jp/ja/laws/view/3870/je.

[31] About Bank of Russia: Legal Status and Functions, website of the Bank of Russia, available at https://www.cbr.ru/eng/about_br/bankstatus/.

[32] Even if It is not self-evident whether central banks are State organs or agencies or instrumentalities, as pointed out, for example, by Ingrid Wuerth, 'Immunity from Execution of Central Bank Assets', *in* Tom Ruys et als. (ed.), *The Cambridge Handbook of Immunities and International Law* (Cambridge University Press, 2019), pp. 266, 278–279, it can be said that they are *presumed* to be so.

The Oligarchs are considered neither State organs nor agencies or instrumentalities of the Russian Government, and equivalent causality is usually hard to establish between Russian aggression and the money of the Oligarchs.

Fifth, some States hesitate, with good reasons, to confiscate the Russian assets due to the constitutional restraints.[33]

Sixth, if a State confiscates Russian assets, it will face legal claims from the Russian owners.[34]

3.6 Exceptional Cases Which Justify the Confiscation

Are there exceptional cases justifying such confiscation? Are 'foreign currency reserves held by a foreign central bank entitled to absolute protection, absent waiver',[35] even if the State to which the bank belongs is an aggressor? The author does not consider confiscation to be absolutely prohibited. Two issues can be considered as the starting points.

First, the immunity enjoyed by central banks applies only to civil proceedings. It is unclear whether this applies to administrative enforcement measures.

Second, as to the assets of the Oligarchs, Article 1 of the Protocol to the Convention for the Protection of Human Rights and Fundamental Freedoms provides: 'Every natural or legal person is entitled to the peaceful enjoyment of his possessions. No one shall be deprived of his possessions, except in the public interest, and subject to the conditions provided for by law and the general principles of international law. The preceding provisions shall not, however, in any way impair the right of a State to enforce such laws as it deems necessary to control the use of property in accordance with the general interest or to secure the payment of taxes, other contributions, or penalties.' States can confiscate the frozen assets of Oligarchs if the measure is 'subject to the conditions provided for by law and by the general principles of international law'.

---

[33] For example, Switzerland says that the confiscation of frozen private assets is inconsistent with the Federal Constitution and the prevailing legal order and violates Switzerland's international commitments. Federal Council has received legal clarifications on frozen Russian assets, website of the Federal Council of the Swiss Government, available at https://www.admin.ch/gov/en/start/documentation/media-releases/media-releases-federal-council.msg-id-93089.html.

[34] For example, Articles 3 and 4 of the Canada- Russia investment agreement provide protections for investors against the taking of property without compensation and provides for the fair and equitable treatment of foreign investors. If Canada seizes and repurposes Russian assets protected by this treaty, it may face legal claims from Russian owners on the basis that their rights as a foreign investor have been violated. Public International Law & Policy Group, Policy Planning White Paper: Repurposing Frozen Russian Assets (2023), pp. 22–23, website of the Public International Law & Policy Group, available at https://static1.squarespace.com/static/5900b58e1b631bffa3671 67e/t/6414c1f9677c52662a32eb8b/1679081977290/2023-03-17+PILPG+-+White+Paper+-+Repurposing+Frozen+Russian+Assets.pdf.

[35] Wuerth, supra note 32, p. 281.

As an exception, in the following hypothetical cases, confiscation might be justified under international law.

First, if the assets of companies, entities, and individuals of State X are expropriated without prompt, adequate, and effective compensation and local remedies by injured companies, entities, and

Individuals are exhausted and fail, and State X can exercise diplomatic protection. When Russia neglects the request for compensation, State X might be able to confiscate the frozen Russian assets and allocate them to the injured companies, entities, and individuals, considering that the immunity enjoyed by central banks is not *jus cogens*. Even if central banks have different legal personalities from those of the government, this cannot be a barrier to consider that the assets of the central bank are part of the government. Considering that central banks can enjoy immunity while not bearing any burdens accompanied by privileges is unfair and contrary to the principle of good faith. In this situation, unjust enrichment does not arise because of confusion, however, a domestic law enabling confiscation is required.

Second, regarding the confiscation of frozen Russian assets for Ukraine's reconstruction, the following points should be confirmed. Ukraine, as the directly injured State, can confiscate Russian assets as Russia absolutely refuses reparation. Ukraine's confiscation did not result in unjust enrichment. To ensure that confiscation by another State, Y, does not cause unjust enrichment, Ukraine's declaration that it can confiscate Russian assets in a foreign State with the cooperation of the State in whose territory the assets are situated and an agreement between State Y and Ukraine concerning the transfer of the confiscated Russian assets to Ukraine is preferable. Confiscation and transfer can be defined as *negotiorum gestio* on the part of State Y.[36]

Although not the assets of the central bank, there was a UN Security Council Resolution which referred to the confiscation of the property of the target State as a non-military enforcement measure. The paragraph 24 of the Security Council Resolution 820 on 17 April 1993 'decides that all States shall impound all vessels, freight vehicles rolling stock and aircraft in their territories in which a majority or controlling interest is held by a person or undertaking in or operating from the Federal Republic of Yugoslavia (Serbia and Montenegro) and that these vessels, freight vehicles, rolling stock and aircraft may forfeit to the seizing State upon a determination that they have been in violation of resolutions 713 (1991), 757 (1992),

---

[36] On 25 April 2022, Andriy Smyrnov, Deputy Head of the Ukraine President's Office proposed mechanisms to recover funds from the Russian Federation frozen abroad to compensate for losses as follows: 'We have several plans to achieve this. The main one is the signing of an international agreement, which will provide for the lifting of immunity from the funds of the Russian Federation and directing them to the affected citizens and legal entities, as well as the restoration of infrastructure. Plan B is the enactment of the relevant law in each jurisdiction where funds have been frozen. In some countries, such bills have already been registered.' *Ukraine has prepared the necessary documents for the launch of a special tribunal on the crime of aggression as soon as possible - Andriy Smyrnov, Website of the President of Ukraine,* available at https://www.president.gov.ua/en/news/ukrayina-pidgotuvala-neobhidni-dokumenti-dlya-yaknajshvidsho-74557.

787 (1992) or the present resolution'. Economic sanctions are not alien to confiscation.

3.7 Additional Remarks Concerning the Confiscation of Frozen Assets of the Russian Central Bank

The following six points have been added as concerns regarding the confiscation of frozen assets by the Russian Central Bank:

First, it must be noted that neither the United Nations Convention on Jurisdictional Immunities of States and Their Property, its commentary, nor domestic law and jurisprudence concerning State immunity have been well prepared for current and ongoing aggression and other serious violations of international law, although they have supposed past wrongful acts. In order for minimising the allegation of violation of international law, it might be wise to avoid the risk and negate jurisdictional immunity as well as immunity from execution in 'unclear' cases. However, such a safe and easy choice may result in unfair profits for the aggressor.

Second, despite Article 21 of the United Nations Convention on Jurisdictional Immunities of States and Their Property, not all assets of the central bank can enjoy absolute immunity from execution. In its remarkable decision Ö 3828-20 (Ascom Goup S.A. et als. v. Ministry of Finance of the Kazakhstan Republic and Kazakhstan Central Bank) dated 18 November 2021 the Supreme Court of Sweden affirmed that the restrictive theory of immunity applied to enforcement against State assets. It found 'no clear support in customary international law that immunity also applies to property which bank controls without there being connection with the bank's mission in terms of monetary policy' and ruled that, for immunity to apply, there had to be a 'clear connection with the central bank's activities in the area of monetary policy'.[37]

Third, concerns regarding the temporary character of countermeasures, when the amount of damage clearly exceeds the amount of the frozen assets, it is possible to situate the confiscation as a preliminary act to set-off.

---

[37] Maria Fogdestram-Aguis and Ginta Ahret, Swedish Supreme Court Weighs in on immunity of Sovereign Wealth Fund Assets under Central Bank Management, *Kluwer Arbitration Blog* (7 March 2022), available at https://arbitrationblog.kluwerarbitration.com/2022/03/07/swedish-supreme-court-weighs-in-on-immunity-of-sovereign-wealth-fund-assets-under-central-bank-man agement/.

The text of the decision (in Swedish) is available at https://www.domstol.se/hogsta-domstolen/avgoranden/2020/81607/. The original Swedish text (paragraph 24) is as follows.

'Det saknas tydligt stöd i internationell sedvanerätt för att absolut immunitet gäller även i fråga om egendom som banken råder över utan att det finns något samband med bankens penningpolitiska uppdrag.' 'Det särskilda skydd som centralbanker bör åtnjuta får därför anses vara begränsat till sådan egendom som har ett klart samband med centralbankens verksamhet på penningpolitikens område.'

Fourth, the bank accounts of embassies. Article 21, paragraph 1 provides that, as with the assets of central banks, assets, including bank accounts of embassies, enjoy immunity from execution. However, the legal character of embassy assets differs from that of central banks. Although embassy assets are usually placed on a reciprocal basis, the assets of the central banks are not. A large amount of money is kept only by the central banks of major currencies as foreign reserves. The amount of money kept in the Russian Central Bank is, if any, limited because the Russian Ruble is not a major currency.

Fifth, the confiscation of frozen assets of Oligarchs for the reconstruction of Ukraine is generally difficult to justify because it conflicts with the right to peaceful enjoyment of his/her possessions, as mentioned above. However, confiscation is not absolutely impossible because Article 1 of the Protocol to the Convention for the Protection of Human Rights and Fundamental Freedoms paves way for confiscation, as an exception, when it meets the requirements of the public interest and conditions provided for by law and the general principles of international law. It is generally difficult to establish a causal link between the activities of Oligarchs and Russian aggression. This differs from high-ranking Russian government officials. However, for Oligarchs who made money through military-related business, the proof might be established rather easily.

Sixth, there is a recent precedent for the de facto confiscation of frozen assets of central banks. On 11 February 2022 US President Biden, under Executive Order 14064, ordered the frozen property of the Afghan Central Bank to be transferred to a consolidated account at the Federal Reserve Bank. Half of the money (3.5 Billion USD) will be for the benefit of the Afghan People and for the Afghanistan's future, and the rest of the money (approximately 3.5 Billion USD) will be for the compensation of US victims of 9/11 terrorism.[38]

3.8 Confiscation of the Frozen Assets of the Russian National Wealth Fund

As to the confiscation of the frozen assets of the Russian National Wealth Fund, the Fund can come under the category of 'other monetary authority of the State' which

---

[38] On 14 September 2022, the United States established the Afghan Fund to disburse assets for the benefit of Afghan people. Taliban and China criticized the creation of the Afghan Fund. Contemporary Practice of the United States (The United States Establishes Fund for the Afghan People from Frozen Afghan Central Bank Assets), 117 *American Journal of International Law (2023)*, p. 144. If the money is withdrawn by Taliban, it would be used against the will of the innocent Afghan people. The action by the United States can be positioned as *negotiorum gestio* for the benefit of the Afghan people and the Afghan Fund would serve to prevent indigenous spoliation by Taliban.

generally enjoys immunity from execution as with central bank.[39] If confiscation of the frozen assets of the Russian Central Bank is possible, there is no reason to treat the Russian National Wealth Fund differently.

4 Possibility of the Management of the Frozen Assets

4.1 The European Commission's Proposal

Lastly, management as distinct from confiscation of the frozen assets is analysed.

On 30 November 2022 the European Commission proposed as follows: 'In the short-term: set up a structure to manage the frozen public funds, invest them and use the proceeds in favour of Ukraine. In the long term, once sanctions are lifted, the Central Bank's assets will need to be returned. This could be linked to a peace agreement that compensated Ukraine for the damages it had suffered. The assets that would need to be returned could be offset against this war reparation.'

This is a realistic idea which avoids the legal risks accompanying confiscation, although the mode of management of frozen funds is unclear. After the leaders' meeting on 30 June 2033 Belgian Prime Minister Alexander De Croo stated that the returns on windfall profits could be €3 billion per year according to the current estimation.[40] The EU has frozen over €200 billion in Russian Central Bank assets, with the bulk held in Belgium.[41] Kamminga aptly points out as follows: 'The Commission's attempt to come up with a creative solution is laudable. The proposed method combines some freezing and confiscation characteristics. Since the proposal envisages that the assets 'would need to be returned', it appears to stop short of confiscation. However, Russia regards this as a disguised form of confiscation. It is unclear what would happen if investments decreased in value. Moreover, the fruits of the investments are likely to be minimal in comparison to Ukraine's needs, so it may be questioned whether they are worth all the trouble. At the time of writing, it is not yet clear whether (a version of) the Commission's proposal will be pursued further'.[42]

---

[39] Article 21 paragraph 1 (c) of the United Nations Convention on Jurisdictional Immunities of States and Their Property provides that 'property of the central bank or other monetary authority of the State' can generally enjoy immunity from execution.

[40] EU Leaders Start Work on Handling Russian Frozen Assets with Caution, homepage of the EURACTIV(1 July 2023), available at https://www.euractiv.com/section/europe-s-east/news/eu-leaders-start-work-on-handling-russian-frozen-assets-with-caution/.

[41] EU Proposal on Using Frozen Russian Funds Delayed to September, homepage of Reuters (21 July 2023), available at https://www.reuters.com/world/europe/eu-proposal-using-frozen-russian-funds-delayed-september-2023-07-20/.

[42] Menno T. Kamminga, Confiscating Russia's Frozen Central Bank Assets: A Permissible Third-Party Countermeasures ?, *Netherlands International Law Review*, vol. 70 (2023), pp. 1, 13.

4.2 The Precedent in the Libyan Central Bank Case

Regarding the possibility of managing frozen assets, the practice in the Libyan Central Bank case is helpful as a precedent.

In Resolution 1970 (2011), the Security Council "decides that Member States *may* permit the addition to the accounts frozen pursuant to the provisions of paragraph 17 above of interests or other earnings due on those accounts or payments due under contracts, agreements or obligations that arose prior to the date on which those accounts became subject to the provisions of this resolution, provided that any such interest, other earnings and payments continue to be subject to these provisions and are frozen."(paragraph 20, emphasis added by the author).

In the Final report of the Panel of Experts on Libya established pursuant to Resolution 1973 (S/2016/209) concerning the asset freeze, the Panel made two Recommendations to the Security Council. Recommendation 8 provides: 'To explicitly allow and encourage the reinvestment of assets frozen under the measures, in consultation with the Government of Libya, in order to protect the value of investments of designated individuals and entities'. Recommendation 9 provides: 'To encourage Member States to urge financial institutions to credit interest payments to frozen assets of designated individuals and entities, in line with normal business practice'. Paragraph 257 of Recommendation 8 points out that there is no bar for fund managers to reinvest assets to achieve the best returns in accordance with their fiduciary duties. Paragraph 258 of Recommendation 9 points out that interest can be paid on deposits in a normal way, provided that it is added to frozen funds and remains frozen. Paragraph 259 states: 'The word 'may' (of the paragraph 20 of the Security Council Resolution 1970) allows banks to avoid paying interest, further diminishing the real value of the assets. The Panel considers that Member States should be encouraged to urge financial institutions to make credit interest payments on frozen assets in line with normal business practice.'

In line with this report, international law does not prohibit investing in frozen assets and giving proceeds to Ukraine for reconstruction. If the investment results in a loss, a fiduciary duty might arise and compensation would be required.

5 Concluding Remarks

The confiscation of the frozen assets of the Russian Central Bank, if realised, will be the most powerful non-military measure against Russia. As mentioned in Sect. 4, confiscation is only lawful when certain requirements are met. However, whether the States take legal risks and proceed with confiscation is still unclear.

In 2019, Tom Ruys pointed out that States did not rely on the doctrine of countermeasures to justify breaches of immunity law, which reflected *opinio juris* on the part of States that perceived immunity rules as a closed system which did not lead to recourse to countermeasures.[43]

However, when facing Russian aggression against Ukraine, the *opinio juris* of the States might change. It seems premature to conclude that immunity is absolute in all situations and eternally protected from countermeasures.

Appendix

On 12 February 2024, the Council of the European Union adopted a decision and a regulation clarifying the obligations of Central Securities Depositories holding assets and reserves of the Russian Central Bank. It is expected that they pave the way for using the profits generated by the Russian assets to finance Ukraine's reconstruction.

---

[43] Tom Ruys, 'Immunity, Inviolability and Countermeasures - A closer Look at Non-UN Targeted Sanctions', in *in* Tom Ruys et als. (ed.), *The Cambridge Handbook of Immunities and International Law* (Cambridge University Press, 2019), pp. 670, 707.

Trade Sanctions Against Russia and Their WTO Consistency: Focusing on Justification Under National Security Exceptions

Fujio Kawashima

Abstract In the wake of Russia's 2022 invasion of Ukraine, around 40 countries/economies, including G7 members, responded to impose a wide range of economic, including trade-related, sanctions on Russia. The question immediately arises as to whether such sanctions violate the WTO agreements or are justified under the relevant national security exceptions. After introducing the material facts of the economic sanctions against Russia as well as the development of WTO jurisprudence on the national security exceptions—particularly, Article XXI(b)(iii) of GATT—this article goes on to analyse the WTO consistency of these trade sanctions against Russia on a country-by-country as well as a measure-by-measure basis. From the standpoint of the "war or other emergency in international relations" and "essential security interests" requirements, countries are categorised according to their geographic proximity and relationship (e.g., military alliances, customs unions, etc.) to the belligerents, while measures are categorised according to their nature and aim from the standpoint of the "necessary to protect" requirement.

1 Introduction

In response to the Russian invasion of Ukraine on February 24, 2022, around 40 countries/economies such as Group of Seven (G7) countries, have since imposed a wide range of economic sanctions on Russia. Such sanctions include, among others, trade measures such as import and export bans, and the suspension of the most-favoured-nation (MFN) treatment. As the countries imposing trade sanctions, as well as the target country, Russia, are all Members of the World Trade Organization (WTO), at first glance, such sanctions may appear inconsistent with the WTO agreements, for instance, the General Agreement on Tariffs and Trade (GATT). However, there is scope for such measures to be justified under the relevant security

---

F. Kawashima (✉)
Graduate School of Law, Kobe University, Kobe, Japan
e-mail: fkawa@port.kobe-u.ac.jp

© The Author(s), under exclusive license to Springer Nature Singapore Pte Ltd. 2024
M. Asada, D. Tamada (eds.), *The War in Ukraine and International Law*,
https://doi.org/10.1007/978-981-97-2504-5_7

157

exception clauses, namely, GATT Article XXI and Article XIV *bis* of the General Agreement on Trade in Services (GATS).

This article first introduces the material facts of the economic sanctions against Russia, and discusses their position in international economic law (Sect. 2). It then briefly introduces the development of the jurisprudence on WTO security exceptions, focusing on GATT Article XXI (Sect. 3). Applying the standards developed in the jurisprudence to the material facts of the trade sanctions against Russia, this article goes on to analyse the WTO consistency of such sanctions on a country-by-country as well as a measure-by-measure basis (Sect. 4). From the standpoint of the "war or other emergency in international relations" and "essential security interests" requirements, countries are categorised according to their position regarding their geographic proximity and particular relationship to the belligerents, such as military alliances, customs unions and so on, while measures are categorised according to their nature and aim from the standpoint of the "necessary to protect" requirement.

2 Material Facts of Economic Sanctions Against Russia and Their Positioning in International Economic Law

2.1 Material Facts of Economic Sanctions Against Russia

A summary of the material facts of the economic sanctions against Russia is as follows.

2.1.1 Countries Concerned

Countries and economies imposing sanctions and countries targeted by them are listed in Table 1 (non-exhaustive list). All countries concerned are WTO Members.

2.1.2 Sectors and Measures Concerned

Sectors that are covered by sanctions include trade in goods, trade in services, investment, settlement, and the movement of persons. In parallel, the types of measures adopted include import and export bans of goods, exclusion from the

Trade Sanctions Against Russia and Their WTO Consistency: Focusing... 159

Table 1 Countries/economies concerned as of August 2023

Imposing	G7 (i.e., Canada, France, Germany, Italy, the EU (representing 27 Members including France, Germany and Italy), Japan, the UK, and the United States), Australia[a], Iceland, Liechtenstein, Moldova, New Zealand[b], Norway, Taiwan, Singapore, South Korea, Switzerland, Ukraine[c]
Targeted	Russia[d]

[a] *See e.g.*, https://www.standard-club.com/ja/knowledge-news/australian-and-new-zealand-sanctions-targeting-russia-4289/

[b] New Zealand Foreign Affairs and Trade, Russia Sanctions, at https://www.mfat.govt.nz/en/countries-and-regions/europe/ukraine/russian-invasion-of-ukraine/sanctions

[c] Letter of the Permanent Representative of Ukraine to the Chairman of the WTO's General Council, 2 March 2022 (notifying the decision to impose a complete economic embargo, "consistent with its national security rights under, inter alia, Article XXI of the GATT 1994, Article XIV bis of the GATS, and Article 73 of the TRIPS Agreement")

[d] Current sanctions also target Belarus which is supporting Russia, the self-proclaimed Donetsk People's Republic and the self-proclaimed Luhansk People's Republic. However, they are outside the scope of this article as they are not WTO Members

SWIFT international settlement network,[1] ban on investment in Russia,[2] ban on entry of persons, and so on.

2.1.3 Reasons for Sanctions

As is explained in more detail elsewhere (*see* Sect. 4.1), there is currently no United Nations Security Council resolution placing an obligation on States to impose sanctions against Russia in response to its aggression against Ukraine. Therefore, the reasons for imposing sanctions vary depending on the imposing party and the types of measures. That being said, seeking to prevent Russia's access to revenue and weapons, as well as access to resources for weapon manufacture, may be regarded as the primary reasons (*See* Sect. 4.4.2, below).

The above facts are key to identifying with which provisions of the WTO Agreements the sanctions in question are inconsistent, and whether they may be justified under the security exceptions.

---

[1] Though it is far from straightforward to establish whether the ban on using the SWIFT international settlement network is inconsistent with WTO rules, it potentially constitutes a violation of GATT Article XI:1 as well as GATS Article XI:1. This article does not explore this point further. For a similar opinion, *see* Kazuyori Ito "Economic Sanctions against Russia and International Law," International Issues, Dec. 2022, p. 27 (*in Japanese*).

[2] For the ban on investment to Russia, *see* the chapter "War in Ukraine and Implications for International Investment Law" of this volume.

Table 2 Japan's trade sanctions against Russia as of August 2023

Date of publication	Contents
Feb. 26, 2022	Export ban on items subject to International Export Control
Mar. 1, 2022	Export ban to Russian military-related entities Export ban on dual-use products incl. semiconductors
Mar. 8, 2022	Export ban on oil refinery machines, etc.
Mar. 16, 2022	Suspension of MFN
Mar. 25, 2022	Export ban on luxury products
Apr. 12, 2022	Import ban on coal, machinery, wooden products, vodka
May 10, 2022	Export ban on emerging technology products incl. quantum computing, 3D printers
June 7, 2022	Export ban on products contributing to strengthening industrial bases incl. lorries and bulldozers
July 5, 2022	Import ban on gold
Sep. 26, 2022	Export ban on products related to chemical weapons, etc. Export ban to 21 designated entities
Dec. 5, 2022[a]	Setting the maximum price of oil originating in Russia
Jan. 27, 2023[b]	Export ban to 49 designated entities Export ban on dual-use products which can strengthen military capacities incl. tear gas, robot, laser welder
Feb. 28, 2023	Export ban to 21 designated entities

[a] https://www.mofa.go.jp/mofaj/press/release/press4_009542.html
[b] https://www.mofa.go.jp/mofaj/press/release/press4_009599.html

2.2 Positioning Sanctions in International Economic Law

For example, Japan, in alignment with G7 sanctions against Russia, has imposed the trade sanctions (Table 2).[3]

---

[3] *See* Prime Minister's Office, *"Measures in Response to Russian Aggression against Ukraine" (in Japanese)*, at https://www.kantei.go.jp/jp/headline/ukraine2022/index.html; Ministry of Economy, Trade and Industry, "On Sanctions against Russia etc." (*in Japanese*), at https://www.meti.go.jp/policy/external_economy/trade_control/01_seido/04_seisai/crimea.html; Ministry of Economy, Trade and Industry, "METI's Supports and Measures related to International Circumstances surrounding Russian Aggression against Ukraine" (in Japanese), at https://www.meti.go.jp/ukraine/index.html.

Trade Sanctions Against Russia and Their WTO Consistency: Focusing... 161

Table 3 Positioning economic sanctions against Russia in international economic law

	Export Ban	Import Ban	Settlement	Investment	Entry Ban
Provisions	GATT XI, I	GATT XI, I	GATT XI, 1 GATS XI, 1	–	– (GATS?)
Justification	GATT XXI	GATT XXI	GATS XIV-2	–	–
Issues/ Comments	Depending on who imposes, reasons and con-tent, etc.	Depending on who imposes, reasons and con-tent, etc.	Only the EU imposes?	No viola-tion of BITs	Targeted per-sons are non-service-providers

BITs bilateral investment treaty/treaties

As all the above concern export and import restrictions applied only to products destined for, or originating in, Russia, preliminarily, it may be concluded that they are inconsistent with either or both Article I, paragraph 1[4] and Article XI, paragraph 1[5] of the GATT.

The foregoing may be summarised as presented in Table 3.

3 Security Exceptions Under GATT Article XXI

3.1 Text of GATT Article XXI

GATT Article XXI provides for as follows:
GATT Article XXI

Article XXI Security Exceptions
Nothing in this Agreement shall be construed

(a) to require any contracting party to furnish any information the disclosure of which it considers contrary to its essential security interests; or

---

[4] Art. I, para. 1: "With respect to customs duties and charges of any kind imposed on or in connection with importation or exportation or imposed on the international transfer of payments for imports or exports, and with respect to the method of levying such duties and charges, and with respect to all rules and formalities in connection with importation and exportation, and with respect to all matters referred to in paragraphs 2 and 4 of Article III, any advantage, favour, privilege or immunity granted by any contracting party to any product originating in or destined for any other country shall be accorded immediately and unconditionally to the like product originating in or destined for the territories of all other contracting parties." (footnote omitted).

[5] Art. XI, para. 1: "No prohibitions or restrictions other than duties, taxes or other charges, whether made effective through quotas, import or export licences or other measures, shall be instituted or maintained by any contracting party on the importation of any product of the territory of any other contracting party or on the exportation or sale for export of any product destined for the territory of any other contracting party."

Table 4 Cases on GATT Article XXI and related provisions

Year	Case	Actions
1970	*Arab Boycott against Israel*	No panel established
1982	*Falkland/Malvinas Islands Dispute*	No panel established
1985	*US — Embargo on Nicaragua*	Panel report but Art. XXI was outside the terms of reference
2016-	*Russia — Traffic in Transit* (DS512)	Panel report adopted in 2019
2018-	*Saudi Arabia — IPRs* (DS567)	Panel report; adoption not sought[a]
2018-	*US — Steel and Aluminium Products* (DS544, etc.)	Panel reports appealed
2020-	*US — Origin Marking (Hong Kong, China)* (DS597)	Panel reports appealed

[a] After Saudi Arabia's appeal of the panel report, on 21 April 2022, Qatar notified the DSB that it had agreed to terminate the dispute, and that it would not seek adoption of the panel report. *See* DS567: *Saudi Arabia — Measures concerning the Protection of Intellectual Property Rights* at https://www.wto.org/english/tratop_e/dispu_e/cases_e/ds567_e.htm.

   (b) to prevent any contracting party from taking any action which it considers necessary for the protection of its essential security interests
      (i) relating to fissionable materials or the materials from which they are derived;
      (ii) relating to the traffic in arms, ammunition and implements of war and to such traffic in other goods and materials as is carried on directly or indirectly for the purpose of supplying a military establishment;
      (iii) taken in time of war or other emergency in international relations; or
   (c) to prevent any contracting party from taking any action in pursuance of its obligations under the United Nations Charter for the maintenance of international peace and security.

3.2 GATT Article XXI Jurisprudence

As witnessed (Table 4), there has been no panel report interpreting security exceptions during the GATT era. However, about 29 years after the establishment of the WTO, four panel reports have so far interpreted GATT Article XXI(b)(iii) and its chapeau, as well as identical provisions in the Agreement on Trade Related Aspects of Intellectual Properties (TRIPS), namely, Article 73(b)(iii) and its chapeau.

However, the Panel Report on *Saudi Arabia — IPRs* (DS567) has not been adopted as the two disputing parties agreed to terminate the dispute following Saudi Arabia's appeal. Both Panel Reports on *US — Steel and Aluminium Products* (DS544, etc.) and *US — Origin Marking (Hong Kong, China)* (DS597) have yet to be adopted as they are currently subject to appeal (by the United States). The Panel

Report on *Russia — Traffic in Transit* (DS512) is the only one that has formally been adopted by the Dispute Settlement Body (DSB). As such, the following subsections mainly focus on the Panel Report on *Russia — Traffic in Transit* (DS512), while also pointing out the commonalities and differences at play among the four panel reports.

3.2.1 *Russia — Traffic in Transit* (DS512)[6]

Since January 2016, Russia has introduced measures to restrict all international cargo transit from Ukraine to Kazakhstan through Russian territory only via the Belarus-Russia border. Ukraine formally filed a complaint within the context of WTO dispute settlement, claiming that these measures were, among other things, in violation of GATT Article V:2. In response, Russia argued that the Panel lacked jurisdiction to evaluate the measures by invoking the GATT security exceptions, namely, Article XXI(b)(iii).[7]

3.2.1.1 Panel Jurisdiction

The panel examined whether the adjectival clause "which it considers" in the chapeau of Article XXI(b) qualifies the determination of the sets of circumstances described in the enumerated subparagraphs of Article XXI(b). The phrase "taken in time of" in subparagraph (iii) describes the connection between the action and the events of war or other emergency in international relations in that subparagraph. The Panel understood this phrase to require that the action be taken during the war or other emergency in international relations. Chronological concurrence is a question of fact—and an objective one for that matter—that is amenable to objective determination. Moreover, the existence of war is also a question of fact that is clearly capable of objective determination. War is one example within the larger category of "emergency in international relations," and it is clear that an "emergency in international relations" can only be understood as belonging to the same category of objective facts that are amenable to objective determination.[8]

Taking into account as context for the interpretation of an "emergency in international relations" in subparagraph (iii), the matters addressed by subparagraphs (i) and (ii) of Article XXI(b), such as a situation of war in subparagraph (iii) itself, all concern defence and military interests, as well as maintenance of law and public order interests. Therefore, an "emergency in international relations" must be understood as eliciting the same type of interests as those arising from the other matters addressed in the subparagraphs of Article XXI(b). These contexts suggest that

---

[6]Panel Report, *Russia — Measures Concerning Traffic in Transit*, WT/DS512/R adopted 26 April 2019.

[7]*Ibid.*, para. 3.2.

[8]*Ibid.*, paras. 7.66–7.73.

political or economic differences between Members are not sufficient, in and of themselves, to constitute an emergency in international relations for the purposes of subparagraph (iii). An emergency in international relations would, therefore, appear to refer generally to situations of armed conflict, latent armed conflict, heightened tension or crisis, or of general instability engulfing or surrounding a state. Therefore, as the existence of an emergency in international relations is an objective state of affairs, the determination of whether the action was "taken in time of" an "emergency in international relations" under subparagraph (iii) of Article XXI(b) is a question of fact, amenable to objective determination.[9] In sum, the Panel considered that the ordinary meaning of Article XXI(b)(iii), in its context and in light of the object and purpose of GATT 1994 and the WTO Agreement more generally, is that the adjectival clause "which it considers" in the chapeau of Article XXI(b) does not qualify the determination of the circumstances in subparagraph (iii). Rather, for action to fall within the scope of Article XXI(b), it must objectively be found to meet the requirements of one of the enumerated subparagraphs of that provision.[10] Article XXI(b)(iii) of the GATT 1994 is not entirely "self-judging" in the manner asserted by Russia. Consequently, Russia's argument that the Panel lacked jurisdiction to review Russia's invocation of Article XXI(b)(iii) must fail.[11]

3.2.1.2 Article XXI(b)(iii)

There was evidence before the Panel that from at least March 2014 and up to at least the end of 2016, relations between Ukraine and Russia had deteriorated to such degree that they were a matter of concern to the international community. By December 2016, the situation between Ukraine and Russia was recognised by the UN General Assembly as having involved armed conflict. Further evidence of the gravity of the situation was the fact that, since 2014, a number of countries had imposed sanctions against Russia in connection to this situation. Consequently, the Panel was satisfied that since 2014 the situation between Ukraine and Russia constituted an emergency in international relations, within the meaning of GATT Article XXI(b)(iii). The Panel also concluded that each of the measures at issue was "taken in time of" an emergency in international relations, within the meaning of GATT Article XXI(b)(iii).[12]

3.2.1.3 Chapeau of Article XXI(b)

The Panel stated that:

---

[9] *Ibid.*, paras. 7.74–7.77.

[10] *Ibid.*, para. 7.82.

[11] *Ibid.*, paras. 7.102–7.103.

[12] *Ibid.*, paras. 7.122–7.126.

Trade Sanctions Against Russia and Their WTO Consistency: Focusing... 165

[T]he question remains whether the adjectival clause "which it considers" in the chapeau of Article XXI(b) qualifies both the determination of the invoking Member's essential security interests *and* the necessity of the measures for the protection of those interests, or simply the determination of their necessity.[13]

"Essential security interests", which is evidently a narrower concept than "security interests", may generally be understood to refer to those interests relating to the quintessential functions of the state, namely, the protection of its territory and its population from external threats, and the maintenance of law and public order internally.[14]

The specific interests that are considered directly relevant to the protection of a state from such external or internal threats will depend on the particular situation and perceptions of the state in question, and can be expected to vary with changing circumstances. For these reasons, it is left, in general, to every Member to define what it considers to be its essential security interests.[15]

However, this does not mean that a Member is free to elevate any concern to that of an "essential security interest". Rather, the discretion of a Member to designate particular concerns as "essential security interests" is limited by its obligation to interpret and apply Article XXI(b)(iii) of the GATT 1994 in good faith. The Panel recalls that the obligation of good faith is a general principle of law and a principle of general international law which underlies all treaties, as codified in Article 31(1) ("[a] treaty shall be interpreted in good faith ...") and Article 26 ("[e]very treaty ... must be performed [by the parties] in good faith") of the Vienna Convention.[16]

The obligation of good faith requires that Members not use the exceptions in Article XXI as a means to circumvent their obligations under the GATT 1994. A glaring example of this would be where a Member sought to release itself from the structure of "reciprocal and mutually advantageous arrangements" that constitutes the multilateral trading system simply by re-labelling trade interests that it had agreed to protect and promote within the system, as "essential security interests", falling outside the reach of that system.[17]

It is therefore incumbent on the invoking Member to articulate the essential security interests said to arise from the emergency in international relations sufficiently enough to demonstrate their veracity.[18]

What qualifies as a sufficient level of articulation will depend on the emergency in international relations at issue. In particular, the Panel considers that the less characteristic is the "emergency in international relations" invoked by the Member, i.e. the further it is removed from armed conflict, or a situation of breakdown of law and public order (whether in the invoking Member or in its immediate surroundings), the less obvious are the defence or military interests, or maintenance of law and public order interests, that can be generally expected to arise. In such cases, a Member would need to articulate its essential security interests with greater specificity than would be required when the emergency in international relations involved, for example, armed conflict.[19]

---

[13] *Ibid.*, para. 7.128.

[14] *Ibid.*, para. 7.130.

[15] *Ibid.*, para. 7.131.

[16] *Ibid.*, para. 7.132.

[17] *Ibid.*, para. 7.133.

[18] *Ibid.*, para. 7.134.

[19] *Ibid.*, para. 7.135.

In the case at hand, the emergency in international relations is very close to the "hard core" of war or armed conflict. While Russia has not explicitly articulated the essential security interests that it considers the measures at issue are necessary to protect, it did refer to certain characteristics of the 2014 emergency that concern the security of the Ukraine-Russia border.[20]

Given the character of the 2014 emergency, as one that has been recognized by the UN General Assembly as involving armed conflict, and which affects the security of the border with an adjacent country and exhibits the other features identified by Russia, the essential security interests that thereby arise for Russia cannot be considered obscure or indeterminate. Despite its allusiveness, Russia's articulation of its essential security interests is minimally satisfactory in these circumstances. Moreover, there is nothing in Russia's expression of those interests to suggest that Russia invokes Article XXI(b)(iii) simply as a means to circumvent its obligations under the GATT 1994.[21]

The obligation of good faith, referred to in paragraphs 7.132 and 7.133 above, applies not only to the Member's definition of the essential security interests said to arise from the particular emergency in international relations, but also, and most importantly, to their connection with the measures at issue. Thus, as concerns the application of Article XXI(b)(iii), this obligation is crystallized in demanding that the measures at issue meet a minimum requirement of plausibility in relation to the proffered essential security interests, i.e. that they are not implausible as measures protective of these interests.[22]

The Panel must therefore review whether the measures are so remote from, or unrelated to, the 2014 emergency that it is implausible that Russia implemented the measures for the protection of its essential security interests arising out of the emergency (emphasis added, footnotes omitted).[23]

[A]ll of the measures at issue restrict the transit from Ukraine of goods across Russia, particularly across the Ukraine-Russia border, in circumstances in which there is an emergency in Russia's relations with Ukraine that affects the security of the Ukraine-Russia border and is recognized by the UN General Assembly as involving armed conflict. In these circumstances, the measures at issue cannot be regarded as being so remote from, or unrelated to, the 2014 emergency, that it is implausible that Russia implemented the measures for the protection of its essential security interests arising out of that emergency ... The Panel finds that Russia had satisfied the conditions of the chapeau of Article XXI (b) of the GATT 1994.[24]

3.2.2 *Saudi Arabia — IPRs* (DS567)[25]

In June 2017, Saudi Arabia severed all relations with Qatar. In response, Qatar filed a complaint within the context of WTO dispute settlement claiming that, among other things, Saudi Arabia's acts and omissions resulting in Qatari nationals being unable

---

[20] *Ibid.*, para. 7.136.

[21] *Ibid.*, para. 7.137.

[22] *Ibid.*, para. 7.138.

[23] *Ibid.*, para. 7.139.

[24] *Ibid.*, paras. 7.144–7.145, 7.148.

[25] Panel Report, *Saudi Arabia — Measures concerning the Protection of Intellectual Property Rights*, WT/DS567/R, 16 June 2020 (adoption not sought).

to protect their intellectual property rights, violate Article 42 of the TRIPS Agreement, because they fail to make available to Qatari nationals civil judicial procedures concerning the enforcement of intellectual property rights, including, among other things, the right to be represented by independent legal counsel; and Article 61 of the TRIPS Agreement, because they fail to provide for the application of criminal procedures and penalties to the wilful commercial scale piracy of a Qatari broadcasting company beIN's copyrighted material. Saudi Arabia counterargued that its actions were justified under Article 73(b)(iii) of the TRIPS Agreement, the wording of which is identical to that of GATT Article XXI(b)(iii).

After finding that Saudi Arabia has acted in a manner inconsistent with Articles 42 and 61 of the TRIPS Agreement,[26] the Panel almost followed the interpretations by the Panel in *Russia — Traffic in Transit* regarding i) "a war or other emergency in international relations" and ii) "taken in time of" in Article 73(b)(iii) of the TRIPS Agreement, as well as iii) the obligation to sufficiently articulate relevant "essential security interests" in the chapeau of Article 73(b) and iv) the link between the actions concerned and the protection of the invoking party's essential security interests,[27] as both parties interpreted Article 73(b)(iii) of the TRIPS Agreement by reference to, and consistently with, the interpretation of GATT Article XXI(b)(iii), as developed by the Panel in *Russia — Traffic in Transit*.[28]

Applying these interpretations to the facts of this dispute, the Panel found that: i) "a situation … of heightened tension or crisis" existed in the circumstances in this dispute (i.e., Saudi Arabia's severance of "all diplomatic and economic ties" with Qatar in the context that Saudi Arabia repeatedly alleged that Qatar had, among other things, repudiated the Riyadh Agreements designed to address regional concerns of security and stability, supported terrorism and extremism, and interfered in the internal affairs of other countries), and is related to Saudi Arabia's "defence or military interests, or maintenance of law and public order interests" (i.e. essential security interests), sufficient to establish the existence of an "emergency in international relations. . .";[29] ii) the measures concerned were "taken in time of war or other emergency in international relations";[30] iii) Saudi Arabia had expressly articulated its "essential security interests," in terms of protecting itself "from the dangers of terrorism and extremism";[31] and iv) the measures aimed at denying Qatari nationals access to civil remedies through Saudi courts, as an aspect of Saudi Arabia's umbrella policy of ending or preventing any form of interaction with Qatari nationals, "meet a minimum requirement of plausibility in relation to the proffered essential security interests" i.e. to protect Saudi citizens and the Saudi population,

---

[26] *Ibid.*, paras. 7.197 and 7.221.

[27] *Ibid.*, paras. 7.241–7.255.

[28] *Ibid.*, para. 7.231.

[29] *Ibid.*, paras. 7.257, 7.258 and 7.263.

[30] *Ibid.*, para. 7.270.

[31] *Ibid.*, para. 7.280.

Saudi government institutions, and the territory of Saudi Arabia from the threats of terrorism and extremism,[32] while the non-application of criminal procedures and penalties to *beoutQ*, i.e., a commercial-scale broadcast pirate, did not have any relationship to Saudi Arabia's policy of ending or preventing any form of interaction with Qatari nationals, and, therefore, failed to "meet a minimum requirement of plausibility in relation to the proffered essential security interests."[33]

3.2.3 *US — Steel and Aluminium Products* (DS544, etc.)[34]

After finding the additional duties on steel and aluminium products imposed by the United States to be inconsistent with GATT Articles II:1(b) and II:1(a) as well as Article I:1,[35] the Panel rejected, as the Panel in *Russia — Traffic in Transit*, the United States' argument that GATT Article XXI(b) is entirely "self-judging" or "non-justiciable", and that the provision contains a "single relative clause" that wholly reserves the conditions and circumstances of the subparagraphs to the judgment of the invoking Member,[36] and also supported the interpretation that an "emergency in international relations" within the meaning of Article XXI(b)(iii) must be, if not equally grave or severe, at least comparable in its gravity or severity to a "war" in terms of its impact on international relations.[37] Applying this interpretation to the case, the Panel could not find that the global excess capacity in steel and aluminium to which the United States referred rose to the gravity or severity of tensions on the international plane so as to constitute an "emergency in international relations" during which a Member may act under Article XXI(b)(iii), and, therefore, found that the inconsistencies of the measures at issue with GATT Articles I:1 and II:1 were not justified under GATT Article XXI(b)(iii).[38]

3.2.4 *US — Origin Marking* (Hong Kong, China) (DS597)[39]

Considering the ordinary meaning, including the grammatical structure, and the context of Article XXI(b), as well as the object and purpose of the covered agreements, the Panel found that the phrase "which it considers" in the chapeau of Article

---

[32] *Ibid.*, paras. 7.284–7.288.

[33] *Ibid.*, para. 7.293.

[34] *See e.g.*, Panel Report, *United States — Certain Measures on Steel and Aluminium Products (China)*, WT/DS544/R, 9 December 2022 (on appeal).

[35] *Ibid.*, paras. 7.47 and 7.59.

[36] *Ibid.*, para. 7.128.

[37] *Ibid.*, para. 7.139.

[38] *Ibid.*, paras. 7.148–7.149.

[39] Panel Report, *US — Origin Marking Requirement (Hong Kong, China)*, WT/DS597/R, 21 December 2022 (on appeal).

XXI(b) does not extend to the subparagraphs and, therefore, Article XXI(b) is only partly self-judging in that the subparagraphs are not subject solely to the invoking Member's own determination. Instead, the subparagraphs are subject to review by a panel, and a finding that the circumstances set out therein do not apply means that the action cannot be justified under the exception.[40] The GATT/International Trade Organization (ITO) negotiating history confirms such reading of the structure of Article XXI(b).[41] The Panel found that Article XXI(b) is not entirely self-judging insofar as the unilateral determination granted to the invoking Member through the phrase "which it considers" in the chapeau of that provision does not extend to the subparagraphs. Instead, the subparagraphs are subject to review by a panel.[42]

The Panel found that the origin marking requirement of the United States accorded to products of Hong Kong, China treatment with regard to marking requirements that was less favourable than the treatment accorded to like products of any third country, and was thus inconsistent with Article IX:1 of the GATT 1994.[43]

The Panel also interpreted the ordinary meaning of the terms in the phrase "emergency in international relations" as suggesting a reference to a state of affairs that occurs in relations between states or participants in international relations that is of the utmost gravity, in effect, a situation representing a breakdown or near-breakdown in relations.[44] The Panel found the United States and Hong Kong, China's international relations to have continued to involve cooperation in a number of policy areas, and trade had carried on between the two, largely as before, with the exception of the origin marking requirement and some export controls. All of this militated against a conclusion of a breakdown or near-breakdown in international relations that the Panel had found to be consonant with an emergency in such relations.[45] Although there was evidence of the United States and other Members being highly concerned about the human rights situation in Hong Kong, China, the Panel stated that the situation had "not escalated to a threshold of requisite gravity to constitute an emergency in international relations that would provide justification for taking actions that are inconsistent with obligations under the GATT 1994."[46]

It is also worth noting that the panel stated in its *dicta* that the open reference to "international relations" suggests that the emergency did not necessarily have to originate in the invoking Member's own territory and bilateral relations; therefore, a war taking place between two or more countries, could also give rise to an emergency in international relations affecting other countries.[47]

---

[40] *Ibid.*, paras. 7.160–7.161.

[41] *Ibid.*, para. 7.175.

[42] *Ibid.*, para. 7.185.

[43] *Ibid.*, para. 7.252.

[44] *Ibid.*, paras. 7.282 and 7.290.

[45] *Ibid.*, para. 7.354.

[46] *Ibid.*, para. 7.358.

[47] *Ibid.*, paras. 7.297 and 7.307.

3.2.5 Commonalities and Differences Among the Four Panel Reports

The three panel reports all take a different approach to interpreting Article XXI(b). While the Panel in *Russia — Traffic in Transit* mainly relied on the nature of the subject-matters in subparagraphs (i) to (iii) of Article XXI(b) which are "subject to objective determination,"[48] the Panels in *US — Steel and Aluminium Products* and *US — Origin Marking (Hong Kong, China)* relied to a greater extent on the grammatical construction or analysis, and the grammatical structure, of Article XXI(b) in reaching their respective interpretations.[49] It should be pointed out, however, that the above reports all share the conclusion that Article XXI(b) is not entirely self-judging,[50] and reject the argument raised by parties that invoked Article XXI(b)(iii) that panels had no jurisdiction to review the merits of invocation. Although the Appellate Body has yet to uphold this point, it is worth noting that all panel reports to date have arrived at this interpretation.

The Panels in *Russia — Traffic in Transit* and *Saudi Arabia — IPRs* concluded that the measures concerned satisfied the requirement of "taken in the time of a war or an emergency of international relations" of Article XXI(b)(iii) and therefore were able to go on to examine whether they satisfied the two requirements in the chapeau of Article XXI(b) that such measures are "necessary" to protect the invoking Member's "essential security interests". The Panel in *Russia — Traffic in Transit* found both to be satisfied, while the Panel in *Saudi Arabia — IPRs*, for the first time, found that requirement concerning "necessary" had not been satisfied in relation to one of the measures. It is worth pointing out that the Panel in *Russia — Traffic in Transit* successfully introduced not too intrusive nor too permissive a standard, in an attempt to strike a delicate balance between the needs to prevent the abuse of national security exceptions and to ensure each Member's sovereignty to define its own national security interests and design measures necessary for their protection.[51]

---

[48] Panel Report, *Russia — Traffic in Transit, supra* note 6, para. 7.77.

[49] Panel Report, *US — Steel and Aluminium Products, supra* note 34, paras. 7.115–7.116; Panel Report, *US — Origin Marking (Hong Kong, China), supra* note 39, paras. 7.34–7.35, 7.89, 7.160, fn 128, 129, 130.

[50] Panel Report, *Russia — Traffic in Transit, supra* note 6, para. 7.102; Panel Report, *US — Steel and Aluminium Products, supra* note 34, para. 7.128; *US — Origin Marking (Hong Kong, China), supra* note 39, paras. 7.160 and 7.309.

[51] *See* Peter Van den Bossche and Sarah Akpofure, "The Use and Abuse of the National Security Exception under Article XXI(b)(iii) of the GATT 1994," *WTI Working Paper* No. 03/2020, pp. 7–8, 25 (evaluating the panel in Russia Traffic in Transit (2019) struck the correct balance between, on the one hand, the sovereign right of Members to determine what their security interests are and how to protect these interests, and, on the other hand, the inherent need for the WTO to avoid abuse of national security exceptions); Viktoriia Lapa, "The WTO Panel Report in Russia — Traffic in Transit: Cutting the Gordian Knot of the GATT Security Exception?", Questions of International Law, May 12, 2020. (evaluating the Panel skilfully dealt with the interpretation of the GATT security exception, and managed to design a flexible framework to accommodate the need for deference towards WTO Members while preventing the abuse of the security exception.) at http:// www.qil-qdi.org/the-wto-panel-report-in-russia-traffic-in-transit-cutting-the-gordian-knot-of-the-

On the other hand, the Panels in *US — Steel and Aluminium Products* and *US — Origin Marking (Hong Kong, China)*, for the first time, denied the existence of "an emergency of international relations" and thus did not need to examine whether the two requirements in the chapeau were satisfied. Neither Panel touched upon the applicability of the principle of good faith to the two requirements in the chapeau, as was applied by Panel in *Russia — Traffic in Transit*. It is therefore necessary to keep a close eye on whether the chapeau of Article XXI(b) continues to be interpreted to function as a minimum safeguard against the abuse of security exceptions.[52]

4 Application to Trade Sanctions Against Russia

4.1 Applicable Provisions to Justify

As there has been no UN Security Council resolution mandating the imposition of sanctions against Russia, GATT Article XXI(c) is not applicable. Therefore, our examination is limited to the applicability of (b)(ii) and (b)(iii) (*See* Sect. 3.1, above).

WTO Members, including Japan, that have imposed sanctions against Russia have not explained the reasons their sanctions are justified. It can be reasonably understood from the viewpoint of litigation strategies that possible justifications should not be disclosed to potential disputing parties until the dispute settlement procedures commence.

However, as circumstances that constitute objective conditions in each provision are different between (b)(ii) and (b)(iii), the "essential security interests," which should specifically be articulated, and the measures "necessary" to protect such interests can vary between the two provisions. In addition, (b)(iii) sets a temporal limitation via the phrase "in time of war or other emergency" while (b)(ii) does not seem to do so via the phrase "relating to the traffic in arms." Therefore, when designing measures that, on their face, may be inconsistent with WTO agreements yet "necessary" to be justified under security exceptions, governmental officials involved in their design should examine in detail based on which provisions such measures may be justified, and try to ensure logical consistency in order to avoid, as well as prepare for, potential WTO disputes.

---

gatt-security-exception/. *See also* Caroline Glöckle, "The second chapter on a national security exception in WTO law: the panel report in *Saudi Arabia — Protection of IPR*," EJIL: Talk!, July 22, 2020, *available at* https://www.ejiltalk.org/the-second-chapter-on-a-national-security-exception-in-wto-law-the-panel-report-in-saudi-arabia-protection-of-ipr/

[52] *See* Separate Opinion of Judge Iwasawa, International Court of Justice, Judgment, Certain Iranian Assets (Islamic Republic of Iran v. United States of America) 30 March 2023, paras. 21–22 (After mentioning the Panel Report in *Russia — Traffic in Transit*, which introduced the principle of good faith in the interpretation of the chapeau of Article XXI(b), introducing the ICJ case law which states that this exercise of discretion is still subject to the obligation of good faith).

If we look at Table 2 (*See* Sect. 2.2, above), most of the sanctions imposed by Japan so far seem more likely to be justified under (b)(iii), while some including export bans to Russian military-related entities and export bans of products related to chemical weapons are likely to be justified under both (b)(ii) and (b)(iii). Therefore, the following sections mainly focus on (b)(iii).

4.2 "In Time of War or Other Emergency of International Relations" in Article XXI(b)(iii)

This section aims to examine whether measures imposed by each country may satisfy the first requirement "in time of war or other emergency of international relations." As summarised earlier (*See* Sect. 3.2.1), the Panel in *Russia — Traffic in Transit* interpreted that whether it is "in time of war or other emergency of international relations" is an objective situation and whether it is "taken in the time" is also an objective fact which can be objectively determined by the panel.[53]

For the purposes of analysis, imposing countries are categorised into the following two groups.

4.2.1 Parties to War or Armed Conflict ("War, Etc.")

The Panel in *Russia — Traffic in Transit* (*See* Sect. 3.2.1), offered the following general statement: "An emergency in international relations would, therefore, appear to refer generally to a situation of armed conflict, or of latent armed conflict, or of heightened tension or crisis, or of general instability engulfing or surrounding a state."[54] It also found that after the 2014 Crimea Crisis, Russia and Ukraine were in a situation of armed conflict.[55] As it was found that there was an "emergency in international relations" which was very close to a war between the complaining party Ukraine and the respondent party Russia which invoked Article XXI(b)(iii), it was apparent that the provision was applicable.

On the other hand, the Panel in *Saudi Arabia — IPRs* (*See* Sect. 3.2.2) considered that "a situation ... of heightened tension or crisis" existed in the circumstance of that dispute by taking into account Saudi Arabia's repeated accusations that Qatar supported terrorism and extremism as background leading to Saudi Arabia's severance of diplomatic and consular relations with Qatar.[56] In that case, there was no finding of a situation very close to a war but an "emergency in international

---

[53] Panel Report, *Russia — Traffic in Transit*, *supra* note 6, para. 7.77. Panel Report, *US — Steel and Aluminium Products (China)*, *supra* note 34, para. 7.148.

[54] Panel Report, *Russia — Traffic in Transit*, *supra* note 6, para. 7.76 (footnote omitted).

[55] Panel Report, *Russia — Traffic in Transit*, *supra* note 6, paras. 7.122–7.123.

[56] Panel Report, *Saudi Arabia — IPRs*, *supra* note 25, paras. 7.257, 7.258, 7.263.

relations" between the two disputing parties was found to exist. Thus, Article 73(b)
(iii) of the TRIPS Agreement—worded in terms identical to Article XXI(b)(iii)—
was found to be applicable.

Based on the above, Ukraine's trade sanctions against Russia in response to the
latter's aggression, can undoubtedly satisfy the requirement of "in time of war or
other emergency of international relations" in Article XXI(b)(iii) as the two potentially disputing countries are in a state of war.

4.2.2 Non-parties to War, Etc.

Justification under security exceptions that has been accepted in WTO jurisprudence
only relates to cases of trade restrictions or suspension of intellectual property
protection between direct parties to a war or an emergency in international relations,
that is, *Russia — Traffic in Transit* and *Saudi Arabia — IPRs*. In the GATT era,
Argentina had argued in the GATT Council that, other than the UK, EEC member
states, Canada, and Australia could not ban imports from Argentina by invoking
GATT Article XXI(b)(iii) in reference to the Falkland/Malvinas Islands Dispute
between Argentina and the UK in 1982.[57] So far, this issue of whether a Member that
is invoking (b)(iii) must be a party to war, etc. has not been resolved in the WTO
jurisprudence.

However, the phrase "in time of a war or an emergency of international relations"
in Article XXI(b)(iii) does not include limiting wording such as "its" war or "its"
emergency. If taking a textual interpretation based on such wording, one may
conclude that a country that is invoking GATT Article XXI(b)(iii) need not be a
party to war, etc. and that any non-party to war, etc. may also argue that it is "in time
of a war or an emergency of international relations."[58] In fact, the Panel in *US —
Origin Marking (Hong Kong, China)* (*See* Sect. 3.2.4), albeit in *dicta*, indicated
some favour towards such interpretation by stating that:

> [w]e recall that, the open reference to "international relations" suggests that the emergency
> does not necessarily have to originate in the invoking Member's own territory and bilateral
> relations. Thus, a war taking place between two or more countries could also give rise to an
> emergency in international relations affecting other countries.[59]

---

[57] *Guide to GATT Law and Practice: Analytical Index*, Updated 6th ed. 1995, p. 605.

[58] Though it is not so clear whether this is based on such a textual interpretation, the following
literature expressly states that a country invoking Article XXI(b)(iii) need not be a party to a war.
Timothy Meyer and Todd N. Tucker, "There are two ways to kick Russia out of the world trade
system. One is more likely to work. Would WTO members change the rules?" *Washington Post*,
March 11, 2022. at https://www.washingtonpost.com/politics/2022/03/11/russia-wto-penalize-
ukraine-conflict/。

[59] Panel Report, *US — Origin Marking Requirement (Hong Kong, China)*, *supra* note 39, para.
7.297. On the other hand, Panel in *Saudi Arabia — IPRs* in Sect. 3.2.2, above, stated that the Panel
considered that "a situation … of heightened tension or crisis" exists in the circumstances in this
dispute, and is related to Saudi Arabia's "defence or military interests, or maintenance of law and
public order interests" (*i.e.* essential security interests), sufficient to establish the existence of an

However, it is very unreasonable for countries that are not geographically close to the parties to war, etc. and totally unrelated to such war, etc. on the other side of the world, to take advantage of the war occurring between two countries and to be permitted to impose trade restrictions on either or both parties to war, etc. This should not be resolved through the requirement of "in time of a war or an emergency of international relations", but through the more comprehensive interpretation of the "its essential security interests" and "necessary to protect" requirements in the chapeau of Article XXI(b) (*See* Sects. 4.3 and 4.4, below).

4.3 *"Its Essential Security Interests" in the Chapeau of GATT Article XXI(b)*

4.3.1 Standard of Review

The Panel in *Russia — Traffic in Transit* stated that, while "it is left, in general, to every Member to define what it considers to be its essential security interests",[60] the discretion of a Member to designate particular concerns as "essential security interests" is "limited by its obligation to interpret and apply Article XXI(b)(iii) of the GATT 1994 in good faith."[61] The Panel also stated that:

> [i]t is therefore incumbent on the invoking Member to articulate the essential security interests said to arise from the emergency in international relations sufficiently enough to demonstrate their veracity...the further it is removed from armed conflict, or a situation of breakdown of law and public order (whether in the invoking Member or in its immediate surroundings), the less obvious are the defence or military interests, or maintenance of law and public order interests, that can be generally expected to arise. In such cases, a Member would need to articulate its essential security interests with greater specificity than would be required when the emergency in international relations involved, for example, armed conflict.[62]

In the case of a party to war, etc., such as Ukraine in the present case, it becomes apparent that "its essential security interests" are related, and even in the case of a total ban by Ukraine, it would be very likely for such measures to be considered "necessary to protect its essential security interests."[63] On the other hand, it is necessary to conduct a more careful examination in the case of non-parties to war,

---

"emergency in international relations." Panel Report, *Saudi Arabia — IPRs, supra* note 25, paras. 7.257, 7.258 and 7.263. This may be interpreted that at the stage of finding an emergency in international relations, it is required to show the relationship to the essential security interests of an invoking party.

[60] Panel Report, *Russia — Traffic in Transit, supra* note 6, para. 7.131.

[61] *Ibid.*, para. 7.132.

[62] *Ibid.*, paras. 7.134–7.135.

[63] *See* Prabhash Ranjan, "Russia-Ukraine War and WTO's National Security Exception," *Foreign Trade Review*, 2022, p.1, p. 8.

etc. For the purposes of the ensuing analysis, non-parties to war, etc. are categorised into the following three groups.

4.3.2 Military Allies of the Parties to War, Etc.

Even if imposing countries are not parties to war, etc. if they are military allies of the parties at war, they can be regarded as being in "a situation ... of latent armed conflict" and thus as at least parties in "an emergency of international relations." In such cases, it is very easy for them to "articulate the essential security interests said to arise from the emergency in international relations sufficiently enough to demonstrate their veracity."

However, although Ukraine has expressed a strong interest in acceding to the North Atlantic Treaty Organization (NATO), it has yet to accede. Therefore, imposing countries that are NATO members cannot argue they are parties in "an emergency of international relations" on the basis of a military alliance with Ukraine.

On the other hand, the United States, Canada, and European countries have repeatedly supplied considerable amounts of arms to Ukraine following the Russian invasion. Therefore, the question arises as to whether they too are belligerent countries. However, it is not considered that countries become belligerent countries on account of supplying arms to the armed forces of a belligerent country.[64]

4.3.3 Countries Neighbouring or Close to the Parties to War, Etc.

Are imposing countries that are not parties involved in war, etc. yet are geographically neighbouring or close to such parties able to invoke Article XXI(b)(iii)? It has been argued that such countries may invoke it to justify their measures.[65]

For example, Moldova (a WTO Member but not a NATO Member), which has imposed some sanctions in line with the EU, may be regarded as reasonably apprehensive of a similar threat of aggression by Russia as it has a sizeable Russian population within its territory, as is also the case with Ukraine. Countries in such a situation may be regarded as being in a "a situation... of latent armed conflict ... or of heightened tension or crisis" and thus as parties experiencing "an

---

[64] Michael N. Schmitt, Providing Arms and Materiel to Ukraine: Neutrality, Co-Belligerency, and the Use of Force, March 7, 2022, at https://lieber.westpoint.edu/ukraine-neutrality-co-belligerency-use-of-force/. *See also* Marko Milanovic, The United States and Allies Sharing Intelligence with Ukraine, EJIL: Talk!, May 9, 2022, at https://www.ejiltalk.org/the-united-states-and-allies-sharing-intelligence-with-ukraine/. For more detail, *see* the chapter "The War in Ukraine Under International Law: Its Use of Force and Armed Conflict Aspects" of this volume.

[65] Kazuhiro Nakatani, "Economic Sanctions against Russia," *Jurist* No. 1575, 2022, p. 115 (supporting the invocation of GATT Article XXI(b)(iii) by countries neighbouring or close to Russia) (*in Japanese*).

emergency of international relations," even if they are not parties to war, etc. In addition, Poland as well as Estonia, Latvia, and Lithuania (the Baltic Three), which are neighbouring or close to Ukraine or Russia or Russia's military ally, Belarus, can be regarded as being reasonably apprehensive of a threat of similar aggression by Russia. In the case of these countries, it is relatively easy to "articulate the essential security interests said to arise from the emergency in international relations sufficiently enough to demonstrate their veracity."

On the other hand, it is not readily determined whether countries such as Germany, France and Italy, which are not geographically neighbouring or close to the belligerent parties, may be regarded as reasonably being apprehensive of such a threat to such a degree as to justify the invocation of security grounds. However, if Poland and the Baltic Three can be regarded as parties in "an emergency of international relations" that are expected to "articulate the essential security interests said to arise from the emergency in international relations sufficiently enough to demonstrate their veracity," then there would be greater scope for trade sanctions uniformly imposed by the EU as a whole to be justified under Article XXI(b)(iii), insofar as these countries have delegated their powers to design and implement trade policy measures to the EU.

In the case of the United States and Japan, both are geographically remote from the areas where the war is taking place, and it is thus far from clear how they may be experiencing a "situation of armed conflict, or of latent armed conflict, or of heightened tension or crisis, or of general instability engulfing or surrounding a state" nor whether they are able to "articulate the essential security interests said to arise from the emergency in international relations sufficiently enough to demonstrate their veracity." However, if Poland and the Baltic Three can be regarded as parties in "an emergency of international relations," and all being NATO members, then there is scope for other NATO members including Canada, Iceland, Norway, the UK, and the United States to also argue to be parties in an "emergency of international relations" and "to articulate the essential security interests said to arise from the emergency in international relations sufficiently enough to demonstrate their veracity." On the other hand, these arguments are not open to Japan, as it is neither a NATO nor an EU member, leading to it being categorised in the final grouping (*see* Sect. 4.3.4, below).

4.3.4 Other Countries

Among the current imposing WTO Members, Japan, Australia, New Zealand, South Korea, Singapore and Taiwan, (Group 4) cannot be categorised in either of the above categories, and, based on the above analysis, it is therefore difficult to regard these as parties in "a war or an emergency of international relations".

Trade Sanctions Against Russia and Their WTO Consistency: Focusing. . . 177

Table 5 Imposing countries/economies as of August 2023

Imposing[a]	G7 (= <u>Canada</u>, *EU (27 Members including* <u>France</u>, <u>Germany</u>, and <u>Italy</u>), **Japan**, <u>UK</u> and <u>US</u>), **Australia**, <u>Iceland</u>, **Liechtenstein**, *Moldova*, **New Zealand**, <u>Norway</u>, **Singapore**, **South Korea**, **Switzerland**, **Taiwan**, *Ukraine*

[a] ***Bolditalic***: Parties to war, etc., and countries in a situation of latent arms conflict; *Italic*: EU member states; <u>Underlined</u>: NATO members; **Bold**: Group 4 countries

4.3.5 Summary

The analysis in the foregoing (*see* Sects. 4.3.1–4.3.4) seeks to clarify the scope of parties in "war or an emergency of international relations" in terms of the ongoing Russian aggression towards Ukraine who is in a position to "articulate the essential security interests said to arise from the emergency in international relations sufficiently enough to demonstrate their veracity." Table 5 summarises that analysis.

4.3.6 Group 4

Regarding countries in Group 4 (*see* Sect. 4.3.4, above), which are not geographically close to the parties to war, it does not seem possible for them to satisfy the requirements of "its essential security interests" directly by the fact that a war is taking place between the other parties; it is, therefore, necessary to more carefully examine their "essential security interests", in order to avoid abuse of the security exceptions. The Panel in *Russia — Traffic in Transit*, made it abundantly clear that: "the further [a Member] is removed from armed conflict, . . . the less obvious are the defence or military interests. . .In such cases, a Member would need to articulate its essential security interests with greater specificity." For example, when countries in Group 4, which are not close to the parties to war, impose import bans from, or export bans to, either of the parties to war, etc., they would be required to more specifically articulate their "essential security interests."[66]

To such end, Group 4 countries such as Japan, Australia, New Zealand and South Korea are likely to attempt to justify their trade sanctions against Russia[67] by arguing that Russia's invasion of Ukraine in 2022 constitutes aggression in violation of Article 2 (4), of the Charter of the United Nations (the UN Charter)[68] and, as the

---

[66] For a similar opinion, *see* Ito, *supra* note 1, p. 28.

[67] For a similar argument, *see* Ranjan, *supra* note 63, p. 9. Also *see* David Collins, "The WTO's Essential Security Exception and Revocation of Russia's Most Favoured Nation Status following the Invasion of Ukraine," *City Law Forum*, March 15, 2022 (suggesting that a Member's essential security interests probably also include the respect for all internationally recognised borders and the prohibition of territorial acquisition by military force. At https://blogs.city.ac.uk/citylawforum/2022/03/15/the-wtos-essential-security-exception-and-revocation-of-russias-most-favoured-nation-status-following-the-invasion-of-ukraine/

[68] Article 2, paragraph 4 of the United Nations Charter: "[a]ll Members shall refrain in their international relations from the threat or use of force against the territorial integrity or political

prohibition of aggression is an obligation *erga omnes*,[69] it also constitutes a threat to the international order[70] and thus amounts to an "emergency in international relations" which involves the "essential security interests" of all WTO Members in general.[71] In the present case, however, the issue arises as to whether WTO dispute settlement, which concerns trade-related rules, is, or should be, able to make findings as to the existence of aggression by a certain country.[72] If such question is being contested between the disputing parties, there would conceivably be criticism of an international organisation specialising in rules related to the economic sphere to be too involved in such political or otherwise highly politicised questions.[73] That being said, this is not unprecedented. In fact, various WTO dispute settlement panels and the Appellate Body have previously adopted the fact findings of other specialised international organisations.[74] In this respect, it is crucial that the United Nations

---

independence of any state, or in any other manner inconsistent with the Purposes of the United Nations."

[69] *Barcelona Traction, Light and Power Co. Ltd (Belgium v. Spain)*, ICJ Reports 1970, p. 32, paras. 33–34.

[70] Government of Canada, Canada cuts Russia and Belarus from Most-Favoured-Nation Tariff treatment, 3 March 2022. "Russia's invasion of Ukraine . . . is a violation of international law and threat to the rules-based international order. Canada is taking further action to ensure those who do not support the rules-based international order cannot benefit from it." At https://www.canada.ca/en/department-finance/news/2022/03/canada-cuts-russia-and-belarus-from-most-favoured-nation-tarifftreatment.html.

[71] Executive Order on Prohibiting Certain Imports and New Investments With Respect to Continued Russian Federation Efforts to Undermine the Sovereignty and Territorial Integrity of Ukraine, March 8, 2022. "[F]inding that the Russian Federation's unjustified. . . war against Ukraine, including its recent further invasion in violation of international law, including the United Nations Charter, further threatens the peace, stability, sovereignty, and territorial integrity of Ukraine, and thereby constitutes an unusual and extraordinary threat to the national security and foreign policy of the United States."

[72] The Panel in *Russia — Traffic in Transit* took a very cautious approach towards this type of finding. Panel Report, *Russia — Traffic in Transit*, *supra* note 6, paras. 7.5, "It is not this Panel's function to pass upon the parties' respective legal characterizations of those events, or to assign responsibility for them, as was done in other international fora. At the same time, the Panel considers it important to situate the dispute in the context of the existence of these events." And, *id.*, para. 7.121, "[I]t is not relevant to this determination which actor or actors bear international responsibility for the existence of this situation to which Russia refers. Nor is it necessary for the Panel to characterize the situation between Russia and Ukraine under international law in general."

[73] Albeit in the direction that contracting parties' right to invoke security exceptions in GATT Article XXI should be respected, *see* the following arguments by the United Arab Republic at the time of the Arabic Boycott against Israel and by Canada at the time of the Falkland/Malvinas Islands dispute. *Guide to GATT Law and Practice*, *supra* note 57, pp. 602, "In view of the political character of this issue, the United Arab Republic did not wish to discuss it within GATT." and 600, "Canada was convinced that the situation which had necessitated the measures had to be satisfactorily resolved by appropriate action elsewhere, as *the GATT had neither the competence nor the responsibility to deal with the political issue* which had been raised" (emphasis added).

[74] *See e.g.*, Appellate Body Report, *United States — Import Prohibition of Certain Shrimp and Shrimp Products*, WT/DS58/AB/R adopted 8 November 1998, para. 132, confirming the exhaustibility of sea turtles by referring to the fact that all of the seven recognised species of sea turtles are

General Assembly Special Session on 2 March 2022 found that the Russian invasion of Ukraine was an aggression in violation of Article 2 (4) of the UN Charter.[75]

It is worth noting that this resolution was adopted in an emergency special session of the General Assembly in response to the failure of the Security Council to adopt a resolution deploring Russia's aggression against Ukraine in violation of Article 2 (4) of the UN Charter, due to Russia vetoing such efforts.[76] Even when the Security Council becomes paralysed, for instance, in case of armed conflict involving a permanent member of the Security Council, and WTO Members are unable to invoke GATT Article XXI(c) as not preventing "any contracting party from taking any action in pursuance of its obligations under the United Nations Charter for the maintenance of international peace and security," there is scope to seek to rely on GATT XXI(b)(iii) instead, based on the existence of a General Assembly resolution expressly acknowledging the occurrence of aggression. If we take this to its conclusion, even Group 4 countries not close to Russia or Ukraine may be able to invoke GATT Article XX1(b)(iii) by referring to General Assembly Resolution ES-11/1 (adopted on 2 March 2022), which deplores Russian aggression against Ukraine.

This will undoubtedly attract considerable criticism to the effect that WTO dispute settlement should refrain from becoming entangled in political or otherwise highly politicised events, even when panels themselves are not directly involved in findings of aggression but rely on the pronouncements of other international organisations or bodies such as the United Nations General Assembly.[77] The Panel in

---

today listed in Appendix 1 of the Convention on International Trade in Endangered Species of Wild Fauna and Flora (CITES). *See also* Panel Report, *Russia — Traffic in Transit, supra* note 6, para. 7.122, confirming an emergency in international relations by referring the recognition by the United Nations General Assembly that the situation between Ukraine and Russia involved armed conflict.

[75] *See* Resolution adopted by the General Assembly on 2 March 2022, ES-11/1, Aggression against Ukraine: "2. Deplores in the strongest terms the aggression by the Russian Federation against Ukraine in violation of Article 2 (4) of the Charter." *See* Valerie Hughes, et al., "Russia Will Challenge Economic Sanctions at the WTO," Bennett Jones Blog, March 22, 2022, where it is argued that Canadian sanctions against Russia can be justified by GATT Article XXI(b) based on Resolution ES-11/1, at https://www.bennettjones.com/Blogs-Section/Russia-Will-Challenge-Economic-Sanctions-at-the-WTO. Hughes, et al. also argue that the phrase "urgent action is needed to save this generation from the scourge of war" in the resolution can serve as a basis to that end.

[76] United Nations, S/2022/155 and S/PV.8979; Resolution 2623 (2022) adopted by the Security Council at its 8980th meeting, on 27 February 2022.

[77] For example, India in the GATT era expressed similar criticism. *Guide to GATT Law and Practice, supra* note 57, p. 608. "India did not favour the use of trade measures for non-economic reasons. Such measures should only be taken within the framework of a decision by the United Nations Security Council. In the absence of such a decision or resolution, there was a serious risk that such measures might be unilateral or arbitrary and would undermine the multilateral trading system." *See also* similar criticism in the following statement regarding economic sanctions against Russia. Joint communiqué following the 21st meeting of the Shanghai Cooperation Organisation (SCO) Heads of Government (Prime Ministers) Council, 1 November 2022. "Unilateral economic sanctions, other than the sanctions approved by the UN Security Council, are inconsistent with the principles of international law and adversely affects third countries and international economic relations." *See also* the chapter "Economic Sanctions Against Russia: Questions of Legality and Legitimacy" of this volume.

Russia — Traffic in Transit, however, found it to be an objective fact that Russia and Ukraine were "in war or other emergency in international relations" since 2014, by taking as evidence the United Nations General Assembly recognition of the situation between Ukraine and Russia as involving armed conflict.[78] Therefore, scope certainly exists for future panels within the context of WTO dispute settlement to also make such findings of fact based on the resolutions of the United Nations General Assembly.

As discussed above, there is scope for trade sanctions against Russia in response to Russia's invasion of Ukraine to be justified by arguing that the invasion constitutes "war or other emergency in international relations" for any WTO Member, including those that are not belligerent countries, and that it is related to their "essential security interests" based on General Assembly Resolution ES-11/1 which deplores Russian aggression in violation of the UN Charter. On the other hand, it is also worth reiterating that even when a war, etc. is taking place, unless there is such a resolution finding an aggression, trade sanctions adopted by any country may not always be justified by arguing that a "war or other emergency in international relations" exists for the invoking party and that such measures are "necessary to protect its essential security interests" (*see* Sect. 4.4, below).

4.4 Measures "It Considers Necessary to Protect" in the Chapeau of GATT Article XXI(b)

4.4.1 Standard of Review

The Panel in *Russia — Traffic in Transit* stated that:

> (t)he obligation of good faith . . . applies not only to the Member's definition of the essential security interests said to arise from the particular emergency in international relations, but also, and most importantly, to their connection with the measures at issue. Thus, as concerns the application of Article XXI(b)(iii), this obligation is crystallized in demanding that the measures at issue meet a minimum requirement of plausibility in relation to the proffered essential security interests, i.e. that they are not implausible as measures protective of these interests. The Panel must therefore review whether the measures are so remote from, or unrelated to, the 2014 emergency that it is implausible that Russia implemented the measures for the protection of its essential security interests arising out of the emergency.[79]

In addition, though its report has not been adopted by the DSB, the Panel in *Saudi Arabia — IPRs* found that, as part of the comprehensive measures to end any direct or indirect interaction between Saudi Arabia and Qatar, the measures to deny Saudi law firms from representing or interacting with Qatari nationals "meet a minimum

---

[78] Panel Report, *Russia — Traffic in Transit, supra* note 6, para. 7.122.

[79] Panel Report, *Russia — Traffic in Transit, supra* note 6, paras. 7.138–7.139.

requirement of plausibility" in relation to the proffered essential security interests, namely, to protect Saudi Arabia itself from the dangers of terrorism and extremism.[80] On the other hand, it also found that the non-application of criminal procedures and penalties to *beoutQ* (i.e., a commercial-scale broadcast pirate in Saudi Arabia), did not have any relationship to Saudi Arabia's policy of ending or preventing any form of interaction with Qatari nationals and, therefore, it was so remote from, or unrelated to, the "emergency in international relations" as to make it implausible that Saudi Arabia implemented these measures for the protection of its "essential security interests."[81]

The above precedents go against the previous understanding that GATT Article XXI(b) is an entirely "self-judging" clause, and demonstrate that panels can examine whether invoking countries meet the necessity test in its chapeau, though it does not reach the level of stringency of the necessity test in GATT Article XX(a), (b) and (d), which examines whether there are less trade-restrictive alternatives that are reasonably available.[82] The standard of review that is applied here is whether the measure at issue meets "a minimum requirement of plausibility", that is to say, whether it is so remote from, or unrelated to, an "emergency in international relations" as to make it implausible that the invoking Member implemented the measure for the protection of its "essential security interests" arising out of that emergency. Under this standard, it is not permitted to examine whether there are less trade-restrictive alternatives, and the test would be similar to the tests of "a close and genuine relationship of ends and means" as to "relating to" in GATT Article XX(g) and of "bring about a material contribution to the achievement of the objective" as a preliminary phase of the necessity test in Article XX(b),[83] or less stringent than those tests.

4.4.2 Application to Trade Sanctions Against Russia

Applying the above standard of review (*see* Sect. 4.4.1), export bans on items 1 to 3 in Table 6 are to diminish Russia's capacity to continue with its war efforts by making it impossible or at least difficult to procure or manufacture weapons, and are thus not so remote from, or unrelated to, Japan's essential security interests in ending Russian aggression in violation of the UN Charter. In addition, the same can be applied to item 4, if it can be categorised along the lines of item 2.

On the other hand, item 5 (export ban on products contributing to strengthening Russia's industrial base), covering a variety of products, cannot necessarily be regarded as an export ban on weapons nor a measure directly making it impossible

---

[80] Panel Report, *Saudi Arabia — IPRs, supra* note 25, paras. 7.284–7.288.

[81] *Ibid.*, paras. 7.289–7.293.

[82] Appellate Body Report, *Brazil — Measures Affecting Imports of Retreaded Tyres*, WT/DS332/AB/R adopted 17 December 2007, para. 156.

[83] Appellate Body Report, *US — Shrimp, supra* note 74, para. 136; Appellate Body Report, *Brazil — Retreaded Tyres, supra* note 82, para.151.

Table 6 Japan's trade sanctions against Russia as of August 2023

	Contents
1	Export ban on items subject to International Export Control (machine tools, carbon fiber, products related to chemical weapons, etc.)
2	Export ban on dual-use products which strengthen military capacity incl. semiconductors, personal computers, telecommunication equipment, etc.)
3	Export ban to Russian military-related entities incl. Ministry of Defence, aircraft manufacturers
4	Export ban on emerging technology products incl. quantum computing, 3D printers
5	**Export ban on products contributing to the strengthening industrial bases incl. lorries and bulldozers**
6	Export ban on oil refinery machines, etc.
7	Export ban on luxury products incl. luxury cars and jewellery, etc.
8	Import ban on coal, machinery, wooden products, vodka, gold, etc.
9	Suspension of MFN incl. tariff increase imposed on crude oil

or difficult for Russia to finance war. Such a measure would certainly call into question whether it can be characterised as weakening the Russian economy in the long term, and thus decreasing Russia's capacity to continue with the war. Item 5 is the only one on which it can be disputed whether it "meet[s] a minimum requirement of plausibility."

Next, both item 8 (import bans) and item 9 (suspension of MFN) are measures aimed at curtailing Russian fiscal revenue from oil and gas exports, and, therefore, at undermining Russia's ability to keep financing the war. Therefore, these measures are not too remote and unrelated to Japan's essential security interests in ending Russian aggression in violation of the UN Charter. Differential treatment towards products, such as introducing an import ban on oil but not gas, is not problematic under the standard of review of the necessity test in the chapeau of GATT Article XXI(b).[84]

On this point, the Panel in *US — Origin Marking (Hong Kong, China)* interpreted the phrase "an emergency in international relations" to refer to "a situation representing a breakdown or near-breakdown in those relations", thus appearing to suggest that a partial restriction of trade cannot be regarded as a breakdown or near-breakdown in international relations.[85] If we were to strictly adhere to this interpretation, even in the case of war or armed conflict and there being an emergency in international relations also for countries other than the belligerents, GATT Article XXI(b)(iii) may not be invoked unless such countries adopt a total ban on both imports and exports. This would seriously impair the self-judging power of

---

[84] In the case of the Agreement on the Application of Sanitary and Phytosanitary Measures (SPS Agreement), inconsistent treatment of similar disease risks between products, such as beef and pork, can be problematic. *See* Article 5, paragraph 5 of the SPS Agreement.

[85] Panel Report, *US — Origin Marking (Hong Kong, China)*, *supra* note 39, paras. 7.290 and 7.354.

Members who invoke GATT Article XXI(b)(iii), and would be inconsistent with the *dicta* of the Panel itself that "the emergency does not necessarily have to originate in the invoking Member's own territory and bilateral relations but could happen more broadly in relations among a wider group of WTO Members."[86] Therefore, the paragraphs of the Panel Report that seem to require a total breakdown in international relations can be interpreted as having in mind scenarios other than war, etc., for instance, the severance of relations as seen in *Saudi Arabia — IPRs*.

5 Concluding Remarks

Given the current strategic competition between the United States and China, and the Russian invasion of Ukraine, the dysfunction of the UN Security Council are becoming patently clear to all. Now the possibility of invoking GATT Article XXI (c) is accordingly diminishing and the need to flexibly interpret GATT Article XXI (b)(iii) as an alternative is rapidly highlighted. In that context, this article's interpretative approach—namely, to consider the fact-finding aspects of an otherwise non-binding UN General Assembly resolution—may have a certain theoretical as well as practical significance. On the other hand, as some of elements of the relevant jurisprudence suggest, it is crucial to interpret security exceptions in a balanced way to prevent their abuse. Currently, we are merely at the starting point of a long journey.

---

[86] *Id.*, paras. 7.297 and 7.307.

WTO Dispute Settlement and Trade Sanctions as Permissible Third-Party Countermeasures Under Customary International Law

Satoru Taira

Abstract The requirements for invoking WTO security exceptions as expounded in recent WTO dispute settlement cases are notably stricter than previously thought by WTO members. Consequently, not all WTO members who have imposed trade sanctions against Russia will be able to invoke these exceptions to justify their actions when accused by Russia of violations of their WTO obligations. This article considers how WTO members who may be unsuccessful in invoking security exceptions may nonetheless be able to justify their measures within the context of WTO dispute settlement under the customary international law on third-party countermeasures. It does so by exploring the scope of the relevant provisions within the Understanding on Rules and Procedures Governing the Settlement of Disputes (DSU) as well as competence of WTO adjudicative bodies (i.e., WTO panels and the Appellate Body) to look beyond the four corners of the WTO covered agreements.

1 Introduction

Many WTO members, including G7 members, have imposed economic sanctions on Russia in response to its invasion of Ukraine. The scope of such sanctions is wide-ranging, affecting trade, investment, and finance. For trade, in particular, the sanctions include not only import and export prohibitions and restrictions of specific goods and services but also comprehensive actions such as the suspension of the most-favoured-nation (MFN) treatment to Russian goods and services.[1] In taking such action that inherently violates WTO agreements, many of these states claim that

---

[1] G7 Leaders' Statement, Berlin, 11 March 2022, at https://www.mofa.go.jp/mofaj/files/100315215.pdf.

For Japan, *see* Law to Amend a Part of the Temporary Tariff Measures Law, adopted and promulgated on 20 April 2022 and enforced on 21 April 2022, Law No. 27.

S. Taira (✉)
Osaka City University, Osaka, Japan

© The Author(s), under exclusive license to Springer Nature Singapore Pte Ltd. 2024
M. Asada, D. Tamada (eds.), *The War in Ukraine and International Law*,
https://doi.org/10.1007/978-981-97-2504-5_8

such action is "necessary to protect [their] essential security interests"[2] and thus appear to assume that they are justified under the, what are known as, 'security exceptions' contained in WTO agreements.[3] Article XXI of the General Agreement on Tariffs and Trade 1994 (GATT 1994) is the standard bearer of such exceptions,[4]

Article XXI Security Exceptions
Nothing in this Agreement shall be construed

   (a) to require any contracting party to furnish any information the disclosure of which it considers contrary to its essential security interests; or

   (b) to prevent any contracting party from taking any action which it considers necessary for the protection of its essential security interests

      (i) relating to fissionable materials or the materials from which they are derived;

      (ii) relating to the traffic in arms, ammunition and implements of war and to such traffic in other goods and materials as is carried on directly or indirectly for the purpose of supplying a military establishment;

      (iii) taken in time of war or other emergency in international relations; or

   (c) to prevent any contracting party from taking any action in pursuance of its obligations under the United Nations Charter for the maintenance of international peace and security.

Regarding this provision, in 2019 the WTO dispute settlement panel in *Russia - Traffic in Transit* for the first time interpreted and applied GATT 1994 Article XXI (b)(iii), thereby confirming the panel's jurisdiction and clarifying the requirements

---

[2] WTO General Council, Joint Statement on Aggression by the Russian Federation against Ukraine with the Support of Belarus, Communication from Albania; Australia; Canada; European Union; Iceland; Japan; Republic of Korea; Republic of Moldova, Montenegro; New Zealand; North Macedonia; Norway; United Kingdom and United States (Joint Statement), 15 March 2022, WT/GC/244.

[3] At the meeting of the Council for Trade in Goods of the WTO, for example, many members sought to justify their measures against Russia under international law, including WTO law, and in particular, the United Kingdom and Australia referred expressly to Article XXI, the 'security exception' of the GATT 1994. *See* Minutes of the Meeting of the Council for Trade in Goods, 21 and 22 April 2022, G/C/M/142. paras. 43.16–43.64 and especially paras.43.21 (for the United Kingdom) and 43.56 (for Australia), 17 June 2022. As for Japan, during Diet deliberations on the amendment of the Temporary Tariff Measures Law (*supra* note 1), the government spokesperson stated that: "We believe that [the withdrawal of MFN treatment] is permissible under international law, including the provisions on security exception in the WTO agreements." Proceedings of the Committee on Finance and Monetary Affairs, House of Councillors, The 208th National Diet of Japan, No. 11, at 7, 19 April 2022.

[4] Article XXI of the GATT 1994 constitutes a security exception concerning trade in goods. For trade in services, Article 14 *bis* of the General Agreement on Trade in Services (GATS) and for intellectual property, Article 73 of the Agreement on Trade-Related Aspects of Intellectual Property Rights (TRIPS Agreement) stipulate security exceptions, using language closely resembling that of GATT Article XXI. For convenience, the focus in this article will be on GATT Article XXI.

for its invocation.[5] The following year, the panel in *Saudi Arabia - IPRs* also confirmed its jurisdiction to consider the defence under Article 73(b)(iii) of the TRIPS Agreement, the security exception under that agreement, and almost entirely upheld the analytical framework and requirements for the invocation of the security exception established by the panel in *Russia - Traffic in Transit*.[6] In addition, several subsequent panel reports examining the defence under GATT 1994 Article XXI(b)(iii) were published one after the other at the end of 2022.[7]

However, the requirements for invoking the security exceptions as expounded in the above precedents are notably stricter than what may have previously been assumed by WTO members; the jurisprudence suggests that the instances where the security exceptions can be invoked would be rather limited. Consequently, it is far from certain that all WTO members that have imposed trade sanctions on Russia may be able to justify their actions by invoking these exceptions.

This article assumes that not all WTO members who have taken measures against Russia will be successful in invoking security exceptions found in WTO law in the event that Russia files a complaint under the WTO dispute settlement procedure alleging that such measures are in violation of WTO law.[8] In such circumstances, the present author considers the question of whether members who may be unsuccessful in invoking security exceptions may still justify their actions within the context of WTO dispute settlement by invoking customary international law on third-party countermeasures.

---

[5] Panel Report, *Russia - Measures Concerning Traffic in Transit*, WT/DS512/R, adopted 5 April 2019 (*Russia - Traffic in Transit*).

[6] Panel Report, *Saudi Arabia, Kingdom - Measures Concerning the Protection of Intellectual Property Rights*, WT/DS567/R, circulated 16 June 2020, mutually agreed solution (*Saudi Arabia - IPRs*), para. 7.241.

[7] Namely, Panel Reports, *United States - Certain Measures on Steel and Aluminium Products*, WT/DS544 (China), 552 (Norway), 556 (Switzerland), 564 (Turkey)/R, circulated 9 December 2022, under appeal (*hereinafter*, only the report of DS544 (China) will be cited as *US - Steel and Aluminium Products*); Panel Report, *United States - Origin Marking Requirement*, WT/DS597/R, circulated 21 December 2022, under appeal (*US - Origin Marking (Hong Kong, China)*).

[8] Russia has indeed alleged that measures taken against Russia by various States "contradict the WTO rules" or amount to "vast and outright violation[s] of WTO rules" at the meeting of the Council for Trade in Goods (Minutes of the Meeting of the Council for Trade in Goods, *supra* note 3, paras. 43.6 and 43.13.). However, at the time of writing of this article, Russia had not sought recourse to WTO dispute settlement. According to Article 23.1 and 23.2 (a) of the Understanding on Rules and Procedures Governing the Settlement of Disputes (DSU) (referred to in Sect. 4.2 of the main text), a finding of violation of a WTO agreement is exclusively within the purview of the WTO Dispute Settlement Body. Therefore, unless Russia has recourse to dispute settlement in accordance with the DSU, the issue of legal justification of measures against Russia essentially does not arise. For the purposes of analysing this hypothetical issue, it is assumed in this article that Russia has sought recourse to WTO dispute settlement.

2 The Possibility of Justification of Trade Sanctions Against Russia Under the GATT 1994 Security Exception

2.1 *The Requirements for Invocation of Article XXI (b)(iii) of the GATT 1994*

Since the measures taken by each state against Russia were not taken as mandatory sanctions under Chapter VII of the United Nations (UN) Charter pursuant to a resolution by the UN Security Council, they cannot be justified under Article XXI (c) of the GATT 1994. Therefore, states taking such measures must be able to justify them under Article XXI(b). In fact, as stated above, such states describe these measures as "necessary to protect [their] essential security interests," which is the wording of the chapeau sentence of paragraph (b), thus appearing to presuppose the possibility of justification under Article XXI(b).[9] However, subparagraphs (i) and (ii) of Article XXI(b) can only be invoked in relation to limited goods and in limited circumstances. Measures that cannot be justified under either of these subparagraphs, especially comprehensive actions such as the suspension of the MFN treatment for goods of Russian origin, would likely require justification under subparagraph (iii) of Article XXI(b). Here, in order to assess the possibility of such a justification, one must first examine the requirements for invoking subparagraph (iii), as expounded in the relevant jurisprudence.

2.1.1 *Russia - Traffic in Transit*

In this case, the complainant, Ukraine, claimed that various Russian restrictions and bans on Ukraine-originating traffic in transit by road and rail across Russia destined for third countries, were inconsistent with Russia's obligations, among others, under Article V of GATT 1994, which provides for 'freedom of transit'.[10] In response to this, Russia invoked Article XXI(b)(iii) of the GATT 1994, asserting that the measures in question were necessary for the protection of its essential security interests taken in response to the emergency in international relations that occurred in 2014, such as the Crimea Crisis,[11] and denied the panel's jurisdiction based on its interpretation that the provision was completely a "self-judging clause".[12]

The panel first stated that considering the logical structure of Article XXI(b) as a whole, subparagraphs (i) to (iii) qualify and limit the exercise of the discretion accorded to WTO members under the chapeau to the circumstances specified in

---

[9] *See* Joint Statement, *supra* note 2; *see* also *supra* note 3.

[10] *Russia - Traffic in Transit*, *supra* note 5, paras. 7.1–7.2.

[11] *Ibid.*, paras. 7.112–7.115. However, Russia did not expressly refer to the Crimean Crisis.

[12] *Ibid.*, para. 7.4.

each subparagraph.[13] Concerning subparagraph (iii), the panel understood the phrase 'take in time of' to require that the action be taken "during" a war or other emergency of international relations, and stated that this chronological concurrence is an objective fact, amenable to objective determination.[14] The panel also stated that the existence of a 'war' is one characteristic example of a large category of an 'emergency of international relations', which is clearly capable of objective determination.[15] The panel further states that an 'emergency in international relations' appears to refer generally to "a situation of armed conflict, or of latent armed conflict, or of heightened tension or crisis, or of general instability engulfing or surrounding a state", and that such situations give rise to "defence or military interests, or maintenance of law and public order interests" for the member in question.[16] For the panel, while political and economic conflicts could occasionally be considered urgent and serious in a political sense, such conflicts will not be 'emergencies in international relations' within the meaning of subparagraph (iii) "unless they give rise to defence and military interests, or maintenance of law and public order interests".[17] Consequently, the panel stated that as the existence of an emergency in international relations is an objective state of affairs, the determination of whether the action was 'taken in time of' an 'emergency in international relations' under subparagraph (iii) of Article XXI(b) is that of an objective fact, subject to objective determination.[18] Thus, the panel identified the requirements of subparagraph (iii) as a) establishing the existence of 'war or other emergency in international relations' and b) the measures in question being 'taken in time of war or other emergency in international relations', as well as clarified the meaning of each of these requirements. At the same time, the panel indicated that the determination of whether these requirements were met is based on objective facts and subject to objective assessment and thereby that the adjectival clause 'which it considers' in the chapeau of Article XXI(b) does not extend to the determination of the circumstances in subparagraph (iii). Consequently, the panel found that it had jurisdiction to determine whether the requirements of Article XXI(b)(iii) of the GATT 1994 had been satisfied.[19]

The panel then stated that the term 'essential security interests' in the chapeau of Article XXI(b) evidently narrower than 'security interests', may generally be

---

[13] *Ibid.*, para. 7.65.

[14] *Ibid.*, para. 7.70.

[15] *Ibid.*, para. 7.71.

[16] *Ibid.*, para. 7.76. In interpreting an 'emergency in international relations', the panel took into account as context the matters addressed by subparagraphs (i) and (ii), and considered that "the matters addressed by those subparagraphs give rise to similar or convergent concerns, which can be formulated in terms of the specific security interests": that is, "defence and military interests, as well as maintenance of law and public order interests". The panel stated that "[a]n 'emergency in international relations' must be understood as eliciting the same type of interests". *Ibid.*, para. 7.74.

[17] *Ibid.*, para. 7.75.

[18] *Ibid.*, para. 7.77.

[19] *Ibid.*, paras. 7.102 and 7.104.

understood to refer to "those interests relating to the quintessential functions of the state, namely, the protection of its territory and its population from external threats, and the maintenance of law and public order internally".[20] The panel noted that because such interests will depend on the particular situation and perceptions of the state in question, and can be expected to vary with changing circumstances, it is left, in general, to every member to define what it considers to be its 'essential security interests'.[21] However, the panel went on to state that member discretion to designate particular concerns as 'essential security interests' is limited by the obligation to interpret and apply Article XXI(b)(iii) in "good faith".[22] The good faith obligation, according to the panel, further requires the invoking member to "articulate the essential security interests said to arise from the emergency in international relations sufficiently enough to demonstrate their veracity."[23] As to the level of this articulation, the panel considered that " the further it is removed from armed conflict, or a situation of breakdown of law and public order, the less obvious are the defence or military interests, or maintenance of law and public order interests, that can be generally expected to arise".[24] In such cases, according to the panel, "a Member would need to articulate its essential security interests with greater specificity than would be required when the emergency in international relations involved, for example, armed conflict."[25]

The panel further stated that the good faith obligation also, and most importantly, demands that the measures at issue meet a minimum requirement of "plausibility" in relation to the proffered essential security interests, that is to say, that "they are not implausible as measures protective of such interests".[26] And, lastly, the panel stated that the conclusion that it is for the member to determine the 'necessity' of the measures for the protection of its essential security interests follows by logical necessity if the adjectival clause 'which it considers' in the chapeau of paragraph (b) is to be given legal effect.[27]

Therefore, regarding the chapeau of paragraph (b), the panel clarified that the determination of 'essential security interests' and the 'necessity' of the measures in question is left to the discretion of the invoking state, but as requirements under this chapeau, the panel made clear that: c) the invoking state must articulate the essential security interests said to arise from the emergency in international relations

---

[20] *Ibid.*, para. 7.130.

[21] *Ibid.*, para. 7.131.

[22] *Ibid.*, para. 7.132. The panel recalled that the obligation of good faith is a general principle of law and a principle of general international law which underlies all treaties, as codified in Articles 26 and 31(1) of the Vienna Convention on the Law of Treaties. *Ibid.*

[23] *Ibid.*, para. 7.134.

[24] *Ibid.*, para. 7.135.

[25] *Ibid.*

[26] *Ibid.*, para. 7.138.

[27] *Ibid.*, para. 7.146.

sufficiently enough to demonstrate their veracity, and that d) the measure must meet a minimum level of plausibility in relation to the proffered essential security interests.

In its conclusion, the panel found that Russia has met all of the above requirements for invoking Article XXI(b)(iii) in relation to the measures at issue.[28] The panel report in *Russia - Traffic in Transit* was adopted by the WTO Dispute Settlement Body (DSB) on 26 April 2019, and thus has some value as a precedent for establishing the analytical framework of, and for clarifying, the requirements for invoking Article XXI(b)(iii).

2.1.2 *Saudi Arabia - IPRs*

In this case, Qatar alleged that Saudi Arabia had violated the TRIPS Agreement by failing to provide adequate protection for the intellectual property rights of a Qatari company. Saudi Arabia invoked the security exception under Article 73(b)(iii) of the TRIPS Agreement.[29] After rejecting Saudi Arabia's request that the panel should decline to exercise its jurisdiction because of the political nature of the current dispute,[30] the panel examined the applicability of the Article 73(b)(iii) security exception.

The panel stated that the interpretation of Article XXI(b)(iii) by the panel in *Russia - Traffic in Transit* gave rise to an analytical framework that can guide the assessment of whether a respondent has properly invoked Article XXI(b)(iii) of the GATT 1994, or, for the purposes of this dispute, Article 73(b)(iii) of the TRIPS Agreement.[31] Thus, the panel in this case reformulated the framework and requirements for invoking Article 73(b)(iii) by stating that panels may proceed by assessing,[32]

(a) whether the existence of a 'war or other emergency in international relations' has been established in the sense of subparagraph (iii) to Article 73(b);
(b) whether the relevant actions were 'taken in time of' that war or other emergency in international relations;
(c) whether the invoking Member has articulated its relevant 'essential security interests' sufficiently to enable an assessment of whether there is any link between those actions and the protection of its essential security interests; and
(d) whether the relevant actions are so remote from, or unrelated to, the 'emergency in international relations' as to make it implausible that the invoking Member

---

[28] *Ibid.*, para. 7.149.

[29] *Saudi Arabia - IPRs*, *supra* note 6, para. 7.1.

[30] *Ibid.*, para. 7.23.

[31] *Ibid.*, para. 7.241.

[32] *Ibid.*, para. 7.242.

considers those actions to be necessary for the protection of its essential security interests arising out of the emergency.

In relation to the above requirement a), the panel considered that "a situation . . . of heightened tension or crisis"[33] had existed in the circumstances of this dispute, and related to Saudi Arabia's "defence or military interests, or maintenance of law and public order interests" (that is to say, to Saudi Arabia's 'essential security interests'), sufficient to establish the existence of an 'emergency in international relations'.[34] Thus, the panel appears to have strictly adhered to the understanding of the panel in *Russia - Traffic in Transit* regarding the meaning of an 'emergency in international relations' and the interests associated with it.

However, it is noteworthy that the panel seems to have slightly changed requirement c) from how it was expounded in *Russia - Traffic in Transit*. That is, according to the panel in *Saudi Arabia - IPRs*, the invoking State must articulate its relevant 'essential security interests' sufficiently to enable an assessment of whether the challenged measures are plausibly connected to the protection of those interests.[35] Thus, the panel clarified that any link between the relevant actions and the protection of essential security interests provides a benchmark to assess the plausibility of the measures in question per requirement d), also expounded in *Russia - Traffic in Transit*.

Furthermore, in relation to requirement d), it was not necessarily clear whether there was any relation between the plausibility of requirement d) and the discretion of the invoking state's necessity determination in the interpretation of the panel in *Russia - Traffic in Transit*. However, the panel in this case seems to have focused on the issue of whether any link between the measures and essential security interests made the invoking State's determination of the necessity plausible, and to have understood such link as a constraint on the discretion of the invoking State's necessity determination.

In its conclusion, the panel found that the requirements for invoking Article 73 (b) (iii) were met in relation to the inconsistency with Article 42 (fair and equitable procedure) and Article 41.1 (availability of enforcement procedures to permit effective action against infringement of IP rights) of the TRIPS Agreement arising from the measures that, directly or indirectly, have had the result of preventing a Qatari company from obtaining Saudi legal counsel to enforce its IP rights through civil enforcement procedures before Saudi courts and tribunals. However, the panel also found that the requirements for invoking Article 73 (b)(iii) had not been met in relation to the inconsistency with Article 61(criminal procedures and penalties) of the TRIPS Agreement arising from Saudi Arabia's non-application of criminal procedures and penalties to a Saudi company who had infringed IP rights of a Qatari

---

[33] *Russia - Traffic in Transit*, *supra* note 5, para.7.76, as cited in *ibid.*, para. 7.257.

[34] *Saudi Arabia - IPRs*, *supra* note 6, paras. 7.257.

[35] *Ibid.*, para. 7.281.

WTO Dispute Settlement and Trade Sanctions as Permissible Third-Party... 193

company.[36] In the event, Qatar did not seek adoption of the panel report as the parties agreed to terminate proceedings.[37]

2.1.3 US - Steel and Aluminium Products

This case concerns additional duties and related measures imposed by the US on steel and aluminium products by reason of its national security under Section 232 of the Trade Expansion Act of 1962. China challenged the consistency of these measures with the US's obligations under the GATT 1994 and the Agreement on Safeguards.[38] The US invoked Article XXI(b)(iii) in response. The panel did not consider that Article XXI (b) was "self-judging" or "non-justiciable" nor that the provision contained a "single relative clause" that wholly reserved the conditions and circumstances of subparagraphs to the discretion of the invoking member.[39]

In assessing the applicability of Article XXI(b)(iii), the panel considered whether the requirement a) was met. However, the panel had a slightly different understanding of the meaning of the phrase 'emergency in international relations' than the earlier two panels discussed in the foregoing. The panel understood this phrase as "situations of a certain gravity or severity and international tensions that are of a critical or serious nature in terms of their impact on the conduct of international relations".[40] The panel also emphasised that the relevant emergency must be 'in international relations' and thus distinguished from an emergency in purely domestic or national affairs.[41] Further, the panel deemed situations must be, if not equally grave or severe, at least comparable in their gravity or severity to a war in terms of their impact on international relations.[42]

Having reviewed the relevant evidence submitted by the US in relation to global excess capacity in steel and aluminium, the panel was not persuaded that the situation to which the US referred rose to the gravity or severity of tensions on the international plane so as to constitute an 'emergency in international relations' during which a member may act under Article XXI (b)(iii).[43] As a result, the panel

---

[36] *Ibid.*, para. 7.294.

[37] *Saudi Arabia - Measures Concerning the Protection of Intellectual Property Rights*, Communication from Qatar, WT/DS657/11, 25 April 2022.

[38] *US - Steel and Aluminium Products*, *supra* note 7, para. 1.1.

[39] *Ibid.*, para. 7.128.

[40] *Ibid.*, para. 7.147.

[41] *Ibid.*, para. 7.173.

[42] *Ibid.*, para. 7.139.

[43] *Ibid.*, para. 7.148.

rejected the US defence under Article XXI (b)(iii).[44] This panel report is currently under appeal.[45]

2.1.4 *US - Origin Marking (Hong Kong, China)*

This case concerns a requirement in US law that imported goods originating in Hong Kong, China be marked to indicate that their origin is 'China' (origin marking requirement). Following the adoption of the Hong Kong Security Law by China in 2020 and certain events in Hong Kong, China, the US President issued an Executive Order, determining that Hong Kong, China was no longer sufficiently autonomous and ordering suspension of differential treatment to that which the US afforded to the People's Republic of China. This led to the adoption of the origin marking requirement at issue. Hong Kong, China claimed the origin marking requirement was inconsistent with the GATT1994, the Agreement on Rules of Origin, and the TBT Agreement, to which the US responded by invoking Article XXI (b)(iii).[46] The panel stated that the phrase 'which it considers' in the chapeau of Article XXI(b) did not extend to the subparagraphs of that provision and, therefore, that the subparagraphs of Article XXI(b) are subject to review by a panel.[47]

In relation to the requirement a), the panel, as was the case with the panel in *US - Steel and Aluminium Products*, had a slightly different understanding of the meaning of the phrase 'emergency in international relations' than the earlier two panels discussed in the foregoing. The panel understood this phrase as referring to "a state of affairs, of the utmost gravity, in effect a situation representing a breakdown or near-breakdown in the relations between states or other participants in international relations."[48] This led it to state that "a panel's inquiry will concern the relations between states and other participants in international relations, and the extent to which underlying circumstances have led to a state of affairs that is of the utmost gravity representing a breakdown or near-breakdown in those relations".[49] Particularly noteworthy is that this panel appears to have tried to cover wider situations than the panel in *Russia - Traffic in Transit*, stating that: "recognizing that each situation will need to be considered on its individual merits, we would refrain from suggesting that an emergency must necessarily involve defence and military interests, as the panel in *Russia - Traffic in Transit* seems to suggest. . . ."[50]

---

[44] *Ibid.*, para. 7.149.

[45] *United States - Certain Measures on Steel and Aluminium Products*, Notification of an Appeal by the United States under Article 16 of the Understanding on Rules and Procedures Governing the Settlement of Dispute (DSU), WT/DS544/14, 30 January 2023.

[46] *US - Origin Marking (Hong Kong, China)*, *supra* note 7, para. 7.1.

[47] *Ibid.*, para. 7.185.

[48] *Ibid.*, para. 7.306.

[49] *Ibid.*, para. 7.307.

[50] *Ibid.*, para. 7.301.

Also interesting is the panel's pointing out that the open reference to 'international relations' suggests that the emergency does not necessarily have to originate in the invoking member's own territory and bilateral relations but could happen more broadly in relations among a wide group of WTO members, and a war taking place between two or more countries could also give rise to an emergency in international relations affecting other countries.[51]

The evidence before the panel indicated that the measures taken by the US vis-à-vis Hong Kong, China had targeted only certain areas of their relations and not others, and that the US and Hong Kong, China's international relations continued to involve cooperation across policy areas. Further, trade has carried on between the US and Hong Kong, China, largely as before.[52] The panel, therefore, concluded that the situation had not escalated to a threshold of requisite gravity to constitute an emergency in international relations, and dismissed the US defence under Article XXI (b)(iii).[53] This panel report is currently under appeal.[54]

2.2 Possibility of Justification of Trade Sanctions Against Russia Under GATT Article XXI(b)(iii)

Among the various measures taken by states against Russia, some trade restrictions on certain goods could indeed be justified by invoking GATT 1994 Article XXI(b) (i) or (ii). However, as mentioned earlier, in terms of comprehensive measures such as the suspension of MFN treatment for Russian goods in general, a question arises whether they can be justified by invoking GATT 1994 Article XXI(b)(iii). Although this author does not attempt to examine this question in detail here,[55] the following issues on the satisfaction of the requirements for invoking GATT 1994 Article XXI (b)(iii) as clarified by the panels in the cases discussed in the foregoing, should be pointed out.

Regarding requirement a) that the invoking state must establish the existence of 'war or other emergency in international relations', it would be straightforward in our case to objectively find the fact of the existence of a 'war or other emergency in international relations' between Ukraine and Russia. The first issue here is to determine whether states taking trade measures against Russia as third parties may

---

[51] *Ibid.*, paras. 7.297 and 7.307.

[52] *Ibid.*, para. 7.354.

[53] *Ibid.*, para. 7.358.

[54] *United States - Origin Marking Requirement*, Notification of an Appeal by the United States under Article 16 of the Understanding on Rules and Procedures Governing the Settlement of Disputes (DSU), WT/DS597/9, 30 January 2023.

[55] For a detailed examination of this problem, *see* the chapter "Trade Sanctions Against Russia and their WTO Consistency: Focusing on Justification Under National Security Exceptions" of this volume.

invoke Article XXI(b)(iii) as justification. All precedents, save for *US - Steel and Aluminium Products*, concern bilateral conflicts involving states invoking Article XXI(b)(iii). It should have been rather straightforward for such states to satisfy requirement a), though in *US - Origin Marking (Hong Kong, China)*, the invoking state, the US, was unable to satisfy this because the panel found that the bilateral situation between the US and Hong Kong, China had not constituted an emergency in international relations.[56] However, in *US - Steel and Aluminium Products*, the invoking state, also the US, referred not to the bilateral relation between the US and China but to the situation of global excess capacity in steel and aluminium. Although the invoking state failed to persuade the panel that the situation constituted an emergency in international relations,[57] this case suggests that a state that has no bilateral conflict with a complaining state may invoke Article XXI(b)(iii) by alleging the existence of an objective situation as an emergency in international relations. Further, the panel in *US - Origin Marking (Hong Kong, China)*, as mentioned earlier,[58] admitted that an emergency need not necessarily originate in an invoking state's own territory and bilateral relations, and that a war taking place between two or more countries could also give rise to an emergency in international relations affecting other countries. Therefore, the first issue can be answered affirmatively: namely, that third states to the dispute between Ukraine and Russia may invoke Article XXI(b)(iii). And such third states can satisfy easily requirement a) of establishing the existence of 'war or other emergency in international relations' because of the objective fact that there is armed conflict between Ukraine and Russia.

However, the second issue is whether third states can establish that the 'war or other emergency in international relations' is objectively affecting their security interests and thus satisfies requirement c), which, according to the panel in *Russia - Traffic in Transit*, mandates that an invoking state articulates its essential security interests sufficiently to demonstrate their veracity. This panel, as mentioned earlier,[59] also defined the term 'essential security interests' generally as "those interests relating to the quintessential functions of the state, namely, the protection of its territory and its population from external threats, and the maintenance of law and public order internally", which clearly include the defence or military interests, maintenance of law and public order interests or are at least close to such interests[60] arising from the situation under requirement a).

Indeed, Russian action could be condemned as aggression against Ukraine in violation of Article 2(4) of the UN Charter and, as such, would appear to constitute a breach of the obligation owed to all UN members or the international community as a whole, that is, a breach of an obligation *erga omnes (partes)*. Therefore, third states

---

[56] *Supra* note 53 and the relevant text.

[57] *US - Steel and Aluminium Products*, *supra* note 7, para. 7.148 and *supra* note 43 and the relevant text.

[58] *Supra* note 51 and the relevant text.

[59] *Supra* note 20 and the relevant text.

[60] *Supra* note 50 and the relevant text.

may allege that the security interests of all states are threatened and thus that requirement c) is satisfied. That being said, there have been no authoritative findings on the part of the UN Security Council or the International Court of Justice (ICJ) of a violation of the UN Charter or a breach of an obligation *erga omnes (partes)* in relation to Russian action. It seems difficult for a panel to admit such an allegation by third states unless it makes such a finding by itself.[61] Furthermore, sanctions by WTO members for a violation of the UN Charter, which is also a breach of an obligation *erga omnes (partes)*, were originally conceived as justified when in pursuance of the obligations under UN Security Council resolutions under GATT Article XXI(c), but not (b).

In reality, third states not directly involved in the dispute may nonetheless be affected in various ways and to varying degrees. Third states adjacent to the conflict area or states that provide arms assistance to either party may be threatened directly in relation to their own defence or military interests, and under a pressing need to protect such interests. Some other third states, however, may be not under such pressure. Although what qualifies as a sufficient level of articulation under requirement c) is not necessarily clear, the panel in *Russia - Traffic in Transit*, as already mentioned, stated that the further the emergency in international relations is removed from armed conflict, the less obvious are the defence or military interests that can generally be expected to arise, and, therefore, an invoking state would need to articulate its essential security interests with greater specificity.[62] Thus, if we follow the logic of this panel, third states seem to need to articulate their essential security interests through convincingly establishing that the situation is objective enough to cause a "heightened tension or crisis"[63] to themselves that actually threatens their defence or military interests.[64] If the invoking State is required to provide such a level of articulation under requirement c), it would appear that at least some third states taking trade sanctions against Russia would have difficulty achieving this level of articulation. The second issue can not necessarily be answered affirmatively.

In relation to this point, it may be argued that it is not difficult to satisfy requirements a) and c) given that Russia has threatened to use nuclear weapons.[65] Indeed, following the onset of the conflict, the nuclear threat has escalated, especially towards Ukraine, a directly involved party, and the NATO states providing

---

[61] We will consider the possibility of such a finding by the panel later at Sect. 4 of this article.

[62] *Supra* notes 24 and 25 and the relevant text.

[63] *Russia - Traffic in Transit, supra* note 5, para. 7.76.

[64] The panel in *US - Steel and Aluminium Product* stated that a situation must be "at least comparable in its gravity or severity to a 'war'" and "international tensions that are of a critical or serious nature in terms of their impact on the conduct of international relations". *Supra* notes 40 and 42 and the relevant text. This statement also seems to suggest that third states must have their own defence or military interests seriously threatened.

[65] Ex., see Andrews Roth, Shaun Walker, Jennifer Rankin, and Julian Borger, "Putin signals escalation as he puts Russia's nuclear force on high alert". The Guardian. Archived from the original on 27 February 2022, https://www.theguardian.com/world/2022/feb/27/vladimir-putin-puts-russia-nuclear-deterrence-forces-on-high-alert-ukraine.

arms assistance. But, for other third states taking trade sanctions, since a certain level of nuclear threat had become normalised even before the outbreak of the current conflict, the difference in the level of threat before and after the conflict may not be as significant. Further, among third states, there might also be states for which the act of taking trade sanctions itself could be seen as a cause for increased levels of tension and threat. Thus, it appears necessary for such third states to delve into a more detailed assessment of the extent of the nuclear threat.

Thus, the requirements for invoking GATT Article XXI (b)(iii), as clarified by the panels in the cases discussed in the foregoing, do not necessarily appear to be ones that can be easily satisfied, and it does not seem that all third states that have taken trade sanctions against Russia may avail themselves of this security exception. Therefore, the question arises whether the measures of states who may be unsuccessful in invoking the security exception could be justified by means other than the security exception. In this article, the author would like to consider next the possibility of invoking customary international law on third-party countermeasures as one such alternative approach.

3 Countermeasures and Third-Party Countermeasures Under Customary International Law

3.1 Countermeasures Under Customary International Law

Countermeasures are means of implementing state responsibility for an internationally wrongful act, and may only be taken by an injured state in order to induce the responsible state to comply with its obligation to cease the internationally wrongful act, if it is continuing, and to provide reparation to the injured state.[66] Countermeasures involve otherwise wrongful conduct, but as a response to internationally wrongful conduct of another state, the wrongfulness of the conduct in question is precluded.[67] The 2001 International Law Commission (ILC) Draft Articles on Responsibility of States for Internationally Wrongful Acts (ARSIWA)[68] are considered as reflecting international customary law. Draft Article 22 of ARSIWA on "Countermeasures in respect of an internationally wrongful act" provides that "[t]he wrongfulness of an act of a State not in conformity with an international obligation towards another State is precluded if and to the extent that the act constitutes a countermeasure taken against the latter State. . . ." Countermeasures are a means of unilateral self-help, traditionally recognised as a unique institution in a decentralised

---

[66] International Law Commission, Draft Articles on Responsibility of States for Internationally Wrongful Acts, with commentaries, in *Yearbook of the International Law Commission* 2001, vol. II, Part Two, as corrected (ARSIWA), p. 128, para. (3) and p. 130, para. (1).

[67] *Ibid.*, p.75, paras. (2) and (4).

[68] *Ibid.*, pp. 31–143.

international community where the legal settlement of disputes is not always guaranteed, and they enable and strengthen the enforcement and normative integrity of international law.[69] However, countermeasures are open to abuse by states claiming to have been harmed due to the actions of some other state as the determining of the 'wrongfulness' of such actions could be subjectively assessed by the claiming state. For this reason, ARSIWA specifies certain conditions as safeguards against abuse in Part III, Chapter 2 "Countermeasures". The main conditions stipulated in Draft Articles 49 through 53 are as follows.

First, an injured state may only take countermeasures against a state responsible for an internationally wrongful act in order to induce that state to cease the wrongful act or fulfil its obligations of reparation for the injury (Draft Article 49(1)). Second, the injured state shall call upon the responsible state to cease the wrongful acts or fulfil its obligation of reparation for the injury, notify it of any decision to take countermeasures and offer to negotiate with that state (Draft Article 52(1)). Third, countermeasures are limited to the non-performance for the time being of international obligations of the state taking the measures towards the responsible state and shall, as far as possible, be taken in such a way as to permit the resumption of performance of the obligations in question (Draft Article 49(2) and (3)). Fourth, countermeasures must be commensurate with the injury suffered, taking into account the gravity of the internationally wrongful act and the rights in question (Draft Article 51). Fifth, countermeasures by threat or use of force are prohibited, and further, countermeasures shall not affect obligations for the protection of fundamental human rights, obligations of a humanitarian character prohibiting reprisals, and other obligations under peremptory norms of general international law (Draft Article 50(1)). Sixth, a state taking countermeasures is not relieved from fulfilling its obligations under any dispute settlement procedure applicable between it and the responsible state (Article 50(2)). Seventh, countermeasures may not be taken, and if already taken must be suspended without undue delay if the internationally wrongful act has ceased or the dispute is pending before a court or tribunal which has the authority to make decision binding on the parties (Draft Article 52(3)).

3.2 Third-Party Countermeasures

Countermeasures under ARSIWA are provided for as the right of the directly injured state of an internationally wrongful act. However, Draft Article 48 of ARSIWA, "Invocation of responsibility by a State other than an injured State", provides in paragraph 1 that any state other than an injured state is entitled to invoke the responsibility of another state if the obligation breached "is owed to a group of

---

[69]Danae Azaria, "Trade Countermeasures for Breaches of International Law outside the WTO", *International and Comparative Law Quarterly*, Vol. 71(April 2022), p. 397.

States including that State, and is established for the protection of a collective interest of the group" or the obligation breached "is owed to international community as a whole". This provision recognises the right of states other than those directly injured to invoke responsibility for breaches of 'obligations *erga omnes (partes)*'. Correspondingly, Draft Article 54 of ARSIWA also provides the following regarding "Measures taken by States other than an injured State",

> This chapter does not prejudice the right of any State, entitled under article 48, paragraph 1, to invoke the responsibility of another State, to take lawful measures against that State to ensure cessation of the breach and reparation in the interest of the injured State or of the beneficiaries of obligation breached.

Regarding this provision, the ILC Commentary states that at the time of drafting in 2001, the international law on countermeasures taken in the general or collective interest was uncertain, and that there appeared to be no clearly recognised entitlement of states other than an injured state to take countermeasures in the collective interest.[70] Due to this situation, Draft Article 54 was included as a saving clause which reserved the position and left the resolution of a matter to the further development of international law. The use of the term "lawful measures" instead of countermeasures was specifically intended not to prejudice any position on this type of measures.[71]

In the ILC, countermeasures taken by states other than the injured state against breaches of obligations *erga omnes (partes)* had been referred to as 'collective countermeasures' or 'multilateral countermeasures',[72] but state practice on this subject at the time of drafting (2001) was considered "limited and rather embryonic".[73] However, prevailing theories up to the present refer to such countermeasures as 'third-party countermeasures', pointing out the extensive and abundant accumulation of state practice. Commentators have argued that third-party countermeasures are currently accepted as customary international law,[74] and that just as with countermeasures by an injured state, the general safeguards regime for countermeasures set forth in Draft Articles 49 to 53 of ARSIWA is applied *mutatis mutandis* to third-party countermeasures to prevent abuse.[75] In state practice to date, third-party countermeasures are normally adopted in response to widely acknowledged breaches of obligations *erga omnes (partes)*, and this is assessed as indicative

---

[70] ARSIWA, *supra* note 66, p. 139, para. (6).

[71] *Ibid.*, p. 139, paras. (6) and (7).

[72] ILC, Summary records of the second part of the fifty-second session, held at Geneva from 10 July to 18 August 2000 in *Yearbook of the International Law Commission* 2000, p. 337.

[73] ARSIWA, *supra* note 66, p. 137, para. (3).

[74] Martin Dawidowicz, *Third-Party Countermeasures in International Law* (Cambridge University Press, 2017), pp. 282–283; Linos-Alexandre Sicilianos, "Countermeasures in Response to Grave Violation of Obligations Owed to International Community," in James Crawford, Alain Pellet and Simon Olleson (eds.), *The Law of International Responsibility* (Oxford University Press, 2010), pp. 1146–1148.

[75] Dawidowicz, *ibid.*, p. 286.

of the significantly reduced risk of abuse associated with the subjective interpretation of wrongful acts.[76]

4 Trade Sanctions Against Russia as Permissible Third-Party Countermeasures

4.1 Problem Setting

As mentioned in the Introduction, this article considers the scenario within which not all WTO members that have taken measures against Russia may successfully invoke security exceptions in response to a Russian complaint within the context of WTO dispute settlement. This article considers whether the measures of states who may be not able to invoke security exceptions may still be justified as third-party countermeasures under customary international law.

The Understanding on Rules and Procedures Governing the Settlement of Disputes (DSU) is understood to contain the special rules (*lex specialis*) provided for in Draft Article 55 of ARSIWA[77] regarding remedies and countermeasures for violations of WTO agreements.[78] Therefore, a preliminary question is whether such special rules preclude customary international law on third-party countermeasures. The DSU also lacks the type of general provisions on the applicable law in WTO dispute settlement, as are found in Article 38 of the Statute of the ICJ. Therefore, the question arises whether panels or the Appellate Body may apply customary international law on third-party countermeasures. Furthermore, since the existence of some prior internationally wrongful act by the state subject to a measure must be found as a minimum for a third-party countermeasure to be lawful, the question also arises whether panels or Appellate Body may apply non-WTO norms such as those pertaining to human rights law, humanitarian law, environmental law, and the law of armed conflict, in order to make such a finding. Whether a respondent may invoke the rules of third-party countermeasures under customary international law as a defence in WTO dispute settlement depends on how these questions are approached. In the following, we will first examine the relationship between the special rules of the DSU and customary international law on third-party countermeasures, before considering the treatment of non-WTO norms under WTO dispute settlement.

---

[76] *Ibid.*, p. 284.

[77] Article 55 of ARSIWA provides that: "These articles do not apply where and to the extent that the conditions for the existence of an internationally wrongful act or the content or implementation of the international responsibility of a State are governed by special rules of international law". ARSIWA, *supra* note 66, p. 140.

[78] Joost Pauwelyn, *Conflict of Norms in Public International law* (Cambridge University Press, 2003), pp. 230–232; Azaria, *supra* note 69, pp. 396–397; ARSIWA, *supra* note 66, p. 140 and n. 818.

4.2 The Relationship Between the Special Rules of the DSU and the Customary Law on Third-Party Countermeasures

The special rules of the DSU are Articles 22 and 23. Article 23, paragraph 1 of the DSU provides that,

1. When Members seek the redress of a violation of obligations or other nullification or impairment of benefits under the covered agreements or an impediment to the attainment of any objective of the covered agreements, they shall have recourse to, and abide by, the rules and procedures of this Understanding.

    Furthermore, paragraph 2 imposes more specific obligations, following the general obligation in paragraph 1,

2. In such cases, Members shall:

    (a) not make a determination to the effect that a violation has occurred, that benefits have been nullified or impaired or that the attainment of any objective of the covered agreements has been impeded, except through recourse to dispute settlement in accordance with the rules and procedures of this Understanding, and shall make any such determination consistent with the findings contained in the panel or Appellate Body report adopted by the DSB or an arbitration award rendered under this Understanding;

    (b) . . .; and

    (c) follow the procedures set forth in Article 22 to determine the level of suspension of concessions or other obligations and obtain DSB authorization in accordance with those procedures before suspending concessions or other obligations under the covered agreements in response to the failure of the Member concerned to implement the recommendations and rulings within that reasonable period of time.

The "suspension of concessions and other obligations" stipulated in Article 23.2 (c) is a countermeasure permitted under the DSU, and Article 22 further stipulates the details of the "suspension of concessions and other obligations" and the procedures for its invocation. Article 23 ("Strengthening of the Multilateral System") seeks to ensure the primacy of the WTO multilateral trade system by prohibiting unilateral measures by members, and members are prohibited from taking unilateral countermeasures without prior recourse to WTO dispute settlement and without the permission of the Dispute Settlement Body (DSB). Articles 22 and 23 of the DSU are special rules within the meaning of Draft Article 55 of ARSIWA, and, to that extent, exclude customary international law on third-party countermeasures.

However, Article 23.1, as worded, only prohibits unilateral measures "[w]hen Members seek the redress of a violation of obligations or other nullification or impairment of benefits *under the covered agreements* or an impediment to the attainment of *any objective of the covered agreements*" (emphasis added). Unilateral countermeasures in relation to broader violations of international law obligations (i.e., other than WTO agreements), such as those considered in this article, do not appear to fall within its scope of application. Therefore, in such cases, there remains room for the application of customary international law on third-party countermeasures for breaches of international obligations outside of those contained in the WTO agreements. It should be noted, however, that scholarly opinion is far from unanimous on this question and can sensibly be grouped in the opposing and the affirming theory camps.

4.2.1 Opposing Theories

Within the opposing camp, Marceau and Wyatt state the following,

> Although the terms of Article 23 of the DSU only require Members not to take unilaterally determined countermeasures in relation to the WTO covered agreements, this wording may also reflect the WTO membership's overall attitude against the taking of unilaterally determined trade countermeasures. Indeed, it would be somewhat odd if the WTO Members were to be lenient regarding unilateral trade measures where taken in the context of breaches of an RTA [i.e., regional trade agreement] provision while maintaining its strict ban on trade unilateralism undertaken for the purposes of enforcing the provisions of the WTO covered agreements. A reading pursuant to which the WTO prohibits trade countermeasures based on unilateral determination, irrespective of the breach they are taken in response to, is therefore, we submit, at least plausible.[79]

Marceau and Wyatt further argue that with respect to GATT 1994, only the general exception under Article XX, the security exception under Article XXI and countermeasures permitted under Article 23 of the DSU may provide justifications to violations of GATT, and that such justifications suffice and do not require further justification under customary international law. Marceau and Wyatt state that "it would be strange if a trade-related measure taken to protect human life were subjected to the good faith test in the chapeau of Article XX, yet a measure portrayed as a trade countermeasure to a breach of a health provision in an RTA were not subjected to any WTO review".[80]

Although arguing under the former GATT regime (i.e., under GATT 1947), Hahn also argues that Article XXI(b)(iii) of the GATT, when interpreted in line with the other escape clauses of the GATT, implicitly excludes the unilateral use of economic measures for the self-enforcement of international law. According to Hahn,

> the wealth of exceptions in the GATT, the various possibilities of the CONTRACTING PARTIES to suspend the application of certain provisions, and the short notice necessary before complete withdrawal suggest that there is no other possibility to evade the obligations of the GATT as a reaction to a preceding violation of international law.[81]

---

[79] Gabrielle Marceau and Julian Wyatt, "Dispute Settlement Regimes Intermingled: Regional Trade Agreements and the WTO," *Journal of International Dispute Settlement*, Vol. 1, No. 1(2010), p. 76.

[80] *Ibid.*, p. 77.

[81] Michael J. Hahn, "Vital Interests and the Law of GATT: An Analysis of GATT's Security Exception", *Michigan Journal of International Law*, Vol. 12(1991), p. 604.

Hahn argues that deciding otherwise implies great potential for instability of the multilateral trading system, and thus undermines GATT's purpose of ensuring stability in international economic relations.[82]

Similarly, Boisson de Chazournes also appears to support the opposing position, although her argument is premised on GATT Article XXIII under the former GATT regime. She states the following,

> En effet, le régime du GATT ne permet pas qu'un fait générateur ne relevant pas du champ d'application de l'Accord général puisse justifier un manquement aux dispositions de l'Accord général, au titre d'un exercice de contre-mesures .... [L]e régime circonscrit l'utilisation de toute mesure en réaction qui enfreindrait une prescription de l'Accord général, que le fait générateur des contre-mesures relève ou qu'il ne relève pas du champ d'application de l'Accord général.[83]

Boisson de Chazournes seems to base her view on the following: on the one hand, under the GATT regime, countermeasures as suspension of concessions or other obligations are strictly limited and regulated under Article XXIII(2);[84] but, on the other hand, the operation of the GATT exceptions [GATT Articles XX and XXI] makes it possible to "decompartmentalise (décloisonnement)" the GATT system to the outside in the sense that measures adopted in accordance with these exceptions can be taken in response to violations of international law not covered by the GATT.[85] Regarding the function of the GATT exceptions, this view aligns with those of Marceau and Wyatt, as well as Hahn.

Furthermore, Bartels argues that while the DSU does not expressly forbid countermeasures under general international law to respond to violations of international law outside of the WTO system, "it does not necessarily follow that such a prohibition might not be implicit in the establishment of a regime excluding resort to unauthorized countermeasures".[86] He points out that although early state practice under the former GATT is not consistent, "the principle that countermeasures are prohibited outside of the GATT exceptions has been confirmed by a substantial and increasingly consistent state practice of justifying trade measures, where relevant, under the relevant GATT exceptions".[87] Bartels, therefore, concludes that coercive

---

[82] *Ibid.*, pp. 603–604.

[83] Laurence Boisson de Chazournes, *Les contre-measures dans les relations internationales économiques* (Editions Pedone, 1992), p. 184. English translation is as follows: "The GATT regime does not permit causal acts that do not fall within the scope of the GATT to justify the violation of the provisions of the GATT in the name of the exercise of countermeasures.... [T]he [GATT] regime circumscribes the use of any reactive measure that would violate a provision of the General Agreement, whether the causal acts of the countermeasures fall within or outside the scope of the General Agreement."

[84] *Ibid.*

[85] *Ibid.*, p. 185. See also *infra* note 93.

[86] Lorand Bartels, "Article XX of GATT and the Problem of Extraterritorial Jurisdiction: The Case of Trade Measures for the Protection of Human Rights," *Journal of World Trade*, Vol. 36, No. 2 (2002), p. 397.

[87] *Ibid.*, p. 400.

WTO Dispute Settlement and Trade Sanctions as Permissible Third-Party... 205

measures in the form of countermeasures are not permitted even when permissible under the rules on state responsibility.[88]

In Japan, Judge Yuji Iwasawa of the ICJ stated the following in 1995, the same year the WTO was established,

> [Article 23.1 of the DSU] only addresses situations "seeking the redress of a violation of obligations or other nullification or impairment of benefits under the covered agreements or an impediment to the attainment of any objective of the covered agreements", so it is not entirely clear whether unilateral retaliations based on violations of international obligations other than those covered agreements are also prohibited by this provision....However, it should be understood that unilateral retaliation taken in contravention of the WTO is not permissible, ...even if it takes place with respect to matters not covered by the WTO Agreements....This is because Article 23.1 [of the DSU] can be read to prohibit retaliation that is inconsistent with the WTO agreements in content without the approval of the Dispute Settlement Body, even if it is based on a violation by the targeted Member of an international obligation other than the covered agreement.[89]

The basis for Judge Iwasawa's statement is not necessarily clear, but it may have been based on his view after detailing the practice of the condemnation of unilateral sanctions during the former GATT era. Furthermore, at the time, there may have been an expectation on the part of WTO members other than the US, including Japan, that Article 23 of the DSU would serve as a containment mechanism for unilateral sanction clauses such as Section 301 of the US Trade Act. This background could provide context for such view.

Therefore, from the standpoint of opposing theories, even though Article 23.1 of the DSU remains silent on violations of obligations other than those flowing from

---

[88] *Ibid.*, p. 402.

[89] Yuji Iwasawa, *Dispute Settlement in the WTO* (Sanseido, 1995), pp. 165–166 (*in Japanese*).

WTO agreements, a WTO member's violation of its WTO obligations as a counter-measure to that prior violation under customary international law would amount to a violation of this provision due to it being a unilateral measure.[90]

4.2.2 Affirmative Theories

Pons states the following in general terms,

> [E]ven in those systems that aspire to being "self-contained regimes" and excluding the operability of the self-help, the principle of speciality restricts the sphere of validity of their specific secondary rules to regulating the outcome of unlawful acts occurring "within" the system, with general international law intervening in regard to the outcome of unlawful acts that occurred "outside" the system.[91]

---

[90] *The 2023 Report on Compliance by Major Trading Partners with Trade Agreements (WTO, FTA/EPA and IIA)* by the Ministry of Economy, Trade and Industry of Japan, in Part II, Chapter 15 'Unilateral Measures' (*in Japanese*) includes the following diagram (https://www.meti.go.jp/shingikai/sankoshin/tsusho_boeki/fukosei_boeki/report_2023/pdf/2023_02_15.pdf, p. 429):

		Content of Unilateral Measure	
		Violation of WTO agreements	No violation of WTO agreements
Content of Dispute	Relating to WTO agreements	(a) The measure constitutes a violation of both Art. 23 of the DSU and any other provision of the WTO agreements.	(b) The measure constitutes a violation of Art. 23 of the DSU.
	Not relating to WTO agreements	(c) The measure constitutes a violation of any provision of the WTO agreements other than Art. 23 of the DSU.	(d)

The Report provides the following explanation regarding this diagram: "With regard to (a) and (b) in the diagram, so long as the issue of the dispute is a violation of the WTO agreements or infringement of its own interests under the WTO agreements by the other party, recourse to WTO dispute settlement in accordance with Article 23 of the DSU is required, and the use of a unilateral measure would be a violation of Article 23 of the DSU. Furthermore, with respect to (a), a violation of the WTO agreements due to the content of the measure is also naturally of concern. As for (c), the measure itself constitutes a violation of the WTO agreements. In other words, for areas other than (d), a violation of Article 23 of the DSU or a violation of the WTO agreements of the unilateral measure itself is always of concern."

In this diagram, the area (c) represents a unilateral countermeasure in response to a violation of international law unrelated to the WTO agreements, through a violation of the WTO agreements. The explanation states that the measure itself constitutes a violation, appearing thus to reject the application of customary international law on countermeasures. However, it does not categorise it as a violation of Article 23 of the DSU and in this point differs from either of the opposing theories discussed in the main text.

[91] Javier Fernández Pons, "Self-Help and the World Trade Organization," in Paolo Mengozzi (ed.), *International Trade Law on the 50th Anniversary of the Multilateral Trade System* (Dott. A. Giuffré Editore, 1999), p. 95.

However, he prefaces this by "as in the case of the GATT/WTO law", thus making it clear that the WTO regime is such an example.[92]

Pons then addresses and criticises the view of Boisson de Chazournes that the security exception under GATT Article XXI would exclude the possibility of invoking customary international law on countermeasures as a way of justifying the suspension of GATT 1947 (*nunc* WTO) obligations as a reaction against any prior violations of international law rules 'outside' the GATT/WTO law and not involving a security issue.[93] According to Pons, such a view would imply in practice that WTO members would have renounced the application of an extensive range of economic countermeasures to react against internationally wrongful acts not affecting their security, as many trade reprisals represent behaviours that are inconsistent with the GATT rules. However, according to Pons, the security exception does not appear to suffice in replacing the operability of customary international law.[94] He states that,

> the fact that certain measures are legitimated as 'treaty exception' is irrespective of the fact that other measures are considered *per se* as 'treaty violation', and silence is upheld concerning their possible justification if these measures respect all the substantial and procedural requirements established by general international law on countermeasures.[95]

Pons further buttresses this view by citing the advisory opinion of the ICJ in the *Namibia Case* on the meaning of 'silence' that "[t]he silence of a treaty [. . .] could not be interpreted as implying the exclusion of a right which has its source outside

---

[92] *Ibid.*, p. 94.

[93] *Ibid.*, p. 97 and n. 106. In this context, Boisson de Chazournes's view that the security exception of the GATT Article XXI justifies the suspension of WTO obligations as a reaction against prior violation of international law rules outside the WTO law and not involving a security issue may be due to her broad interpretation of 'other emergency in international relations' in subparagraph (b) (iii).

[94] *Ibid.*

[95] *Ibid.*, pp. 97–98.

the treaty, in general international law, and is dependent on the occurrence of circumstances which are not normally envisaged when a treaty is concluded."[96]

Ultimately, Pons states that,

> [t]he solution probably does not consist of redefining the content of the 'security exceptions', but rather of assuming that the operability of general international rules on countermeasures can justify, by itself, a suspension of the WTO obligations as a reaction against a prior internationally wrongful act on the fringe of special provisions.[97]

Pauwelyn, who argues in favour of allowing defences based on non-WTO law against claims for violation of the WTO agreements, also points out that the contracting out of international law on countermeasures under the DSU is only in respect of countermeasures taken in response to a breach of WTO rules, and that the DSU is silent on countermeasures taken in response to breaches on other (i.e., non-WTO) norms/rules. Pauwelyn argues that the suspension of WTO obligations as a countermeasure is valid under international law, and ought to be recognised also as valid within the context of WTO dispute settlement.[98]

Azaria points out that the panels in *Russia - Traffic in Transit* and *Saudi Arabia - IPRs* (discussed earlier, cf., Sect. 2) interpreted the terms 'essential security interests' and 'emergency in international relations' in GATT Article XXI(b)(iii) and Article 73(b)(iii) of TRIPS Agreement very narrowly, so that the security exceptions apply only to a much narrower range of circumstances than have traditionally given rise to countermeasures,[99] and disagrees with the opposing theories that argue that countermeasures under customary international law for breaches of non-WTO obligations overlap with, and are intended to be excluded by, security exceptions.[100] Azaria acknowledges that where a WTO member uses force against another WTO member, the 'essential security interests' of some WTO members other than the injured WTO member may be threatened, owing, for instance, to geographic proximity or ensuing refugee flows. However, Azaria argues that GATT Article XXI(b)(iii) would not apply in relation to WTO members whose essential security interests are not threatened, but that in all such situations trade restrictions would be available to

---

[96] *Legal Consequences for States of the Continued Presence of South Africa in Namibia (South West Africa) notwithstanding Security Council Resolution 276 (1970)*, Advisory Opinion, *ICJ Report* 1971, p. 47, para. 96, cited by Pons, *supra* note 91, p. 98, n. 108. However, Bartels points out that "insofar as this opinion merely recognizes that general international law applies to treaties to the extent that it has not been contracted out of by the parties, it does not help to answer the question whether the WTO members have contracted out of their right to take countermeasures under general international law". Bartels, *supra* note 86, pp. 398–399.

[97] Pons, *supra* note 91, p. 98–99. On the other hand, in conclusion, Pons approaches the position of the opposing camp on the basis that the rules of customary international law on countermeasures do not apply because the jurisdiction and applicable law of the panel and the Appellate Body will be bound within the "four corners of WTO law". *Ibid.*, pp. 101–104.

[98] Pauwelyn, *supra* note 78, p. 232.

[99] Azaria, *supra* note 69, p. 404.

[100] *Ibid.*, p. 401.

WTO members only and to the extent that they are permissible countermeasures under customary international law.[101]

Furthermore, Azaria draws attention to the opinion of the Appellate Body in *Mexico-Soft Drinks*.[102] In that case, Mexico had alleged US violations of NAFTA obligations, arguing that its own countermeasures in the form of suspensions of WTO obligations taken in response were justified under GATT Article XX(d)[103] on the basis that they were intended to secure US compliance with international obligations. The Appellate Body rejected Mexico's defence on the ground that 'laws or regulations' within the meaning of Article XX(d) "refer to the rules that form part of the domestic legal order of the WTO Member invoking the provision and do not include the international obligations of another WTO Member."[104] Azaria argues that according to the Appellate Body, countermeasures in response to a violation of international obligations by another WTO member cannot be justified under the general exception in Article XX(d),[105] which must also mean that this provision does not overlap with the function of countermeasures under customary international law.[106]

What is more, the Appellate Body stated that Mexico's interpretation of the term 'laws or regulations' as including another WTO member's international obligations would logically imply that a WTO member could invoke Article XX(d) to also justify measures designed 'to secure compliance' with that other member's WTO obligations,[107] adding the following,

> Mexico's interpretation would allow WTO Members to adopt WTO-inconsistent measures based upon a unilateral determination that another Member has breached its WTO obligations, in contradiction with Articles 22 and 23 of the DSU and Article [XXIII(2)] of the GATT 1994.[108]

Azaria, thus, points out that the Appellate Body made it clear that the DSU has expressly displaced the right to take unilateral countermeasures for breaches of WTO obligations.[109] She states, however, that the DSU remains silent on whether it also displaces countermeasures under customary international law for breaches of

---

[101] *Ibid.*, p. 406.

[102] Appellate Body Report, *Mexico-Tax Measures on Soft Drinks and Other Beverages*, WT/DS308/AB/R, adopted 24 March 2006 (*Mexico-Soft Drinks*).

[103] Article XX(d) reads as follows: '... nothing in this Agreement shall be construed to prevent the adoption or enforcement by any contracting party of measures: (d) necessary to secure compliance with laws or regulations which are not inconsistent with the provisions of this Agreement, including those relating to customs enforcement, the enforcement of monopolies ..., the protection of patents, trade marks and copyrights, and the prevention of deceptive practices.'

[104] *Mexico-Soft Drinks*, *supra* note 102, para. 75.

[105] Azaria, *supra* note 69, p. 391.

[106] *Ibid.*, p. 412.

[107] *Mexico-Soft Drinks*, *supra* note 102, p. 32, para. 77.

[108] *Ibid.*

[109] Azaria, *supra* note 69, p. 412.

non-WTO obligations, and questions the notion that WTO members had intended to exclude countermeasures under customary international law for breaches of non-WTO obligations while failing to include provisions expressly displacing such countermeasures, in the way that they had done so for displacing countermeasures in response to breaches of WTO obligations. After all, Azaria argues, their failure to do so suggests that they had not displaced countermeasures under customary international law for breaches of non-WTO obligations.[110]

In the context of recent practice, Furculita points out that the European Commission asserts the legality of its proposal for the Anti-Coercion Instrument (ACI) published in December 2021[111] on the basis of customary international law on countermeasures.[112]

The ACI proposal enables the European Union (EU) to take countermeasures, including suspension of tariff concessions, the imposition of new or increased custom duties, and the introduction or increase of restrictions on the importation or exportation of goods, which would otherwise be violations of WTO agreements, when a third country applies or threatens to apply measures affecting trade or investment aimed at demanding a particular act from the EU or an EU member state that amount to measures of economic coercion to such an extent that they violate the principle of non-interference under customary international law.

Furculita suggests that behind the ACI proposal lies the European Commission's understanding of Article 23 of the DSU as follows: Article 23 of the DSU as *lex specialis* mandates the use of WTO dispute settlement to the exclusion of customary international law on countermeasures. Nevertheless, it does so only when WTO members "seek the redress of a violation [...] under the covered agreements".[113] Indeed, the panel in *US - Certain EC Products*[114] had expressly stated that "the criterion for determining whether Article 23 is applicable is whether the Member that imposed the measure was 'seeking the redress of' a WTO violation",[115] and the panel in *EC - Commercial Vessels*[116] had also stated that "the phrase 'seek the

---

[110] *Ibid.*

[111] European Commission, "Proposal for a Regulation of the European Parliament and of the Council on the protection of the Union and its Member States from economic coercion by third countries," 8.12.2021, COM(2021)775 final, at https://trade.ec.europa.eu/doclib/docs/2021/december/tradoc_159958.pdf. This proposal was adopted with some modification as Regulation (EU)2023/2675 on 22 November 2023, at https://eur-lex.europa.eu/eli/reg/2023/2675/oj.

[112] Cornelia Furculita, "Guest Post: Does EU's Anti-coercion Instrument violate Art. 23 of the DSU?", *International Economic Law Policy Blog* (posted on 21 February 2022), at https://ielp. worldtradelaw.net/2022/02/guest-post-does-eus-anti-coercion-instrument-violate-art-23-ofthe-dsu.html#_ftn2.

[113] *Ibid.*

[114] Panel Report, *United States - Import Measures on Certain Products from the European Communities*, WT/DS165/R, adopted 10 January 2001 (*US - Certain EC Products*).

[115] *Ibid.*, para. 6.21.

[116] Panel Report, *European Communities - Measures Affecting Trade in Commercial Vessels*, WT/DS301/R, adopted 20 June 2005 (*EC - Commercial Vessels*).

WTO Dispute Settlement and Trade Sanctions as Permissible Third-Party... 211

redress of a violation...' covers any act of a Member in response to what it considers to be a violation of a WTO obligation by another Member".[117] Furculita claims that, pursuant to that understanding, the European Commission is seeking to take countermeasures against economic coercion measures by third countries that violate the principle of non-interference under customary international law, regardless of whether such measures simultaneously violate WTO agreements. Thus, she states that since the countermeasures imposed under the ACI do not seek the redress of a violation of the WTO Agreement, the *lex specialis* in the form of Article 23 of the DSU would not apply to that extent and that they would be lawful insofar as they meet the requirements for countermeasures under customary international law.[118] Therefore, it could be reasonably argued that the European Commission is of the view that, on the basis of customary international law on countermeasures, it would be able to justify EU countermeasures under the ACI that otherwise violate WTO agreements, even within the framework of WTO dispute settlement.

In sum, opposing theories deny the possibility of invoking customary international law on countermeasures, arguing that Article 23.1 of the DSU expressly or impliedly prohibits unilateral countermeasures, and that any countermeasures in the form of a violation of the WTO agreements must be authorised by the DSB in accordance with the DSU, or justified by the general exception of GATT Article XX or the security exception of GATT Article XXI. Conversely, affirmative theories argue that the language of Article 23.1 of the DSU only explicitly prohibits unilateral countermeasures against violations of obligations under the WTO agreements, and that the key customary international legal right of states to take countermeasures against violations of non-WTO obligations cannot be assumed as waived under the DSU. Underlying the opposing theories is the notion that the existence, under WTO law, of general and security exceptions to WTO obligations suffices for the purposes of addressing the question of permissible countermeasures in response to violations of non-WTO obligations. Recourse to customary international law on countermeasures is therefore excluded. This may be particularly understood against the backdrop of the historically prevalent view that security exceptions are self-judging, and that the term 'other emergency of international relations' under the security exceptions is broad enough to afford wider discretion to members invoking the security exceptions. However, the fact that recent panels interpreting the security exception appear to have overturned such a broad understanding of security exceptions rather narrows the scope of situations in which security exceptions can be successfully invoked. This has also been the starting point for this article. Countermeasures under customary international law are a significant, if not the only, means of enforcing and preserving the normative integrity of international obligations outside the WTO[119] in a decentralised international community. Indeed, third-party countermeasures can play an ever more critical role in seeking rectification of widely acknowledged

---

[117] *Ibid.*, para. 7.196.

[118] Furculita, *supra* note 112.

[119] Azaria, *supra* note 69, p. 423.

breaches of obligations *erga omnes (partes)* such as the prohibition of use of force, particularly when authoritative bodies like the UN Security Council are paralysed due to veto use. In this sense, the present author espouses Azaria's contention that the assertions made under the opposing theories—namely, that such countermeasures are precluded by Article 23.1 of the DSU—must be based on clear evidence.[120] Silence seems to work in favour of the affirmative theories.

4.3 The Treatment of Non-WTO Law in WTO Dispute Settlement

In the first place, questions arise whether panels and the Appellate Body can justify a measure that violates the WTO agreements by applying customary international law on third-party countermeasures, and further, whether they can apply international law other than WTO law to establish the existence of prior internationally wrongful acts. It has been held as self-evident that, under the DSU, the substantive jurisdiction of panels and the Appellate Body is limited to claims under the WTO agreements and does not extend to claims under non-WTO law including customary international law.[121] On the other hand, there has been active academic debate on whether the defending member can invoke non-WTO law as a defence when a claim of violation of the WTO agreements is filed, and whether non-WTO law may be the applicable law in that sense.[122]

However, as far as their practice is concerned, WTO panels and the Appellate Body have, in fact, applied customary international law referred to as so-called secondary norms, and legal scholarship generally accepts such norms as necessary for the fulfilment of judicial functions. For example, Van Damme states that general international law includes general principles of law such as good faith and due process, customary principles and rules on treaty formation, interpretation and application, and the principles on state responsibility. According to Van Damme, such norms share the characteristic that they are not intended to regulate a particular type of behaviour; rather, they are about how international law—including WTO law—should be created, applied, interpreted, and enforced. She states, therefore, that

---

[120] *Ibid.*

[121] Isabelle Van Damme, "Jurisdiction, Applicable Law, and Interpretation", in Daniel Bethlehem, Donald Mcrae, Rodney Neufeld, Isabelle Van Damme (eds.), *The Oxford Handbook on International Trade Law* (Oxford University Press. 2009), pp. 298–300.

[122] Pauwelyn, *supra* note 78; Pauwelyn, "The Role of Public International Law in the WTO: How Far Can We Go?", 95 *Am J Int'l L* 535 (2003); Joel Trachtman, "The Jurisdiction of the WTO", 98 *American Society of International Law Proceedings* 139 (2004). For a discussion of the controversy between Pauwelyn and Trachtman, *see* Satoru Taira, "Applicable Law in the WTO Dispute Settlement Procedure - Can Multilateral Environmental Agreements become Applicable Law?", *Hogaku Zassi* (*Journal of Law and Politics of Osaka City University*), Vol. 54, No. 1, pp. 161–197, 2007 (*in Japanese*).

such norms are in the nature of "general law to apply generally" insofar as they have not been specifically excluded.[123] Therefore, panels and the Appellate Body, as judicial bodies, may rather be seen as being required to apply the law of state responsibility, including the rules on countermeasures. For this reason, our discussion here proceeds on the assumption that the law of state responsibility regarding third-party countermeasures is applicable, at least as a secondary norm.[124] However, the question remains whether panels and the Appellate Body can interpret and apply substantive non-WTO norms to establish the existence of prior internationally wrongful acts.

Mexico-Soft Drinks is a rare instance where such a question was addressed. As mentioned earlier, in this case, Mexico alleged a US violation of NAFTA, and raised a defence under GATT Article XX(d) that its violations of the WTO Agreement were intended to secure US compliance of NAFTA obligations. Had Mexico invoked customary international law on countermeasures instead of GATT Article XX(d), the Appellate Body would have been compelled to determine whether such customary international law was indeed applicable. However, the Appellate Body effectively addressed this question with the following supplemental opinion,

> Mexico's interpretation would imply that, in order to resolve the case, WTO panels and the Appellate Body would . . .have to assess whether the relevant international agreement has been violated. WTO panels and the Appellate Body would thus become adjudicators of non-WTO disputes. . . . [T]his is not the function of panels and the Appellate Body as intended by the DSU.[125]

Thus, this supplemental opinion suggests that even if customary international law on countermeasures were to be invoked as a defence, such a defence would be inadmissible because WTO panels and the Appellate Body would not be competent to make determinations of the existence of prior violations of non-WTO norms, which would be a prerequisite for admitting such a defence.[126]

Kuijper, commenting on this case, states that, assuming that Mexico had relied on customary international law on reprisals (i.e., countermeasures), the Appellate Body, which has declared itself that the WTO does not exist in "clinical isolation" from general international law,[127] would need,

---

[123] Van Damme, *supra* note 121, p. 319.

[124] Rules on countermeasures are included in ARSIWA, which is said to deal with secondary norms, but these rules can also be considered primary norms when they concern the wrongfulness of a conduct. The distinction between primary and secondary rules was not always rigorously applied by the ILC. Eric David claims, however, that the codification of the rules on responsibility would have been incomplete without dealing with rules relating to circumstances precluding wrongfulness. Eric David, "Primary and Secondary Rules", in James Crawford et al. (eds.), *supra* note 74, pp. 31–32. In this article, the approach of the ILC is followed, and the function of rules on countermeasures, as pointed out by Van Damme, is taken into account. *See also* Azaria, *supra* note 69, p. 396 and n. 34.

[125] *Mexico-Soft Drinks*, *supra* note 102, para. 78.

[126] Azaria, *supra* note 69, p. 391.

[127] Appellate Body Report, *United States - Standards for Reformulated and Conventional Gasoline*, WT/DS2/AB/R, adopted 20 May 1996, p. 17.

214 S. Taira

at the very least to take seriously the question whether WTO law has become a totally reprisal-free zone in international law, or whether in exceptional circumstances reprisals for breaches of law elsewhere in the international system may entitle a WTO Member to ignore its obligations under the WTO [a]greement[s], without being automatically condemned under the dispute settlement system.[128]

Kuijper then goes on to criticise the Appellate Body's supplemental opinion in the following terms,

Surely it was not necessary for the Appellate Body to rule in all detail on the NAFTA sugar dispute, but merely to decide whether Mexico *prima facie* had a strong case with its argument that the United States had acted illegally…, so that a credible case for reprisal could be made. This cannot be too difficult for a high-powered institution like the Appellate Body and remains well within other interpretations the Appellate Body has given of non-WTO agreements, because it could not avoid doing so in the context of a WTO dispute.[129]

Davey and Sapir also criticise the supplemental opinion of the Appellate Body. According to them, while a panel might in the circumstances envisaged by the Appellate Body have to make a determination for its own purposes as to whether the US was acting consistently with NAFTA, such a determination would not be a determination of rights under NAFTA; it would only be a preliminary step in making a WTO ruling.[130] Davey and Sapir go on to state that,

---

[128] Pieter-Jan Kuijper, "Does the World Trade Organization Prohibit Retorsions and Reprisals? Legitimate 'Contracting Out' or 'Clinical Isolation' Again?" in Merit E. Janow, Victoria Donaldson and Alan Yanovich (eds.), *The WTO: Governance, Dispute Settlement and Developing Countries* (Juris Publishing, Inc., 2008), p. 706.

[129] *Ibid.*, p. 707.

[130] William J. Davey and Andre Sapir, "Soft Drinks case: the WTO and regional agreements", *World Trade Review*, Vol.8, No. 1 (2009), p. 18. The authors refer to *EC-Bananas III* as a similar situation, where the panel (and the Appellate Body) had to take a position on the meaning of the Lomé Convention in order to rule on whether an EC measure was covered by the so-called Lomé waiver, which permitted EC measures to be taken under the Lomé Convention. *European Communities - Regime for the Importation, Sale and Distribution of Bananas*, WT/DS27/AB/R, paras. 167–178, adopted 25 September 1997.

> [w]hile WTO panels and the Appellate Body cannot definitively determine rights and obligations under non-WTO agreements, absent some provision so providing, they can refer to and analyse such agreements to the extent it is necessary to determine rights and obligations under the WTO agreements.[131]

These criticisms are worth noting. They point out that WTO panels and the Appellate Body can interpret non-WTO law to determine rights and obligations under WTO law even without considering non-WTO law as applicable law.[132] Thus, when customary international law on third-party countermeasures is raised as a defence, and when WTO panels or the Appellate Body have a *prima facie* conviction by reference to non-WTO law as to the existence of some prior wrongful act, it can be argued that the illegality of violations of the WTO Agreement is negated subject to the satisfaction of other requirements for the countermeasure to be lawful.

5 Conclusion

In this article, assuming the situation in which not all WTO members who have imposed trade sanctions against Russia are able to successfully invoke WTO security exceptions as a defence against possible violations on their part of the WTO agreements, we have explored whether members who may be unsuccessful in invoking security exceptions may still be able within the context of WTO dispute settlement to justify their actions under the customary international law on third-party countermeasures.

As a result, the present author would like to propose the following general overview. First, we can support the view that Article 23.1 of the DSU only amounts to the special rules on countermeasures against violations of WTO agreements, and that it cannot be interpreted as excluding customary international law on third-party countermeasures against violations of non-WTO norms. Second, the rules on third-party countermeasures under customary international law are considered to be applicable by WTO panels and the Appellate Body as secondary norms, as are the other rules of ARSIWA. And third, it is possible for panels and the Appellate Body to justify a measure in violation of WTO agreements as a third-party countermeasure

---

[131] *Ibid.*

[132] Pauwelyn points out how *Mexico-Soft Drinks* highlights, in some cases, the line between jurisdiction, applicable law and treaty interpretation is blurry: '[S]urely, WTO panels do not have jurisdiction to decide claims of violation under a non-WTO treaty (say, NAFTA or CITES), but when does an assessment of a WTO claim that is within the jurisdiction of a WTO panel (say, a claim of violation of GATT Article III and a defense under GATT Article XX) with reference to a non-WTO treaty, cross the line from permissible treaty interpretation (or assessing a WTO claim in the context of applicable law beyond the WTO treaty) to that of impermissible adjudication of "non-WTO disputes"?'

Joost Pauwelyn, "Interplay between the WTO Treaty and Other International Legal Instruments and Tribunals: Evolution after 20 Years of WTO Jurisprudence", Posted: 12 Feb 2016, Last revised: 26 Jul 2017, https://papers.ssrn.com/sol3/papers.cfm?abstract_id=2731144.

under customary international law if they are convinced of the *prima facie* existence of a prior international wrongful act by reference to substantive non-WTO norms.

If WTO dispute settlement does not accept customary international law on third-party countermeasures as applicable norms, a measure that is lawful in the macrocosm of the international legal system will end up being unlawful in the microcosm of the WTO.[133] Would WTO members caught in such predicament really want to remain in such a microcosm?

Although there are no authoritative findings of illegality by the UN Security Council or the ICJ regarding Russia's invasion of Ukraine, a UN General Assembly resolution adopted on 2 March 2022,[134] while not legally binding, condemns in the strongest possible terms "the aggression by the Russian Federation against Ukraine in violation of Article 2(4) of the Charter," and thus indicates that, at the very least, the UN General Assembly considers a violation of Article 2(4) of the UN Charter to exist. Given the fact-finding competence of WTO panels, they could adopt findings of fact of other competent organisations, including the UN General Assembly, as *prima facie* evidence of the existence of prior wrongful acts on the part of Russia,[135] thus enabling panels and the Appellate Body to consider trade sanctions against Russia as permissible third-party countermeasures under customary international law.

---

[133] Nakatani argues that WTO dispute settlement bodies, responsible for the "subsystem", should also consider broader international law, which is the "system" as a whole. Kazuhiro Nakatani, "Economic Restrictions due to National Security Concerns and International Law", *International Economic Law (Yearbook of the Japan Association of International Economic Law)*, No. 31, pp. 123–124 (2022) (*in Japanese*).

[134] Resolution adopted by General Assembly on 2 March 2022, A/RES/ES-11/1, 18 March 2022, p. 3.

[135] In practice, the panel in *Russia - Traffic in Transit* referred to UN General Assembly resolutions as evidence that the situation in that case was a matter of concern to the international community and involved armed conflict. *Russia - Traffic in Transit, supra* note 5, para. 7.122.

War in Ukraine and Implications for International Investment Law

Dai Tamada

Abstract Russia's 2022 invasion of Ukraine has sent shockwaves across the international community, not least the international investment community and the arbitration world. A flurry of disputes has arisen not only in connection to harm to the interests of foreign investors in Ukraine and Russia but also in relation to sanctions—including asset freezing measures—imposed by many western and aligned states. This article outlines the typology of arising cases, and discusses the principal arguments, outcomes and challenges of means of redress (typically, arbitration) that appear to be at play.

1 Introduction

A number of investment disputes have arisen following Russia's 2022 invasion of Ukraine[1] that may be grouped into four types, namely: i) disputes between Ukrainian investors and Russia directly arising from the 2022 Russian invasion of Ukraine and the annexation of Crimea in 2014 (Ukrainian investors v. Russia); ii) disputes arising from Russia's measures preventing foreign investors in Russia from divesting (foreign investors v. Russia); iii) disputes arising from measures taken by Ukraine against Russian investments (foreign investors v. Ukraine); and iv) disputes that may arise from asset freezing measures on the part of Western states against Russian nationals and businesses (Russian investors v. Western states). It is necessary to analyse such disputes in light of applicable bilateral investment treaties (BITs)

NB., the following two URLs are omitted in footnotes: *Investment Arbitration Reporter* (https://www.iareporter.com/) and *Nikkei Newspaper* (in Japanese) (https://www.nikkei.com/).

[1] Professor Masahiko Asada's legal evaluation of Russia's 'military operation' is also discussed in this book.

D. Tamada (✉)
Graduate School of Law, Kyoto University, Kyoto, Japan
e-mail: tamada@law.kyoto-u.ac.jp

© The Author(s), under exclusive license to Springer Nature Singapore Pte Ltd. 2024
M. Asada, D. Tamada (eds.), *The War in Ukraine and International Law*,
https://doi.org/10.1007/978-981-97-2504-5_9

before moving on to discuss the relevant legal issues and notions including that of 'effective control' of territory, the balance between sanctions and energy security, and the legal status of central banks under BITs.

2 Ukrainian Investors v. Russia

The Russian invasion of Ukraine has been greatly damaging for Ukrainian investors who have since sought to recover their losses via investment arbitration under the existing Russia-Ukraine BIT.[2] For instance, Rinat Akhmetov, a Ukrainian businessman, has had interests in many industrial sectors in Ukraine (e.g., metals, mining, energy, media, telecommunications, agriculture, transportation, logistics, etc.), through SCM (Ukraine's largest investment group), and is reported considering redress under investment arbitration for alleged losses (over USD 4.6 billion) due to Russia's invasion.[3]

2.1 Investment Arbitration Cases Arising from the Annexation of Crimea

There have been ten arbitration cases arising from Russia's annexation of Crimea in 2014 that are likely to have significant implications for subsequent disputes flowing from Russia's 2022 invasion of Ukraine.

---

[2] Agreement between the Government of the Russian Federation and the Cabinet of Ministers of Ukraine on the Encouragement and Mutual Protection of Investments (signed in 1998 and entered into force in 2000), at https://investmentpolicy.unctad.org/international-investment-agreements/treaties/bit/2859/russian-federation%2D%2D-ukraine-bit-1998-.

[3] Vladislav Djanic, "Ukrainian Businessman Foreshadows Billion-Dollar Claim Against Russia over War Losses", *Investment Arbitration Reporter* (May 26, 2022). It is also reported that Rinat Akhmetov initiated arbitration against Russia in 2023, targeting the unlawful actions of Russia between 2014 to 2017, and onwards. Vladislav Djanic, "Ukraine's Richest Man Initiates BIT Arbitration against Russia over Interference with Donbas Assets", *Investment Arbitration Reporter* (April 11, 2023).

Claimant	Submission	Russia	Subject and decisions (NB., Published decisions are underlined)
Aeroport Belbek[4]	2015	Absent	Expropriation of airport management rights: **Partial Award** [24/2/2017] (jurisdiction affirmed);[5] **Award on Responsibility** [4/2/2019]; Hague Appeal Court **Judgment** [19/7/2022] (rejected Russia's claim to set aside).
Privatbank[6]	2015	Absent	Prohibition of bank business and expropriation: **Partial Award** [24/2/2017] (jurisdiction affirmed); **Responsibility Award** [4/2/2019]; Hague Appeal Court **Judgment** [19/7/2022].
Lugzor[7]	2015	**Present**	Real estate expropriation (details unknown).
Ukrnafta[8]	2015	Absent	Oil reservoir expropriation: **Jurisdiction Award** [26/6/2017]; **Merits Award** [12/4/2019]; Swiss Federal Tribunal **Judgment** [12/12/2019].
Stabil[9]	2015	Absent	Oil reservoir expropriation: **Jurisdiction Award** [26/6/2017]; **Merits Award** [12/4/2019] (damages ordered); Swiss Federal Tribunal **Judgment** [12/12/2019]; US District Court **Judgment** [9/4/2022] (recognition of award).
Everest Estate[10]	2015	Absent	Real estate expropriation: **Jurisdiction Award** [20/3/2017]; **Merits Award** [2/5/2018]; Hague Appeal Court **Judgment** [19/7/2022] (Russia's claim declined).

(continued)

---

[4] *Aeroport Belbek LLC and Mr. Igor Valerievich Kolomoisky v. Russian Federation*, PCA Case No. 2015-07, at https://www.italaw.com/cases/3826.

[5] It is reported that the tribunal avoided addressing the issue of the lawfulness of the annexation of Crimea under international law, and affirmed the application of the BIT by applying the effective control criterion. Luke Eric Peterson, "In Jurisdiction Ruling, Arbitrators Rule that Russia is Obliged under BIT to Protect Ukrainian Investors in Crimea Following Annexation", *Investment Arbitration Reporter* (March 9, 2017). The finding of the tribunal seems identical to that in *PrivatBank v. Russia*.

[6] *PJSC CB PrivatBank and Finance Company Finilon LLC v. Russian Federation*, PCA Case No. 2015-21, at https://www.italaw.com/cases/3970.

[7] *Limited Liability Company Lugzor and Others v. Russian Federation*, PCA Case No. 2015-29, at https://www.italaw.com/cases/6345. Although Russia did not initially appear in the arbitration proceedings, it later decided to appear before the tribunal.

[8] *PJSC Ukrnafta v. The Russian Federation*, UNCITRAL, PCA Case No. 2015-34, at https://www.italaw.com/cases/4032.

[9] *Stabil LLC and Others v. Russian Federation*, UNCITRAL, PCA Case No. 2015-35, at https://www.italaw.com/cases/4034.

[10] *Everest Estate LLC et al. v. the Russian Federation*, PCA Case No. 2015-36, at https://www.italaw.com/cases/4224.

Claimant	Submission	Russia	Subject and decisions (NB., Published decisions are underlined)
Oschadbank[11]	2016	Absent	Bank branch expropriation: **Award** [26/11/2018] (damages of USD 1.1 billion)
Naftogaz[12]	2016	**Present**	Oil and gas assets expropriation: **Partial Award** [22/2/2019]; Hague Appeal Court **Judgment** [19/7/2022] (Russia's claim dismissed; partially approved); **Final Award** [12/4/2023].
Krymenergo[13]	2018	**Present**	Electricity distribution business expropriation (details unknown).
Ukrenergo[14]	2019		Electricity generation facilities expropriation (details unknown).

The outcomes in the above cases point towards the following points. First, all fell within the scope of the Russia-Ukraine BIT and the 1976 UNCITRAL Arbitration Rules. Consequently, awards are, in principle, not made public. In several of the above cases, tribunals found Russia to be in breach of BIT obligations, and further determined the amount of compensation, although no case has resulted in compensation payments by Russia. Second, arbitral awards share identical conclusions, probably due to cross-references among tribunals.[15] Third, when it comes to the geographical requirement of investment (i.e., the 'territory' where investments are hosted/located), tribunals have typically avoided definitively addressing the issue of territorial sovereignty of Crimea. Fourth, tribunals have not examined Russia's claims as to why such measures were justified or are otherwise permissible under certain exceptions potentially available to Russia.[16] Fifth, Russia had initially been absent from the arbitration proceedings in the earlier cases, allegedly for fear of a possible unfavourable finding on the legal status of Crimea under international law.[17] Subsequently, once this concern was mitigated, Russia began to commit itself

---

[11] *Oschadbank v. Russia*, PCA Case No. 2016-14, at https://www.italaw.com/cases/7491.

[12] *NJSC Naftogaz of Ukraine et al. v. the Russian Federation*, PCA Case No. 2017-16, at https://www.italaw.com/cases/4381.

[13] *DTEK Krymenergo v. Russia*, PCA Case No. 2018-41, at https://investmentpolicy.unctad.org/investment-dispute-settlement/cases/1022/dtek-v-russia.

[14] *Ukrenergo v. Russia*, PCA Case No. 2020-17, at https://www.italaw.com/cases/7563.

[15] Some cases are dealt with by different tribunals in parallel. For example, *Belbek v. Russia* and *PrivatBank v. Russia* are dealt with by different tribunals but composed of the same arbitrators, and the two tribunals rendered the resulting awards on the same day.

[16] The *Stabil v. Russia* tribunal did not examine the possibility of Russia's justification (e.g., security exception or necessity), possibly due to Russia being absent in the proceedings and therefore having not advanced any justification for its acts.

[17] Ila Rachkov and Elizaveta Rachkova, "Crimea-Related Investment Arbitration Cases against Russia before International Investment Arbitration Tribunals", 4 *Moscow Journal of International Law* (2020) p. 145, at https://www.mjil.ru/jour/article/view/384?locale=en_US.

to the arbitral proceedings.[18] At the time of writing, Russia is not entirely ignoring investment arbitrations but is rather presenting its legal views, and seeking to justify its position through arbitral proceedings. As to future cases arising in connection to annexed regions, it is certainly possible that Russia will opt to attend related arbitration proceedings.[19]

2.2 Requirement Ratione Loci of Investment

2.2.1 The Requirement of 'Territory' Under BIT

A persistent controversial legal issue in the disputes under review is the legal status of the location where an investment in question is established, namely, Crimea and other regions annexed by Russia. Article 1 (1) of the Russia-Ukraine BIT provides that:

> "Investments" shall denote all kinds of property and intellectual values, which are put in by the investor of one Contracting Party [Ukraine] *on the territory of the other Contracting Party* [Russia] in conformity with the latter's legislation [. . .] (emphasis added).

For Ukrainian assets in Crimea to fall within the definition of investment under the BIT, they must exist 'on the territory' of Russia. In this sense, the legal status of the location of the property, currently under military occupation by Russia, is a preliminary and essential issue before tribunals. On this issue, scholars have generally taken the position that under international law Crimea remains part of Ukraine and, therefore, that arbitral tribunals must deny their jurisdiction.[20] What is more, scholars argue that Russia's annexation of Crimea is a breach of *jus cogens* and, therefore, tribunals are obliged not to recognize its consequences. Against these positions, however, the tribunals have admitted their jurisdiction on the following grounds.

---

[18] IA Reporter, "Awards under Russia-Ukraine BIT Surface", *Investment Arbitration Reporter* (Oct 3, 2022). Interestingly, in *Naftogaz v. Russia*, Russia was absent from the jurisdictional phase, though it raised objections to jurisdiction. *Naftogaz v. Russia* (2019), para. 2.

[19] In the *Allegations of Genocide* case (Ukraine v. Russia) before the ICJ, Russia raised preliminary objections on 3 October 2022. This may amount to evidence of Russia's intention to commit itself to ICJ proceedings. *Allegations of Genocide under the Convention on Prevention and Punishment of the Crime of Genocide (Ukraine v. Russia)*, Order of 7 October 2022.

[20] Patrick Dumberry, "Requiem for Crimea: Why Tribunals Should Have Declined Jurisdiction over the Claims of Ukrainian Investors against Russia under the Ukraine-Russia BIT", 9 *Journal of International Dispute Settlement* (2018) 506–533.

2.2.2 Criteria of 'Territory': Legal Steps and Physical Control

On this issue, the *PrivatBank v. Russia* tribunal stated that the 'effective de facto control', namely, the mere presence of Russian troops in Crimea, does not satisfy the 'territory' requirement under Article 1(1) of the BIT.[21] It then elaborated on the applicable criteria of 'territory', as follows:

> the critical consideration is likely to be an appreciation of *settled, long-term control* over the territory in question by the State [. . .]. Evidence of such settled, long-term control may come, inter alia, as in this case, both from *legal steps* taken by the State [. . .] to formalise, and constitutionalise, its control, and by *settled, long-term physical manifestations* of control (emphasis added).[22]

It is made clear that the notion of 'settled, long-term control' is the essence of the 'territory' under BIT, which is constituted by: i) a legal element, namely, legal steps of Russia to formalise and constitutionalise its control; and ii) a physical element, namely, the settled, long-term, physical manifestations of control, such as the physical presence of the military occupation. The tribunal justified the application of these exacting criteria by emphasising the 'settled' nature of investments protected under the BIT. By applying these criteria, the tribunal concluded that, on 21 March 2014 (i.e., the date on which the Incorporation Law was enacted by the Parliament of the Russian Federation), Crimea was to be treated as part of the 'territory' of Russia for the purposes of the BIT.[23]

2.2.3 Criteria of 'Territory': Jurisdiction and de facto Control

Later, in a similar way, the *Stabil v. Russia* tribunal concluded that Crimea was a 'territory' of Russia for the purposes of the BIT, by stating that:

> there can be no doubt that the Russian Federation has established *effective control* over Crimea, by taking *physical control* coupled with *legal steps*. It is equally clear that the Respondent considers Crimea as part of its sovereign territory; it treats it as such in its *national law* and claims sovereignty vis-à-vis the international community (emphasis added).[24]

Within the structure of the above reasoning, the presence of physical control and legal steps on the part of Russia amount to effective control which satisfies the 'territory' requirement under the BIT. The tribunal then turned its attention to treaty interpretation rules to conclude that:

---

[21] *PrivatBank v. Russia* (2017), para. 191.

[22] Ibid., para. 192.

[23] Ibid., para. 195.

[24] *Stabil v. Russia* (2017), para. 132.

War in Ukraine and Implications for International Investment Law

the ordinary meaning of the term "territory" includes areas over which the Contracting Parties exercise *jurisdiction* and *de facto control*, even if they hold *no lawful title* under international law (emphasis added).[25]

If the term 'jurisdiction' (*Stabil v. Russia*) can be understood as 'legal steps' (*PrivatBank v. Russia*), there are parallels between the two cases in terms of the 'territory' requirement, in the sense that the tribunals require two elements, namely, the legal and physical elements be present in order for the 'territory' requirement under Article 1(1) of the BIT to be satisfied.

2.2.4 Application of the Criteria to Donbas

If the tribunals were to apply the legal element and the physical element to Donbas,[26] the following issues would arise. First, even though two breakaway Ukrainian regions declared independence in 2014 (namely, Lugansk and Donetsk), the Donbas region had not been militarily occupied by Russia prior to 2022. This means that there had been no effective de facto control by Russia at the material time.[27] Second, since February 2022, there have been multiple missile attacks by Russia on Ukrainian cities, including Kyiv, however, they do not satisfy both criteria of the 'territory' requirement. Third, since 24 February 2022, East Ukraine (i.e., Luhansk and Donetsk) has been under Russian military occupation, and, thereafter, so has South Ukraine (i.e., Kherson and Zaporizhzhya). Although this fact may satisfy the criterion of effective de facto control, another criterion (namely, the legal element) was yet to be satisfied. However, as Russia officially annexed four regions (namely,

---

[25] Ibid., para. 146.

[26] A series of arbitral awards relating to Crimea have been criticised on the ground of their incompatibility with the obligation not to recognise the unlawful annexation of Crimea. Felix Krumbiegel, "The Applicability of the Russia-Ukraine Bilateral Investment Treaty to Crimea in the Light of the Duty of Non-recognition in International Law", 38 *Journal of International Arbitration* (2021) p. 669.

[27] It is said that, in light of the legal status of Donbas between 2014 and 2020, it had been a Ukrainian territory, without any de facto control by Russia and, therefore, was beyond the scope of the application of the Russia-Ukraine BIT. Stefan Lorenzmeier and Maryna Reznichuk, "Investment law and the Conflict in the Donbas Region: Legal Challenges in a Special Case", in Tobias Ackermann and Sebastian Wuschka (eds.), *Investments in Conflict Zones: the Role of International Investment Law in Armed Conflicts, Disputed Territories, and 'Frozen' Conflicts* (2020) pp. 434–435.

Donetsk, Luhansk, Kherson, and Zaporizhzhya) in October 2022 through legal acts,[28] the two criteria have since been satisfied.[29]

2.2.5 Nationalisation of the Zaporizhzhya Nuclear Power Plant

There has been an actual case involving an investment dispute arising from Russia's nationalisation of the Zaporizhzhya nuclear power plant. This is the biggest nuclear power plant in Europe, owned and managed by Energoatom, a Ukrainian national nuclear energy generating company. By the Presidential Order of 5 October 2022, Russia established a state-owned company to which it transferred the Zaporizhzhya nuclear power plant.[30] It was reported that Energoatom had sent a notice of arbitration to Russia on the basis of the Russia-Ukraine BIT (claiming USD 3 billion in damages).[31] The issue as to whether the 'territory' requirement is satisfied is most likely to arise. First, as Zaporizhzhya had already been incorporated into Russia, the first element (i.e., the legal element) would be satisfied.[32] Second, as the plant itself has been under the control of Russia's troops since March 2022, the second element (i.e., the physical element) would also be satisfied. Thus, the tribunal would likely be inclined to find that the location of the power plant can be understood as 'territory' of Russia for the purposes of the BIT, and that Russia's nationalisation, without any compensation, amounts to an unlawful expropriation.

---

[28] Four oblasts were annexed by Russia via a series of domestic measures of Russia: namely, a Presidential statement (September 30, 2022), the signature of the President of the relevant documents (i.e., the annexation treaties) (October 4, 2022), and the approval of Russia's parliaments (October 3 and 4, 2022).

[29] Among the four incorporated oblasts, Donetsk and Zaporizhzhya have not been entirely occupied by Russia and, thus, this fact does not satisfy the second criterion (i.e., the physical element).

[30] Nikkei Newspaper (October 6, 2022), "Zaporizhzhya nuclear power plant, nationalized by Russia, Order of President Putin".

[31] Lisa Bohmer, "Energoatom puts Russia on notice of arbitration dispute in relation to treatment of Zaporizhzhia Nuclear Power Plant and other assets in the context of the war in Ukraine", *Investment Arbitration Reporter* (April 16, 2023).

[32] The date of nationalisation (October 5, 2022, i.e., the date of the declaration by President Putin) was almost the same as that of the incorporation of the four oblasts. This fact may raise doubt as to whether there was 'settled, long-term control' prior to incorporation. On this point, it is worth recalling that, in *PrivatBank v. Russia*, the tribunal stated that 'settled, long-term control' was 'crystallized' on March 21, 2014, namely, the date of implementation of the incorporation law of Crimea (para. 194). If applied to the Zaporizhzhya case, it will be possible to take the nationalisation under Russian law as the 'crystallization' of 'settled, long-term control'.

2.2.6 Time of the Establishment of Investments

In addition to the 'territory' requirement, Article 1(1) of the BIT also requires that, in order to protect Ukrainian investments, they be established 'in conformity with [Russia's] legislation'. There have been two approaches to the material time for applying this requirement. *One* approach is that this is the initial time of establishing investments; as they were all established under Ukraine legislation at the initial time, they do not seem capable of satisfying that requirement. The *other* approach treats the time of initiating the arbitral procedure or the time of the alleged breach of BIT as material;[33] consequently, the investments, already under the effective de facto control of Russia, may satisfy the territory requirement. Arbitrators were divided over this in *Naftogaz v. Russia* (2019). The majority took the latter approach to conclude that the investments in question were established in conformity with Russia's legislation at the 'date of the alleged breach' of the BIT.[34] On the other hand, one arbitrator, the minority, took the former approach to conclude that, at the initial time, the investments were not established in conformity with Russia's legislation, but with Ukraine's.[35] Taken in conjunction with the legal element of the 'territory' requirement (i.e., the annexation legislation enacted by Russia), it seems realistic to take the latter approach, rather than the other. In future cases arising from Donbas, the tribunals are likely to continue adopting the latter approach to affirm their jurisdiction.

2.3 *Breach of Substantive Obligations*

The Russia-Ukraine BIT provides several substantive obligations which are likely to be at issue in future cases; such obligations include those concerning: 'complete and unconditional legal protection' (Article 2(2)); national treatment and the most-favoured-nation treatment (Article 3); expropriation (Article 5(1));[36] and free transfer of property (Article 7). It should be noted that, in *Stabil v. Russia* (2019), the tribunal rather succinctly concluded that there had in fact been an unlawful expropriation by Russia under Article 5,[37] while avoiding to make findings on other

---

[33] Tobias Ackermann and Sebastian Wuschka, "The Applicability of Investment Treaties in the Context of Russia's Aggression against Ukraine", *ICISD Review*, vol. 38, no. 2 (2023), pp. 468–469.

[34] *Naftogaz v. Russia* (2019), para. 165.

[35] Dissenting Opinion of Professor Dr. Maja Stanivuković, paras. 129–130.

[36] Article 5(1): "Investments made by investors of one Contracting Party in the territory of the other Contracting Party shall not be expropriated, nationalized or subject to other measures equivalent in effect to expropriation, except in cases where such measures are taken in the public interest under due process of law, are not discriminatory and are accompanied by prompt, adequate and effective compensation."

[37] *Stabil v. Russia* (2019), para. 259.

claims.[38] In light of the nature and scale of Russia's measures, tribunals are likely to easily conclude that there have been breaches of obligations under the BIT, and, in particular, that there have been unlawful expropriations.

2.4 Dispute Settlement Procedure

The Russia-Ukraine BIT provides two means of dispute settlement: investor-State and State-State. As to the former, the disputing parties first 'shall exert their best efforts to settle that dispute by way of negotiations' (Article 9(1)) and, should this fail, the investor may resort to: a) a competent court or an arbitration court of the Contracting Party (i.e., Russia), on whose territory the investments were carried out; b) the Arbitration Institute of the Chamber of Commerce in Stockholm (SCC); or c) an 'ad hoc' arbitration tribunal under the Arbitration Regulations of the UNCITRAL (Article 9(2)). As the first choice is unlikely to prove effective in protecting Ukrainian investments, investors are in reality left with two options. As was the case relating to Crimea, the Donbas cases are likely to be submitted to the third option (i.e., UNCITRAL arbitration). Even if such an option is exercised, favourable investor-claimant arbitral awards are likely to face subsequent execution issues, as investors would need to seek the award recognition and enforcement in third-country courts. This matter will be discussed separately in relation to possible future cases under the Japan-Russia BIT (see Sect. 3.3.3).

In addition to investor-State arbitration, State-State dispute settlement (Article 10) is also available to Contracting Parties. In the case of impasse of investor-State arbitration, or in parallel to such arbitrations, it is possible for the Government of Ukraine to resort to State-State arbitration.[39]

2.5 Security Exception and the Law of Armed Conflict

The Russia-Ukraine BIT does not provide for security exceptions, which regulate the application of the BIT in times of war or armed conflict. That being said, Article 6 of the BIT contemplates such events in mentioning the most-favoured-nation (MFN) treatment in the case of damage 'as a result of war, civil disturbances or other similar circumstances'. This mention suggests that the BIT is supposed to be applicable even in times of 'war' or similar circumstances. However, considering the limited

---

[38] Ibid., para. 260.

[39] Peter Tzengt, "Sovereignty over Crimea: A Case for State-to-State Investment Arbitration", 41 *Yale Journal of International Law* (2016) pp. 466–468.

protection of investment under Article 6 (namely, damages in the case of war on the basis of MFN), it is not certain whether full compensation principle, based on the Hull formula, would be applied to loss to investors caused by the armed activities of Russia.

3 Foreign Investors v. Russia

3.1 Withdrawal of Foreign Investors from Russian Business

Since Russia's invasion of Ukraine, many foreign investors (mainly those of the United States, the European Union and Japan) have withdrawn from Russia. In response, Russia has attempted to prevent such sudden and widespread divestment by taking a variety of measures.

3.2 Russia's Measures Against Divestment

3.2.1 The External Administration Bill

On 12 April 2022, the External Administration Bill (also known as the 'Expropriation' Bill) was presented to the Russian Parliament (Duma).[40] It provides that should a business in an 'essential' industrial sector in which more than 25% of its shares are owned by businesses of an 'unfriendly' State[41] withdraw from Russian business, an external administrator would be appointed to initiate a restructuring or insolvency procedure through which it may be sold to another enterprise or the Russian Federation at a low price. It seems that this proposed legislation is aimed at pre-empting withdrawal on the part of foreign investors from Russia, and, in case of withdrawal, at facilitating the transformation of their businesses. Once enacted, however, this legislation will allow direct expropriation, and, in turn, give rise to investment disputes[42] most likely to be submitted to arbitration.

3.2.2 Sakhalin II

Sakhalin II, a Russian liquified natural gas (LNG) project, was once managed by Sakhalin Energy Investment Company Ltd (Bermuda), and its shares once owned by

---

[40] At https://www.izvoznookno.si/Dokumenti/AKTUALNO/2022/Pregled-stanja-ruskega-gospodarstva-%2012042022.pdf. At the time of writing, this bill had yet to be enacted.

[41] The Russian Federation Government Directive No. 430-r (March 5, 2022), at http://government.ru/en/docs/44745/. Japan is included in the list of 'unfriendly' States.

[42] Nikkei Newspaper (Mar 12, 2022 and Apr 2, 2022). Asahi Shinbun Digital (April 13, 2022).

Gazprom (Russia; 50% plus 1), Shell (UK; 27.5% minus 1), Mitsui & Co., Ltd. (Japan; 12.5%), and Mitsubishi Corporation (Japan; 10%). In February 2022, Shell expressed its intention to withdraw from Sakhalin II.[43] By Presidential Order No. 416 of 30 June 2022, Russia established a Russian Limited Liability Company (Sakhalin Energy LLC), which will take over the rights and obligations of Sakhalin Energy Investment Company.[44] By this Order, the equity partners listed above were required to seek Russian Government permission to retain their respective shareholdings. The requests on the part of the two Japanese companies were finally approved by Russia,[45] therefore, resulting in no investment dispute, at least publicly.

3.2.3 Sakhalin I

In the case of another oil and gas project, Sakhalin I, its shares were owned by ExxonMobil (US; 30%), SODECO (Japan; 30%),[46] Rosneft (Russia; 20%), and ONGC (India; 20%). On 1 March 2022, ExxonMobil expressed its intention to withdraw from this project.[47] Against this backdrop, by Presidential Decree No. 520 of 5 August 2022,[48] Russia prohibits foreign investors of 'unfriendly' States in the financial and energy sectors from conducting any transaction (operation) resulting in the acquisition, modification, termination, or creation of any encumbrance over the rights to own, use, or dispose of securities, or participation interests in share capitals or in certain Russian legal entities. The Sakhalin I project was included within the scope of Decree No. 520 (Article 2(c)). Due to this Decree,

---

[43] Shell, "Shell announces intent to withdraw from Russian oil and gas", at https://www.shell.com/media/news-and-media-releases/2022/shell-announces-intent-to-withdraw-from-russian-oil-and-gas.html.

[44] Executive Order No. 416 of the President of the Russian Federation (June 30, 2022), at http://en.kremlin.ru/acts/news/68792.

[45] Decree of the Government of the Russian Federation (August 26, 2022) No. 2442-r, at http://publication.pravo.gov.ru/Document/View/0001202208300034; Decree of the Government of the Russian Federation (August 31, 2022) No. 2474-r, at http://publication.pravo.gov.ru/Document/View/0001202208310010.

[46] SODECO (i.e., Sakhalin Oil and Gas Development Co., Ltd.) shares are mainly owned by Ministry of Economy, Trade and Industry (METI), Itochu Co., JAPEX (Petroleum Exploration Co., Ltd.), and Marubeni Co. among others.

[47] ExxonMobil, "ExxonMobil to discontinue operations at Sakhalin-1, make no new investments in Russia" (March 1, 2022), at https://corporate.exxonmobil.com/News/Newsroom/News-releases/2022/0301_ExxonMobil-to-discontinue-operations-at-Sakhalin-1_make-no-new-investments-in-Russia.

[48] Presidential Decree (August 5, 2022), at http://publication.pravo.gov.ru/Document/View/0001202208050002.

War in Ukraine and Implications for International Investment Law   229

ExxonMobil is barred from selling its shares in Sakhalin I,[49] and, reportedly, is now attempting to initiate an investment arbitration against Russia.[50] As the U.S.-Russia BIT has yet to enter into force,[51] there is no other prospect for arbitration save for by mutual agreement. In addition to the above measure, by way of Presidential Decree No. 723 of 7 October 2022,[52] Russia has established a new company to which it transferred the business of Sakhalin I in a similar manner it did with Sakhalin II. Japan and Japanese business sought to retain their interests in Sakhalin I and, as was the case with Sakhalin II, were permitted to do so.[53]

3.3 Japan-Russia BIT

Should Japanese investors suffer from any harmful measures taken by Russia, investment arbitration under the Japan-Russia BIT[54] would be a means to seek redress.

---

[49] Bloomberg News (August 6, 2022), at https://www.bloomberg.co.jp/news/articles/2022-08-05/RG5EA5DWX2PS01.

[50] Damien Charlotin, "ExxonMobil Threatens Arbitration against Russia over Difficulties in Exiting Oil and Gas Project", *Investment Arbitration Reporter* (September 1, 2022).

[51] Treaty between the United States of America and the Russian Federation concerning the Encouragement and Reciprocal Protection of Investment (1992), at https://investmentpolicy.unctad.org/international-investment-agreements/treaty-files/2236/download. This agreement has yet to be ratified by Russia.

[52] Reuters, "Putin orders seizure of Exxon-led Sakhalin 1 oil and gas project" (October 8, 2022), at https://www.reuters.com/world/europe/russias-putin-signs-decree-setting-up-new-operator-sakhalin-1-tass-2022-10-07/.

[53] The Japan Times (November 15, 2022), "Russia allows Japan to keep stake in Sakhalin-1 oil and gas project", at https://www.japantimes.co.jp/news/2022/11/15/business/economy-business/sakhalin-japan-stake/.

[54] Agreement between the Government of Japan and the Government of the Russian Federation concerning the Promotion and Protection of Investments (signed on November 13, 1998, entered into force on May 27, 2000), at https://www.mofa.go.jp/mofaj/gaiko/treaty/pdfs/A-H12-1631_1.pdf#page=3.

3.3.1 Key BIT Clauses

The Japan-Russia BIT contains substantive clauses, not unlike normal BITs that include: the definition of 'investment' (Article 1), MFN treatment (Article 3(1)), national treatment (NT) (Article 3(2)), fair and equitable treatment (Article 3(3)), expropriation provisions (Article 5),[55] and the freedom of transfer (Article 8). With regard to dispute settlement, Article 11(2) provides three options: i) ICSID arbitration so long as the ICSID Convention is in force between Japan and Russia; ii) arbitration under the ICSID Additional Facility Rules; and iii) UNCITRAL arbitration. While Japan has ratified the ICSID Convention, this is not the case with Russia. As a result, only the last two options are open to Japanese investors.

3.3.2 National Security Exception

The protocol of the Japan-Russia BIT contains the following security exception (Article 5(1)):

> Notwithstanding the provisions of paragraph 2 of Article 3 of the Agreement [i.e., NT], each Contracting Party shall reserve the right to determine economic fields and areas of activities where activities of foreign investors shall be excluded or restricted, in accordance with its applicable laws and regulations, in case *it is really necessary for the reason of national security* (emphasis added).

This provision gives rise to the following issues. First, as its scope is expressly limited to the NT clause (Article 3(2)), it does not seek to extend to breaches of any other BIT provisions. Second, was it 'really necessary for the reason of national security' to prevent foreign investors from withdrawing from Russia? Third, to invoke the national security exception (Article 5(1)), Russia would have to determine what are any 'new economic fields and areas of activities' within the scope of the exception, which it should then 'notify [to Japan]' (Article 5(3)). Japan may argue that since it has not received any such notification, Russia cannot rely on the exception clause.

3.3.3 Execution of Arbitral Awards

Even if Japanese investors were to obtain an arbitral award in their favour, they would still have to face the thorny issue of its enforcement and execution. Article 11(3) of the Japan-Russia BIT provides that:

---

[55] Article 5: 'Investments and returns of investors of either Contracting Party shall not be subjected to expropriation, nationalization or any other measure the effect of which would be tantamount to expropriation or nationalization, within the territory of the other Contracting Party unless such measures are taken for a public purpose and under due process of law, are not discriminatory, and are taken against prompt, adequate and effective compensation'.

War in Ukraine and Implications for International Investment Law   231

> The decision of arbitration shall be final and binding upon both parties to the dispute. This decision shall be executed *by the applicable laws and regulations* concerning the execution of decision in force in the country in whose territories such execution is sought (emphasis added).

It is clear enough that Russia, a Contracting Party to this BIT, is obliged to execute all of the arbitral awards, whatever their content. However, crucially, this is subject to the 'applicable laws and regulations' of Russia which could potentially provide Russia some convenient loopholes. For instance, Russia has enacted Federal Law No. 171-FZ of 8 June 2020[56] to amend its commercial procedural law to the effect that its commercial court possesses the exclusive jurisdiction on disputes arising from anti-Russia sanctions, and that any award and judgment of foreign courts cannot be executed in Russia.[57] Nonetheless, there is still room for Japanese investors to argue that investor-State arbitral awards fall outside the scope of that amended regime since they are not related to anti-Russia sanctions.

If Japanese investors fail to obtain a decision to execute the arbitral award in Russia, they will have to seek execution in third countries. First, the 1958 New York Convention entitles Japanese investors to request the enforcement of an arbitral award,[58] subject to the 'public policy' exception (Article 5(1)(b)).[59] Second, the final hurdle is State immunity. The New York Convention obliges States to execute arbitral awards 'in accordance with the rules of procedure of the territory where the award is relied upon' (Article 3). Such 'rules of procedure' normally include the customary international law rule of state immunity, as broadly codified in the UN Immunity Convention.[60] With regard to the immunity of State property in a third country, Article 19(c) of the Convention provides that:

> No *post-judgment* measures of constraint, such as attachment, arrest or *execution*, against property of a State may be taken in connection with a proceeding before a court of another State unless and except to the extent that: (c) it has been established that the property is

---

[56] Freshfields Bruckhaus Deringer, "An Unofficial Translation of the Russian Federal Law on Amendment of the Arbitazh (Commercial) Procedure Code of the Russian Federation to Protect the Rights of Individuals and Legal Entities in view of the Restrictive Measures Introduced by Foreign States, State Associations and/or Unions and/or State (Interstate) Institutions of Foreign States or State Associations and/or Unions", at http://ssl.freshfields.com/noindex/documents/0720/Federal-law-No-171-FZ.pdf.

[57] With regard to a commercial arbitration between a Spanish railway company and a Russian state-owned railway enterprise, on 27 June 2022, a Russian court denied the execution of the ICC arbitral award, in accordance with the 2020 Law. Vladislav Djanic, "CIS Round-Up: Russian Court Deems Arbitration Clauses Unenforceable against Sanctioned Entities, New Cases, Concluded Disputes, and an ECtHR Ruling", *Investment Arbitration Reporter* (October 6, 2022).

[58] Article 3: 'Each Contracting State shall recognize arbitral awards as binding and enforce them in accordance with the rules of procedure of the territory where the award is relied upon [...]'.

[59] Article 5(2)(b): 'Recognition and enforcement of an arbitral award may also be refused if the competent authority in the country where recognition and enforcement is sought finds that: (b) The recognition or enforcement of the award would be contrary to the public policy of that country'.

[60] United Nations Convention on Jurisdictional Immunities of States and Their Property (adopted in 2004, not yet in force).

specifically in use or intended for use by the State *for other than government non-commercial purposes* and is in the territory of the State of the forum, provided that post-judgment measures of constraint may only be taken against property that has a connection with the entity against which the proceeding was directed (emphasis added).

If Japanese investors equipped with an arbitral award were to then obtain an execution judgment in a third country in which they could identify Russian property not used for 'government non-commercial purposes', there would be room to realise the execution of that arbitral award. Third, it must be noted, however, that, pursuant to Article 21(1)(c) of the UN Convention,[61] the assets of the Central Bank of Russia, largely frozen in many Western countries, are exempt from execution.

4 Foreign Investors v. Ukraine

Since the invasion by Russia, the Ukrainian Government has seized Russian assets in its territory, causing harm to Russian investors and third-country investors who may conceivably be seeking redress on the basis of applicable BITs in force. On 11 May 2022, Ukrainian President, Mr. Zelenskyy, issued Presidential Order No. 326 allowing the seizure of assets of Russian banks in Ukraine, which the Ukrainian Parliament approved on 12 May 2022.[62] Subsequently, shares of the subsidiary of Sberbank and Vnesheconombank (VEB) were seized. The two banks have since expressed their intention to have recourse to arbitration against Ukraine in accordance with the Russia-Ukraine BIT, by alleging unlawful expropriation.[63]

Besides Russian investors, there will be third-country investors who may seek to initiate investor-State arbitration against Ukraine, given that the latter's seizure measure extends to assets indirectly related to Russia. In fact, AMIC Energy, an Austrian company, has reportedly submitted a dispute for arbitration on the ground that the Ukrainian Government (the Bureau of Economic Security of Ukraine:

---

[61] Article 21(1)(c): "The following categories, in particular, of property of a State shall not be considered as property specifically in use or intended for use by the State for other than government non-commercial purposes under article 19, subparagraph (c): (c) property of the central bank or other monetary authority of the State".

[62] Проект Закону про затвердження Указу Президента України "Про рішення Ради національної безпеки і оборони України від 11 травня 2022 року "Про примусове вилучення в Україні об'єктів права власності Російської Федерації та її резидентів, at https://itd.rada. gov.ua/billInfo/Bills/Card/39594.

[63] Vladislav Djanic, "Two Russian Banks Threaten Treaty Arbitration against Ukraine Following Seizure of their Assets in the Context of the Ongoing Russia-Ukraine War", *Investment Arbitration Reporter* (May 12, 2022). At the time of writing, it was not certain whether the two banks had initiated arbitration.

War in Ukraine and Implications for International Investment Law   233

ESBU) has begun to seize AMIC Energy assets in Ukraine merely because it 'is connected to the Russian Federation'.[64] The claimant will be able to rely on the Austria-Ukraine BIT,[65] the Energy Charter Treaty, and the ICSID Convention.

5   Russian Investors v. Western States

5.1   *Investment Disputes Arising from Sanctions*

As 'sanctions' against Russia mainly take the form of asset-freezing or seizure of assets, this inevitably gives rise to investment disputes, both State-State and investor-State. Outside the context of the war in Ukraine, the *Iranian Assets* case before the ICJ arose following U.S. asset-freezing measures against Iran.[66] As an investor-State case, the Central Bank of Iran attempted to initiate arbitration against South Korea, which had frozen USD 7 billion worth of assets, in accordance with the U.S. sanctions law.[67] In the context of the Russian invasion of Ukraine, Western countries have imposed sanctions against Russia and its nationals, which have given rise to investment disputes: i) Rosneft v. Germany, which will arise due to Germany's decision to place Rosneft's two German subsidiaries (Rosneft Deutschland GmbH and RN Refining and Marketing GmbH) under trusteeship;[68] ii) Volga-Dnepr Cargo Airlines (Russian airline) v. Canada, which has arisen due to Canada's decision to seize the airplane of the Russian airline company;[69] and iii) Russian investors v. Belgium and Luxembourg, which will be lodged under the Belgium/Luxembourg-Russia BIT, arising due to measures to freeze the assets held by two European central securities depositories (namely, Clearstream and Euroclear).[70]

---

[64] Lisa Bohmer, "Seizure of Gas Stations Allegedly Linked to Russian Interests Prompts Threat of Investment Arbitration against Ukraine", *Investment Arbitration Reporter* (August 20, 2022).

[65] Agreement between the Republic of Austria and Ukraine on the Requirement and Mutual Protection of Investments, at https://investmentpolicy.unctad.org/international-investment-agreements/treaties/bit/282/austria%2D%2D-ukraine-bit-1996-.

[66] *Certain Iranian Assets (Islamic Republic of Iran v. United States of America)*, Judgment (March 30, 2023).

[67] Damien Charlotin, "South Korea Round-Up", *Investment Arbitration Reporter* (July 31, 2023). According to South Korean media, on 10 August 2023, the U.S. and Iran reached agreement on the release of assets subject to several conditions. Chosun Online (August 12, 2023), at https://www.chosunonline.com/site/data/html_dir/2023/08/12/2023081280018.html.

[68] Lisa Bohmer, "Rosneft is Preparing Investment Arbitration Claim against Germany over the State's Decision to Place the Company's Assets under Trusteeship", *Investment Arbitration Reporter* (April 16, 2023).

[69] Lisa Bohmer, "Russian Airline Files Notice of Dispute over Canada's Decision to Seize Aircraft", *Investment Arbitration Reporter* (April 16, 2023).

[70] Lisa Bohmer, "Russian Investors are Reportedly Contemplating Treaty Claims over Freezing of Their Assets Held by European Central Securities Depositories", *Investment Arbitration Reporter* (June 19, 2023).

Many other cases are likely to be submitted by Russian investors against Western States, on account of sanction measures in response to Russia's invasion of Ukraine. As we shall see below, Japan will not be an exception.

5.2 Asset Freeze Measure of Japan (Financial Measures)

Since 26 February 2022, Japan has implemented economic sanctions against Russia, which are divided into three categories:[71] asset freeze measures; prohibition on exports to specific Russian entities; and prohibition on exports of certain items that may contribute to the enhancement of Russian industrial capacities. The first measures ('financial sanctions') comprise: payment restrictions and capital transaction restrictions. In relation to the latter, a permission system will be applied to capital transactions (namely, contracts of deposit, trust, and money loan) with the individuals and entities designated by a Ministry of Foreign Affairs Notice. Anyone prohibited under the permission system will effectively have their assets frozen, having the effect of prohibiting the transfer of assets owned by Russian individuals and entities in Japanese bank accounts. As at the time of the latest list (28 February 2023), targets of asset freeze measures include: 683 individuals, 129 groups, and 12 specific banks.[72] This includes banks, finance companies and military companies, and expands not only to state/public functionaries and politicians but also to civilians. The most effective measure was against the Central Bank of Russia, which was added to the list on 1 March 2022.[73] Consequently, the Central Bank of Russia has been barred from transferring its foreign exchange reserves held in Japanese banks to any other financial bodies.[74]

5.3 Potential Issues Under the Japan-Russia BIT

Japan's measures may give rise to investment disputes under the Japan-Russia BIT on the following issues. First, under the BIT, the term 'investors' includes 'physical persons', namely 'nationals of Japan' and 'citizens' of Russia (Article 1(4)(a)), and 'company' (Article 1(4)(b)) which seemingly corresponds to legal/juridical persons.

---

[71] The Japanese Government's measures of sanction, at https://www.kantei.go.jp/jp/headline/ukraine2022/index.html.

[72] Japan MOFA, Measures based on the Foreign Exchange and Foreign Trade Act regarding the situation surrounding Ukraine (February 28, 2023), at https://www.mofa.go.jp/press/release/press4e_003221.html.

[73] Notice of the Ministry of Foreign Affairs (March 1, 2022), at www.mofa.go.jp/mofaj/files/100308181.pdf.

[74] Nikkei Newspaper (February 28, 2022), "Freezing Russia's foreign exchange reserves, amounting to USD 27 to 34 billion".

The most controversial issue will be whether the Central Bank of Russia may be regarded as a 'company'. The BIT broadly defines the term 'company' as 'corporations, partnerships, companies and associations whether or not with limited liability, whether or not with legal personality and whether or not for pecuniary profit' (Article 1(3)). In this regard, it is not entirely clear whether the Central Bank of Russia constitutes a 'company' under this definition. On the one hand, if a tribunal adopts the *Broches* test,[75] which has been used by investment tribunals to focus on the *nature* of the act in question (namely, the possession of assets in foreign banks),[76] the Central Bank of Russia may be characterised as a 'company' under the BIT.[77] On the other hand, if the tribunal adopts the approach taken by the ICJ in the *Iranian Assets* case (2023), which focuses on the *sovereign function* of the act in question, in that case, taken by the Central Bank of Iran,[78] the Central Bank of Russia may not be characterised as a 'company'. Second, Article 1(1) of the Japan-Russia BIT defines the term 'investments' as 'every kind of asset'. There is no doubt that this includes a variety of assets belonging to Russian investors that have been frozen by Japan, including those of the Central Bank of Russia. Third, while Japan's asset freeze measures do not necessarily amount to direct expropriation, their effect of impairing the use and enjoyment of such assets, may constitute indirect expropriation,[79] which, in the absence of compensation, may amount to unlawful expropriation (Article 5(1)). Fourth, as the measures in question intentionally only target Russian individuals and entities, they give rise to questions of NT (Article 3(2)) and MFN treatment (Article 3(1)). From the foregoing, it is not unrealistic to expect investment disputes to arise from the asset freeze measures taken by Japan. Fifth, Japanese sanctions against Russia include a ban on *outward* investment in Russia,[80] in a similar way to the UK ban.[81] As this prohibition is prior to the establishment of an investment, it is outside the scope of the applicable BIT.

---

[75] Aron Broches, "The Convention on the Settlement of Investment Disputes between States and Nationals of Other State", 135 *Recueil des cours de l'Académie de droit international de la Haye* (1972) pp. 354–355.

[76] For example, *Československá Obchodní Banka A.S. v. The Slovak Republic*, ICSID Case No. ARB/97/4, Decision on Objections to Jurisdiction, Award (May 24, 1999), para.20.

[77] It should be noted that the Broches test has been applied and developed in ICSID cases given that it was originally the interpretation of Article 25 of the ICSID Convention.

[78] The ICJ stated that the operations of Bank Markazi (i.e., the Central Bank of Iran) are "merely a way of exercising its *sovereign function* as a central bank" (emphasis added) and, due to this, this bank cannot be characterised as a 'company' under the 1955 Treaty between the US and Iran. *Certain Iranian Assets (Islamic Republic of Iran v. United States of America)*, Judgment (30 March 2023), paras. 50–53.

[79] For example, *Stabil v. Russia* (2019), para. 225.

[80] The Japanese Government, "Prohibition of New Outward Direct Investment to the Russian Federation" (April 12, 2022), at www.mofa.go.jp/mofaj/files/100330732.pdf.

[81] The UK Government imposed pressure on BP to terminate its business with Rosneft. Washington Post (February 27, 2022), "BP to 'exit' its $14 billion stake in Russian oil giant in stark sign that Western business is breaking ties over Ukraine invasion", at https://www.washingtonpost.com/business/2022/02/27/bp-russia-rosneft-ukraine/.

6 Conclusions

A variety of investment disputes have arisen or may potentially arise consequent to Russia's invasion of Ukraine (and the prior annexation of Crimea). In line with the analysis provided in the foregoing, it may be worth noting the following points.

First, investment disputes between Ukrainian investors and Russia have already been submitted to arbitration, and similar cases are expected to arise in the future. While investment arbitration itself is not enough to stop ongoing Russian aggression, it may contribute to weakening Russia's legal position in many cases against it.[82]

Second, although Russia initially did not appear in arbitrations concerning investments in Crimea, it subsequently engaged in selective participation in such proceedings. In that sense, arbitrations will provide a further forum for Russia to present its legal views, not only towards opposing investors-claimants but also towards the international community.[83] It is necessary to keep a close eye on Russia's attitude and reaction towards investment arbitration in future cases.

Third, the relationship between international investment law and the law of armed conflict can arise as a key issue within and beyond investment arbitration. In general, BITs do not typically contain national security exceptions. Even when they do, the content of such exceptions remains quite unclear or insufficient to deal with cases arising due to armed conflict. On the one hand, therefore, it seems reasonable to take BITs as applying even when armed conflict is at play. On the other hand, it is important to be mindful of the significant discrepancy between international investment law (setting a high level of protection for investments) and the law of armed conflict (tolerating incidental damage to civilian properties insofar as it is proportionate to military necessity).

---

[82] Cameron Miles, "Lawfare in Crimea: Treaty, Territory, and Investor-State Dispute Settlement", *Arbitration International* (2022) (advance access publication October 3, 2022) pp. 14–16, at https://doi.org/10.1093/arbint/aiac009.

[83] As mentioned earlier, UNCITRAL arbitration is confidential and the content of proceedings is not made public. That being said, details of arbitration proceedings including awards regularly enter the public domain through related domestic court proceedings.

Part III
Conclusion

Reflections on War in Ukraine and International Law

Martins Paparinskis

The starting point for my reflections is the call by Masahiko Asada in the conclusion of Chapter 'The War in Ukraine Under International Law: Its Use of Force and Armed Conflict Aspects' for 'focus on how to respond to this unprecedented crisis in the rule of law and what to do with it in order to avoid its recurrence'. The whole volume may be read as an extended response, applying the vocabulary of public international law to explain, in predominantly doctrinal terms, the war in Ukraine and the responses thereto by the international legal process. The authors do so with an eye to what one might call the 'traditional' topics of international law: use of force, countermeasures, individual criminal responsibility, and international courts and tribunals. That is not the only disciplinary perspective that could be taken, nor the only framing and the choice of topics—public international law is not just a discipline of crisis, as famously pointed out by Hilary Charlesworth.[1] But one need not take this important point about the plurality of values and interests in various fields of international law too far for the sake of contrarianism. Public international law does play an important role in shaping the way how international crises are addressed *and* is in turn particularly likely to be shaped by them.[2] Indeed, in the otherwise very different contemporary crises one reads about in the frontpages of daily newspapers, the one recurrent theme is the importance attributed by the relevant actors to the tools and mechanisms of international law. The docket of the

---

[1] H Charlesworth, 'International Law: A Discipline of Crisis' (2002) 65 Modern Law Review 377.
[2] MM Mbengue and J D'Aspremont (eds), *Crisis Narratives in International Law* (Brill Nijhoff 2022).

M. Paparinskis (✉)
UCL, London, UK

International Law Commission, Geneva, Switzerland
e-mail: m.paparinskis@ucl.ac.uk

© The Author(s), under exclusive license to Springer Nature Singapore Pte Ltd. 2024
M. Asada, D. Tamada (eds.), *The War in Ukraine and International Law*,
https://doi.org/10.1007/978-981-97-2504-5_10

International Court of Justice (ICJ and the Court) illustrates the point well.[3] So it has been for the war in Ukraine.

The volume is set in the particular context summarised by the ICJ in the 2024 judgment on preliminary objections in the case concerning *Allegations of Genocide under Convention on the Prevention and Punishment of the Crime of Genocide (Ukraine v. Russian Federation) (Allegations of Genocide).* The Court noted the armed conflict between Ukrainian armed forced and forces linked to two entities that referred to themselves as the 'Donetsk People's Republic' and the 'Luhansk People's Republic' between the spring of 2014 and 2022;[4] Russian Federation's recognition of these entities as independent States on 21 February 2022[5] and conclusion with them of what it itself referred to as two 'Treaties on Friendship, Cooperation and Mutual Assistance' on 22 February;[6] launch in the morning of 24 February of what it described as a 'special military operation' in Ukraine[7] [explained in the letter to the United Nations (UN) Secretary General as 'measures taken in accordance with Article 51 of the Charter of the United Nations in exercise of the right of self-defence'];[8] after which the armed conflict between the Russian Federation and Ukraine continued to the day the judgment was rendered.[9] This conflict between the Russian Federation and Ukraine has been addressed in the framework of several

---

[3] *Alleged Violations of the 1955 Treaty of Amity, Economic Relations, and Consular Rights (Iran v US)* (Preliminary objections) [2021] ICJ Rep 9; *Application of the Convention on the Prevention and Punishment of the Crime of Genocide (The Gambia* v. *Myanmar)* (Preliminary objections) [2022] ICJ Rep 477; *Application of the International Convention on the Elimination of All Forms of Racial Discrimination (Armenia* v. *Azerbaijan)* (Order of 17 November 2023) [2023] ICJ Rep <https://www.icj-cij.org/sites/default/files/case-related/180/180-20231117-ord-01-00-en.pdf>; *Arbitral Award of 3 October 1899 (Guyana* v. *Venezuela)* (Order of 1 December 2023) [2023] ICJ Rep <https://www.icj-cij.org/sites/default/files/case-related/171/171-20231201-ord-01-00-en.pdf>; *Obligations of States in respect of Climate Change (Request for an Advisory Opinion)* (Order of 15 December 2023) [2023] ICJ Rep <https://www.icj-cij.org/sites/default/files/case-related/187/187-20230420-ORD-01-00-EN.pdf>; *Application of the Convention on the Prevention and Punishment of the Crime of Genocide in the Gaza Strip (South Africa* v. *Israel)* (Order of 26 January 2024) [2024] ICJ Rep <https://www.icj-cij.org/sites/default/files/case-related/192/192-20240126-ord-01-00-en.pdf>; *Allegations of Genocide under the Convention on the Prevention and Punishment of the Crime of Genocide (Ukraine* v. *Russian Federation: 32 States intervening)* (Preliminary objections) [2024] ICJ Rep <https://www.icj-cij.org/sites/default/files/case-related/1 82/182-20240202-jud-01-00-en.pdf>; *Legal Consequences arising from the Policies and Practices of Israel in the Occupied Palestinian Territory, including East Jerusalem* (Order of 3 February 2024) [2024] ICJ Rep <https://www.icj-cij.org/sites/default/files/case-related/186/186-20230203-ORD-01-00-EN.pdf>.

[4] *Allegations of Genocide* Preliminary objections ibid [29].

[5] Ibid [30].

[6] Ibid [31].

[7] Ibid [31]-[32].

[8] Ibid [33].

[9] Ibid [35].

universal and regional international institutions,[10] including the UN General Assembly, which in Resolution ES-11/1 of 2 March 2022 deplored 'in the strongest terms the aggression by the Russian Federation against Ukraine in violation of Article 2 (4) of the [United Nations] Charter'.[11] (This is not to understate the importance of international law in addressing various aspects of the conflict in 2014–2022, which may be of relevance also for the present inquiry, but the focus in the volume is on the developments since February 2022).[12]

The first layer of analysis addresses directly the rules on the use of force in three complementary ways. Tatsuya Abe reviews the historical record of use of force by the Soviet Union and Russia against the benchmarks of the UN Charter (concluding that in most cases it raised significant concerns about lawfulness, albeit not uniquely so by comparison to the practice of other powerful States), Asada adopts the inter-State perspective of *jus ad bellum* and neutrality in the current war, while Claus Kress considers individual criminal responsibility for the crime of aggression.

In relation to use of force, it is often helpful to consider whether the judgement on its lawfulness requires taking a position on a major issue of legal principle—a different question from whether it is politically and legally controversial or factually contested.[13] Asada does not, overall, face questions of principle in reaching the conclusion that the applicable rules on the use of force were breached by the Russian Federation in February 2022 (despite some factual ambiguity over the precise character of the claim made in the address of its President that was forwarded to the Secretary-General in the letter noted in the second paragraph).[14] The particular question of permissibility of use of force for the recovery of territory—on which the reasonableness of disagreement is reflected in the negative answer by the only international tribunal to directly address the issue,[15] dismissed in turn by the leading

---

[10] *Allegations of Genocide under the Convention on the Prevention and Punishment of the Crime of Genocide (Ukraine* v. *Russian Federation)* (Order of 16 March 2022) [2022] ICJ Rep 211 [19].

[11] UNGA Res 'Aggression against Ukraine' (2 March 2022) UN Doc A/RES/ES-11/1 [2].

[12] See *Dispute Concerning Coastal Rights in the Black Sea, Sea of Azov, and Kerch Strait (Ukraine* v. *Russian Federation)*, PCA Case no 2017-06, Award Concerning the Preliminary Objections of the Russian Federation, 21 February 2020; App nos 20958/14 and 38334/18 *Ukraine* v. *Russia (*Re *Crimea)* [GC] (Decision of 16 December 2020); *Application of the International Convention for the Suppression of the Financing of Terrorism and of the International Convention on the Elimination of All Forms of Racial Discrimination (Ukraine* v. *Russian Federation)* [2024] ICJ Rep <https://www.icj-cij.org/sites/default/files/case-related/166/166-20240131-jud-01-00-en.pdf>, and generally L Hill-Cawthorne, 'International Litigation and the Disaggregation of Disputes: Ukraine/Russia as a Case Study' (2019) 68 ICLQ 779.

[13] M Wood, 'The Law on the Use of Force: Current Challenges' (2007) 11 Singapore Yearbook of International Law 1, 3.

[14] *Allegations of Genocide* Preliminary objections (n 3) [33]. Cf. CR 2023/17 34 [3]-[10] (Zabolotskaya); CR 2023/19 53 [29]-[33] (Cheek).

[15] Eritrea-Ethiopia Claims Commission, Partial Award: *Jus Ad Bellum*—Ethiopia's Claims 1–8 (2005) 26 RIAA 457 [11].

contemporary scholar[16]—ultimately, for Asada, might not need to be answered on the facts. Conversely, it is important in practice to know how the traditional regime of neutrality, predicated upon the distinction between peace and war,[17] fits with the modern *jus contra bellum,* particularly regarding the status and obligations of actors providing military assistance to parties to an international armed conflict. The much-missed James Upcher, with whose work Asada engages, has powerfully shown that the stratum of State practice in relation to neutrality in contemporary law is richer and more sophisticated than often appreciated, and it may well be that developments in relation to war in Ukraine push States to clarify their position both on the rules and the relevant considerations in their application.[18]

Aggression raises questions of both State responsibility for unlawful use of force and individual criminal responsibility for the crime of aggression,[19] and Kress' chapter addresses the latter aspect. Is there a gap in the international law and institutions for addressing the war in Ukraine, which may be filled by the creation of the Special Tribunal for the Crime of Aggression against Ukraine? For Kress, while an appropriate amendment of the Statute of the International Criminal Court (ICC) would be the most principled path,[20] a good legal and policy case could be made for the creation of an *ad hoc* Special Tribunal. Some questions regarding the character and powers of such a body have been posed in clear terms. The UN Legal Counsel de Serpa Soares has noted that:

> he was aware of the discussions taking place among States on the possible establishment of a special international tribunal on the crime of aggression against Ukraine, with or without the involvement of the United Nations. ... In any discussion on the possible involvement of the United Nations in such an initiative, Member States would have to answer three preliminary questions: first, whether the General Assembly had the power to adopt a binding resolution on the establishment of such a tribunal; second, if so, what kind of majority would be needed; and, third, whether such a resolution could waive the immunity of Heads of State under customary international law.[21]

Other public interventions may have been less helpful, including the occasional reference to hybrid or internationalized tribunals—in the view of some, juridically meaningless, since the categories of criminal courts are exhausted by the

---

[16]C Gray, 'Eritrea/Ethiopia Claims Commission Oversteps its Boundaries: A Partial Award?' (2006) 17 EJIL 699, 710–714. For a somewhat different view, see C Yiallourides, M Gehring, and J-P Gauci, *The Use of Force in relation to Sovereignty Disputes over Land Territory* (BIICL 2018).

[17]See L Oppenheim, *International Law: Peace* (Volume I, Longmans, Green, and Co. 1905); L Oppenheim, *International Law: War & Neutrality* (Volume II, Longmans, Green, and Co. 1905).

[18]J Upcher, *Neutrality in Contemporary International Law* (OUP 2020).

[19]M Wong, 'Aggression and State Responsibility at the International Criminal Court' (2021) 70 ICLQ 961.

[20]For background, M Wong, 'The Activation of the International Criminal Court's Jurisdiction over the Crime of Aggression: International Institutional Law and Dispute Settlement Perspectives' (2020) 22 International Community Law Review 197.

[21]Provisional summary record of the 3622nd meeting of the International Law Commission (11 May 2023) UN Doc A/CN.4/SR.3622 10–11.

Reflections on War in Ukraine and International Law

'international' and 'municipal' dyad.[22] And yet others reflect well-known and often long-standing discussions on the law of immunities, in which Kress himself has been an influential participant. These topics include the best construction of the sixth sentence of paragraph 61 of the ICJ's judgment in *Arrest Warrant of 11 April 2000,*[23] the persuasiveness or otherwise of the ICC Appeals Chamber's Judgment in *Jordan Referral re Al-Bashir Appeal,*[24] and various aspects of the International Law Commission's (ILC) work on the topic of immunity of State officials from foreign criminal jurisdiction (to be addressed in the second reading in 2024).[25]

I noted in the first paragraph of these reflections the trend for contemporary crises to be brought to the ICJ, with the war in Ukraine as a prominent example. Dai Tamada addresses the *Allegations of Genocide* case, with an eye to the provisional measures indicated and interventions by States. I appeared before the Court on behalf of one of the intervening States so I will not say anything about the substance of the chapter,[26] except to emphasise the formal distinction between a *declaration of intervention* (filed by a State which desires to avail itself of the right of intervention conferred upon it by Article 63)[27] and an *intervention*, composed of written observations and observations in the course of the oral proceedings on the subject-matter of the intervention (submitted by the intervening State, i.e. the State whose declaration is admissible).[28] Tamada's fine-grained discussion of the procedure of the Court also illuminates a broader point about the systemic character of public international law, including its rules on peaceful settlement of international disputes. By way of example, the Court's order on provisional measures took note of General Assembly Resolution ES-11/1,[29] and was in turn recalled in the preambular recital to Resolution ES-11/5.[30] Judicial settlement may be a very visible aspect of the international legal landscape, but it is only one in the open-ended list of means of peaceful

---

[22] R O'Keefe, *International Criminal Law* (OUP 2015) 86–88.

[23] *Arrest Warrant of 11 April 2000 (DRC* v. *Belgium)* [2002] ICJ Rep 3 para 61 ('an incumbent or former Minister for Foreign Affairs may be subject to criminal proceedings before certain international criminal courts, where they have jurisdiction').

[24] *The Prosecutor* v. *Omar Hassan Ahmad Al-Bashir,* Judgment in the Jordan Referral re Al-Bashir Appeal, 6 May 2019.

[25] For the first reading text and commentaries, see 'Text of the draft articles on immunity of State officials from foreign criminal jurisdiction adopted by the Commission on first reading' in *Report of the International Law Commission Seventy-third session (18 April–3 June and 4 July–5 August 2022)* UN Doc A/77/10 [68]. Comments by States are available at <https://legal.un.org/ilc/guide/4_2.shtml#govcoms>.

[26] *Allegations of Genocide* Preliminary objections (n 3) [23].

[27] Article 82 of the Rules of the International Court of Justice.

[28] Ibid art 86.

[29] *Allegations of Genocide under the Convention on the Prevention and Punishment of the Crime of Genocide (Ukraine* v. *Russian Federation)* (Order of 16 March 2022) [2022] ICJ Rep 211 [76].

[30] UNGA Res 'Furtherance of remedy and reparation for aggression against Ukraine' (14 November 2022) UN Doc A/RES/ES-11/5.

settlement of international disputes.[31] An important truth about the contemporary international dispute settlement is that it works as an interconnected system, and must be evaluated on these terms.[32]

Another important truth about public international law is that it is a decentralised legal order. Of course, States and other actors coordinate their conduct through various forms of international cooperation, particularly in and through the UN when topics of universal importance are at issue. But if the relevant UN organs are perceived as unable to act, States may fall back on the default mode of decentralised conduct, either unilateral or coordinated outside the UN, as was the case with adoption against the Russian Federation after February 2022 of measures that have also been described as 'sanctions'. The place of these measures in public international law is addressed in two chapters: Mika Hayashi and Akihiro Yamaguchi consider economic sanctions against Russia, while Kazuhiro Nakatani deals with freezing, management, and possible confiscation of Russian (State) assets. Authors are interested, rightly, in how international law characterises these measures, since the position in the legal systems of actors adopting them can neither insulate such measures from international responsibility nor trigger it necessarily; these are simply distinct queries.[33]

Hayashi and Yamaguchi and Nakatani (as well as Satoru Taira in a later chapter) also refer, with some caution, to what the ILC Special rapporteur James Crawford called countermeasures by States other than the injured State[34] (or, to sacrifice some technical precision for elegance, 'third-party countermeasures'). This approach is warranted by the methodological questions raised, both for identification of customary international law and for confirmation whether, in fact, the putative power has been asserted in the particular circumstances. Nor are these challenges surprising, in light of the generally strong hesitation of States to explicitly use the language of countermeasures in explaining their conduct. By way of an example, the United States appears, with one exception,[35] not to have characterised in such terms the blocking of the Iranian assets in response to the seizure of the US embassy in Tehran in 1979, even though its rationale and practicalities of implementation were broadly

---

[31] 'Text of the draft guidelines on settlement of disputes to which international organizations are parties provisionally adopted by the Commission at its seventy-fourth session' in *Report of the International Law Commission: Seventy-fourth session (24 April–2 June and 3 July–4 August 2023)* UN Doc A/78/10* 37 Draft guideline 2(c).

[32] *Application of ICSFT and CERD* (n 12) [396]-[398].

[33] 'Draft articles on responsibility of States for internationally wrongful acts', *Yearbook of the International Law Commission 2001 (Volume II Part Two)* UN Doc A/CN.4/SER.A/2001/Add.1 (Part 2) 76 art 3 (but see Commentary 7).

[34] 'Fourth report on State responsibility, by Mr. James Crawford, Special Rapporteur' in *Yearbook of the International Law Commission 2001 (Volume II Part One)* UN Doc A/CN.4/SER.A/2001/ Add.1 (Part 1) 1 [70].

[35] IUSCT, *Iran and the US*, B1 Partial Award No 382, 31 August 1988 [28], [31].

in line with what would be called for by substantive and procedural criteria of countermeasures.[36]

Vaughan Lowe memorably described international trade and investment law more than a decade ago as 'two of the most fecund and febrile areas of legal practice',[37] and the creativity of the practitioners of international economic law has only increased since then. Three authors consider how dispute settlement in contemporary international economic law may affect the war in Ukraine. Two chapters address the perspective of the World Trade Organization (WTO): Fujio Kawashima focuses on justification of 'sanctions' against Russia under the national security exception in Article XXI of the General Agreement on Tariffs and Trade (GATT), while Taira addresses their permissibility in the guise of third-party countermeasures. Article XXI of GATT contains interpretative multitudes, both historically[38] and in recent dispute settlement practice, and Kawashima's call for a balanced approach is certainly attractive—although that benchmark itself may mean different things to different actors, as reflected in submissions in recent WTO disputes.

If Article XXI is unavailable, Taira suggests permissibility of invocation of countermeasures as a matter of secondary rules, which is an argument that would go with the grain of some of the aspects of the law of State responsibility.[39] Whether bodies of limited jurisdiction could easily characterise conduct outside their *ratione materiae* jurisdiction as *prima facie* wrongful for the purposes of deciding on countermeasures would likely be subject to greater disagreement. Some inspiration for that discussion could be drawn from recent judicial decisions in other settings,[40]

---

[36] *United States Diplomatic and Consular Staff in Tehran (US v Iran)* ICJ Pleadings 316 (Owen on behalf of the US) ('the United States came forward with a peaceful response which it considered totally appropriate under accepted principles of international law and comity among nations. … having in mind Iran's unlawful detention of American hostages, the President of the United States simply froze all Iranian assets in United States control for the time being …. At the same time the Government of the United States has made it clear that once the hostages have been released the United States will be willing to open negotiations looking toward a mutual settlement of claims, which in turn will lead to the lifting of the freeze. In the meantime, the United States regards the freeze of Iranian assets as a justified, prudent and proportional measure of restraint in the circumstances'). Cf. 2001 ILC articles on responsibility of States for internationally wrongful acts (n 33) arts 49, 51, 53; CD Guymon (ed), *Digest of United States Practice in International Law 2021* (Office of the Legal Adviser, United States Department of State 2022) 767–768.

[37] V Lowe, 'Function of Litigation in the International Community' (2012) 61 ICLQ 209, 210.

[38] M Pinchis-Paulsen, 'Trade Multilateralism and U.S. National Security: The Making of the GATT Security Exceptions' (2020) 41 Michigan Journal of International Law 109.

[39] M Paparinskis, 'Equivalent Primary Rules and Differential Secondary Rules: Countermeasures in WTO and Investment Protection Law' in T Broude and Y Shany (eds), *Multi-Sourced Equivalent Norms in International Law* (Hart Publishing 2011) 259, 280–287.

[40] *Appeal relating to the Jurisdiction of the ICAO Council under Article II, Section 2, of the 1944 International Air Services Transit Agreement (Bahrain, Egypt and UAE v. Qatar)* [2020] ICJ Rep 172 [49]. See CR 2019/16 15 [6], [22] (Petrochilos); 28 [2], [34], [37] (Shaw); 56 [17] (Akhavan); CR 2019/17 16 [9], [11] (Lowe).

including on the *Monetary Gold* principle.[41] The final chapter by Tamada considers the implications for investment law. In the wilderness of investment arbitration, much depends on the facts and framing of particular disputes, but one important factor noted in the chapter is the weight to be given to existing awards in the cases regarding Crimea, which may seem more persuasive on some points of public international law than others.

I started my observations by reference to Asada's call for identification of challenges and ways to prevent their recurrence—the mischief and the cure, so to speak. Law on the use of force and neutrality, individual criminal responsibility for the crime of aggression, resort to international dispute settlement by particular interested actors, reactions by the broader community, and possible calibration of that reaction by specialised fields of international law are the features of the normative landscape that will have to be engaged with by those reflecting on Asada's challenge. It is important to neither understate nor overstate the role of international law in that process. Law is not the only relevant benchmark, in international relations just as in any other setting of human endeavour, but it will be important for calibrating the discussion and framing the response.[42] At the same time, the arc of international politics does not necessarily bend towards compliance with rules of international law, even of foundational character or implemented through universal international institutions. A historical example of some regional salience is the expulsion of the Soviet Union from the League of Nations in 1939 for 'the aggression which it has committed against Finland'; one actor in this interaction effectively perished soon afterwards, while the other went to be foundational for the post-World War Two legal order.[43] Ultimately, the viability and effectiveness of public international law depends upon the long-term conviction and conduct of its key actors, particularly States. In the shorter term, this volume will be an indispensable guide for lawyers that navigate pragmatism and idealism in thinking through the challenges posed by the war in Ukraine and the future of the rule of law in the international legal order.

---

[41] *Dispute concerning delimitation of the maritime boundary between Mauritius and Maldives in the Indian Ocean (Mauritius/Maldives)* [2021] ITLOS Rep [247]; *Arbitral Award of 3 October 1899 (Guyana v. Venezuela)* (Preliminary objections) [2023] ICJ Rep <https://www.icj-cij.org/sites/default/files/case-related/171/171-20230406-JUD-01-00-EN.pdf> [97]-[107]; also M Paparinskis, 'Long Live *Monetary Gold* *Terms and Conditions Apply' (2021) 115 AJIL Unbound 154, 157–158. But see *Black Sea* (n 12) [167]-[196].

[42] J Crawford, 'Chance, Order, Change: The Course of International Law' (2013) 365 Hague Recueil 13, 46–47.

[43] (1939) 20 LNOJ 506, 508; (1939) 20 LNOJ 531–541. See C Tams, 'Article 6' in B Simma et al (eds), *The Charter of the United Nations: A Commentary* (Volume I, 3rd edition OUP 2012) 374, 375.

Printed in the USA
CPSIA information can be obtained
at www.ICGtesting.com
LVHW011823041124
795688LV00003B/331